ORAL TRADITIONAL LITERATURE

LITERATURE

A Festschrift For Albert Bates Lord

ORAL TRADITIONAL LITERATURE

LITERATURE

A Festschrift For
Albert Bates Lord

John Miles Foley
Editor

1981

Slavica Publishers, Inc.

See the last pages of this book for a list of some other books from
Slavica; for a complete catalog with prices and ordering
information, write to:

Slavica Publishers, Inc.
P.O. Box 14388
Columbus, Ohio 43214

GR
72
.07

ISBN: 0-89357-073-7.

Text set by Eleanor B. Sapp.

Printed in the United States of America.

CONTENTS

11422

DEDICATION

It is a great pleasure to dedicate this volume to
Albert Lord, both in grateful acknowledgment of his monumental contribution to the field of oral literature research and in sincere appreciation of his personal example of integrity and humanism in the academic profession.
In bringing these essays together as a *Festschrift*, we
seize a rare opportunity in literary history: the chance
to honor not simply a significant theorist or prolific
critic but rather a true originator. For as crucial to
the oral theory as Milman Parry's bold and brilliant
first steps most certainly were, it has been Albert
Lord's clear-eyed, patient, and equally brilliant studies
that have created and defined the discipline of oral
literature. This book, then—or at least whatever in it
may be worthy—is his, and we hope he is pleased.

ACKNOWLEDGMENTS

First among those deserving thanks for their assistance with this *Festschrift* are the authors whose essays
comprise it. Fifteen of them (Patricia Arant, David
Bynum, Francelia Clark, Robert Creed, Joanne Foley, John
Foley, Donald Fry, William González, Joseph Harris,
Edward Haymes, Deirdre La Pin, John Miletich, Gregory
Nagy, Alain Renoir, and Bruce Rosenberg) joined in pre-
senting oral versions of their papers in Albert Lord's
honor in a series of sections on Oral Literature at the
Thirteenth Congress of the Medieval Institute in Kalama-
zoo, Michigan on May 5-7, 1978; revised texts of these
presentations, along with contributions by Joseph Duggan,
Barbara Halpern, and John Niles and a closing essay by
Albert Lord, make up the greater part of this volume.

I wish also to express my gratitude to my institution, the University of Missouri, for a University Research Council Grant which subvented part of the cost of
preparing the manuscript for publication. In addition,
the president of Slavica Publishers, Charles Gribble, deserves much credit for committing his press to publishing
the full and unbowdlerized manuscript of the *Festschrift*,
and particularly for preserving the original languages
and alphabets quoted by contributors, a rare standard in
these days of tight budgets and transliteration. I would
also thank the scholars who read the book for the press;
their comments and suggestions have been very helpful in
preparing final copy.

Less immediate but equally important to the fact and
eventual shape of the *Festschrift* is the year which I
spent as a Visiting Fellow at the Milman Parry Collection
of Oral Literature at Harvard University in 1976-77. Under the direction of Albert Lord and David Bynum, I was
able to work on a firsthand basis with oral epic texts in
Serbo-Croatian. I am very grateful to the American
Council of Learned Societies for making that year of
study possible.

Some *eaxlgesteallan* must be specially acknowledged:
David Bynum, for his assistance with Albert Lord's bibliography and also for his generous and learned counsel
over the years; Donald Fry, for his help with the Old
English bibliography as well as his dependably illuminat-
ing insights on this and other projects; Barbara Halpern,
for sharing a productive collaboration in both field work

and analytical writings; Anne Lebeck, now deceased, for teaching me to hear Homer's music with a Keatsian ardor (though she could not wait to teach us more); and Alain Renoir, for his intelligent advice and unflagging encouragement on the *Festschrift*.

One further word. This book could not have been done without Robert Creed, Albert Lord's student and my mentor, who taught me how to do it and who gave me the place and the time to do it. *Et merci bièn, mon amie musicale.*

Rocheport, Missouri
September 30, 1980.

ABBREVIATIONS

JOURNALS

AA	*American Anthropologist*
ABäG	*Amsterdamer Beiträge zur älteren Germanistik*
AfricaL	*Africa* (London)
AfrLS	*African Language Studies*
AI	*American Imago*
AJA	*American Journal of Archaeology*
AKG	*Archiv für Kulturgeschichte*
AM	*Annuale Mediaevale*
AN	*Acta Neophilologica* (Ljubljana)
ANF	*Arkiv för nordisk filologi*
Anglia	*Anglia: Zeitschrift für englische Philologie*
APh	*Archives de philosophie*
ArchN	*Archaeological News*
Arv	*Arv: A Journal of Scandinavian Folklore*
ASch	*The American Scholar*
ASUL	*American Studies in Uralic Linguistics*
Atlantic	*Atlantic Monthly*
BBA	*Bonner Beiträge zur Anglistik*
BGDSL	*Beiträge zur Geschichte der deutschen Sprache und Literatur*
BHS	*Bulletin of Hispanic Studies*
BMGS	*Byzantine and Modern Greek Studies*
BRAB	*Boletín de la Real Academia de Buenas Letras de Barcelona*
BRMMLA	*Bulletin of the Rocky Mountain Modern Language Association*
BS	*Balkan Studies*
CalSS	*California Slavic Studies*
CASS	*Canadian-American Slavic Studies*
CEAfr	*Cahiers d'études africaines*
ChauR	*Chaucer Review*
CHum	*Computers and the Humanities*
CJ	*Classical Journal*
CL	*Comparative Literature*
CN	*Cultura Neolatina* (Modena)
Comitatus	*Comitatus: Studies in Old and Middle English Literature*
CompC	*Comparative Criticism*
Cor	*La Corónica*

CP	*Classical Philology*
CT	*The Comparatist*
CW	*Classical World*
DA(I)	*Dissertation Abstracts (International)*
DArch	*Dossiers de l'archéologie*
DQ	*Denver Quarterly*
EA	*Études anglaises*
ELH	*English Literary History*
ELN	*English Language Notes*
EnSt	*Englische Studien*
ES	*English Studies*
ESA	*English Studies in Africa*
ESC	*English Studies in Canada*
ESMEA	*Essays and Studies by Members of the English Association*
FIRL	*Forum at Iowa on Russian Literature*
FMLS	*Forum for Modern Language Studies*
FP	*Filološki pregled* (Belgrade)
GRM	*Germanisch-romanische Monatsschrift*
HES	*Harvard English Studies*
HLB	*Harvard Library Bulletin*
HR	*Hispanic Review*
HSCP	*Harvard Studies in Classical Philology*
HSS	*Harvard Slavic Studies*
HudR	*The Hudson Review*
IAN	*Izvestija Akademii Nauk S.S.S.R., Serija literatury i jazyka* (Moscow)
IFMJ	*International Folk Music Journal*
IJSLP	*International Journal of Slavic Linguistics and Poetics*
ISS	*Indiana Slavic Studies*
JAF	*Journal of American Folklore*
JAP	*Journal of American Philology*
JEGP	*Journal of English and Germanic Philology*
JFI	*Journal of the Folklore Institute*
JHS	*Journal of Hellenic Studies*
Knji	*Književnost* (Belgrade)
L&S	*Language and Style*
LTR	*La Table ronde*
MAE	*Medium Ævum*
MGS	*Michigan Germanic Studies*
MHr	*Mlada Hrvatska*
MLN	*Modern Language Notes*
MLR	*Modern Language Review*
MM	*Maal og Minne*
MP	*Modern Philology*

MS	*Mediaeval Studies*
MScan	*Mediaeval Scandinavia*
N&Q	*Notes & Queries*
NAWG	*Nachrichten von der Akademie der Wissenschaften in Göttingen*
Neophil	*Neophilologus*
NLH	*New Literary History*
NM	*Neuphilologische Mitteilungen*
NRFH	*Nueva Revista de Filología Hispánica*
NSSVD	*Naučni sastanak slavista u Vukove dane*
NUm	*Narodna umjetnost* (Zagreb)
NYTBR	*New York Times Book Review*
NZK	*Naukovi zapysky naukovo-doslidčoju katedry istoriji ukrajins'koj kul'tury*
Olifant	*Olifant: a Publication of the Société Rencesvals, American-Canadian Branch*
OSP	*Oxford Slavonic Papers*
PacQ	*Pacific Quarterly*
P&R	*Philosophy and Rhetoric*
PAPS	*Proceedings of the American Philosophical Society*
PIMA	*Proceedings of the International Musicological Association*
PLL	*Papers on Language and Literature*
PMLA	*Publications of the Modern Language Association of America*
PMMLA	*Papers of the Midwest Modern Language Association*
Poetics	*Poetics: International Review for the Theory of Literature*
PQ	*Philological Quarterly*
Prilozi	*Prilozi za književnost, jezik, istoriju i folklor*
PTL	*Poetics and the Theory of Literature*
RAL	*Research in African Literatures*
REtS	*Revue des études slaves*
RFE	*Revista de Filología Española*
RNL	*Review of National Literatures*
RPh	*Romance Philology*
RUS	*Rice University Studies*
Saga-book	*Saga-book of the Viking Society for Northern Research*
SAV	*Schweizerisches Archiv für Volkskunde*
SEEJ	*Slavic and East European Journal*
SEER	*Slavonic and East European Review*
SP	*Studies in Philology*

SR	*Slavic Review*
SS	*Scandinavian Studies*
TAPA	*Transactions of the American Philological Association*
TLS	*Times Literary Supplement*
TRHS	*Transactions of the Royal Historical Society*
TSL	*Tennessee Studies in Literature*
TSLL	*Texas Studies in Literature and Language*
UCCS	*University of Cincinnati Classical Studies*
UCPCP	*University of California Publications in Classical Philology*
UCPMP	*University of California Publications in Modern Philology*
UCTSE	*University of Cape Town Studies in English*
ULCSB	*University of London Classics Studies Bulletin*
UR	*Umjetnost riječi*
UTQ	*University of Toronto Quarterly*
WF	*Western Folklore*
WS	*Die Welt der Slaven*
YCS	*Yale Classical Studies*
ZDA	*Zeitschrift für deutsches Altertum und deutsche Literatur*
ZNŽO	*Zbornik za narodni život i običaje*

BOOKS AND SERIES

AnthBC	*An Anthology of Beowulf Criticism*, ed. by Lewis E. Nicholson (Notre Dame, rpt. 1966)
A-SP	*Anglo-Saxon Poetry: Essays in Appreciation (for John C. McGalliard)*, ed. by Lewis E. Nicholson and Dolores W. Frese (Notre Dame, 1975)
BP	*The Beowulf Poet*, ed. by Donald K. Fry, Jr. (Englewood Cliffs, 1968)
BrodeurSts	*Studies in Old English Literature in Honor of Arthur G. Brodeur*, ed. by Stanley B. Greenfield (Eugene, 1963)
CH	*A Companion to Homer*, ed. by Alan J. B. Wace and Frank H. Stubbings (London, rpt. 1969)

EETS	Early English Text Society
EsAr	*Essential Articles for the Study of Old English Poetry*, ed. by Jess B. Bessinger, Jr. and Stanley Kahrl (Hamden, 1968)
FFC	Folklore Fellows Communications (Helsinki)
Franciplegius	*Franciplegius: Medieval and Linguistic Studies in Honor of Francis Peabody Magoun, Jr.*, ed. by Jess B. Bessinger, Jr. and Robert P. Creed (New York, 1965)
Haymes	*A Bibliography of Studies Relating to Parry's and Lord's Oral Theory* (Cambridge, Mass., 1973)
KlMisc	*Studies in English Philology: a Miscellany in Honor of Frederick Klaeber*, ed. by Kemp Malone and Martin B. Ruud (Minneapolis, 1929)
MHV	*The Making of Homeric Verse: the Collected Papers of Milman Parry*, ed. by Adam Parry (Oxford, 1971)
OEL	*Old English Literature: Twenty-two Analytical Essays*, ed. by Martin Stevens and Jerome Mandel (Lincoln, rev. 1976)
OEP	*Old English Poetry: Fifteen Essays*, ed. by Robert P. Creed (Providence, 1967)
OL&F	*Oral Literature and the Formula*, ed. by Benjamin A. Stolz and Richard S. Shannon (Ann Arbor, 1976)
OLSE	*Oral Literature: Seven Essays*, ed. by Joseph J. Duggan (New York, 1975)
OPMPC	*Occasional Publications of the Milman Parry Collection*, ed. by David E. Bynum, forthcoming
RadJAZU	*Rad jugoslavenske akademije znanosti i umjetnosti*
S&T	*Spontaneity and Tradition: a Study in the Oral Art of Homer*, by Michael N. Nagler (Berkeley, 1974)
S-CHS	*Serbo-Croatian Heroic Songs (Srpskohrvatske junačke pjesme)*, 4 vols., coll., ed., and trans. by Milman Parry, Albert B. Lord, and David E. Bynum (Cambridge, Mass. and Belgrade, 1953-54; Cambridge, Mass., 1974)
Singer	*The Singer of Tales*, by Albert B. Lord (1960; rpt. New York, 1968 et seq.)

SmithSts   *Early English and Norse Studies Presented to Hugh Smith in Honour of His Sixtieth Birthday*, ed. by Arthur Brown and Peter Foote (London, 1963).

TWW   *The Winged Word: a Study in the Technique of Ancient Greek Oral Composition as Seen Principally through Hesiod's* Works and Days, by Berkley Peabody (Albany, 1975)

PREFACE

At a dinner on May 6, 1978, attended by many of the contributors to this volume, John Foley asked me to introduce Albert Bates Lord. I did so with a toast that went something like this:

> Hal wes þu, Albert, eallbeorht hlaford,
> beo þu weaxende in Wyrde fæþme,
> wisdome gefylled werum to nytte.[1]

(As I recall explaining at the time, there is a variant with equal manuscript authority of the last halfline: *wifum to nytte*.)

I don't think my Old English toast—based, I now confess, on a passage in the great charm of land fertility—is an entirely inappropriate celebration of a great and fertile scholar. Albert Lord has waxed full of wisdom gratefully drawn upon by many of us for nearly three decades. I put myself in his debt with every article I publish, every paper I deliver, nearly every class I teach.

My acquaintance with Albert Lord began nearly thirty years ago when I was a graduate student at Harvard. Since what has become a friendship began rather inauspiciously, I hope I may be forgiven for telling at some length about the first time I saw him and heard him speak, and something of what that occasion has led to.

It was at a seminar on Old English poetry conducted by another great teacher, the late Professor Francis P. Magoun, Jr. Professor Magoun informed us that he had invited a colleague from the Slavic Department to speak to us. We were puzzled, and became more so when Magoun informed us that Lord had been collecting "songs" from illiterate "singers" in small towns and villages in Yugoslavia. What could this man have to say to us, students as we were of the sophisticated poetry of Anglo-Saxon England?

As it turned out, Professor Lord had something awful in store for us. He played recordings of *guslari* sawing away on—did we hear him right?—their *one*-stringed instruments while they intoned their sing-songs. I think most of us in that seminar were shocked. I know I was. I refused to believe that such awful noises could tell me anything at all about the subtle text of *Beowulf* I pored over in Klaeber's third edition.

What I didn't know at the time was this: by the end of Professor Lord's presentation I was already hooked.

It took some time for the insidious addiction to begin to take effect. At first I simply did what Magoun told us to do: I went to the Harvard Archive on the top floor of Widener Library and read Professor Lord's recently completed dissertation (1949), "The Singer of Tales." There, along with underlined and underdashed passages from "singers" whose names I refused to try to pronounce, was a passage from my beloved *Beowulf*—similarly underlined and underdashed! Worse still, there was a passage from sacrosanct *Homer* treated in the same way!

Puzzled, I checked out Milman Parry's published articles, following up references to them in Lord's dissertation. If a *classicist* had been able to make something out of those noises—had even travelled into the backwoods of Yugoslavia to *collect* them—maybe there was something to them.

When Albert Lord published the first two volumes of *Serbo-Croatian Heroic Songs* in 1953 and 1954, I was already following his lead in "The Singer" and ferreting out formulas in *Beowulf*. Albert Lord's quiet insistence that there *were* formulas to be found in the Old English poem, his willingness to serve as reader for my dissertation on the subject, and Professor Magoun's enthusiastic encouragement, all had had their effect.

Albert Lord is best known for *The Singer of Tales*, the seminal book that grew out of his already seminal dissertation. But he has done many other things, too. Besides editing and translating the immensely important *Ženidba Smailagina sina* (*The Wedding of Smailagić Meho*) of Avdo Medjedović in volumes III and IV of *Serbo-Croatian Heroic Songs*, he has been for many years now at work on a study of traditional oral poetry in the Balkans that will take us back to Homer and beyond. All of us look forward eagerly to what promises to be a work of importance equal to or greater than anything he has already published. In the meantime I find myself going back again and again to his writings, particularly *The Singer of Tales*. Each time I do, I discover something I had missed or slighted before.

I'll conclude this preface with two examples to demonstrate the importance of reading again and again the writings of this careful and subtle thinker. Both of my examples are from *The Singer of Tales*.

In his chapter on the formula, Lord deals briefly
with Milman Parry's concept of "thrift." Parry argues
that a singer will demonstrate his thrift by not having
"two formulas, metrically equivalent, which express the
same essential idea" (*Singer*, p. 50). In the course of
tracing "the essential idea" of a single formula through
some nine thousand lines of songs performed by the *guslar* Salih Ugljanin, Lord comes to the following conclusion:

> Our brief excursion into the principle of
> thrift in actual oral composition among Yugoslav
> singers has served to emphasize the context of
> the moment when a given line is made. In order
> to understand why one phrase was used and not
> another, we have had to note not only its meaning,
> length, and rhythmic content, but also its sounds,
> and the sound patterns formed by what precedes and
> follows it. We have had to examine also the
> habits of singers in other lines, so that we may
> enter his mind at the critical creative moment.
> We have found him doing more than merely juggling
> set phrases. Indeed it is easy to see that he
> employs a set phrase because it is useful and
> answers his need, but it is not sacrosanct. What
> stability it has comes from its utility, not from
> a feeling on the part of the singer that it can-
> not or must not be changed. It, too, is capable
> of adjustment. In making his lines the singer is
> not bound by the formula. The formulaic tech-
> nique was developed to serve him as a craftsman,
> not to enslave him. (pp. 53-54).

It has taken me a long time to begin to realize
what I think is going on in this passage. In the midst
of pursuing one of Parry's tests for orality, Lord finds
and quietly states the importance of *sound-patterning* in
controlling the singer's performance. In the same
chapter that contains the famous and often-copied
"charts" with their underlined "formulas" and underdashed "systems," Lord here demonstrates, and later develops, the *aesthetic* control of sound-patterning. The
guslar is no slave to the scholarly notion of the formula. He is instead hooked into a tradition that is
constantly hooking thoughts together by means of alliteration, assonance, consonance, rhyme.

Oral traditions, as Albert Lord studies them, turn out to be not just the sometimes strange-sounding performances of backwoods performers, but the expression of patterns recognized and recreated by the human mind. Salih's or Avdo's mind and vocal tract shaped these passages; Lord's eyes and ears and mind explore the passages so that he can report to us what we might otherwise miss.

What I begin to learn from reading and listening to Albert Lord is this: humankind has travelled on its immensely long journey from savannah to civilization by keeping track of its past through sound-patterning. We have not lost our ability to detect and respond to sound-patterning, even though we pay little attention to the process now. What Albert Lord has done is to listen patiently to, transcribe, and scrutinize thousands of lines of Salih Uglijanin's performances, and those of other *guslari* of Yugoslavia. In doing so, Lord shows us the way into the past that lies in our own minds.

In another chapter in *The Singer of Tales* he shows us another way to begin the exploration of our past. Again, he does so quietly. In his chapter on the theme he writes as follows:

> It is a curious fact in the Yugoslav tradition, that when a hero has been absent for a long period, or even when a long war is an element in the story, whether the hero has been in that war or not, a deceptive story, or its vestige, and a recognition, or its vestige are almost invariably to be found in the same song. Some force keeps these elements together. I call it a "tension of essences."
>   The Odyssean story of return after long absence entails disguise, deceptive story, and recognition. The Yugoslav return songs have the same grouping of elements. This grouping is, of course, to be expected because it is the basic narrative of the tale. There are, however, songs that are not fundamentally return songs but that contain some if not all of these elements.... This group of themes (long war, disguise, deceptive story, recognition) tends to maintain an identity of its own even when it is not ostensibly the main theme of the story.... (p. 97).

Again, I have found it necessary to quote at some length. But then that is easy to do when one is quoting such a careful thinker-stylist as Albert Lord. In shaping that beautiful phrase "tension of essences," he has done more than put together a phrase: he has shaped an important tool for probing humankind's past.

That past does not separate but instead joins Salih Ugljanin and Homer, not directly, but indirectly, for they are cousins descended from speakers of the Indo-European tradition. They were also human beings responding to some inner need to *keep* together things that they deeply felt *belong* together. This is part of what Lord's phrase "tension of essences" tells us.

Albert Bates Lord's written and spoken words are, to paraphrase Keats, loaded with ore. I find myself learning this fact anew each time I read or reread his subtle, careful, profound writings, or reflect on what I have heard him say with equal care, thought, and profundity.

Now I find myself thinking: what will he tell us about thousands of years of traditional oral poetry in the Balkans, and how will he phrase his telling?

Robert P. Creed
Shutesbury, November 1979

NOTE

[1]Too literally,

    Be hale, Albert,   all-bright lord,
    be fertile   in Fate's bosom,
    filled with wisdom   for the use of men.
(Ed.)

A BIBLIOGRAPHY OF THE WRITINGS OF ALBERT BATES LORD

1936

"Homer and Huso I: The Singer's Rests in Greek and Southslavic Heroic Song," *TAPA*, 67(1936), 106-13

1938

"Homer and Huso II: Narrative Inconsistencies in Homer and Oral Poetry," *TAPA*, 69(1938), 439-45

1948

"Homer and Huso III: Enjambement in Greek and Southslavic Heroic Song," *TAPA*, 79(1948), 113-24

"Homer, Parry, and Huso," *AJA*, 52(1948), 34-44; rpt. in *MHV*, pp. 465-78

1951

Serbo-Croatian Folk Songs, with Béla Bartók (New York: Columbia University Press, 1951)

"Yugoslav Epic Folk Poetry," *IFMJ*, 3(1951), 57-61

"Composition by Theme in Homer and Southslavic Epos," *TAPA*, 82(1951), 71-80

1953

"Homer's Originality: Oral Dictated Texts," *TAPA*, 84(1953), 124-34

1953-54

Novi Pazar: English Translations and *Novi Pazar: Serbocroatian Texts*, Serbo-Croatian Heroic Songs, vols. 1-2, coll. with Milman Parry, ed. and trans. by Albert Lord (Cambridge, Mass. and Belgrade: Harvard University Press and the Serbian Academy of Sciences, 1953-54)

1954

"Notes on *Digenis Akritas* and Serbocroatian Epic," *HSS*, 2(1954), 375-83

1956

"Avdo Medjedović, Guslar," *JAF*, 69(1956), 320-30

1956 (Contd)

"The Role of Sound-Patterns in Serbo-Croatian Epic," in *For Roman Jakobson* (The Hague: Mouton, 1956), pp. 301-5

1959

"The Poetics of Oral Creation," in *Comparative Literature: Proceedings of the Second Congress of the International Comparative Literature Association*, ed. Werner P. Friederich (Chapel Hill: University of North Carolina Press, 1959) pp. 1-6

1960

The Singer of Tales (Cambridge, Mass.: Harvard University Press, 1960), rpt. in paperback (New York: Atheneum, 1968 et seq.)

1962

"Homeric Echoes in Bihać," *ZNŽO*, 40(1962), 313-20
"Homer and Other Epic Poetry," in *CH*, pp. 179-214
"The Epic Singers," *Atlantic*, 210(1962), 126-27

1963

"Nationalism and the Muses in Balkan Slavic Literature in the Modern Period," in *The Balkans in Transition: Essays on the Development of Balkan Life and Politics Since the Eighteenth Century*, ed. by Charles and Barbara Jelavich (Berkeley: University of California Press, 1963), pp. 258-96

1964

"Ivo Andrić in English Translation," *SR*, 23(1964), 563-73

1965

"Beowulf and Odysseus," in *Franciplegius*, pp. 86-91

1967

"Homer as Oral Poet," *HSCP*, 72(1967), 1-46

"The Influence of a Fixed Text," in *To Honor Roman Jakobson: Essays on the Occasion of His Seventieth Birthday (11 October 1966)*, vol. 2, Janua Linguarum, Series Maior, 32 (The Hague: Mouton, 1967), pp. 1199-1206

1969

"The Theme of the Withdrawn Hero in Serbo-Croatian Oral Epic," *Prilozi*, 35(1969), 18-30

1970

"Tradition and the Oral Poet: Homer, Huso, and Avdo Medjedović," in *Atti del Convegno Internazionale sul Tema: La Poesia epica e la sua formazione* (Rome: Academia Nazionale, 1970), pp. 13-28

1971

"Homer, the Trojan War, and History," *JFI*, 8(1971), 85-92

"Some Common Themes in Balkan Slavic Epic," in *Actes du Premier Congrès des Études Balkaniques et Sud-Est Européennes* (Sofia, 1971), pp. 653-62

"An Example of Homeric Qualities of Repetition in Medjedović's 'Smailagić Meho'," in *Serta Slavica: Gedenkschrift für Alois Schmaus*, ed. by Wolfgang Gesemann *et al.* (Munich: Rudolf Trofenik, 1971), pp. 458-64

1972

"The Effect of the Turkish Conquest on Balkan Epic Tradition," in *Aspects of the Balkans: Continuity and Change*, ed. by Henrik Birnbaum and Speros Vryonis, Jr. (The Hague: Mouton, 1972), pp. 298-318

"History and Tradition in Balkan Oral Epic and Ballad," *WF*, 31(1972), pp. 53-60

1974

The Wedding of Smailagić Meho (Ženidba Smailagina sina), by Avdo Medjedović, coll., ed., and trans. with Milman Parry and David Bynum, Serbo-Croatian Heroic Songs (Srpskohrvatske junačke pjesme), vols. 3-4 (Cambridge, Mass.: Harvard University Press, 1974)

Editor, *The Multinational Literature of Yugoslavia* (New York: St. John's University, 1974), also issued as *RNL*, 5(1974)

"The Nineteenth-Century Revival of National Literatures: Karadžić, Njegoš, Radičević, The Illyrians, and Prešeren," in *The Multinational Literature of Yugoslavia*, pp. 101-11

"Perspectives on Recent Work on Oral Literature," *FMLS*, 10(1974), 187-210, rpt. in *OLSE*, pp. 1-24

1976

"The Heroic Tradition of Greek Epic and Ballad: Continuity and Change," in *Hellenism and the First Greek War of Liberation (1821-30): Continuity and Change*, no. 156 (Thessaloniki: Institute for Balkan Studies, 1976), pp. 79-94

"The Traditional Song," in *OL&F*, pp. 1-15

"Folklore, 'Folklorism,' and National Identity," in *Balkanistica: Occasional Papers in Southeast European Studies*, III(1976), ed. by Kenneth E. Naylor, (Columbus, Ohio: Slavica Publ., 1978), pp. 63-73

"Studies in the Bulgarian Epic Tradition: Thematic Parallels," in *Bulgaria Past and Present: Studies in History, Literature, Economics, Music, Sociology, and Linguistics*, Proceedings of the First International Conference on Bulgarian Studies (University of Wisconsin, Madison, May 3-5, 1973), ed. by Thomas Butler (Columbus, Ohio: American Association for the Advancement of Slavic Studies, 1976), pp. 349-58

1977

"Parallel Culture Traits in Ancient and Modern
Greece," *BMGS*, 3(1977), 71-80

1978

"The Gospels as Oral Traditional Literature," in
*The Relationships among the Gospels: an Interdis-
ciplinary Dialogue*, ed. by William O. Walker, Jr.
(San Antonio: Trinity University Press, 1978), pp.
33-91

Forthcoming

"Memory, Fixity, and Genre in Oral Traditional
Poetries," in the present volume

"Interlocking Mythic Patterns in *Beowulf*," in *Old
English Literature in Context: Ten Essays*, ed. by
John D. Niles (London and Totowa, New Jersey:
Boydell-Brewer and Rowman & Littlefield, 1980)

THE ORAL THEORY IN CONTEXT

Oral literature research has become a field of its own. It now speaks crucially to literatures as diverse as ancient Greek, early Chinese, Vedic Sanskrit, various African traditions, Serbo-Croatian, Old English, medieval French and Spanish, Eskimo, medieval Arabic, and the folk-preaching of the American rural South.[1] In addition, the vigorous and eclectic methodology developed in the course of this research draws from the resources of a number of disciplines, among them literary criticism, linguistics, history, and anthropology. The field of oral literature may thus be said to be interdisciplinary in the best sense of the term; it represents a creative fusion of several more classical ways of thinking which answers a perceived need and which fills a lacuna in our literary understanding.

The basic reason for this dramatic emergence is clear enough: from our point of view as a very literate, typographic culture, the idea of a literary text as oral in origin is a truly fascinating one. We are confronted with a virtual anomaly, a story or narrative which proceeds out of a context we find unfamiliar, perhaps uncomfortably so. What presents itself is not the usual phenomenon of an object text, but rather a continuous *tradition* of text-making and -remaking which has, in effect, no texts (as we understand them) until the performance of this or that moment in time is written down and the process is, for better or worse, frozen. The creature comforts of the author's study, the musing over and revising of sentences or verses, the changes suggested or made at various points in editing or proof—all of these ritual *accoutrements* of the more "usual" mode of literary creation become impertinent, in fact misleading. We encounter in the oral text something very different from the closely worked prose of Henry James or even the variorum edition of Yeats' poems; we encounter a literary document of great historical or diachronic depth, a kind of oral palimpsest which evolved to its manuscript form not as a visible record but as audible sound. This document thus presents us with an intriguing and complex riddle which the culturally egocentric etymology of our term "literature" itself suggests: how can a non- or preliterate people have and maintain an art which we know only in its post-literate form, and what is the signifi-

cance of the discrepancy between these oral and written
types of narrative?

The answers to these questions, and even the fact
that the questions may be phrased in this way, are the
direct results of what has come to be known as the
Parry-Lord oral theory. In fact, as we shall see, this
designation, like most rubrics, is descriptively inadequate in a number of ways. The research which these two
scholars have made possible is in many respects no longer
"theoretical"; while there may be differences of opinion
over its exact application to and significance for "dead
language" traditions, the unique kinds of information it
has provided about the structure and meaning of many ancient and medieval works is a matter of record. And, of
course, the great many fieldwork projects on oral tradition either undertaken or in the process of being undertaken all over the world again speak without qualification to the ontology of terms like "oral" and "traditional" as applied to literature. Also, as we shall see
in detail below, the field of oral literature falls
naturally into two periods, and this division depends
upon the respective activities of the discipline's orig-
inators. Milman Parry's *thèses* inaugurated the field in
1928. Albert Lord's monumental *The Singer of Tales*,
published in 1960, had a staggering comparative impact
upon many areas of scholarly endeavor; it essentially
secured and broadened what Parry had begun. In what
follows I will attempt to trace the early achievements
of Milman Parry (Part I); the continuing contribution of
Albert Lord (Part II); the history of formulaic and thematic studies in Old English, as an example of the oral
theory's influence on comparative literature (Part III);
and prospects for future research, as indicated by the
essays in this volume (Part IV). It is hoped that this
survey, brief though it must be, will indeed place the
oral theory in context and, in adumbrating its central
importance to humanistic studies in general, will reveal
its manifold possibilities for future investigations of
all kinds.

I. Milman Parry and the Homeric Question

What confronted Milman Parry in 1923,[2] and had confronted every other classicist since the systematic
study of the Homeric texts began, was a problem which
may at first sight seem surprisingly simple. Straight-

forwardly put, the celebrated "Homeric Question" amounts
to this: "Who was Homer?" or even "Was there a 'Homer'?"
While literary researchers may wonder at the apparent ignorance involved in asking such a disarmingly preliminary
kind of question, there was no reasonable answer available to Parry, or at least nothing that he could consider
reasonable. Ancient evidence on "Homer"—his origins,
ancestry, and date—is remarkably contradictory; as J. A.
Davison[3] reminds us, "by the early fifth century [B.C.]
several different cities were already claiming to have
been Homer's birthplace" (p. 235). The exact functions
and identities of the "singer" (*aoidós*) and professional
reciter or "rhapsode" (*rhapsōidós*) were no clearer,[4] and a
so-called "Peisistratean Recension"—hypothetically the
first text of Homer, thought to have been written down at
the Panathenaic Festival in sixth century B.C. Athens—
remains today an educated guess. The quandary had only
deepened in 1795 with the publication of Wolf's *Prolegomena ad Homerum*.[5] Here was a scholarly presentation
of evidence that what we know as the Homeric corpus must
have been preserved orally for hundreds of years before
being committed to manuscript; writing could not have
existed at the time of composition, Wolf argued, so his
conclusion was an empirical necessity.

The nineteenth century saw the advent of what has
come to be known as the "Analyst-Unitarian" controversy,
an avatar of the same Homeric Question and, significantly, the form in which Parry was to come to grips with it.
The first, and historically the earlier, of these
schools sought to "analyze" the *Iliad* and *Odyssey* into
levels or strata, and to isolate an original nuclear text
which was thought to have been added to, subtracted from,
and generally worked over by later generations of editors
and interpolators.[6] The task of the Analysts, then, was
to separate the poems into their chronological and geo-
graphical-dialectal parts, most often by locating what
were taken as narrative inconsistencies, dialect usages,
and archaeological infelicities. Their implicit answer
to the Homeric Question was, in effect, that there had
been many "Homers," many contributors to the texts which
have reached us. The Unitarians, on the other hand,
argued for a single author, for, as Adam Parry recon-
structs their position, "the Homeric poems [were] works
of art too great, their dramatic structure [was] too perfect, their characterization too consistent, to have been
the more or less random conglomeration of a series of

poets and editors" (p. xviii).[7] Dismissing many of the
philological details pursued in great depth by their opposition, the Unitarians visualized an individual craftsman comfortably like more modern poets.

Milman Parry's great achievement lay in the fact
that he was able to ignore this controversy and, interpreting then contemporary linguistic studies in a new
way,[8] posit an ongoing traditional *process* instead of
either a series of nonintegrated stages involving a
mélange of poets, editors, and interpolators or an individual act of poetic creation. As early as his M.A.
thesis of 1923, we find the following description of this
process: "Just as the story of the Fall of Troy, the tale
of the House of Labdakos, and the other Greek epic legends were not themselves the original fictions of certain
authors, but creations of a whole people, passed through
one generation to another and gladly given to anyone who
wished to tell them, so the style in which they were to
be told was not a matter of individual creation, but a
popular tradition, evolved by centuries of poets and
audiences, which the composer of heroic verse might follow without thought of plagiarism, indeed, without knowledge that such a thing existed."[9] This was the way in
which Parry first conceived of the poetic tradition, but
he was careful even then not to strip Homer of his "freedom of expression,"[10] for he made it clear that such a
hypothesis as his "does not mean that personal talent
had no effect on style, nothing to do with the choice and
use of the medium whereby an author undertook to express
his ideas.... It does mean, though, that there were certain established limits of form to which the play of
genius must confine itself." (p. 421). His comparison of
this formulaic style to the conventions underlying Greek
sculpture directed attention away from modern ideas of
the individual artist romantically searching for *le mot
juste* toward the ritual depth of the artist working within his tradition.

The French *thèses*, *The Traditional Epithet in Homer:
an Essay on a Problem of Homeric Style* and *Homeric Formulae and Homeric Meter*,[11] advanced these preliminary
conceptions significantly, initiating a method which was
to characterize Parry's writings—a meticulous attention
to evidence with which to ballast his hypotheses. In *TE*
he first defined the "formula" as "an expression regularly used, under the same metrical conditions, to express
an essential idea" (p. 13)[12] and then adduced his proof

in the form of Homeric noun-epithet combinations. A
great many distinctions of type and placement in the line
were made, and comparisons were drawn between the traditional, formulaic poems of Homer and the literary *Argo-
nautica* and *Aeneid* of Apollonius and Virgil. In *FM* he
submitted various kinds of metrical inconsistencies in
the Homeric hexameter to a formulaic scrutiny, concluding
at one point that "formulary diction can be likened to a
net of which each mesh is a single formulary expression:
the form of each will be adapted to that of the meshes
surrounding it" (p. 225). Besides explaining metrical
problems in a new way and continuing his description of
tradition, Parry was pointing the way to the diachronic
analyses of the text which have emerged in recent years.[13]

Parry's next major works, and they have proven over
time to be his most seminal, were "Studies I" and
Studies II."[14] In the former he first anchored the concept of "thrift" securely in the context of traditional
style[15]: "Unless the language itself stands in the way,
the poet—or poets—of the Homeric poems has—or have—
a noun-epithet formula to meet every regularly recurring
need. And what is equally striking, there is usually
only one such formula. An artifice of composition of
this variety and of this thrift must have called for the
long efforts of many poets who all sought the best and
easiest way of telling the same kind of stories in the
same verse-form." (p. 266). And, most important of all,
he also first suggested in "Studies I" that critics di-
vest themselves of preconceptions formed on the basis of
experience with *written* literature, and that they treat
Homer as *oral* literature: "The first move in this attempt to rebuild the Homeric idea of epic poetry will be
to show that the *Iliad* and the *Odyssey* are composed in a
traditional style, and are composed orally, then to see
just how such a poetry differs from our own in style and
form.... We shall find then, I think, that this failure
to see the difference between written and oral verse was
the greatest single obstacle to our understanding of
Homer, we shall cease to be puzzled by much, we shall no
longer look for much that Homer would never have thought
of saying, and above all, we shall find that many, if
not most of the questions we were asking, were not the
right ones to ask." (p. 269).

In "Studies I" Parry went on to describe the structure and texture of what he called the "traditional oral
style," offering both tabulations and morphologies of

formulas within the Homeric epics, as well as comparisons
with nontraditional poetries. His formulaic analyses of
Iliad I.1-25 and *Odyssey* i.1-25 make up part of this
data, which, as a whole, leads him to a line of reasoning: "Whatever means of composition we could suppose for
Homer, it could only be one which barred him in every
verse and in every phrase from the search for words that
would be of his own finding. Whatever reason we may
find for his following the scheme of the diction, it can
only be one which quits the poet at no instant. There is
only one need of this sort which can even be suggested—
the necessity of making verses by the spoken word." (p.
317). "Studies II" concentrated on demonstrating that
the Homeric language was not simply a collection of dia-
lects, but was itself a traditional "poetic dialect"
used only for oral epic composition: "...the whole of the
two poems [the *Iliad* and *Odyssey*], with perhaps a few
rare verses excepted, are the work of one or a number of
Ionic singers using, at about the same time, the same
traditional style, which was itself an Arcado-Cyprian
and Aeolic creation" (p. 361).

        Having for all practical purposes laid the Analyst-
Unitarian conflict to rest and having proposed a radical
new theory of poetic composition for Homer, Parry, together with Albert Lord, now turned what was once a
Homeric Question into a Oral Traditional Question. Their
field expeditions to Yugoslavia, about whose oral tradition Parry had heard from Matija Murko,[16] were intended
to test hypotheses developed for the "dead language"
texts of ancient Greek in the living laboratory of South
Slavic oral epic. As the result of the original collecting trips in 1933-35 and subsequent field work done later
by Lord and David Bynum, the Milman Parry Collection of
Oral Literature at Harvard University now houses the
largest collection of Serbo-Croatian oral narrative song
in existence.[17] Milman Parry had made a momentous beginning, both in his conception of a Homeric oral tradition and in his plans for testing that conception comparatively.

II. Albert Lord and the Oral
Traditional Question

        It would be difficult indeed to overestimate the
influence of Albert Lord on studies in literature, philology, folklore, and anthropology. The modulation of the

Homeric Question into the Oral Traditional Question was
begun by his and Parry's fieldwork in Yugoslavia, but it
was secured by Lord's *The Singer of Tales*. Along with
his editions of *Serbo-Croatian Heroic Songs* and a long
and rich series of articles on allied subjects, *Singer*
has stimulated productive research in a great many fields
and for a great many scholars; there is as yet no sign
that the activity engendered by these writings has
reached its peak. The promise of Milman Parry's beginning is being fulfilled and augmented by the ongoing research and scholarship of Albert Lord.[18]

The collecting trips of the thirties had resulted in
a unique sample of Serbo-Croatian oral texts, but Parry
was not to live to carry out the analyses he intended.[19]
Lord began in 1936 a series of papers dealing with specific problems in the Homeric poems which could be addressed by analogy to the Yugoslav oral tradition. In
the first of these papers,[20] he confronted the hypothesis
that the book divisions in Homer were in some sense
"chants" or chapters of heroic song. Did the singer
choose an appropriate (or at least what we, dealing with
the literary "chapter," would see as appropriate) place
to stop his performance, and was there in fact any evidence of a "performance unit" in the *Iliad* and *Odyssey*?
Referring to Parry's unpublished "The Falsity of the Notion of Chants in the Homeric Poems,"[21] he demonstrated
that the Yugoslav *guslar* may stop at almost any point,
either to rest from his considerable physical exertion
or simply because of the audience situation: "Breaks
which are the result of external circumstances are quite
beyond control, can come at no fixed point in the story,
and therefore form no fixed narrative unit. But when the
singer stops of his own accord with the purpose of resting and taking up the song later, he can choose his place
in the narrative.... He will not ordinarily drop it in
the middle of a sentence, nor in the midst of some minor
action; but because of the progressive style of composition, the addition of theme upon theme, the singer has no
difficulty in finding places to stop, and once he has
made up his mind to stop, it is never necessary for him
to go on for any length of time to find a convenient
spot." (110).[22] Near the end of this essay Lord makes an
important comment about comparative context: "Nor does
Homer suffer, as some would have us think, from this comparison with what is sometimes disparagingly called 'folk
epic.' Rather, I believe, he emerges an even greater

figure, because we are no longer seeking to compare him
with the literary geniuses of another kind of tradition,
but are trying to see him in his own time and place."
(113).[23]

    In the second article in this series,[24] he considers
the problem of narrative inconsistencies, the textual
"blemishes" upon which the Analysts in part founded their
theories of strata. He explains textual incongruities by
describing how the theme, defined here as "a subject
unit, a group of ideas, regularly employed by a singer,
not merely in any given poem, but in the poetry as a
whole" (410),[25] becomes progressively more stable and
self-sufficient: "But two of these units may be put together in the same poem because they are fitting, and yet
they contain details which are incongruous. This, of
course, does not upset the singer, intent as he is on the
theme on which he is working at the moment." (411). A
third aspect of Homeric style that Lord clarifies by comparative reference to Serbo-Croatian oral epic is that of
enjambement.[26] Showing how "the heroic decasyllable line
of the Southern Slavs contains the unit of thought of the
singer even more rigorously than the Homeric hexameter"
(114), he explains that "the answer to the question of
why necessary enjambement is more frequent in Homer than
in the Southslavic poetry, therefore, is that Homeric
style is richer in traditional devices for carrying the
thought beyond the end of the line" (123). All three of
these early "Homer and Huso" studies participate in establishing Lord's comparative methodology, a procedure
which combines copious and detailed evidence with imaginative, far-ranging analysis.

    A few years later a comparative survey of tradition-
al units appeared in "Composition by Theme in Homer and
Southslavic Epos."[27] In addition to illustrating how
"the theme and the formula are distinct units, even if at
times they coincide" (73), Lord offered a second definition for the theme: "a recurrent element of narration or
description in traditional oral poetry. It is not restricted, as is the formula, by metrical considerations."
(73). He also sets forth in this article the outlines
of a process he will later describe in detail—the singer's appropriation of the tradition[28]: "In the early
stages of learning the young singer learns both themes
and formulas, but his attention is fixed chiefly on the
latter.... But, even as his knowledge of formulas, which
is vague in the period of absorption which precedes his

first taking the accompanying instrument in his hand and
opening his mouth to sing, is sharpened to precision by
the act of singing his first song, so his idea of themes
is given shape as he learns new songs and perhaps ultimately creates songs of his own. The real function of
the theme is to be found in that phase of transmission
which covers the learning of a song by a singer in the
later stages of his training or by an accomplished singer
and in the creation of a new song. Once a singer has a
command of the common themes of the tradition, he has
merely to hear a song which is new to him only to be able
to perform it himself." (73-74). He goes on to distinguish between "essential" and "ornamental" themes, giving
examples from both ancient Greek and Serbo-Croatian
texts, concluding that "both poets have a short and a
long way of expressing the same fundamental theme by employing varying degrees of ornamentation. Homer's skill
in using this type of theme in proper perspective and
with telling effect is no small part of his peculiar
genius." (79).[29]

  Serbo-Croatian Folk Songs, co-authored with Béla
Bartók,[30] presented a sample of the so-called "women's
songs" (*ženske pjesme*) in the Serbo-Croatian tradition,
that is, the shorter lyric songs performed by women and
young men without the accompaniment of the *gusle*. Lord's
section of the book contains the texts and translations
of 75 of these women's songs, together with an introduction which describes the circumstances of their collection, especially in the Gacko region. Some of the lyrics
are sung on particular occasions, such as weddings and
other ritual times, or as lullabies; the majority are
love songs which could be performed at any time. Parry
and Lord concentrated on recording epic and Lord's analyses have treated primarily the heroic material, so this
edition of and commentary on the folk or lyric poems is
particularly valuable in bringing another aspect of the
tradition to light.

  "Homer's Originality: Oral Dictated Texts"[31] furnished an answer to the opinion that Parry's work was an
attack on Homer's genius. Lord's close study of actual
sung performances as compared to poems taken down from
dictation produced a number of new insights. First, the
formulaic repertory exhibits a good deal of variation:
"We now know that creation and re-creation occur on the
formula level much more extensively than Parry had at
first thought" (127). After noting how the theme and

story as a whole show a similar amount of variation, Lord
concludes that "the oral technique not only allows freedom for change and creation but aids in providing the
means by which the singer may exercise his creative imagination if he so desires. His medium is not so restrictive that he is stifled by his tradition." (128).[32] Arguing by analogy from his experience in collecting both
sung and dictated epics, Lord then makes the case for the
Homeric poems as oral dictated texts, as songs written
down from performance. He bases his claim primarily on
the greater length and quality of such texts in Serbo-
Croatian tradition: "The chief advantage to the singer of
this manner of composition is that it affords him time to
think of his lines and of his song. His small audience
is stable. This is an opportunity for the singer to show
his best, not as a performer, but as a storyteller and
poet. He can ornament his song as fully as he wishes and
is capable.... The very length of the Homeric poems is
the best proof that they are products of the moment of
dictation rather than that of singing. The leisureliness
of their tempo, the fullness of their telling, are also
indications of this method." (132-33).

     In 1953 and 1954 the first two volumes of *Serbo-
Croatian Heroic Songs* appeared, no. I entitled *Novi
Pazar: English Translations* and no. II *Novi Pazar:
Serbocroatian Texts.*[33] Besides the poems themselves,
these volumes offer an introduction to the field work and
index to Parry Collection holdings, conversations with
the singers whose songs are published therein, and a
great many helpful summaries and notes. Lord's clearly
stated criteria for selection of material account for the
composition of I and II: "In investigating an oral epic
tradition, it is necessary to begin with a study of the
songs of an individual singer and then to proceed to a
consideration of the other singers in the same district.
One thus sees the singer both as an individual and in relation to the community of singers to which he belongs.
For that reason our selected texts will be published by
districts, and within each district the songs of a single
singer will be grouped together." (I, p. 16). The material gathered together in this first sampling from Novi
Pazar presents the scholar with a much more extensive
referent of known oral song than does either the ancient
Greek or any of the continental or insular medieval literatures. While no one would argue that the Novi Pazar
songs are of the quality of the *Iliad* or *Beowulf* or the

Chanson de Roland, it should also be remembered that—
virtually by definition—few poems of any period or literature can be said to equal or surpass the very best
that these traditions have to offer. These "first
fruits" from the Parry Collection were published to give
slavists and comparatists the opportunity to study the
metamorphosis of formula, theme, and story pattern from
song to song and from singer to singer within a defined
geographical area, a local tradition. This they do exceedingly well.[34] As far as approaching the Homeric
poems in terms of length and aesthetic quality, this
task was left to volumes III and IV and Avdo Medjedović.[35]

  Lord's article on Avdo[36] is a paean to all great
traditional singers. Included in the biography are some
remarkable statistics. We learn, for instance, that
Avdo had in 1935 a repertoire of 58 epics and that he
dictated one song of 12,323 lines ("The Wedding of
Smailagić Meho") and sang another of 13,331 lines
("Osmanbey Delibegović and Pavičević Luka")[37] —both, in
other words, about the length of the *Odyssey*. In discussing Medjedović's fondness for elaboration, Lord remarks with justice that "Avdo's songs are living proof
that the best of oral epic singers are original poets
working within the tradition in the traditional manner"
(323-24). After illustrating Avdo's techniques of ornamentation and flashback, he then recounts Parry's experiment of having the greater singer present when another
guslar was performing a poem which Avdo had not heard
before: "When it was over, Parry turned to Avdo and
asked him if he could now sing the same song, perhaps
even sing it better than Mumin, who accepted the contest
good-naturedly and sat by in his turn to listen. Avdo,
indeed, addressed himself in his song to his 'colleague'
(*kolega*) Muminaga. And the pupil's version of the tale
reached to 6,313 lines, nearly three times the length of
his 'original' on his first singing!" (327).[38] Lord recorded some epics from Avdo during the 1951 trip; though
ill, he still managed "over fourteen thousand lines in
about a week's time" (329). This most Homeric of *guslari* was fittingly honored by Nikola Vujnović's *kudos*:
"'Onda kad ne bude Avda medu živima, neće se naći niko
ko bi bio ovakav za pjevanje'—'When Avdo is no longer
among the living, there will be no one like him in singing'" (329-30).

  In the same year of 1956 Lord took up a fundamental

aspect of oral tradition in "The Role of Sound-Patterns
in Serbo-Croatian Epic."[39] He shows in this article that
not only syntactic parallelism but also alliteration and
assonance patterns help to guide the poet in his formula
usage and deployment. These sound clusters, groupings
marked by phonemic redundancy, seem to be organized by a
"key word," which "is, as it were, the bridge between
idea and sound" (302). A detailed explication of sound
patterning in a passage from Salih Uglanin's *Song of Bagdad* illustrates how the patterns "are clustered around
the essential ideas which come successively to the singer's consciousness as he tells the story" (303). Far
from working against the formulas, then, sound aids the
singer in the formulaic expression of "essential ideas"
and adds another dimension to the compositional process.
This rather short paper thus proves to be a significant
one, both in the effect it has on later theory and in
focusing attention on the oral/aural reality of traditional narrative song.[40]

Lord again treated sound patterns and their role in
oral epic composition in an article which appeared three
years later, "The Poetics of Oral Creation."[41] In addition to comments on formula, theme, acoustic sequence,
and syntactic balance, however, he also discussed the
continuing force of myth in epic, using the example of
the *guslar* Sulejman Fortić's versions of *The Song of Bagdad* (*S-CHS* II, nos. 22 and 23) as illustration. He
showed how "Đerdelez Alija has taken over a theme belonging to the god who dies and goes, or is lost or banished,
to the other world and who is sought, when disaster
threatens, to save his people by return.... *Fortić does
not know this, of course,* but the force of the myth pre-
vails." (6). Through the singer's art the myths of times
long past are maintained alive and vital, and the poetics
of oral epic derive ultimately from their continuing influence: "Perhaps the most fundamental of [the poetic
values of oral poetry] come from the myth, or myths,
which first determined the themes of oral narrative
poetry, which provided the story material and gave it
significance. For the myths brought it into being and
kept it living long after they themselves had officially
been declared dead." (*idem*).

To try to assess the impact of *The Singer of Tales*
on the scholarly world would be an impossibly complex
and lengthy task in any format, not to mention the few
paragraphs available here. Suffice it to say that the

book has held its position as the *fons et origio* of oral
literature research for nearly twenty years; it will always be the single most important work in the field, for,
simply put, it began the field. Lord's methodology is
straightforward: he applies the personal experience of a
living oral tradition in Yugoslavia to earlier literatures, illustrating by analogy the traditional oral form
and structure of those literatures. Following the introduction with a chapter on the performance and training of the *guslar*, he sketches in the usual milieu and
social setting of epic singing and describes three stages
in the poet's "apprenticeship." The first period is one
of listening; at an early age "the themes of the poetry
are becoming familiar to him, and his feeling for them is
sharpened as he hears more and as he listens to the men
discussing the songs among themselves. At the same time
he is imbibing the rhythm of the singing and to an extent also the rhythm of the thoughts as they are expressed in song." (p. 21). The second stage starts with
the boy's initial attempts at singing: "It begins with
establishing the primary element of the form—the rhythm
and melody, both of the song and of the gusle or the
tambura (a two-stringed plucked instrument). This is to
be the framework for the expression of his ideas." (p.
21). The third period dates from the time a singer can
perform more than one song all the way through and can
add or subtract ornamentation to suit his performance to
the audience and the situation.

     Lord's remarks on the formula in Chapter 3 assume
Parry's latter definition, "a group of words which is
regularly employed under the same metrical conditions to
express a given essential idea," which he supplements
with phrases of his own, such as the formula being "the
offspring of the marriage of thought and sung verse"
(p. 31), and a large number of examples from Serbo-
Croatian oral tradition. In conceiving of the formulaic
repertoire as a kind of oral poetic language and stress-
ing the formative function of rhythm and melody, he
points the way to a dynamic view of the formula, a view
that emphasizes the active multiformity of the substitutable phrase.[42] After showing "the way in which the formulaic style enters into the consciousness of a young
singer as he learns to use it for the telling of tales"
(p. 45), Lord moves on to describe and exemplify the
technique of formulaic analysis. His examination of
songs by Salih Ugljanin (see *S-CHS* I and II) proves

that "in making his lines the singer is not bound by the
formula. The formulaic technique was developed to serve
him as a craftsman, not to enslave him." (p. 54). Near
the end of this chapter he enters briefly on a discussion
of sound-patterning, syntactic parallelisms, and word-
boundary patterns, all of which are shown to act as
guides for the poet as he works his way forward formulaically. All evidence indicates that "the poetic grammar
of oral epic is and must be based on the formula" (p.
65).[43]

I will pass over discussion of the "theme" at this
point, since Lord's comments on this unit are quoted extensively in Part III, and go on to Chapter 5, "Songs
and the Song." Here we confront most clearly the differences between our "literary" view of the oral epic
poem and the poem as it exists in tradition, as "a flexible plan of themes" (p. 99). Our concept of "the original" becomes oblique: "Each performance is the specific
song, and at the same time it is the generic song. The
song we are listening to is 'the song'; for each performance is more than a performance; it is a re-creation"
(p. 101). Using examples from the Parry Collection, and
especially the songs of Avdo Medjedović, Lord illustrates
the fairly conservative oral structure of the song and
its fluid parts; even from the same singer, stability
from one performance to the next is likely to lie not at
the word-for-word level of the text, but at the levels of
theme and story pattern. Modes of variation include
elaboration, simplification, change in order within a
series, addition or omission of material, substitution of
themes, and, frequently, different ways of ending the
song. Our usual notion of "text" must be modified considerably, for "in a variety of ways a song in tradition
is separate, yet inseparable from other songs" (p. 123).

In the sixth chapter, "Writing and Oral Tradition,"
the various kinds of interfaces between the worlds of
print and song are addressed. Lord's most important
single point, however, is to debunk an assumption which
we as members of a highly literate culture implicitly
make: "When writing was introduced, epic singers, again
even the most brilliant among them, did not realize its
'possibilities' and did not rush to avail themselves of
it. Perhaps they were wiser than we, because one cannot
write song. One cannot lead Proteus captive; to bind him
is to destroy him." (p. 124). The very fluidity which is
the life of traditional song can exist only when no fixed

text exists; once *a* performance becomes "*the* song," the
variorum nature of tradition ceases to play its role. Of
course, as Lord mentions, such a fixed text could be
elicited from a singer without disturbing his participation in the tradition, but the elicited text must be as-
sessed in its true context, not as *the* poem. However,
when literacy enters the picture, the traditional ways
of composing oral epic—formula, theme, story pattern—
lose their *raison d'être*. Even the fixed text itself, if
made available for memorization (as it was among younger
guslari even in 1933-35), spells death for the tradition.
In either case, composition soon comes to focus on a single model, usually a model committed to memory, and the
multiforms which make up the tradition fall away. Indeed, as Lord notes with reference to a number of European literatures, "oral tradition did not become transferred or transmuted into a literary tradition of epic,
but was only moved further and further into the background, literally into the back country, until it disap-
peared" (p. 138).

     The final four chapters of *The Singer of Tales* apply
the theoretical principles derived from the Serbo-Croatian tradition to ancient Greek and medieval epic. They
include formulaic and thematic analysis of the *Iliad* and
Odyssey, Beowulf, the *Chanson de Roland,* and *Digenis
Akritas.* Lord argues very cogently for these poems as
oral traditional poems, and discusses the hypothesis
against the background of what is known about the history
of their transmission. There are also in these pages—
especially those devoted to Homer—unique insights into
the larger structure and meaning of these great works,
insights made possible by an understanding of the true
nature of the texts which have reached us in fixed form.
As only one example, I quote from Lord's comments on the
overall structure of the *Odyssey*: "There seems to be
evidence ... of a version in which Telemachus met his
father at Pylos and returned with him, and another version in which he met Odysseus at Eumaeus' hut. They
have been put together in oral tradition as we have it in
this song of Homer's. The result is duplication often
with one element in the duplication being vestigial or
partial, and hence an apparent postponement and suspense,
or an inconsistency." (p. 174).[44] Finally, Lord places a
closing emphasis on the terms which define the new Question: "Yet after all that has been said about *oral* composition as a technique of line and song construction, it

seems that the term of greater significance is *tradition-al*. Oral tells us 'how,' but traditional tells us 'what,' and even more, 'of what kind' and 'of what force.' When we know how a song is built, we know that its building blocks *must* be of a great age. For it is of the *necessary* nature of tradition that it seek and maintain stability, that it preserve itself. And this tenacity springs neither from perverseness, nor from an abstract principle of absolute art, but from a desperately compelling conviction that what the tradition is preserving is the very means of attaining life and happiness. The traditional oral epic singer is not an artist; he is a seer." (p. 220).

Two years after the first printing of *The Singer of Tales*, Lord commented on striking similarities of detail in the Serbo-Croatian "return song" and the *Odyssey* in his article "Homeric Echoes in Bihać."[45] Working specifically with a song dictated by Franje Vuković, "The Captivity of Šarac Mehmedagha" (Parry no. 1905), he related an episode in the Serbo-Croatian epic to scenes in the Homeric poem. An enumeration of points of contact between the two ends with this conclusion: "It would seem that the first part of the episode, the encounter with the women at the well, is paralleled by the encounter with Nausicaa in Phaeacia; and that the second part, deceptive story and recognition, is paralleled in Ithaca. The two have been telescoped by the Yugoslav singer, or by his tradition; or, perhaps, they have been separated and elaborated by the Greek tradition." (319). The essay closes with a brief look at another "deceptive tale," that which Odysseus tells to Athena just after he lands at Ithaca; the same scene also contains elements of the "Nausicaa theme," wherein the hero meets a woman or women near the well, and thus acts as a structural mid-point in the *Odyssey*.[46] On the basis of these descriptions, Lord asks the question which they beg—whether there is a continuous tradition of "return songs" in the Balkans from at least Homeric times. Though proceeding with characteristic caution, he affirms the possibility: "Stories, or their narrative essences, cling tenaciously together and pass easily from language to language, providing only that there is a singing tradition. I like to think that in 'The Captivity of Šarac Mehmedagha' and in other similar songs in the Yugoslav tradition one is hearing the *Odyssey* or other similar songs, still alive on the lips of men, ever new, yet ever the same." (p. 320).

"Homer and Other Epic Poetry"[47] offers a context for
Homeric oral narrative by setting the *Iliad* and *Odyssey*
against the backdrop of epic from all over the world and
from as early as 2000 B.C. Lord recapitulates many of the
analyses and descriptions carried out at length in *Sing-*
er, adding useful comparative remarks like the following:
"The Homeric hexameter is a longer line than [those of
the Serbo-Croatian, Old French, and Old English poet-
ries], and the number of places in it where a diaeresis
or caesura may occur multiplies the possible lengths for
formula units. Its basic formula structure is more varied even than that of the Old Germanic line. Yet it is
still fundamentally a system of parts of lines and of
whole lines." (p. 187). He also illustrates in detail the
multiformity of the theme and song and places Homer in an
oral tradition, a tradition which by its very nature
would not consider the use of writing in the composition
of epic: "Were one to discover epics written in Linear B
having all the characteristics of oral narrative poetry,
one would have uncovered another period of collecting.
We know now that the answer to whether the Homeric poems
are oral or not lies in the analysis of their style and
not in the presence or absence of writing, or even in the
presence or absence of a literary tradition." (p. 197).
In the final sections of this essay, Lord gives examples
of sound patterns in Homer, suggests connections between
epic song and ritual, and describes the functions of the
epic as history, teaching, and entertainment.[48]

One of Lord's most wide-ranging and important articles, "Homer as Oral Poet,"[49] appeared in 1967. His
first point is the effect of literacy upon oral tradition, made in answer to Adam Parry's "Have We Homer's
Iliad?". He summarizes: "First, if the singer is well
established in the oral technique, he is not likely to
be much attracted by reading or writing." And, "second,
the singer in the 25- to 50-year age group, who is well
steeped in the traditional oral technique before he acquires the idea of the fixed text, may be able for a
time to continue to compose in the oral manner." Finally, "third, the singer who is not secure in the oral
technique, no matter what his age, when the newer ideas
come to him, will succumb quite easily to the concept of
the fixed text, and he will rapidly lose whatever ability he had in oral composition." (5). Thus the influence
of the *pesmarica* ("songbook") makes itself felt, differ-
entially and over time, to the eventual destruction of

the oral tradition.   Of course, this topic leads naturally into the next: the value of the Serbo-Croatian analogy
to studies of Homer.   Here Lord shows that T.B.L. Web-
ster's hypothesis that "literacy killed the Yugoslav
poets because it brought them into touch with a higher
culture" and that "there is no reason why it should have
had the same effect on Greek oral poets"[50] is undocument-
ed and critically uninformed.   Likewise, he demonstrates
the limits of Adam Parry's understanding of the situation
in the latter's characterization of Serbo-Croatian oral
epic as a "backwoods phenomenon,"[51] affirming the integrity of the Moslem epic tradition from the rise of the
Ottoman Empire.[52]

At the heart of the disagreement over whether quantitative formula analysis can prove Homer's orality,
Lord believes, lies a fatal variation in definition and
application.   Taking studies by Joseph Russo and G. S.
Kirk as *pieds à terre*,[53] he shows that available data
does indeed point toward a significant correlation between formula density and orality, but that more analysis
and less speculation are needed.   He then describes the
kinds of investigations undertaken for medieval texts
and Serbo-Croatian songs, in the latter category both
oral and imitation oral texts.   Lord's own techniques
and an additional method developed by David Bynum suc-
cessfully distinguish between the oral and imitation
poems.   In comparing the formula density of samples taken
from the *Batrachomyomachia* and the *Iliad*, Lord finds the
Homeric poem much more formulaic and takes this quality
as proof of its orality.[54]   What informs all of his
analyses are concerns for a fair amount of material, a
(presumed) single singer, and careful definitions of
formula and formulaic.[55]   The remainder of the article
focuses on specific instances of what Lord feels is
"subjective interpretation" of Homer, impressionistic
explication which goes against the traditional nature of
the poems.   His arguments in response to the ideas of
Kirk and Anne Amory Parry[56] are too detailed to treat in
summary fashion, but we may say that meticulous research
into the formulaic structure of the passages involved
sheds a new and truer—because objective—light on their
meaning.   Lord's caveat speaks to the need for more of
this kind of study: "Surely one of the vital questions
now facing Homeric scholarship is how to understand oral
poetics, how to read oral traditional poetry.   Its
poetics is different from that of written literature

because its technique of composition is different. It
cannot be treated as a flat surface. All the elements
in traditional poetry have depth, and our task is to
plumb their sometimes hidden recesses; for there will
meaning be found. We must be willing to use the new
tools for investigations of themes and patterns, and we
must be willing to learn from the experience of other
oral traditional poetries. Otherwise "oral" is only an
empty label and "traditional" is devoid of sense. Together they form merely a facade behind which scholarship can continue to apply the poetics of written literature." (46).

The next two articles in chronological sequence both
concentrated mainly on the larger paradigm of oral story
structure, that which Lord has called the "story pattern."[57]   As he says in "The Theme of the Withdrawn Hero
in Serbo-Croatian Oral Epic,"[58] "my basic assumption is
that in oral tradition there exist narrative patterns
that, no matter how much the stories built around them
may seem to vary, have great vitality and function as
organizing elements in the composition and transmission
of oral story texts" (18). In fact, he believes the
story pattern treated in this essay, which involves the
five-element sequence of Absence, Devastation, Return,
Retribution, and Wedding, to be as old as the Indo-
European oral tradition and to be preserved in, for example, the Homeric *Odyssey*. Tracing the pattern in a
number of Serbo-Croatian oral epics, significantly from
both the Moslem and Christian singing traditions, he is
able to illustrate the multiformity in narrative of this
simple elemental sequence and the connection between the
Yugoslav poems and "similar stories sung in Homer's day,
and even from generations before him" (30).

Although his primary interest in "Tradition and the
Oral Poet: Homer, Huso, and Avdo Medjedović"[59] turns to
the relationship between history and the epic, Lord's
methodology again touches on the story pattern in a comparative context. After a convincing demonstration of
how an oral story text cannot be reconstructed from
"later" variants because of the fluidity of themes and
sequences and the anachronism of tradition as a whole,
he discusses duplication and agglomeration, two processes by means of which stories evolve within tradition.
He shows that "there is a kind of interpenetration between songs, a kind of exchange from one to another, as
it were. A song is a conglomerate of elements more or

less loosely joined together for a time, always capable
of losing some of its elements to another conglomerate
with a somewhat similar, though not exactly the same,
configuration.... An interweaving of elements in this
way is the normal method of formation and of continual
re-formation of 'songs' in oral traditional narrative."
(p. 22).[60] He then applies these findings to the *Odyssey*
and locates duplications of arrival and shipwreck. The
final emphasis rests on the primacy of the story pattern,
on the mythic paradigm which precedes and even gives
shape to historical facts: "Historical events cannot
give to a pattern the intensity and force needed for it
to survive all the changes of tradition. These changes
are not the corruption of time, but the constant rein-
terpretation of succeeding generations and societies.
Not corruption, but constant renewal and revivification.
The patterns must be suprahistorical in order to have
such force. Their matrix is myth and not history; for
when history does have an influence on the stories it
is, at first at least, history that is changed, not the
stories." (pp. 27-28).

The relationship between myth and historical event
remained the central concern in three of Lord's next
four articles. In the first of these, "Homer, the Trojan War, and History,"[61] he takes issue with both Denys
Page's and M. I. Finley's interpretations of the Iliadic
catalogs of Achaeans and Trojans,[62] arguing that any
theme, including a catalog, will exhibit variation over
time and therefore cannot be expected to preserve "historical fact." A comparative look at Avdo Medjedović's
catalogs in "The Wedding of Smailagić Meho" and "Osmanbey
Delibegović and Pavičević Luka" proves that the accuracy
of the oral epic, as we understand the concept of accuracy, is not absolute: "Fact is present in the epic, but
relative chronology in the catalogue is confused. Time
is telescoped. The past of various times is all as-
sembled into the present performance.... Oral epic presents a composite picture of the past." (90-91). The
second of the papers studied "The Effect of the Turkish
Conquest on Balkan Epic Tradition."[63] Along with a useful geographical and historical survey of Moslem oral
epic from earliest times, Lord considers the Turkish
elements now part of the Serbo-Croatian singing tradition. His comments range from particular lexical
glosses to the more general phenomenon of the "ceremonial
elegance and brilliance of the Balkan epic which seems to

have entered with the Turkish Moslem culture" (p. 307).
In addition, he relates the "return song" story pattern
to "the vegetation pattern of death and resurrection, the
dying god who returns" (p. 311) and concludes that
"thanks to the conservatism of the Moslemized bards of
the Balkans, the oldest mythic patterns of oral epic were
preserved, elaborated, and strengthened" (p. 318). And
finally, in "History and Tradition in Balkan Oral Epic
and Ballad,"[64] Lord again instances "The Wedding of
Smailagić Meho" to suggest the primacy of myth in epic,
that "history *enters into* or is in its general characteristics reflected in oral epic and ballad tradition,
rather than originating it" (60).

In 1974 the long-awaited text and translation of
"The Wedding of Smailagić Meho," dictated by Avdo
Medjedović in July of 1935, was published by Lord and
David Bynum as the third and fourth volumes of *Serbo-
Croatian Heroic Songs*. This is the epic which Lord had
previously described in a number of articles, the most
Homeric of Yugoslav epic songs both in length and in
traditional quality.[65] In the translation and especially in the original language, the consummate skill of
Avdo—his ability to sing a great song *within a tradition of singing* which also includes, inevitably, lesser
songs—shines through, affording a view of a master poet
in perfect control of his medium. His characteristic
ornamentation gives a sense of fullness to the poem, an
effulgence and dynamism that derive directly from the
Protean possibilities which form the context for its
making and reveal the depth of its roots in tradition.
In coming to grips with Avdo's art, we can see most
clearly the poetic reality behind the theoretical message of *The Singer of Tales* and understand the comparison of the Serbo-Croatian and ancient Greek traditions
in a new light. Lord and Bynum incorporate a very helpful and informative apparatus: the translation volume
(III) includes essays on Avdo and his originality, conversations with the singer, notes, and appendices covering related texts, while the original text volume (IV)
adds material on Avdo's background, his repertory, conversations (in Serbo-Croatian), and notes. In short,
these volumes and the poem they present offer a unique
view of a monumental epic, an *oral* and *traditional* epic
which deserves careful scholarly attention from slavists
and comparatists alike.

A collection of essays edited by Lord, *The Multi-*

national Literature of Yugoslavia[66] also appeared in
1974. His own contribution, "The Nineteenth-Century
Revival of National Literatures: Karadžić, Njegoš,
Radičević, The Illyrians, and Prešeren" (pp. 101-11),
offers an overview of the complex group of traditions at
the root of more modern Yugoslav literature. Of special
interest are his comments on the oral traditional context of important events and trends in the nineteenth
century; for instance, he notes that "the literary language chosen by Vuk and by the writers of the Illyrian
movement in Zagreb was neither the dialect of Zagreb nor
that of Belgrade but that of oral literature in Herzego-
vina" (p. 103). Included as well are a brief listing of
significant collections of oral literature from the
period, an account of "purely literary" original writings by individuals, and placement of those individuals
in their contemporary context. The primary value of
this article lies in the sketch it gives of the movement
from oral to written in the nineteenth century; much remains to be done with this crucially important interface
between literatures.

Lord's "Perspectives on Recent Work on Oral Literature"[67] surveys contributions to research in a number of
literatures, among them Serbo-Croatian, Russian, Alba-
nian, modern Greek, Central Asiatic, various African
linguistic communities, Ugaritic, Sumerian, early Chinese, Sanskrit, medieval Greek, Old Irish, ancient
Greek, Old French, and Old English. Much more than a
bibliographical supplement, this essay treats many problems in depth, especially in the last three literatures
listed above. Two points on Homeric tradition and the
Yugoslav analogy are particularly noteworthy. Lord reminds us in commenting on Bernard Fenik's study of the
Iliad[68] that "the South Slavic singers have taught us a
great deal about the mechanics of oral composition of
traditional narrative verse or song, and we should be
willing to acknowledge ... at least that much of a debt
to them" (p. 12). But also, he goes on, "we have been
able to see in the modern Balkans the *whole* of a tradition and that over a long period of time—not just two
songs from one singer but many songs from many singers
...." (p. 12). This wider view is valuable indeed,
since "we do not have enough of the tradition outside
of Homer's poems to judge, on our own, pragmatically,
Homer's relationship to his tradition" (p. 13).[69]

Comparative extension of theories and observations

based on the Homeric texts took another direction in
Lord's 1976 article, "The Heroic Tradition of Greek Epic
and Ballad: Continuity and Change."[70] In this essay he
traces Greek oral song from its ancient beginnings
through its medieval transformations to its modern forms,
making the point that the tradition preserves as well as
discards, continues as well as changes. Comparisons are
drawn between the medieval hero Digenis Akritas and the
classical Herakles, shifts in language and religion (and
the resultant syncretism of pagan and Christian in medieval times) are described, and the various modern modu-
lations in narrative pattern typical of the Akritic and
klephtic songs are exemplified. In brief compass, then,
this article documents "the progression in time, with
both continuity and change, from long and intricate epic
in ancient times, through drastic changes in form in the
medieval period, which did not involve changes in story
elements and patterns, in spite of vast social, political
and religious changes, to a modern sense of history and
the development of a new tradition of historical songs,
side by side with a hauntingly elegiac and deeply moving
oral tradition of lyrico-balladic *klephtic* panegyrics
and laments drawn from the lives of the *armatoloi* and
klephts and the brave bands of *pallikars*" (pp. 93-94).

Lord's "The Traditional Song" was presented to a
colloquium on "Oral Literature and the Formula" in 1974
and published in 1976.[71] Once again he focuses on large
narrative patterns, this time in "Bojičić Alija Rescues
Alibey's Children" (*S-CHS* no. 24), the *Odyssey*, "The
Wedding of Smailagić Meho," the fourteenth-century Old
Turkish romance of Sajjid Batthal, and the *Iliad*. A
comparison is drawn between Bojičić Alija and Telemachus
on the basis of their similar backgrounds and roles within the poems; Lord detects a single story pattern involving "(1) father absent or dead, (2) challenge, (3)
helper-donor, (4) borrowed equipment, and (5) journey"
(p. 4) cast in two different narrative situations. He
then relates the stories of two more initiatory heroes—
Meho and Dschaafar (Batthal)—to the same pattern. Lord
also explains Achilles as a participant in this mythical
structure, understanding the special armor, which, he
feels, outstrips Hector's importance, as a traditional
precursor to Achilles' fight against the river, a supernatural opponent: "If we approach the *Iliad* as a traditional song, then it is possible to see in the divine
armor and in the fight with the river a vestige of the

ancient pattern of the battle of the supreme god for power against a primordial water dragon" (p. 13). What we
have in the poem is thus a composite structure: "The
tale of human vengeance, according to this view, became
entangled with the dragon-slaying pattern at some point
in the past" (p. 14). His closing remarks on Meho indicate the diachronic depth and multiform nature of the
Serbo-Croatian epic as well: "Thus, even within the
limited scope of the early portions of The Wedding of
Smailagić Meho one can see the interweaving of ritual
and mythic patterns which give a traditional depth to
the modern song. For Meho is an initiatory hero, and
at the same time also the dragon-slayer of divine implications with a holy crusade to bring divine order and
salvation to his people, and finally he is a maiden-
saving dragon-slayer." (p. 15).

Some of the comparative points raised in the 1976
essays were again addressed in a paper that appeared the
next year, "Parallel Culture Traits in Ancient and Modern
Greece."[72] Here Lord investigates the possible continuity of the ancient and modern Greek traditions through
analysis of narrative pattern and formula. He also relates the Greek and Serbo-Croatian traditions through
(a) "songs containing supernatural elements whose protagonists are historical figures of the past" (tales of
Digenis Akritas and Marko Kraljević) and (b) historical
and elegiac songs (72). The argument from formula, intended to indicate a relationship between the Homeric
hexameter and the 15-syllable *politikos* line, proceeds
from a study of metrical word-position; Homeric and
Digenis Akritas formulas are placed side by side to illustrate their agreement in the constraints placed on
the positioning of τέκνον and ἀκούω. His conclusions
about continuity are in principle quite convincing, and
they open up many new areas for research at levels of
oral traditional structure from formula to story pattern.

Lord's most recent essay, "The Gospels as Oral
Traditional Literature,"[73] is a long and experimental
application of oral literary methodology to a new subject. He begins by reiterating and developing earlier
ideas about the primacy of mythic patterns and their
shaping function in the determination of what we are
accustomed to call "history." A number of biographical
events in the gospels are shown to proceed from generic
life patterns common to oral texts such as the *Theogony*,
the Babylonian *Enuma Elish*, and many others. By weighing

common and divergent themes, he seeks to establish the
traditional character of each gospel and at the same time
to indicate their lack of dependence on a single archetype. The remainder of the study is devoted to a comparative analysis of traditional motifs and verbal correspondence in Matthew, Mark, and Luke. Carefully taking
note of the necessarily tentative nature of conclusions
based on this bold first step in an unexplored direction,
Lord then summarizes: "As I see it at the moment, the
events in Jesus' life, his works and teachings, evoked
ties with 'sacred' oral traditional narratives and narrative elements that were current in the Near East and in
the eastern Mediterranean in the first century A.D.
These were stories whose deepest meanings were concerned
with: (a) establishing order in the world by invoking
divine models and divine intervention, and (b) assuring,
as part of this order, a continuation of life for a
humanity that was puzzled by and anxious about its own
mortality." (p. 91).

This section of the introduction is only temporarily
complete. For Albert Lord's contribution is not only a
seminal but a continuing one, as the last essay in the
present volume attests. We all anticipate his further
writings on oral literature,[74] and especially his book
in progress on the history of Balkan oral epic. As we
pass on to Part III, it is well to remember that the virtual explosion of research in Old English formulaic and
thematic structure since 1953 is the direct result of
his (and Francis P. Magoun's) thinking, and, furthermore, that Old English is but one of many literatures
now better understood and appreciated because he encouraged us to ask the Oral Traditional Question.

III. The Oral Theory and Old English Poetry

In tracing the origins and development of the oral
theory in Old English poetry,[75] we must be aware of what
preceded the revolutionary effect of Parry's and Lord's
work. For, as in the case of Homeric epos, earlier
scholars writing on Anglo-Saxon verse had much to say
about the commonplaces of word, line, and scene. I will
therefore distinguish two clearly differentiated periods:
(1) Formulaic Structure and the Text (1878-1948), and
(2) Oral Traditional Theory (1949-1978).

Formulaic Structure and the Text (1878-1948)

The well-known proposals of Albert Lord and Francis
P. Magoun, Jr.,[76] which open the second of our two periods, have roots in nineteenth-century Germany, specifically in the "Higher Criticism" whose objectives were
the establishment of text and author and the provision
of a critical apparatus. These early studies make very
little or nothing of the possible orality of the poems
they examine, occasionally suggesting sung or recited
performance but always assuming a prior written record
which serves as the basis for the performance. Editors
and commentators have much to say about the "formula,"
very loosely conceived and defined, but for a few distinct and limited purposes only: (1) to solve the complex puzzle of authorship and interpolator(s) and thus
(2) to assess interrelationships among poems in the same
literature or language family. To put it another way,
the chronological strata which occupied the Analyst and
Unitarian classicists have their counterparts in the
Lieder and *Fortsetzungen* of the leading Germanists of
this era. Questions of style, methods of composition,
and the like are not addressed, simply because they are
not the concerns of the "Higher Criticism."[77]

Though other somewhat earlier studies touch on similar problems,[78] the first instance of close attention
to formulaic language is the "*Formelverzeichnis*" appended
to Eduard Sievers' edition of the Old Saxon *Heliand*.[79]
The opening section of this compendium, the *synonymischer
Teil*, has as its criterion for inclusion what the Parry-
Lord definition of the formula will later call the "essential idea." Thus a phrase such as "geng thâr âband
tô, *sunna te seðle*" stands alongside "thê liohto
giuuêt *sunna te seðle*" (*Hel* 3422 and 4232, respectively;
italics mine), but also alongside "uuarth âband cuman,
naht mid neflu" (5748). A great many cross-references
to related ideas in the *Heliand* and in Old English poems,
all made according to this same criterion, fill out the
listing. Sievers also includes a *systematischer Teil*,
wherein phrases are arranged by grammatical categories.
Though both sections are of limited use to us today, the
assumptions underlying the editor's arrangement of
materials fairly represent the rather inexact concept
of "formula" typical of the most of the period.

Indeed, though it would be a long time before a real
sense of definition and systemic theory would make

formulaic investigations at least somewhat more precise,
in 1879 F. Charitius was already arguing for attention to
phrases rather than single words or synonyms. In "Über
die angelsächsischen Gedichte vom hl. Guthlac,"[80] he
wrote: "Man könnte diese beispiele [single words only]
noch häuften; es lässt sich aber schon aus dem eben
angeführten zur genüge ersehen, wie unsicher es ist, aus
dem vorkommen oder nichtvorkommen eines einzelnen wortes
auf den autor eines gedichtes schlüsse machen zu wollen"
(300). On the question of establishing Cynewulf's authorship of *Guthlac B*, he continued: "Eine weitaus
sichere grundlage für einen beweis bieten die phrasen
und wortverbindungen" (301). Examples drawn from *Guthlac
B* and from *Elene, Christ,* and *Juliana* follow, examples
which are brought together because of their similarities
in wording, grammatical type, "essential idea," or a
combination of these. Near the end of his essay,
Charitius introduced a sample of repeated verses and
lines, calling attention to this "*phraseologische
material*" as another basis for his stance on authorship.[81]

    The question of what comprised the Cynewulf canon
also motivated a series of studies by Gregor Sarrazin.
The first of these, "Beowulf und Kynewulf," published
in 1886,[82] demonstrated verbal correspondences between
Beowulf and the Cynewulfian poems and developed three
possible explanations for the congruency: either (1) the
poet or the last interpolator of *Beowulf* was an imitator
of Cynewulf's, or (2) vice versa, or (3) "dass Kynewulf
und der verfasser des Beowulf identisch sind" (531).
Perhaps surprisingly, Sarrazin favored the third of his
possibilities[83]; he was not long, as we shall see, in
being challenged for that choice. But the most important feature of his study, for our purposes, is a comment made almost in passing on the relationship between
Parallelstellen and the ideas they embody. In explaining his sample of evidence, Sarrazin says: "Ich könnte
die zahl der parallelstellen noch bedeutend vermehren,
wenn ich alle fälle anführen wollte, *in denen ähnliche
gedanken ähnlich ausgedrückt sind*; absichtlich habe ich
nur solche berücksichtigt, wo wörtliche anklänge
vorliegen" (548; italics mine). "In them [the *Parallelstellen*] like thoughts are expressed alike"; this and
other concepts of the necessary relationship between the
idea and its expression will reappear throughout the development of the oral theory. Here the assumption is

one of absolute correspondence, for, even though the
parallelisms in question are not formally defined, most
examples show similarities at the verbal as well as
ideational level.

In the same year that Sarrazin's first article appeared, Adolf Banning published his *Die epischen Formeln
im Bêowulf. I Teil: Die verbalen Synonyma.* [84] Much in
the manner of Sievers' "*Formelverzeichnis*," Banning's
table of "synonyms" includes a variety of kinds of related phrases. Thus, while under the heading of *Abend
werden* he can group "syððan æfen-lêoht under heofenes
hâdor beholen weorded" (*Bwf* 413b-14) and "syððan æfen
cwom" (1235b), he can also place under *abstossen (vom
Lande*) the formulaically unrelated examples "guman ût
scufan ... wudu bundenne" (215b, 216b) and "gewat en ŷð-
nacan, Dena land ofgeaf" (1905). He sees these similarities as an affirmation of Müllenhof's five-part schema
for the composition and structure of *Beowulf*. [85] By contrast, Sarrazin's second contribution to the "Higher
Critical" tradition, *Beowulf-Studien: ein Beitrag zur
Geschichte altgermanischer Sage und Dichtung,* [86] argues
strenuously for a unified *Beowulf*: "In der Composition
der beiden Lieder lässt sich eine auffallende
Ähnlichkeit, ja man kann sagen, ein Parallelismus nicht
verkennen" (p. 79). [87] In seeking once again to place
Beowulf in the context of the Cynewulfian canon, Sarrazin
assembles an impressive array of dictional evidence, much
of it at the level of the repeated or nearly repeated
verse.

Of the early comparative studies in the same vein,
Richard M. Meyer's *Die altgermanische Poesie nach ihren
formelhaften Elementen beschrieben,* [88] is the most atten-
tive to the different kinds of repetitions which characterize early Germanic poems. Working from the assumption that "die vielmalige Wiederholung desselben Wortes
scheint für die Poesie der uncivilisirten Völker von
grosser Bedeutung und ist vielleicht sogar für die
älteste Epoche einer jeden Poesie bezeichnend" (p. 227),
he examined repetition at the levels of the word, verse,
line, and group of lines, and in many cases attempted to
show how these phenomena emerged from the overlay of
metrical features on natural language characteristics. [89]
Meyer is also unusually explicit about exactly what he
is analyzing; in fact, he offers definitions of many of
his terms, a practice up to this point virtually unknown. [90] Because of his care in these matters, and also

because of the comparative evidence he marshals, Meyer's
work marks a significant step forward in the analysis of
formulaic structure.

In 1889 Johannes Kail issued a reply to Sarrazin's
assertions of the year before.[91] He disagreed with the
interpretation of *Parallelstellen* as "ein charakter-
istikon für einen bestimmten autor," suggesting instead
that such correspondences were simply another example of
a universal phenomenon, that *Parallelstellen* were part
of "epic style." In particular, he continued, "bei den
Germanen speziell war für die ausbildung stehender
phrasen die alliteration ein wichtiges förderungsmittel"
(37). Kail displayed examples of first and second verse
repetitions, some of them admitted to the sample on account of their semantic congruency, some because of syntactic pattern. Finally, he recognizes that the
religiösen Formeln cannot have come into being at the
same time as other elements in what he terms the *Phrasenvorrat*: "sie müssen also zu jenen phrasen gehören, welche
eine spätere übertragung oder eine selbständige entwick-
lung auf englischem boden sind" (38). From the historical point of view, Kail's contribution thus consists
only secondarily in his primary goal—to refute Sarrazin's claim that the *Beowulf* poet (or "Interpolator B")
is Cynewulf. His main accomplishment is the hypothesis
of a *Phrasenvorrat* which developed over time as part of
the epic style. Though oral theory is still many years
away, the basis for a *tradition* is laid as early as 1889.

Of course, controversy was just as much a part of
formulaic scholarship in this period as it continues to
be today, and Sarrazin was not long in joining battle
with his adversary. In 1892 he published his third study
on Cynewulf and repetitive phrasing, "Parallelstellen in
altenglischer Dichtung,"[92] which amounts to a response to
Kail. Sarrazin felt that the simplest explanation of an
obvious stylistic consistency was the hypothesis of a
single author. Turning to Kail's own evidence, he
charged "er die zahl und die qualität der 'parallelstellen' nicht genügend in betracht zog" (192).[93]
Sarrazin employed the same method, and made the same
assumptions, in his comparative study of *Beowulf* and
what he referred to as "Cynewulf's *Andreas*," which appeared five years later.[94] His group of *Übereinstim-
mungen*, much enlarged from that presented in *Beowulf-
Studien*, includes various sorts of repetitions. In examining the first few lines of the two poems, he picks

up the obvious parallels in phrasing, but misses the only
really generative substitution system which they share—

on _ X _ - <u>dagum</u>,

where the alliterating element X can be adjusted according to the stave in the other half-line. Other examples
vary from verbatim repetitions to widely disparate
phrases which have in common only a single word.

    Just before the turn of the century another study of
the formulaic structure of *Andreas* appeared, and with it
the first real notion of the aesthetic function of repeated phraseology. E. C. Buttenweiser[95] put it this
way: "der einzige Anhaltspunkt bei einer Verfasser-
schaftsfrage [kann] nur der sein, dass der eine Dichter
diese Gedanken [the *Parallelstellen*] logischer und
passender einführt als der andere, dass er beim Auswählen
aus dem Ausdrucksvorrat, bei der Anordnung der Formeln
mehr Geist und Geschmack zeigt und im Bau seiner Verse
grössere Glätte und Vollendung ... zustande bringt" (p.
62). Some time after the publication of Buttenweiser's
book, a monograph by Ernst Otto[96] opened up another
direction in structural analysis of Old English poems.
Though not addressed specifically to formulaic patterns,
Otto's work disclosed typical, recurring elements at the
level of narrative and characterization. He found, for
example, four typical *Charaktertypen*—God, the king, the
retainer, and the monster—and related them to what he
construed as Anglo-Saxon ideals.[97]
    In 1923 John S. P. Tatlock turned his attention to
"epic formulas" in the writings of the Middle English
poet Layamon. In the more extensive[98] of two articles
published that year, he found in Layamon's *Brut* "an extraordinary profusion of epic formulas, full of flavor
and charm, contributing as much as anything to the marked
individuality of the poem" (494). Here we have a combination of earlier descriptions: Sarrazin's *bestimmten
Autor* uses formulaic phrases with an aesthetic edge
Buttenweiser would approve. Tatlock's data is very
thorough indeed, and, in what represents a clear step
forward in studies of this type, he insists upon a more
rigorous concept of the formula: "Every alliterating
phrase, even if repeated in one or more poems, is not a
formula; certainly not a mere couple of words, found now
together, now some distance apart; still less a mere
type of phrase, of which the words vary" (494, n. 1).[99]

Another novel suggestion is his hypothesis on the effect
of this phraseology, that "formulas are magnifying and
imposing, no mere convenience, but often a means of em-
bellishment" (513). He then went on to compare the recurrent phrase to a recurrent motif in a musical score,
only qualifying this analogy by reserving for Layamon
the control to defer and the ability to make new phrases
in any situation.

But, for our purposes, Tatlock's most significant
inclusion was his description—meant to be comparative
to Layamon, and thus to be historical—of formula usage
in the Anglo-Saxon poems. On this point he differed
considerably from other investigators: "The [Anglo-Saxon]
poet used certain types of phrases a great deal, phrases
with a general resemblance to each other, and used some
exact repetition of his own or others' words. But the
'Epische Formeln' of which numerous collections have
been made for this or that poem recur comparatively seldom, sometimes no doubt unconsciously; indeed it is difficult to fancy what some students have meant by an epic
formula, or to justify their use of the term. On the
whole the earlier poet cultivated variety and ingenuity
of phrasing. He was more inclined to present the same
situation over again in different words, than a different situation in the same words." Indeed, he went on,
"Anglo-Saxon poetry in general is sophisticated and not
popular, produced in large part by professionals and
scholars, and the complexity of the verse ... and its
uniformity through several centuries, and other uniform-
ities of style, point to a conscious Arts Poetica."(515-
16).[100] The picture is one too familiar from later writings as well, of an artist largely the prisoner rather
than the master of his idiom. Though he understands the
Old English poet as having available what Kail termed a
Phrasenvorrat, Tatlock believes that "considering the
extreme convenience of alliterating formulas to a man
writing alliterating verse, the Anglo-Saxon poet must
have been constantly praying Ne nos inducas in tenta-
tionem" (517).

The final section of this article continues the
comparative description in Middle English, other early
Germanic literatures, Old French, Old Spanish, and
ancient Greek. From this basis he comments generally
on the use of formulas: "The usage ... appears in the
beginnings of a literature,... near the head of the written documents of the peoples involved. The usage bears

the marks of oral delivery, and assisted it. It goes
with singing more than reciting, and with that more than
reading." (528). He anticipates more modern distinctions,
such as that between the generic and the particular, in
assessing the impact of formulaic phraseology: "The use
of language which carries the mind back to like occasions before contributes to the simple, impersonal air
which is one of the charms of earlier poetry. The well-
tried phrase for what is usual leaves the full sharpness
of the attention for what is fresh." (529). Tatlock's
meticulous scholarship advanced formulaic criticism in a
number of ways and, though some of his more subjective
judgments were to be overturned, his attention to detail,
evidence, definition, and the comparative view is worthy
of praise.

Francis P. Magoun, Jr. is, of course, well known by
all scholars of Old English poetry, and especially for
his 1953 article, "The Oral-Formulaic Character of Anglo-
Saxon Narrative Poetry,"[101] which formally introduced the
theories of Albert Lord and Milman Parry. But a much
briefer paper by Magoun reveals that in 1929 he was already interested in probing the formulaic structure of
Beowulf and Old Norse verse. In "Recurring First Elements in Different Nominal Compounds in *Beowulf* and in
the *Elder Edda*,"[102] he is very close to assuming a tradition of verse-making when he suggests that "the tendency
to make recurrent use of the same first compounding elements no doubt arose in seeking alliterative words" (p.
77). After offering a group of example multiform phrases
from each literature, he comments: "An interesting and
enlightening study could be made of an examination of all
OE poetry to determine the extent to which nominal compounds are used for *stuðlar* [alliterative staves or
positions], to what extent for *hǫfudstǫfur* [headstaves]
(cf. *Háttatal*, §I). This might ultimately lead to an
understanding of the *actual technique of composition*."
(p. 77; final italics mine). The point here is that
Magoun sees the outline of a process, of a tradition,
behind phraseological structure; twenty-four years later,
stimulated by the brilliant findings of his colleague
Albert Lord, he will turn these outlines into his seminal
first statement of oral theory in Old English.

Another essay in the *Klaeber Miscellany* of 1929,
"Epithetic Compound Folk-Names in Beowulf," by W. F.
Bryan,[103] also treated the question of the formation of
diction, but from a different perspective. Bryan at-

tempted to prove that these compounds were not mechani-
cally determined by the requirements of the alliterative
verse form, as the conventional opinion had it, but that
they were "chosen by the poet with especial reference to
the specific situation in which they are used" (p.
123).[104] His examination of specific examples draws attention to what he sees as the poet's artistry: "Nor was
the poet driven to alliteration on *g* through lack of
some other phrase than *in gēar-dagum* to express the notion of 'in days of old'; *in ǣr-dagum*, for example, with
vocalic alliteration, was used in this sense by other
Old English poets [ref. to Grein's *Sprachschatz*[105]]. If
he had wished to use a less specifically warlike, more
generally commendatory name for the Danes, he might have
called them *Ār-Dene,* and *Hwæt, wē Ār-Dena in ǣr-dagum*
would have been structurally satisfactory. But the poet
of *Beowulf* wished to summon all the associations that
had been collected about a fierce and successful warrior
folk, and he named them *Gār-Dene*." (pp. 123-24). Bryan
was wrestling with the same question of structural de-
terminism versus poetic freedom that has long plagued
formulaic studies in Old English, and which was also becoming a concern of Homeric scholarship at about the
same time.[106]

With this account we come to the end of the first
period in the history of formulaic criticism in Old English poetry.[107] The next important event, and it will
prove to be far the most telling in the one hundred years
of scholarship summarized here, is Albert Lord's dissertation, "The Singer of Tales." I thus place the mark of
division between the two periods at its date of submis-
sion in 1949, for from that time onward there is a shift
in critical interest and method away from enumeration of
the perceived *Parallelstellen* and establishment of the
text toward the new questions of the orality and tradition which underlie repeated elements at all levels of
the poetry. Investigations of formulaic structure cease
to be subservient to "Higher Critical" concerns of text,
author, and apparatus; rather they seek explanations of
phrase and narrative generation, viewing the text as the
result of a traditional process rather than the patch-
work product of scholarly poet-interpolators. The formulaic method, whether understood as oral or not, gains
the status of an idiom, of a poetic dialect in which and
through which traditional poems are made. This series of
apercus we owe primarily to the insights of Albert Lord.

Oral Traditional Theory (1949-1978)

In presenting the history of the oral theory in this
second period, it will be convenient to observe a bibli-
ograpical distinction between studies focusing primarily
on the formula and those focusing primarily on the
theme.[108]

The Formula

The real history of the oral formula in Old English
poetry begins with Lord's 1949 dissertation, later revised into *The Singer of Tales*, wherein he presented a
formulaic analysis of lines 1473-87 of *Beowulf* (see
Singer, p. 199). His definition of the formula is that
which Milman Parry constructed for Homeric poetry, "a
group of words which is regularly employed under the same
metrical conditions to express a given essential idea."
Lord acknowledges the newness of his approach with respect to earlier criticism of Anglo-Saxon poetry and
carefully stipulates that "it is beyond the scope of this
chapter to do more than to indicate, as I have tried to
do with the Homeric poems, some lines of investigation,
and to suggest, often I fear only tentatively, some possible results" (p. 198).[109]
        In 1953 Francis P. Magoun, Jr., in his classic "The
Oral-Formulaic Character of Anglo-Saxon Narrative Poetry," asserted that "the recurrence in a poem of an appreciable number of formulas or formulaic phrases brands
the latter as oral, just as a lack of such repetitions
marks a poem as composed in a lettered tradition. Oral
poetry, it may be safely said, is composed entirely of
formulas, large and small, while lettered poetry is never
formulaic." (84). His analysis of lines 1-25 of *Beowulf*
includes "formulaic systems," which Parry defined as "a
group of phrases which have the same metrical value and
which are enough alike in thought and words to leave no
doubt that the poet who knew them used them not only as
a single formula, but also as formulas of a single type"
("Studies I," in *MHV*, p. 275). With these definitions
in hand, Magoun claimed that over 70% of his sample occurs elsewhere within the Anglo-Saxon poetic corpus of
some 30,000 lines. In fact, he found a limitation even
in this figure, for "were the surviving corpus, say,
twice as big and if, above all, we had other songs of
any extent dealing with anything like the same thematic

material, there might well be almost nothing in the language here used that could not be demonstrated as traditional" (88-89). While denying the importance for Germanic verse form of the dictum of formulaic "thrift,"
originally introduced by Parry as a characteristic feature of Homeric style,[110] Magoun transposed all other
definitions advanced by the oral theory directly from
the Homeric to the Old English poetic canon. Hypotheses
and conclusions developed for the *aoidós* and tested at
the side of the *guslar* were now applied, without discernible modification, to the *scop*.

In his next article, "Bede's Story of Cædman: the
Case History of an Anglo-Saxon Oral Singer,"[111] Magoun
makes the same assumptions of definition in seeing the
legendary Cædmon as a practicing oral poet. The apparent miracle which Bede reports is not the account of a
supernatural gift, for "whatever he did hear would have
been composed in the traditional manner out of the standard reservoir of formulas and themes and in conformity
with the traditional metrical patterns to which alone
the singers could have sung" (57). Magoun's only other
article which deals specifically with the formula is
"Two Verses in the Old English Waldere Characteristic
of Oral Poetry."[112] Here the argument is simpler and
yet far-reaching; he contends "that this common occurrence of *wine Burgenda* and *vin Borgunda* merely tells us
that Anglo-Saxon and Old-Icelandic singers—no doubt all
Old-Germanic singers of the Migration period and after—
knew the fact that Gúþhere-Gunthere-Gunnar had ruled the
Burgundians and had at their command this obvious means
of saying so in a just measure of verse" (218).[113]

Challenges to these new ideas of the formula and
the singer arose almost immediately. Claes Schaar pointed out in 1956 that "the proposition 'all formulaic poetry is oral' does not follow, either logically or psy-
chologically, from the proposition 'all oral poetry is
formulaic'."[114] He adduced the argument, to be repeated
many times afterward, of ostensible literary borrowing,
especially in the so-called Cynewulfian poems,[115] an argument Magoun had anticipated and answered by relying on
formula count as the ultimate test of traditional and
oral composition ("Oral-Formulaic Character," 104). In
1960 Kemp Malone joined Schaar in casting his weighty
vote against the singer theory in a review of a monograph by Godfrid Storms.[116] Commenting upon Storms' assumption that *Beowulf* was orally composed, Malone says:

"Here Dr. Storms goes sadly astray. The *Beowulf* poet was
no minstrel, strumming a harp and composing verse as he
strummed. He was a sophisticated literary artist, who
gave careful thought to what he was doing and did not
rest content until he found the right words for what he
had in mind. The use of traditional diction is one
thing; improvisation is something else again. The two
need not go together and in *Beowulf* they most emphatical-
ly do not." (204). In an article which appeared a year
later,[117] he asserted that "Magoun's heterodox views
about Cædmon spring from his dictum that 'formulas are
created only slowly and no one singer ever invents many,
often none at all.' This dictum works well enough when
applied to a singer who keeps to the traditional themes
but it does not work at all when applied to a singer who
breaks with tradition by choosing Christian themes. Who-
ever composed the first Christian song in English had to
make up his formulas as he went along." (195).

     While the dissenters to the oral theory were making
themselves heard, the proponents were gathering strength.
In 1955 Robert P. Creed, a student of Magoun's, completed a formulaic analysis of all of *Beowulf*.[118]   Basing
his determination upon the poem itself rather than the
entire poetic corpus, and employing Magoun's definitions
and methodology, he showed that *Beowulf* was indeed highly formulaic.[119]   His "The *Andswarode*-System in Old English Poetry" appeared in 1957[120]; here Creed argued that
this particular formulaic system serves as a kind of
"oral quotation mark" at the opening of a speech. After
illustrating the various forms which the *andswarode*-
pattern takes, he remarks that "in each of these cases
the singer appears to be aware of the solution to the
problem of saying 'so and so answered him' elsewhere employed either by himself or by other singers of the tradition. In each of these cases the singer has solved
the problem in a whole line, or, more properly, a verse-
pair system." (524). In "*Beowulf* 2231a: *sinc-fæt
(sohte)*,"[121] and again in "*Genesis* 1316,"[122] he used the
oral-formulaic theory to discuss manuscript readings
from a new and promising angle.

     Creed's next article, "The Making of an Anglo-Saxon
Poem,"[123] included important alterations in Magoun's
(that is, Parry's) definition of the formula for Old
English. After setting its length at between a single
syllable and a line and a half, he assigned it the following characteristics: "The essential quality of a

formula is not its memorable sound—although some formulas are, even for us, memorable—but its usefulness to the singer. To be useful to a singer as he composes rapidly a phrase or word must suggest to him that it belongs at only *one* point, or possibly two points, in his verse or line; that is, it must be a significant segment of his rhythm. To be useful to the singer every phrase or word which is metrically significant should also be a syntactic unit, that is, if it is not a polysyllable which by itself makes a whole verse or whole 'crowded' measure, it should be at least a phrasal group or a clause." (142). Having added these tradition-dependent characteristics, Creed redefines the formula as "a word or group of words regularly employed under certain strictly determined metrical conditions to express a given essential idea" (143).[124]

The major thrust of this article, however, is the re-making, in the traditional style, of *Beowulf* 356-59. Creed's illustration has become a *locus classicus* for critics on both sides of the debate over the oral-formulaic nature of Old English poetry. Robert D. Stevick, in his "The Oral-Formulaic Analyses of Old English Verse,"[125] applauds the enthusiasm but censures the lack of rigor which he feels is evident in the studies of the singer theorists. Using the analogy of improvisational jazz, he challenges Creed's insistence on total, phrase-by-phrase re-making in the traditional performance: "Moreover, in a traditional oral (or musical) art form— as opposed to a tradition perpetuated in writing or notation—memory of past performances will have a very large effect on any further performance.... But composition in improvisational art, for traditional themes handled repeatedly by professional performers, can hardly be conceived of entirely as fresh creation measure-by-measure, phrase-by-phrase, line-by-line, as Creed has represented it. In fact, Creed's reconstruction equally suits the procedure of a lettered poet composing pen-in-hand in a formulaic manner." (398).[126]   R. F. Lawrence echoed Stevick's opinion when, in "The Formulaic Theory and its Application to English Alliterative Poetry,"[127] he wondered "if [Creed] can effectively use the oral techniques in the privacy of his study, then how much more effectively might the Anglo-Saxon monk have done likewise?" (pp. 177-78, n. 27).

Creed responded to these two critics and to others by admitting that oral composition did, to some extent,

depend upon the memory of earlier performances; "yet some
simplification of the complexity of the interaction of
tradition and the traditional singer-poet may well be
necessary if we are to try to understand something of the
nature of the singer as artist, that is as shaper of the
tradition, and not simply as performer, that is trans-
mitter of the tradition" ("Additional Remarks," in *BP*,
p. 152). To the charge that he was imitating a lettered,
monkish poet, he answered: "I should like to point out
that the 'monk' who was as much concerned as I was about
possible substitutions of the sort I have suggested
above either performed the same elaborate and painstaking operations I performed with the aid of Grein-Köhler-
Holthausen's *Sprachschatz* or was a singer-poet thoroughly
trained in the tradition" (*idem*). Creed's only other
piece to deal directly with the formula, "The Art of the
Singer: Three Old English Tellings of the Offering of
Issac,"[128] examines, from the point of view of just such
a singer-poet, the one prose and two poetic versions of
the Biblical episode, illustrating the aural effects in-
corporated by the *scopas* and including a text of the
Genesis A passage marked for performance.

  In 1953 Robert E. Diamond, another student of
Magoun's, completed a dissertation on the formulaic
character of the so-called Cynewulf poems.[129] The substance of that thesis appeared six years later in "The
Diction of the Signed Poems of Cynewulf,"[130] in which he
claimed that "a detailed analysis of the diction of these
poems [*Elene, Juliana, Fates of the Apostles*, and *Christ
II*] indicates that they were composed in the traditional
formulaic style" (228). Using Magoun's definitions, he
discovered a high percentage of repetition: "Checking
for verses or verse parts repeated only within the 5194
verses (i.e., 2598 typographic lines) of the four signed
poems of Cynewulf reveals that 2224 verses, or 42.8 per
cent, are demonstrably formulaic.... Included in this
figure are 1037 verses, or 19.9 per cent, which are
demonstrable whole-verse repeats." (234). Although these
figures are important as an index of repetition within a
body of verse usually ascribed to a single author,
Diamond's article contains another assertion more important to the development of the oral-formulaic theory.
Echoing Schaar's comments on the interrelationship between "formulaic" and "oral," he contended that "on the
basis of internal evidence alone (there is no external
evidence), it is impossible to determine whether the

Cynewulf poems were composed orally and written down by a
scribe, were composed with pen in hand in the ordinary
modern way, or were composed by a learned poet who was
making use of the traditional poetic formulas handed down
to him from an age when all poems were oral. Although it
seems unlikely that this question can ever be settled to
anyone's satisfaction, it is possible, by examining the
diction of such a poem, to determine whether it was composed in the traditional formulaic style." (229).

In an earlier article, "Heroic Diction in *The Dream
of the Rood*,[131] Diamond had made a slightly more cautious
statement of the same opinion: "Whether or not *The Dream
of the Rood* and other such poems were composed orally or
with pen in hand can probably never be settled to anyone's satisfaction, but they reflect a kind of oral-
formulaic diction, handed down from generation to generation, added to a little here and a little there, comprising a common stock of formulaic phrases which enabled the poets to express almost any idea in correct
verses, without casting about for a felicitous turn of
expression" (pp. 4-5). The apparent contrast between
the subject and diction of *The Dream of the Rood* is thus
explained as the product of a traditionally trained
poet's attempt at a new kind of song, for "if he set
himself to compose a song on a Christian subject, it was
natural that diction reflecting an earlier society should
creep in" (p. 5).[132]

Diamond examines what he assumes to be literary—
though formulaic—translation in *The Diction of the
Anglo-Saxon Metrical Psalms*.[133] His methodology consisted of checking a random sample from the 5000 lines
of the Paris Psalter against the entire Old English
poetic corpus, and he found that "of these 305 verses,
151 (49.5%) are demonstrably formulaic, including 72
(23.6%) whole-verse repeats" (p. 6). His conclusion
stresses the importance of the metrical and alliterative
pressure of the moment of composition: "While it can be
urged that the psalter poet was untalented and unimagina-
tive, and surely no one will be found to claim that his
work is worthy to be placed alongside such masterpieces
as *Beowulf* and the elegies, nevertheless, a detailed
analysis of his diction makes one fact very clear; much
of the choice of words depends more on mechanical considerations than on taste or 'inspiration.' Is it not
likely that there is more of this element of mechanical
compulsion in even the great Anglo-Saxon poems than is

usually recognized?" (p. 8).

In "The Diction of the Old English *Christ*,[134] his
most recent contribution to formulaic studies, Diamond
takes on the much-debated problem of the authorship and
unity of the three poems collectively called *Christ*.
After discussing former opinions, whose bases range from
paleography to metrical analysis, he turns to an examination of the four signed poems to determine the body of
what he calls "Cynewulf formulas." Having made this collection of phraseology, Diamond then compares his control group of Cynewulfian diction to *Christ I* and *III*,
the unsigned poems in the problematic trilogy. Because
of a large discrepancy between control and test groups,
he feels that "we may assume with some confidence that
Christ I and *Christ III* are not by Cynewulf," though the
figures for the first and third sections are themselves
so close that "they may be the work of the same poet,
who may have sought to provide Cynewulf's poem, *Christ
II*, with a setting, much as an artisan might provide a
setting for a gem" (p. 307).

Another scholar who has greatly influenced the evolution of the oral-formulaic theory in Old English poetry is William Whallon. Drawing from a knowledge of
ancient Greek and Hebrew as well as Anglo-Saxon, he has
produced several important comparative studies.[135] In
"The Diction of *Beowulf*,"[136] reacting against those who
would deprive the formula of meaning because of its consummate usefulness,[137] he maintained that "a formula
need not be held meaningless merely because it was selected with little conscious reflection. Time-savers
though the periphrastic expressions are, they may nevertheless be handsome or ironic or humorous." (310). After
an analysis of the epithets accorded Odysseus and Beowulf, he argues that the many violations of Parry's law
of thrift in the Old English poem[138] are evidence for
the relative youth of the Anglo-Saxon poetic tradition:
"Further centuries of poeticizing in the same tradition
might have augmented the language with useful formulas
it lacked, and might also have limited the use of certain
distinctive kennings for the epic hero; further centuries would at least have cast many replaceable kennings
into oblivion. As the language stands, however, some
prosodic needs have too many solutions, some have none;
greater neatness, uniqueness, and inevitability would
appear desirable on the one hand, and greater amplitude
on the other." ("Diction," 318).

In 1965 Whallon's "Formulas for Heroes in the *Iliad*
and in *Beowulf*" appeared.[139]   His main point here was
that "while the formulaic epithets for heroes of the
Iliad are true to individual character but indifferently
appropriate to context, the formulaic kennings for the
heroes of *Beowulf* are true to generic character but significantly appropriate to context" (96; italics deleted).
In "The Idea of God in *Beowulf*,"[140] he claims that the
language of the poem is not so thoroughly Christianized
as others have thought[141] : "To a Bede in the epic audience the language of the poet might have contained suggestions of orthodox doctrine, but the larger part of the
audience must have understood *halig god* in the same manner as *ginnheilog goð* was understood by the audience of
the *Voluspá*. For the old poetic formulas gave the oral
tradition a religious continuity not easily broken."
(23). The same general theses about thrift, appropriateness to context, and the conservatism of Old English
poetic diction are refined and developed at length in his
*Formula, Character, and Context: Studies in Homer, Old
English, and Old Testament Poetry.*[142]

The next year Alison Jones published her useful
study, "*Daniel* and *Azarias* as Evidence for the Oral-
Formulaic Character of Old English Poetry,"[143] in which
she proposed a new solution to the textual riddle posed
by these two closely related poems. Discarding earlier
paleographical and source-based explanations, she claimed
that "the two poems show differences which are more at-
tributable to the lapses of memory of an 'oral singer'
than to anything else, yet they are so similar that they
must at the same time stem from the same 'original'
poem." (95). Though we can avoid the prejudicial judgment that variation means a "lapse of memory," Jones'
conclusions, based as they are on a meticulous examination of what she considers formulaic phraseology shared
by *Daniel* and *Azarias*, have considerable weight.[144]

The mid-1960s brought a discernible shift in focus
to oral-formulaic theory, and not a few scholars—often
in reaction to the imposition of verbal and metrical constraints which they felt were too rigid—began to argue
for a syntactic definition of the formula.[145] Though the
taxonomical line could easily be drawn in a number of
other places, I choose to draw it here and to separate
the critics described above at least nominally from the
new group, who will be called the "Syntacticians." The
dissertations of Wayne O'Neil (1960)[146] and Godfrey

Gattiker (1962)[147] laid the groundwork for the new
school, as they described, respectively, the composition
of the Old English elegies and *Beowulf* in terms of syntactic formulas. Frederic Cassidy's "How Free Was the
Anglo-Saxon Scop?"[148] assimilates the data from these
theses and moves toward a new concept of the formulaic
method. Using O'Neil's definition of a syntactic frame
as "a recurrent morphemic and relational frame into which
the words of a verse fit" ("Oral-Formulaic Structure,"
p. 83), Cassidy remarks: "Recent investigation has shown,
however, that the verbal formula rests upon one or another of a limited number of archetypal syntactic patterns, each furnishing a 'frame' by means of which a very
large and theoretically unlimited number of differently
worded formulas may be produced" (p. 78). In the process
he quotes the following statistics: "But now a large body
of Old English poetry, consisting of the elegies (709
lines) and all of *Beowulf* (3182 lines), has been examined
with rather remarkable results; for it turns out that Old
English verse is built upon only twenty-five syntactic
patterns, six of which are noun-centered and five verb-
centered frames of frequent occurrence, five adjective-
centered and five adverb-centered frames of less common
occurrence, and five other minor types" (*idem*). Through
the use of such internalized, pre-conscious patterns, he
reasons, the *scop* was much freer than had been commonly
thought: "As to details, he had a stock of convention-
alized verbal formulas to draw upon, some suited to
specific points in the performance ... but others too
which were free to be used wherever appropriate. It is
these which have proved less rigid than some have
thought, because, as we now see, all verbal formulas were
referable to archetypal syntactic frames: the verbal details could change, not only unstressed elements but even
stressed ones as in formulaic systems, within the steady-
ing patterns of the syntax." (p. 83).[149]

Donald C. Green continued the work of the Syntacticians in his dissertation, "The Syntax of the Poetic
Formula in a Cross-Section of Old English Poetry."[150] In
an attempt to discover the interrelationships among formulas, metrical types, and syntactic frames, he examined
*Beowulf, The Finnsburh Fragment, Juliana, Fates of the
Apostles, The Phoenix, Exodus, The Battle of Maldon*, and
five short poems of the *Anglo-Saxon Chronicle*, all with
the aid of a computer. Many of the results are reported
in his "Formulas and Syntax in Old English Poetry: a

Computer Study."[151]   Green finds evidence which, he
claims, points toward confirmation of the syntactic
frame theory, and indicates new directions for future
studies of this type: "Whether the factors examined in
the present study can be used to establish the relative
dating of two or more given poems, or that they are or
are not by the same author, is not yet clear, but the results at least suggest what extensions of the research
might be profitable. It seems fairly certain that the
degree to which a given poem is formulaic is not a useful indicator.... The analysis of favored metrical
types, on the other hand, may well be much more significant in distinguishing the practice of one author from
another.... Much the same conclusion would be reached
on the basis of favored syntactic frames: *Juliana* and *The
Fates of the Apostles* differ considerably in the proportion of the whole which each syntactic type constitutes."
(91-92, 93).

An important critic who will, for the sake of convenience, be discussed along with the Syntacticians is
Stanley B. Greenfield. In 1963 he published a pioneering
study, "Syntactic Analysis and Old English Poetry,"[152]
which dealt with the syntax of a single sentence in *The
Wanderer*. Concentrating on syntactic features and word-
order arrangements, he commented: "I am convinced that
the Old English poet, orally or in writing, had some
flexibility in these matters; and that he could use and
did use, consciously or unconsciously, these linguistic
counters, as he did diction, formulas, and themes, to
contribute uniquely, in many cases, to his poetic effect"
(378). His investigation continued in "Grendel's Approach to Heorot: Syntax and Poetry,"[153] in which he remarked: "To assert, as I have done, that the poet's
manipulation of diction and syntax achieves subtle poetic
effects in bringing Grendel, Beowulf, and the warriors
from a polarity of position, action, and attitude to confrontation in Grendel's vision of the band within the
hall is not to deny, of course, that verse formulas or
even syntactic formulas abound in the passage. But formulas of whatever sort, as Quirk and I and others have
been trying to show, were but counters for the Old English poet to use either conventionally, in the worst
sense of that word, or brilliantly and strikingly, as the
Beowulf poet has used them in presenting Grendel's approach to Heorot." (p. 283).[154]

The article by Randolph Quirk to which Greenfield

makes reference is "Poetic Language and Old English
Meter."[155]   After a fine discussion of aesthetics and
formulaic composition, Quirk concludes: "It should therefore be emphasized that, while formulaic utterances and
habitual collocations are the necessary starting point in
the study of early alliterative poetry, they are *only* the
starting point. The very fact that he could depend on
his audience having a firm expectation of certain de-
pendences and determined sequences involving metre, vocabulary, and grammar gave the poet his opportunity to
stretch linguistic expression beyond the ordinary poten-
tialities of prose, and to achieve a disturbing and
richly suggestive poetry." (p. 171). It should be noted
that these conclusions stem from his definition of the
formula as "a habitual collocation, metrically defined,
which is fundamental to linguistic expression, namely
the expectation that a sequence of words will show lexical congruity, together with (and as a condition of)
lexical and grammatical complementarity" (pp. 150-51).[156]

Greenfield declared his opposition to many of the
oral-formulaic theorists in his "The Canons of Old English Criticism" (see note 137). Disagreeing with Creed
on the validity of his re-making of *Beowulf* 356-59, and
with Whallon on the meaning of Old English kennings and
epithets, Greenfield also has a word for syntactic pattern analysis: "Cassidy claims that the notion of the
syntactic frame should give us 'a firmer concept of the
formula.' *Au contraire*: the idea of the formula as '*a
group of words which is regularly employed under the same
metrical conditions to express a given essential idea*'
disintegrates almost entirely, not only because of the
flexibility the frames allow the poet in the choice of
verbal phrases and their own flexibility in regard to
grammatical inversion (e.g., AN or NA; or N_1N_2 or N_2N_1)
and verse types (most can occur in any of the five major
Sievers categories), but because of their own 'non-fix-
ity' with respect to the syntactic relations they enjoy
in their own half-lines, or in the contexts of their own
sentence structures." (149).

Serious doubts about the oral nature of Old English
poetry were raised in 1966 by Larry D. Benson's "The
Literary Character of Anglo-Saxon Formulaic Poetry."[157]
On the basis of his analysis of the metrical preface to
Alfred's *Pastoral Care*, *Riddle 35*, the macaronic
Phoenix, and *The Meters of Boethius*, which are shown to
have approximately the same formula content as *Beowulf*

and the Cynewulf poems, he argues for an Old English corpus which is *both* formulaic *and* literary: "From [the
poems mentioned above] we can see that not only can literate poets write formulaic verse, they can write it pen
in hand in the same way any writer observes a literary
tradition" (337). Because of these examples, he continues, "we must use the greatest caution in assuming the
oral composition of any surviving Old English poem"
(340). Benson's closing comments point in what he considers the most worthwhile direction: "Because Old English poetry is formulaic, our study of it must begin with
the exciting and useful techniques developed by students
of oral verse, but because this poetry is also literature, our study need not end there" (340).

Since Benson's article appeared, later studies have
deepened our understanding of how the supposed poet-
translator of the *Meters* practiced his craft. In his
Poetic Diction in the Old English Meters of Boethius,[158]
Allan A. Metcalf used the relative density and position
of "exclusively poetic" words to describe how the author
moved from prose to poetic versions. A comparison with
Beowulf, *Judith*, and *The Battle of Maldon* led him to argue that "while the *MBo* poet worked from a text, the
other poets composed independently" (p. 147). Three
years earlier, however, John W. Conlee [159] had used the
high formulaic density of the *Meters* to claim, along with
Benson, that "Old English poetry was created within a
lettered tradition which had thoroughly assimilated the
formulaic style" (579). In 1975 Pierre E. Monnin completed a dissertation[160] which subjects the *Meters* to a
formulaic and computerized metrical analysis; his findings indicate separate authorship of prose and poetic
versions and an overall unity for the poetic text.

To return to the chronological survey, in 1969 Ann
C. Watts, in her *The Lyre and the Harp: a Comparative
Reconsideration of Oral Tradition in Homer and Old English Epic Poetry*,[161] found fault with the "imperfect application" (see espec. pp. 63-125) of Parry's and Lord's
discoveries to Old English poetry.[162] She claimed
"first, that the original theory has not been rigorously
or consistently applied to Old English poetry although
one is given to understand that it has; second, that the
practice of analogy has not been adequately tested or
measured by those who believe Old English poetry to be
oral in its composition" (p. 64). After criticizing the
Magoun school for varying and inaccurate definitions of

the formula and formulaic system, she stated: "Rules for
one will not fit the other. Any comparative investigation, whether of epithets or of other verbal arrangements, finally ends not only in a recognition of the distinct characters of the two traditions of poetry but in
uncertainty about the oral nature of Old English poetry."
(p. 124). Her new definition of the formula is "a repeated sequence that fills one of Sievers' five basic
rhythmical types" (p. 90); that of the formulaic system
is "two or more phrases of a similar Sievers verse-type,
syntactical pattern, and lexical significance, which may
differ in an important element according to alliterative
substitution, or context, or a type of narrative super-
fluity" (p. 144).

In the same year Jess B. Bessinger's and Philip H.
Smith's *A Concordance to Beowulf*[163] appeared, fulfilling
in part Magoun's call for tools with which to carry on
formulaic analysis. In addition to prefatory material
and a checklist of homographs, this computer-generated
directory contains a complete word-by-word concordance,
a sample "key word in context" display, and a tabulation
of headwords in order of decreasing frequency. Bessinger and Smith finished the massive job of listing the
entire poetic corpus in 1978 with the publication of *A
Concordance to the Anglo-Saxon Poetic Records*, which
followed by exactly one hundred years the appearance of
Sievers' early "*Formelverzeichnis*." The concordance
should have a unique and lasting effect on Old English
formulaic studies by replacing the Grein-Köhler-
Holthausen *Sprachschatz* with a thorough and very usable
reference.[164]

In 1972 Patrick Conner attempted to describe a
transformational grammar for the Anglo-Saxon poetic language in his "Schematization of Oral-Formulaic Processes
in Old English Poetry."[165] He defines the formula as
"the product—one half-line in length—of a grammar of
poetic diction superimposed upon a grammar of the spoken
language" (206). He then proceeds to isolate the semantic, syntactic, and phonological components of this grammar in order to display the dynamics of what he terms a
very "organic" system.

I have intentionally delayed discussion of Donald
K. Fry's ideas until now—beyond the chronologically appropriate spot—because I believe his contribution to be
one of the furthest advances to date. In his "Old English Formulas and Systems,"[166] after a survey of contem-

porary critical opinion, Fry turns his attention first to
the formulaic system. He argues that "systems are based
on substitutions of key words in relation to other key
words; in actual practice, systems seem to be built mostly upon the two stressed elements of the half-line, only
one of which needs to alliterate. One stressed element
is a constant, and the other is varied to meet the needs
of alliteration, unless the constant itself alliterates,
in which case the poet may choose the variable element
without regard to its initial sound." (202). The system,
a generative entity of verbal, metrical, and syntactic
definition, [167] also has a definite length: "Systems seem
to occur in half-line lengths in Old English poetry. Any
unit smaller than one verse fails to show a consistent
pattern of substitution spaces linked to a constant word
or words in a certain form with alliterating words filling the blanks.... On the other hand, units larger than
one half-line do not show a consistent simplicity, both
in the number of blanks to be filled and in the number of
alliterating words required." (203).

Using Lord's description of the Serbo-Croatian
singer's learning process, Fry points out that a traditional poet learns only the "basic mold," from which he
generates formulas: "Theoretically, if two poets use
exactly the same formula, each could have produced it
from a different system, depending on his training; furthermore, a very clever poet could probably produce one
formula by analogy from two systems" (201). He then defines the mold, or formulaic system, as "a group of half-
lines, usually loosely related metrically and semantically, which are related in form by the identical relative
placement of two elements, one a variable word or element of a compound usually supplying the alliteration,
and the other a constant word or element of a compound,
with approximately the same distribution of non-stressed
elements" (203; italics deleted).

Fry thus sees formulas as creations of systems,
every "new phrase" depending for its generation on some
"basic mold." He acknowledges that most of this generation takes place before a given performance, for "an
experienced composer will have ready in his mind thousands of formulas which need no more modification than
the addition of a particle or two, or an inflection, if
even that much; these formulas were produced, perhaps by
him or perhaps hundreds of years before by earlier
poets, from systems" (203). But if the poet has nothing

in his *wordhord* to suit his present purpose, "he will
produce a new formula ('new' in the sense that he has
not heard or used it before, or has failed to remember
it) from some system he has learned" (203). Having illustrated the systemic origin of the formula and having
admitted the possibility of Benson's argument for literary character, Fry redefines the formula as "a group of
words, one half-line in length, which shows evidence of
being the direct product of a formulaic system" (204).

In a later article, "Some Aesthetic Implications of
a New Definition of the Formula,"[168] he applies the conclusions just summarized to some troublesome passages in
Beowulf. Fry attempts to resolve the disagreement between Creed and Greenfield by showing that artistic mer-
it may be assigned both to the formula and to the single
word, for "the poet chose the best systems to express his
intended meaning and substituted the individual words in
the various slots of the systems" (519). While qualifying Greenfield's interpretation of *recedes muþan* in
Beowulf 724a, he contends that "this process of determining systems does uphold Greenfield's conviction that
the study of individual words and grammatical structures
in Old English poetry is a valid critical procedure; in
fact it expands it somewhat. We can also observe how
the poets choose particular systems to fit the context of
the passage and add to them alliterating words chosen
from the traditional wordhoard." (522).

Fry's latest article to deal primarily with the
formula, "Cædmon as a Formulaic Poet,"[169] is a re-examination of the "miracle" Magoun attempted to explain in
1955. After a verse by verse "system analysis" of
Cædmon's Hymn against the background of the entire corpus, Fry remarks: "But I find it more likely that the
half-lines in the corpus originated in systems Cædmon
used than that Cædmon originated the systems himself.
That would be a miracle. Cædmon did begin Old English
vernacular poetry, the value of which Abbess Hild and
her scholars immediately recognized.... I suspect that
Hild grasped the potential of converting the secular
poetry of the Germans to Christian uses, in the spirit
of Pope Gregory's admonition to Abbot Melitus to convert
pagan temples into churches, because the English 'will be
able to banish error from their hearts and be more ready
to come to the places they are familiar with, but now
recognizing and worshipping the true god.' Cædmon did
just that." (pp. 60-61).

In 1973 Thomas Gardner[170] described a literate
Beowulf-poet, one who quite consciously and carefully
set up aesthetically reverberative oppositions of words
and narrative units. Understanding the audience as a
still traditional group able to react to formulas and
attempting to show the wide spectrum of formulaic association (beyond the confines of Fry's "systems"), he
contends that the usual concepts of "formula" and "type-
scene" need expansion: "The recurrence of a given word
in a group of related contexts seems more often than not
to depend more upon a cluster of key words or concepts
than a similarity of subject matter" (117). His findings point, he feels, to one conclusion: "the *Beowulf*
poet manipulated his formulaic materials in such a way
that they achieved conspicuous variety, and this requires
skill.... He was not a prisoner of the oral-formulaic
tradition. He was free to think about the words he was
using and all indications are that he did." (121). And
this freedom and technique, Gardner claims, suggest a
literate poet: "I do not see how it could have been just
memory alone. I suspect that the eye also played its
part." (126).

Three years later James P. Holoka advanced a cognate
argument in his "The Oral Formula and Anglo-Saxon Elegy:
Some Misgivings."[171] His formulaic analysis of the usually paired elegies "The Wife's Lament" and "The Husband's Message," performed according to the method used
by Magoun in his 1953 article, did not isolate strictly
defined formulas, but rather a series of "allusive verbal
nuances one associates with literate artistry" (571). He
concluded that these echoes "are more likely the result
of conscious premeditation than of repetition induced by
the exigencies of improvisation" (571). Holoka claims
that this result is only to be expected, given the discrepancies between the epic and briefer elegiac genres:
"Certainly a skilled singer, one who could run on for
thousands of verses without (we must suppose) serious
breakdown, could easily enough hold in his mind, *in toto,*
a set piece of some one hundred verses; he could review,
polish, revise, rework until finally his method closely
approximated that of his more educated counterpart. Thus,
short, elegiac poems could conceivably attain a fixity
indistinguishable from that of a written text." (572).[172]

John S. Miletich's "The Quest for the 'Formula': a
Comparative Reappraisal,"[173] provides bibliographical
assistance and some comments on Old English. Speaking

in the context of Watts' work on Anglo-Saxon and Lord's
comparative studies, he observes that "whether the meter
is syllabic, tonic-alliterative, or quantitative, the
syntactic pattern must be the same if the statistical results are to be comparable" (116). He also feels that
"in a consistent application of the Parry-Lord theory, we
must conclude that *Beowulf* was not orally composed"
(117). In calling for more lengthy analyses of known and
hypothetically oral and non-oral texts, Miletich cautions
that "this kind of formative work would help to establish
more definite analytic categories appropriate to a wider
variety of texts. Comparative statistical analyses will
be possible only with such uniformity." (123).

In 1974 a conference on "Oral Literature and the
Formula" was held at the University of Michigan. The
proceedings of those meetings include an essay of mine,
"Formula and Theme in Old English Poetry,"[174] which offers a new approach to the formulaic nature of *Beowulf*.
Using computer analysis, I was able to determine that
there exists a level of purely metrical formula below
the level of verbal structure, "a single rhythmic template which generates 94% of all lines metrically recov-
erable from the unique manuscript and the Thorkelin
transcriptions" (p. 207). Whereas investigators from
1878 onward had been concerned with the semantic or syntactic surface of formulaic diction (a surface which, I
stress, is *visible*), we now have evidence that a more
fundamental level of template exists—"a rhythmic underlay, one whole poetic line in length with verse (half-
line) substitution, which predetermines the structure of
its verbal counterpart the formula" (p. 219; italics
deleted). I ended the section on the formula by reasoning that, because this template is strictly an oral/aural
phenomenon, it is safe to grant at least a functionally
oral status to *Beowulf*: "This is not to say that the discovery of the template proves Old English poetry to be
oral, in the usual sense of 'entirely unlettered'.... I
shall not claim that any poem in the Anglo-Saxon canon
is an actual oral performance of an unlettered *scop*. I
shall insist, however, that, if any or even all of the
Old English poets were lettered, they depended to a much
more significant degree on aural intake and oral output
than on visual apprehension and written expression; they
were not literary artists." (p. 220).[175] Two years later
my "A Computer Analysis of Metrical Patterns in *Beowulf*"[176] described in detail the data processing project

which produced, among other results,[177] the discovery of
the metrical formula. Tables and graphs of the relative
densities of various rhythmic patterns suggest the sub-
tlety of the aural dimension of *Beowulf*.

Geoffrey R. Russom's "Artful Avoidance of the Useful
Phrase in *Beowulf, The Battle of Maldon,* and *Fates of the
Apostles*"[178] also appeared in 1978. After reviewing some
features of oral theory, particularly as described in
works by Lord, Kirk, Whallon, and Watts,[179] he concen-
trates on proving that the poets of these three poems
were intentional and original manipulators of Old English
traditional diction and that the oral theory is lacking
because it cannot account for such artistry. Comparing
passages from the Anglo-Saxon poems to the Iliadic Catalog of Ships and the frequently occurring Serbo-Croatian
theme of the letter, Russom attaches considerable significance to Parry's principle of "economy," which he
states is violated time and again in the Old English
texts. He writes, for example, in commenting on the Old
English *Seasons for Fasting:* "Here, as in Homer's catalogue, the most frequently repeated concepts are the
most fixed in poetic form. If oral theory is correct,
the same principle should hold true for all sequential
structures in Old English formulaic verse. Wherever repeated ideas cluster most thickly, we should observe an
especially heavy concentration of repeated formulas. In
Beowulf, Maldon, and *Fates*, however, we find exactly the
contrary. The heaviest concentration of repeated concepts is accompanied by a total elimination of useful
repetition." He goes on: "We have to deal with deliberately varied diction." (378). Because he feels that this
situation "can only be explained by the operation of
analogy in the mind of a poet who had mastered a formulaic diction, and who placed a high value on varied expression" (387), Russom sees the oral theory as an inadequate explanatory system, both for Old English and for
oral literature in general. He prefers to confront the
Anglo-Saxon tradition on its own terms, positing in
place of the Parry-Lord hypothesis a view of the poets
of *Beowulf, Maldon,* and *Fates* which leaves them free to
depart consciously and originally from their tradition:
"Where one ancient phrase would have done, they stocked
their memories with several. Where a ready-made formula
would have served, they were willing to create a new
line by analogy. Their diction stands out as superior
because they knew more of the tradition than singing

demanded, and controlled it with greater facility."(390).

Of the articles now in press which have to do with
the formula in Anglo-Saxon, I will mention three. The
first, my "Epic and Charm in Old English and Serbo-
Croatian Poetry,"[180] starts with a brief review of the
origins of formulaic and thematic studies in ancient
Greek and proceeds to a discussion of another level of
regularity in oral traditional literature, that of "sound
patterns."[181]   Selections from songs by *guslari* in the
Parry Collection illustrate the guiding function of these
acoustic patterns (even to the point of "misguiding" the
singer at times), and comparative reference is made to
various kinds of aural redundancies in Old English poems,
among them "cued" alliteration and morphemic repetition
(or "responsion"[182]).   I then turn to a comparison of
Yugoslav charms, collected in rural Serbia in 1975 by our
research team of anthropologists and specialists in oral
literature,[183] and the surviving Old English spells, both
of which are shown to draw their power from the fact of
their oral performance. Both *galdor*, the Anglo-Saxon
term for verbal magic, and *bajanje*, the Serbo-Croatian
counterpart, derive from Indo-European roots associated
with the production of meaningful sound. From a synchronic point of view, analysis reveals many and similar
kinds of sound patterns and formulaic structures in the
two charm traditions, among them repetition of key
morphs, sequences of "nonsense" syllables which nonetheless obey various euphonic laws, a kind of metonymic personification, and extended formulaic series. I find, in
short, that "whether from the Old English or Serbo-Croatian tradition, and whether used for curing eruptions
of the skin, recovering stolen cattle, or revivifying
barren land, all of these charm excerpts have one feature in common: they depend for their magic on oral performance and sound patterns" (italics deleted; 86).

Donald Fry's "Old English Formulaic Statistics"[184]
is intended primarily as a reply to Miletich's "The
Quest for the 'Formula'," summarized above. Fry praises
the diversity of formulaic studies in many literatures
and at the same time applauds Miletich's call for rigor
in comparison, but he also offers the opinion that "one
person's rigor may become another person's rigidity.
Literatures do differ and require exactly tailored analyses within the formulaic framework." Noting that criteria based on Parry's original definition of the formula
do not apply well to Old English,[185] that the general

anonymity of Anglo-Saxon poets makes individual profiles
within the tradition impossible, and that the syntactical, lexical, and contextual parameters of Old English
are significantly different from those of other traditional poetries, he demonstrates that Miletich's demands
for precision are undercut by his failing to take into
account the poetics of Anglo-Saxon verse: "Old English
poetry proves too complex for statistical formulaic
analysis as now practiced. So long as comparative studies remain based on Parry's definition, which does not
fit the Old English evidence, we must excuse Anglo-Saxon
poetry from such comparisons."

Last among the forthcoming articles on the formula
to be mentioned here is my "*Beowulf* and Traditional Narrative Song: the Potential and Limits of Comparison."[186]
The major thrust of this study aligns with that of my
contribution to this *Festschrift* and also with Fry's emphasis in his latest piece: in comparing oral traditional
literatures, we must be wary of the oversimplification
and reductionism toward which uncritical demonstrations
of similarities can lead; we must consider the *differences* as well as the *similarities* among oral literatures,
and we must do so with philological precision and
methodological imagination. In the first part of this
essay, that which deals briefly with the formula in comparative terms, I argue for a view of the traditional
phrase which takes each particular tradition into account, that is, which conceives of the formula not as an
archetype or *Ur*-form common to all oral traditions but
more immediately as a creature of a particular prosody,
euphony, and so forth. While "the formula" may at some
generic level be just such a universal phenomenon, we
cannot carry on valid comparison among literatures without penetrating beyond this generic sameness to underlying, tradition-dependent idiosyncrasies. Each poetry,
as well as the field of oral literature research in general, deserves these distinctions.

The Theme

The history of the oral theme in Old English poetry
also begins with Albert Lord's 1949 dissertation, later
to become *The Singer of Tales*. Defining "themes" as
"the groups of ideas regularly used in telling a tale in
the formulaic style of traditional song" (*Singer*, p. 68),
Lord clearly and precisely explicated the dynamics of

large narrative units in Serbo-Croatian oral tradition
and applied his findings to Homeric Greek, Old English,
Old French, and modern Greek texts.[187]   Though his original proposals have undergone occasional modifications in
the hands of some Anglo-Saxon scholars, his basic principles still govern current research. For this reason it
is appropriate to start this section of the survey with a
selection of his comments on the theme:

> There is nothing in the poet's experience (or in
> ours if we listen to the same song from several
> singers and to the same singer telling the same
> song several times) to give him any idea that a
> theme can be expressed in only one set of words.
> Those singers whom he has heard have never repro-
> duced a theme in exactly the same words, and he
> has no feeling that to do so is necessary or even
> normal practice. The theme, even though it be
> verbal, is not any fixed set of words, but a
> grouping of ideas. (p. 69).

> In building a large theme the poet has a plan of
> it in his mind beyond the bare necessities of
> narrative. There are elements of order and bal-
> ance within themes. The description of an as-
> sembly, for example, follows a plan proceeding
> from the head of the assembly and his immediate
> retinue through a descending hierarchy of nobles
> to the cupbearer, who is the youngest in the
> assembly and hence waits upon his elders, but
> ending with the main hero of the story. This
> progression aids the singer by giving him a
> definite method of presentation. (p. 92).

> In all these instances one sees also that the
> singer always has the end of the theme in his
> mind. He knows where he is going. As in the
> adding of one line to another, the singer can
> stop and fondly dwell upon any single item with-
> out losing a sense of the whole. The style
> allows comfortably for digression or for enrich-
> ment. (p. 92).

> Although the themes lead naturally from one to
> another to form a song which exists as a whole
> in the singer's mind with Aristotelian beginning,

middle, and end, the units within this whole, the
themes, have a semi-independent life of their own.
The theme in oral poetry exists at one and the
same time in and for itself and for the whole
song. (p. 94).

Lord also locates themes specifically in *Beowulf*: "repeated assemblies with speeches, repetition of journeying
from one place to another, and on the larger canvas the
repeated multiform scenes of the slaying of monsters"
(pp. 198-99).[188]

Francis P. Magoun, Jr., and Stanley B. Greenfield
first anchored Lord's comparative observations in example. In his 1955 article, "The Theme of the Beasts of
Battle,"[189] Magoun isolated a theme which pervades Old
English poetry: "namely, the mention of the wolf, eagle,
and/or raven as beasts attendant on a scene of carnage"
(83). In order to illustrate the possible variation, he
collected all twelve occurrences in the poetic corpus and
subjected them to a formulaic analysis, claiming that
"the formulas and formulaic systems will be seen to divide up in two ways, those particularly relevant to the
subject matter of the theme and those of general usefulness" (90). In a subsequent piece, "Some Notes on
Anglo-Saxon Poetry,"[190] Magoun identified two more Old
English themes ("the grateful recipient" and "the gesture
of the raised shield and/or brandished spear"), specu-
lated on a particular theme in the *Kalevala* ("the temporary misinterpretation of a sight or sound"), and commented on the heavily traditional diction of *The Battle
of Maldon*.

Greenfield's "The Formulaic Expression of the Theme
of 'Exile' in Anglo-Saxon Poetry,"[191] also appeared in
1955. After listing several examples of exile "images,"
Greenfield noted: "Despite the fact that the exile figures are so different in kind and character ... the expressions of their plights are clearly cast in similar
molds" (201). He argued that the traditional identity
of the theme rests on the consistent usage of four aspects: (1) status, (2) deprivation, (3) state of mind,
and (4) movement in or into exile (201). Extending his
definition of originality in formulaic diction—"the degree of tension achieved between the inherited body of
meanings in which a particular formula participates and
the specific meaning of that formula in its individual
context" (205)—to originality in the handling of

formulaic themes, he then closed with a brief examination of the exile pattern in *The Wanderer* and *The Seafarer*.[192]

Reaction to these new ideas was almost immediate. Adrien Bonjour sought a compromise between the "singer school" and the literary critics of Anglo-Saxon poetry in his "*Beowulf* and the Beasts of Battle"[193] by championing Greenfield's notion of originality within a tradition. On the basis of this assertion, he claimed that "the originality of the *Beowulf* scop is fully confirmed" (569). For, while in all of the other parallel passages cited by Magoun the "Beasts of Battle" theme precedes a real fight of some sort, "in *Beowulf*, on the other hand, the theme is never used in connection with any of the numerous battle scenes which come into focus throughout the poem; and when it appears, there is only a passing reference to warfare at that, still hidden in the haze and dream of things to come" (568). If other singers used the "beasts" only in a conventional manner, the *Beowulf* poet used them to prophesy the Geats' destiny in what was still a traditional manner. Bonjour ended with the suggestion, later elaborated by many,[194] that almost certainly Cynewulf—and, therefore, perhaps the author of our text of *Beowulf*—was a lettered *and* formulaic poet.

The next important study of the theme to appear, and it proved to be a truly seminal one, was David Crowne's "The Hero on the Beach: an Example of Composition by Theme in Anglo-Saxon Poetry."[195] Applying Lord's earlier ideas on the theme (see note 189) to the Old English *Andreas* and its sources, he concluded that "the poem, however, is not simply a versified translation of some one of the prose versions, but is a vigorous re-creation of the foreign story within the traditional native idiom" (366). Crowne defined the unit which informs such a traditional re-making as "a stereotyped way of describing (1) a hero on the beach (2) with his retainers (3) in the presence of a flashing light (4) as a journey is completed (or begun)" (368). He quoted an example of the same pattern in *Beowulf* (1802a-6) to illustrate thematic flexibility, and argued against Krapp's explanation of the similarities between *Beowulf* and *Andreas* as a literary borrowing[196] by suggesting that "the characteristics of thematic composition allow us to conclude that the likenesses are merely evidence of common oral tradition" (372).

In 1961 Robert P. Creed, in his "On the Possibility

of Criticizing Old English Poetry,"[197] asked a much-re-
peated question about the product of oral composition:
"how can a tissue of formulas, of repeated verses and
significant parts of verses, be a great poem?" (98).   He
then answered his own question not by attempting to find
originality in the poetic formula, but by claiming that
"it is on the level of the theme that we can legitimately
expect to find differences in the work of mature singers
which has survived to us" (99).   Creed located the art of
the singer in the articulation—varied with each occurrence—of thematic patterns, for "there is *no* distance
between the many appearances of a given theme within a
tradition.   That is to say, every time a singer performs
the same theme he and his audience hear and appreciate
that performance against the music of all other performances of that theme" (101).[198]   In a later article, "The
Singer Looks at His Sources,"[199] he examined occurrences
of the "theme of the singer" in the *Iliad,* the *Odyssey,*
and *Beowulf.*   In each case he saw the poet linking himself with an earlier singer to establish a traditional
connection between himself and the events he is recounting: "We are thus left to listen to these passages with
an impression of Homer and the Anglo-Saxon singer glanc-
ing back at these moments to what they would apparently
have us believe are the primary sources of their great
sings—Demodocus and the Danish singer." (52).

Some years later Jeff Opland[200] was to re-examine
the evidence and come to complementary conclusions: "The
testimony furnished by the poem must be evaluated within
the context of what can be learned from all extant Old
English and Anglo-Latin sources, from a comparative study
of Germanic and Indo-European literatures, and from a
comparative study of analogous traditions surviving today.   Only after due consideration has been given in this
context, and after allowance has been made for the probability of change in the tradition, should scholars accept the evidence that *Beowulf* affords us of the practice
of poetry in Anglo-Saxon England." (466-67).[201]

Robert E. Diamond discussed themes of war, sea voyages, the comitatus, and cold weather in his 1961 article, "Theme as Ornament in Anglo-Saxon Poetry."[202]   Including extremely detailed supporting evidence for each
example, he illustrated the multiform nature of the traditional units, molded as they are by each singer for a
different narrative purpose.   But perhaps the most interesting parts of this essay are (1) his explanation of

why the *Andreas* and the *Seafarer* poets have employed no
set sea-voyaging themes and (2) his comments on the nature of influence in a traditional poetry. Diamond saw
these two poems as works in which particular poetic purposes have overridden the conventionality of a simple
"set piece" such as that of the sea voyage. As for influence among poems, he remarked: "Recent studies of Old
English poetry tend to discount the likelihood that any
one Anglo-Saxon poem consciously echoes any other. The
more we find out about formulaic diction, the stronger
the assumption that all the poets drew on the same stock
of traditional diction. The paradox is that the more we
understand about the way these poems were put together,
the less certainty we can pronounce on the relationships
of the poems to each other." (392).

Alain Renoir brought aesthetics to the fore with
his 1962 article, "Point of View and Design for Terror
in *Beowulf*."[203] Directing his attention toward the visual *tour de force* of Grendel's approach to Heorot, he
writes: "In this necessity to evoke immediate visualiza-
tion lies a fundamental difference between the Old-
English poet and his modern counterpart: whereas the
latter *writes for readers* who may proceed through the
text at their own leisure and go back over any passage
as often as necessary, the former *sings for listeners*
who will never have a second chance if they miss anything
on the first hearing" (p. 155). Later he continues: "If
we recall that the entire passage contains only one suggestion of sound, whose effect is to emphasize transition in the otherwise purely visual account, we must
further conclude that the terror which the scene so
powerfully evokes in the audience is entirely the result
of masterfully selected visual details consistently presented from the most immediately effective point of
view" (p. 166). This focus on the uniquely arresting
movement and texture of oral traditional narrative also
characterized a paper published the next year, "The
Heroic Oath in *Beowulf*, the *Chanson de Roland*, and the
Nibelungenlied,"[204] in which Renoir examines in detail
the shape of the warrior's boast in three different traditions.

The purpose of George Clark's "The Traveler Recognizes His Goal: a Theme in Anglo-Saxon Poetry,"[205] is
similar to that of Diamond's article, namely "to point
out a theme, 'the traveler recognizes his destination,'
to examine its structure, and by doing so demonstrate

that Anglo-Saxon poets were able to control and manipulate its materials for consciously artistic ends" (646).
In speaking, for example, about the life of Abraham as
related in *Genesis A*, Clark described "the poet's medi-
ation between the traditional mould and borrowed stories,
and [one] can feel that the poet controls both at a real
though modest level of competence" (649). We may compare what he says about *Beowulf* to Bonjour's statements
concerning the handling of thematic material: "In two
instances, the *Beowulf* poet's development of the theme
of the traveler's arrival is thoroughly conventional, and
illustrates that poetic brilliance in exploiting the
techniques of oral poetry is manifested not only in the
re-handling of traditional materials, but also in the
perfect fusion of the traditional theme with the narrative structure and emotional tone of the poet's fable"
(655).

In his "Beowulf and Odysseus,"[206] Albert Lord pointed
out the thematic similarity of the passages leading up to
the story of Euryalus and those preparatory to the Unferth episode. He identified the submerged schema, more
prominent in Yugoslav songs, of "winning a wife" as a
structurally important theme in both the *Odyssey* and
Beowulf: "The examples of the narrative sequence which
we have been investigating seem to indicate that it is
useful and has meaning both on the return of the hero to
his home to set everything in order and to remarry his
wife and on the outward journey of the young hero to win
a wife. In *Beowulf* the pattern has remained in spite of
the loss in this heroic Germanic society of the purpose
of winning a wife or returning to one. Perhaps
Wealtheow's role is vestigial." (p. 91). Explaining the
resemblances in pattern in terms of a common Indo-European epic tradition, he commented: "The story patterns
in such a tradition are very old, amazingly stable, surprisingly alive, whether we observe them in the eighth
century B.C., the eighth century A.D., or in our own
time" (p. 91).[207]

In 1966 Donald Fry began a series of articles on the
theme with "The Hero on the Beach in *Finnsburh*."[208] He
sought to confirm Renoir's argument in "Oral-Formulaic
Theme Survival: a Possible Instance in the *Nibelungenlied*" by advancing lines 2-12 of the *Finnsburh Fragment*
as a chronological intermediate between the "hero on the
beach / at the door" themes in *Beowulf* and the
Nibelungenlied: "In view of this dual possibility of the

theme's transmission before and after the invasion, the
case for its survival from the time of the composition of
Andreas and *Finnsburh* to that of the *Nibelungenlied* is
greatly strengthened" (31).   In an essay that appeared a
year later, "The Heroine on the Beach in *Judith*,"[209]   Fry
illustrated the flexibility of the same theme in its application to the Biblical figure.   In concert with his
ideas on the generative nature of the formulaic system
and the equivalence of its variants, he spoke against
the concept of a "norm" for the theme: "Because we do
not know what 'norms' governed conventional Old English
poetry, we must regard all the passages as equally legitimate and conventional variant treatments of the same
narrative materials" (179).[210]   Placing the emphasis on
the aesthetics of the theme, he then listed three of its
uses and effects.   The first is association: "Actually
themes prove to be a mnemonic device as much for the
audience as for the poet; they provide the audience with
a supply of associations, which are used by the poet to
enrich the narrative" (181).   Second, he described the
structural character of the unit, by which the theme
"allows and even justifies the inclusion of details
otherwise unnecessary ... to the plot and gives them a
fitness and unity by means of the thematic structure"
(183).   Third, the themes contribute to the overall
unity and continuity of the poem.

Fry published his most influential study along these
lines, "Old English Formulaic Themes and Type-Scenes,"[211]
in 1968.   He distinguished two kinds of traditional units
in the poetry: the "type-scene" was defined as "a recurring stereotyped presentation of conventional details
used to describe a certain narrative event, requiring
neither verbatim repetition nor a specific formula content," while the "theme" was "a recurring concatenation
of details and ideas, not restricted to a specific event,
verbatim repetition, or certain formulas, which forms an
underlying structure for an action or description"
(53).[212]   With these concepts in hand, he focused on the
"approach-to-battle" pattern[213] in his "Themes and
Type-Scenes in *Elene* 1-113."[214]   Here Fry showed that
"the traditional formulaic poet using type-scene construction gains certain advantages from his medium.   By
manipulating recognized patterns already rich in association, he affords himself possibilities for unity, symmetry, suspense, foreshadowing, and larger connotations
from imagery." (41).   In practice, he claimed that

"despite their similarity, we can see that themes represent a form of structural device different from type-
scenes. The latter involves a narrative event; the former a state of being or situation. A plot can be made up
of a series of events, or type-scenes, but themes are
always static. No action occurs in them as part of their
essential form or content; they are no more than con-
catenations of imagery. Therefore, themes can only underlie narrative structures, such as type-scenes, and
provide a framework into which the poet may weave enrich-
ing details."(40).[215]

The meaning of thematic repetition in context is
also discussed by Paul B. Taylor in his "Themes of Death
in *Beowulf*."[216] He describes the role of the narrative
commonplace in the parallelism and identification of elements, in the sense which the unit conveys of previous
contexts, and in the unification of the work of art. With
similar concerns Fredrik J. Heinemann examined what he
saw as the comic inappropriateness of the *Judith* poet's
traditional diction in his "*Judith* 236-291a: a Mock
Heroic Approach-to-Battle Type-Scene."[217] After a careful analysis of these lines, in which he subdivided the
type-scene into smaller units called *topoi* (after an unpublished paper by Creed[218]), Heinemann remarked that
"although the poetry is formulaic and highly conventional, it is not therefore mechanical. *Judith* 236-291a re-
futes many such charges and reveals that a formulaic
poet can be knowledgeable about the tradition and capable of stretching its limits to achieve his own poetic
ends." (96).

In 1971 Lee C. Ramsey published "The Sea Voyages in
Beowulf,"[219] an analysis of the structure of a very common thematic unit with emphasis on its abstract pattern
rather than verbal correspondence. He claimed that "the
important similarities between the two sea-voyaging
scenes are narrative: that is, they are similarities in
events and in the sequence of events" (54) and that "these
passages clearly illustrate the type of similarities and
differences which we have come to associate with oral-
formulaic themes and type-scenes: general correspondence
without actual repetition" (54). Ramsey follows these
comments with an explication of Scyld's and Beowulf's
funerals against the traditional background of the sea-
voyaging type-scene.[220]

Albert Lord's "Perspectives on Recent Work on Oral
Literature" contains a section on Old English poetry, in

which he argues against the orality of the "Christian
poems":

> Although the composers of these poems might have
> known the saints' legends from sermons, i.e.,
> not necessarily in written form, yet it is nor-
> mal to assume that they knew them from some writ-
> ten source, for example, the Latin versions that
> were to be found in the monasteries. I would
> also like to suggest the possibility that in these
> poems, namely, the religious ones, a new body of
> formulas to express the new ideas of the Chris-
> tian poetry was beginning to be developed on the
> model of the oral traditional poetry. I am
> tempted to call the religious poetry 'transi-
> tional' or perhaps 'mixed.' If that is the cor-
> rect term, it applies not only to formulas but
> to themes as well.
>
>   If the religious poems were truly oral tradi-
> tional songs, I would expect to find a higher
> degree of verbal correspondence among the vari-
> ous instances of a theme within a given poem,
> after making due allowance for adjustment to
> the specific position in the poem which it
> occupies. (23).[221]

His notion of the theme clearly includes a measure of
verbal correspondence, as is especially evident in the
following remarks: "The theme as *subject* alone is too
general for our very special purposes. But if by theme
one means a repeated narrative element together with its
verbal expression, that portion of a poem, an aggregate
of specific verses, that tells a certain repeated part
of the narrative, measureable in terms of lines and even
words and word combinations, then we find ourselves dealing with elements of truly oral traditional style."[222]

    A 1976 essay by Alain Renoir, "Oral Theme and Writ-
ten Texts,"[223] continued his studies of the survival of
themes from one tradition to another. Renoir located
the same theme in Catullus' *Poem IV, The Dream of the
Rood,* and *The Husband's Message*, describing the commonplace as "an elongated, man-made, wooden object of any
size ... with a pragmatic effect upon the speaker of the
poem or a protagonist thereof ... speaks up to tell how
it once had a previous existence under the form of one
or more live trees" (340-41). After bringing to light

similar narrative clusters in Homer and Virgil and weighing the possible explanations, he argued that "both the classical and Anglo-Saxon texts have independently drawn upon the same theme, thus conforming to an established pattern which has been mentioned above in respect to the *Odyssey* and *Beowulf* and offering us the practical advantage of enabling us to bypass the nearly insoluble problems likely to plague any attempt to determining the indebtedness of formulaic materials" (344). The interface between oral structures and written texts has long been a shadowy and ill-defined one, and many more studies like Renoir's are needed to help us understand just what the dynamics of the transition are.[224]

In the same year I suggested a tradition-dependent basis for the theme in "Formula and Theme in Old English Poetry." Working from a comparative point of view and using examples from the Christian poems *Andreas* (the "scourging" sequence) and *Elene* (the "tradition" sequence), I proposed the stressed root morpheme as the most fundamental datum of the Anglo-Saxon narrative pattern: "The repetitive element of the Homeric theme, the unit of verbal correspondence, is either (1) the whole line or (2) the caesura-bound partial line; the same may be said for the Serbo-Croatian theme, although available evidence here points toward (2) as the more frequently occurring unit. The corresponding element in the Old English theme is the 'stave-root.' By this term I mean to indicate *principally the roots of alliterating words, although non-alliterating words may at times be included.*" (p. 221). On this basis only, I maintained, may we apply Lord's criterion of verbal correspondence to Old English; to continue to expect all literatures to answer definitions fashioned for ancient Greek and its close prosodic relative Serbo-Croatian is an error in true comparison.[225] Toward the end of the essay I commented briefly on the ritual nature of traditional oral units of composition, noting that "echoes from one occurrence of a given theme reverberate not simply through the subsequent linear length of the given poem, but through the collective mythic knowledge of the given culture. Under these circumstances, we may have to revise our thinking about 'mistakes' and 'inconsistencies,' for example. In addition, ... usefulness and aesthetics need no longer preclude one another's existence; they merge in the ritual unity of traditional art." (p. 232).

H. Ward Tonsfeldt also brought a comparative per-

spective to his analysis of "Ring Structure in *Beowulf*."[226] Referring to the works of van Otterlo, Notopoulos, and Whitman,[227] he illustrated in some detail the
Beowulf poet's use of this avowedly oral structure first
described in the Homeric texts. Tonsfeldt's most convincing argument rests in his judgment that "we clearly
need an aesthetic rather than a mechanical explanation
to account for the ring structures in *Beowulf*" (446),
combined with his demonstration that the Finnsburh episode functions as a structural microcosm for the poem as
a whole. Indeed, it seems that this function is characteristic of ring-composition throughout *Beowulf*. By
showing how this figure "delineates a rhetorical unit
rather than a narrative one" (451), he is able to move
beyond structural analysis to poetics.

The next year my "The Oral Singer in Context: Halil
Bajgorić, *Guslar*"[228] appeared, bringing the Serbo-Croatian analogy to bear directly on the Old English and
ancient Greek traditions by working from previously unedited Parry Collection texts. After a discussion of
the "ideal singer" described by many *guslari* and his
possible relationship to figures such as the Anglo-Saxon
Widsith and Deor, I turn to comparisons of themes in
the three traditions. The first comparison, involving
the "heroic oath" theme in two versions of Bajgorić's
Marko i Nina od Koštuna and in its two fully orchestrated
occurrences in *Beowulf*, uncovers one sort of pattern:
"Both the Serbo-Croatian and Old English themes, then,
reveal a highly structured underlay of motifs, elements
which combine in a fairly regular sequence to form the
larger, integral unit. These themes are alike in their
dependence on the underlays, and also in their relative
lack of dependence on verbal correspondence. In fact,
only a very few elements have a slight morphemic or
formulaic resemblance between occurrences. This situation is typical of Anglo-Saxon verse units, whose
verbal correspondence is in most cases locally echoic
and centered on ictus-bearing morphemes rather than on
whole-line or colonic formulas. The same situation is
typical of some Serbo-Croatian themes, and atypical of
others." (240). The second comparison, which sets
Bajgorić's theme of "Readying the hero's horse" alongside
the Odyssean "feast scene," detects another kind of pattern, one which involves dense verbal correspondence.
As do related essays summarized in the section on the
formula, this comparative study of the theme emphasizes

the importance of giving each tradition its due.

The notion of tradition-dependence is also paramount in my "*Beowulf* and Traditional Narrative Song: the Potential and Limits of Comparison." In the part of this article concerned with the theme, I examine four versions of the "Shouting in Prison" multiform taken from the previously unedited songs of the Parry Collection singer Mujo Kukuruzović and the two occurrences of the "sea voyage" in *Beowulf*. The opening analysis corroborates Lord's observation that both narrative sequence and verbal correspondence characterize the Serbo-Croatian theme; I find as well that (1) "as might be expected given the colon structure underlying formula generation, the verbal agreement between instances is largely in terms of whole lines or cola," (2) "though the narrative sequence seems to remain almost absolutely constant and to oversee the thematic progress of the story, in rare cases ... a unit can be transposed, provided that the narrative logic is maintained," (3) "verbal correspondence is not of uniform density throughout the theme or from instance to instance; certain motifs are much more stable formulaically than others," and (4) "variation in verbalization of the theme can take a number of forms, among them what may be termed 'formulaic variance,' in which lines and part-lines recombine and permute according to systemic principles, and 'ornamentation,' in which a non-narrative, paratactic gloss not necessary in itself but rather complementary to a necessary element is included." The Beowulfian sea voyage also exhibits a definite narrative sequence of elements or motifs, but verbal correspondence between occurrences takes a tradition-dependent form—not the repetition of colonic formulas as in Serbo-Croatian or ancient Greek, but the echo of single root morphemes. In short, "neither the sea voyage nor 'Shouting in Prison' is less a theme for its similarity to or difference from its counterpart; rather each theme is actualized in a form governed by the prosody of the tradition involved."[229]

IV. New Directions

The essays in this volume exemplify the continuing development of oral literature research and scholarship. They document recent advances in field work coverage and indicate how methodologies for interpreting ancient, medieval, and contemporary texts are still in the process

of formation. Ranging widely over many different literatures, their authors illustrate the explanatory power of
the oral theory in novel and exciting ways, from the
coming into being of the *Iliad* and *Odyssey* poems, to the
relationship between repeated phrase and mythic structure
in *Beowulf*, to the phenomenology of the tale-telling act
in central Africa. The papers speak to both familiar and
unfamiliar problems with fresh critical insights, illum-
inating individual texts through attention to the traditions from which those texts take their meaning.

Five of the articles are concerned primarily with
Old English poetry. Robert P. Creed's "The *Beowulf*-Poet:
Master of Sound-Patterning" deals with five levels of
oral traditional structure—phoneme, formula, enjambement, theme, and song—after the manner of Berkley Peabody's recent *The Winged Word*, and explores in depth the
importance of oral tradition in the making and meaning of
the poem. In "Feasts and Anti-Feasts in *Beowulf* and the
Odyssey," Joanne De Lavan Foley discovers in *Beowulf* a
recurrent mythic structure which rationalizes the use of
formulas having to do with "sleeping and feasting," and
then extends her method to a cognate analysis of feasts,
their disruption, and their restoration in the *Odyssey*.
John Miles Foley's "Tradition-dependent and -independent
Features in Oral Literature: a Comparative View of the
Formula" considers the Old English formula against the
background of its Homeric Greek and Serbo-Croatian
counterparts and offers a new definition sensitive to
the prosody and natural language characteristics of
Anglo-Saxon. In "The Memory of Cædmon," Donald K. Fry,
Jr. brings together theories of memory, Bede's story of
Cædmon, and Eric Havelock's reconstruction of the educative reality of Homer; the result is a bold synthesis
suggesting how formulaic verse served as a means of religious instruction in Anglo-Saxon England. John D.
Niles re-examines Fry's concept of the "formulaic system" in Old English poetry, using Homeric diction as a
comparative context and emphasizing precision of definition and generativity, in "Formula and Formulaic System
in *Beowulf*."

In another contribution on Germanic literature,
"Satire and the Heroic Life: Two Studies (*Helgakviða
Hundingsbana* I, 18 and Bjorn Hítdœlakappi's *Grámagaflím*),"
Joseph Harris examines the place of satire in the heroic
patterns of Helgi and Bjorn from two perspectives, those
of traditional narrative structures and the "ideological

matrix supporting those structures." Edward R. Haymes'
focus in "Oral Composition in Middle High German Epic
Poetry" is one of both genre and *ambiance*: he sees the
courtly epic as nontraditional and literate and the
heroic epic, specifically the *Nibelungenlied*, as traditional and oral or oral-derived. Gregory Nagy also argues from a social and historical reality by way of the
oral theory toward a literary critical reality in "An
Evolutionary Model for the Text Fixation of Homeric
Epos"; in his view the texts of the *Iliad* and *Odyssey*
which have reached us attained their fixed form in the
social context of eighth century B.C. Panhellenism. In
"Narrative as Precedent in Yorùbá Oral Tradition,"
Deirdre La Pin brings modern critical methods and her
field work experience in sub-Saharan Africa to bear on
the function of narrative in a living oral culture, showing how the story structure constitutes a readily available referent for action and personal behavior.

Serbo-Croatian oral epic, which of course provided
the first living analog for the oral composition of the
Homeric poems, furnishes comparative material for a discussion of theme in Old English and Yugoslav traditional
poetry in Francelia Clark's "Flyting in *Beowulf* and Rebuke in *The Song of Bagdad:* the Question of Theme." In
"Genealogy as Genre in a Serbian Village," Barbara K.
Halpern adds another dimension to the understanding of
oral culture in Yugoslavia with a sociolinguistic analysis of genealogical "poems" which she collected in the
region of Šumadija. Extending the oral theory to another
Slavic literature, Patricia Arant incisively probes the
structure of the oral theme and illustrates its inner
logic in "The Intricate Web: Thematic Cohesion in Russian
Oral Traditional Verse Narrative." The Serbo-Croatian
tradition also plays a significant part in John
Miletich's "Hispanic and South Slavic Traditional Narrative Poetry and Related Forms: a Survey of Comparative
Studies (1824-1977)," which presents a thorough review
of previous research and a summary of some of the author's own work on oral literature. William González'
concern in "The Religious Ballad of New Mexico and the
Canary Islands: a Comparative Study of Traditional Features" is to establish a common oral poetic tradition
still shared by two originally related groups of speakers now widely separated geographically.

The interaction of oral tradition and historical
reality is Joseph Duggan's general subject in "Legitima-

tion and the Hero's Exemplary Function in the *Cantar de mio Cid* and the *Chanson de Roland*; by seeking out the contemporary sociological context of the medieval Spanish and French epics, he is able to offer readings which explain the two heroes as cultural models of mythic and mimetic significance. In "Oral-Formulaic Context: Implications for the Comparative Criticism of Mediaeval Texts," Alain Renoir offers an intriguing alternative to literary theories involving both the customary kinds of context and the current notion of "decontextualization": using as illustration the theme of oral performance in the *Odyssey*, *Beowulf*, and the *Song of Hildebrand*, he suggests oral-formulaic structure as a context free from assumptions of geography, chronology, and influence. David E. Bynum reassesses contemporary literary and anthropological thinking in "Myth and Ritual: Two Faces of Tradition," with particular emphasis on the universal aspects of the concept of marriage and on diachronic and synchronic views of myth and ritual. Finally, in "Oral Literature and the Middle Ages," Bruce Rosenberg describes the importance of folktale analysis in the interpretation of medieval texts and comments on the variety of forms taken by oral literatures and also on the need for more data from field ethnographers, linguists, and psychologists.

Albert Lord's essay, "Memory, Fixity, and Genre in Oral Traditional Poetries," which I add at the end of this volume in his honor, explores some vexed issues in oral literature research with typical clarity and grace. In discussing the possible role of memorization, he indicates by example how Serbo-Croatian singers respond in typical formulaic ways as they make their songs, and that they do not learn these regular responses by rote. He demonstrates further that it is the constancy of the underlying "essential ideas" which make a text appear fixed, with the degree of absolute version-to-version fidelity depending on a host of factors relating to the singer and song. Of particular importance for the comparatist are his remarks on the relative fixity attainable in various individual genres, and in non-narrative as opposed to narrative types of poetry. All in all, Lord's essay treats some long-disputed problems in an authoritative way, and I am very pleased to be able to include it in this *Festschrift*.

Taken together, then, these essays represent a still evolving discipline, one which in the fifty years since its inception has demonstrated time and again its singular potential for explicating many literatures on many levels, but at the same time one which by its very nature holds out manifold possibilities for future growth. The happy paradox is this: the more we are able to discover about these singers of tales, the more they have to tell us.

NOTES

[1]See *Haymes* and, for example: *TWW*; Ching Hsien-Wang, *The Bell and the Drum: Shih Ching as Formulaic Poetry in an Oral Tradition* (Berkeley, 1974); Gregory Nagy, *Comparative Studies in Greek and Indic Meter* (Cambridge, Mass., 1974); Ruth Finnegan, *Oral Literature in Africa* (Oxford, 1970); *Singer*; Francis P. Magoun, Jr., "The Oral-Formulaic Character of Anglo-Saxon Narrative Poetry," *Speculum*, 28(1953), 446-67; Joseph J. Duggan, *The Song of Roland: Formulaic Style and Poetic Craft* (Berkeley, 1973); Ruth Webber, "Formulistic Diction in the Spanish Ballad," *UCPMP*, 34, no. 2(1951), 175-277; Michael J. Zwettler, *The Oral Tradition of Classical Arabic Poetry* (Columbus, 1978); and Bruce A. Rosenberg, *The Art of the American Folk Preacher* (New York, 1970).

[2]See note 9.

[3]"The Homeric Question," in *CH*, pp. 234-66. I will make no attempt to give a thorough history of the Ques-

tion, for which the reader is directed to the Davison essay and Adam Parry's "Introduction" to *MHV*, pp. ix-lxii. For the latest and fullest bibliography, see, in addition to *Haymes* (and its supplement in a review by Samuel J. Armistead in *MLN*, 90[1975], 296-99), James P. Holoka, "Homeric Originality: a Survey," *CW*, 66(1973), 257-93.

[4]Davison draws from the scattered earliest evidence "the strong assumption that for the Greeks of the period down to about 450 B.C. Homer was a real person who had lived at latest in the early seventh century and had composed a large number of narrative poems of the highest quality which were still being recited by professional rhapsodes, and especially by a group of people who lived in Chios and called themselves *Homeridae*, thus claiming to be the poet's descendants" (p. 235). See further Davison, "The Transmission of the Text," in *CH*, pp. 218-19.

[5]Friedrich August Wolf, *Prolegomena ad Homerum sive de Operum Homericorum Prisca et Genuina Forma Variisque Mutationibus et Probabili Ratione Emendandi*, 3rd ed. by R. Peppmüller (Halle, 1884).

[6]See, as perhaps the most accomplished example of this line of textual study, Ulrich von Wilamowitz-Müllendorf, *Die Ilias und Homer* (Berlin, 1916). See also Part III of this "Introduction," where the "Higher Criticism" of Old English texts, which shared the Analysts' concerns of authorship and establishment of the text, is discussed in some detail.

[7]See, for example, J. A. Scott, *The Unity of Homer* (Berkeley, 1921).

[8]Of this important catalyst Adam Parry writes: "... the effect of linguistic examination was the reverse of what had been intended by those who practised it: instead of discernible layers of language which would correspond to fixed stages of composition, they succeeded in demonstrating the homogeneity of the dialect mixture." Quoting Witte's remark that "the language of the Homeric poems is a creation of epic verse," he goes on: "For if the tradition created an artificial language, that language, with its forms of diverse date and diverse place, could have been used at one time by one poet to create one work." (pp. xx-xxi).

[9]"A Comparative Study of Diction as One of the Elements of Style in Early Greek Epic Poetry," in *MHV*, p. 421.

[10] The problem of constraint and freedom in formulaic

style has still not been satisfactorily solved, largely, I believe, because scholars are in the habit of regarding formulas as confining rather than as associational and referential. If we were aware of the echoic potential of tradition, perhaps by experiencing first-hand a number of known oral epics in a known oral tradition, we would be in a better position to comment.

[11] *L'Épithète traditionnelle dans Homère: Essai sur un problème de style homérique* (Paris, 1928), trans. in *MHV*, pp. 1-190, hereafter *TE*; *Les Formules et la métrique d'Homère* (Paris, 1928), trans. in *MHV*, pp. 191-239, hereafter *FM*.

[12] Later modified in "Studies I" (in *MHV*, p. 272) to: "a group of words which is regularly employed under the same metrical conditions to express a given essential idea."

[13] See espec. *TWW* and Nagy, *Comparative Studies*.

[14] "Studies in the Epic Technique of Oral Verse-Making. I. Homer and Homeric Style," *HSCP*, 41(1930), 73-147, rpt. in *MHV*, pp. 266-324; and "Studies in the Epic Technique of Oral Verse-Making. II. The Homeric Language as the Language of an Oral Poetry," *HSCP*, 43(1932), 1-50, rpt. in *MHV*, pp. 325-64.

[15] See also *TE*, pp. 7, 16.

[16] Murko was present, through the agency of Parry's director A. Meillet, at the *soutenance* in 1928, following the completion of *TE* and *FM* (see "Ćor Huso: a Study of Southslavic Song," in *MHV*, p. 439). Murko's published works on oral tradition in Yugoslavia include: *Bericht über eine Bereisung von Nordwestbosnien und der angrenzenden Gebiete von Kroatien und Dalmatien behufs Erforschung der Volksepik der bosnischen Mohammedaner* (Vienna, 1913); *Bericht über eine Reise zum Studium der Volksepik in Bosnien und Herzegowina im Jahre 1913* (Vienna, 1915); *La Poésie populaire épique en Yougoslavie au début du XXe siècle* (Paris, 1929); "Nouvelles observations sur l'état actuel de la poésie épique en Yougoslavie," *REtS*, 13(1933), 16-50; and *Tragom srpskohrvatske narodne epike (putovanja u godinama 1930-32)*, 2 vols. (Zagreb, 1951). Another importance influence on Parry was Marcel Jousse's "Le Style oral rhythmique et mnémotechnique chez les Verbo-moteurs," *APh*, 2(1924), cahier IV, 1-240.

[17] See note 19.

[18] To attempt a thorough assessment of and commentary on Lord's work is beyond the scope of this introduction.

I will try instead to place some of his most important
writings in the foreground, and to indicate to some extent their significance for the oral theory.

[19] Parry left behind the unfinished manuscript of
"Ćor Huso: a Study of Southslavic Song"; the abstract of
a paper to have been presented at the 1935 meetings of
the American Philological Association, "Homer and Huso I:
the Singer's Rests in Greek and South Slavic Heroic
Song," *TAPA*, 66(1935), xlvii, rpt. in *MHV*, p. 420; and
seven pages of a projected book-length study, entitled
"The Singer of Tales." Lord later presented and published a paper derived from Parry's abstract and augmented by his own thoughts (see note 20). Lord's "Homer,
Parry, and Huso," *AJA*, 52(1948), 34-44, rpt. in *MHV*, pp.
465-78, summarizes Parry's writings, reviews the collection of texts gathered during various stages of field
work, and prints the seven manuscript pages left by
Parry. The fullest description of the early collecting
trips is Lord's "Introduction" to *S-CHS* I, pp. 3-20. On
the 1950-51 trip, see his "Yugoslav Epic Folk Poetry,"
IFMJ, 3(1951), 57-61, which includes comparative analysis
of songs from the same singer, gathered in 1933-35 and
1950-51. For an overview, see David E. Bynum, "Child's
Legacy Enlarged: Oral Literary Studies at Harvard Since
1856," *HLB*, 22(1974), 27-48.

[20] "Homer and Huso I: the Singer's Rests in Greek and
Southslavic Heroic Song," *TAPA*, 67(1936), 106-13. Huso
Husović was, as Lord tells us, a great singer of a past
generation: "Many of the oldest singers that we found had
known and heard him, and legend pictures him riding in
brilliant array with his gusle from town to town, from
region to region, singing his songs—much like the Greek
Homer revealed to us by the words of the *Contest of Homer
and Hesiod*, περιερχόμενος ἔλεγε τὰ ποιήματα" (107).

[21] From "Ćor Huso," pp. 454ff.

[22] In working with songs from the Milman Parry Collection, in some cases with the same singer whom Lord
mentions in this article (Ibrahim Bašić), I found much
corroborating evidence for this view. In "The Traditional Structure of Ibro Bašić's 'Alagić Alija and Velagić
Selim'," *SEEJ*, 22(1978), 1-14, I showed how the *guslar*
"will not resume his song at just any point. Rather he
'backtracks' to the last traditional boundary and, after
a brief proem for continuance, begins anew from that
boundary. This usually means reverting to the beginning
of the last theme or subthematic structure and identify-

ing it as a starting point." (7).

[23] These criteria for comparison have not been heeded by those who would discount the Yugoslav analogy on the basis of what they feel is the obvious difference in "quality" between the available samples of Homeric and Serbo-Croatian epic; see, for example, G. S. Kirk, *The Songs of Homer* (Cambridge, 1962), espec. pp. 83ff., and Adam Parry, "Have We Homer's *Iliad*?" *YCS*, 20(1966), 177-216, espec. 212-16.

[24] "Homer and Huso II: Narrative Inconsistencies in Homer and Oral Poetry," *TAPA*, 69(1938), 439-45.

[25] See Parry's early notions on the theme in his review of Walter Arend's "Die typischen Scenen bei Homer," in *CP*, 31(1936), 357-60, rpt. as "On Typical Scenes in Homer," in *MHV*, pp. 404-7; and "Ćor Huso," espec. pp. 448-51.

[26] "Homer and Huso III: Enjambement in Greek and Southslavic Heroic Song," *TAPA*, 79(1948), 113-24. See further *TWW*, pp. 118-67.

[27] *TAPA*, 82(1951), 71-80. This article, notably, was one of Magoun's sources in his "The Theme of the Beasts of Battle in Anglo-Saxon Poetry," discussed below in Part III.

[28] As Parry put it in "Ćor Huso" (p. 450), "the singer embraces the tradition, and what is true of one is true of the other."

[29] On unessential "decoration" of the story, Lord remarks (74): "[The singers] consider this ornamentation as good and admirable, but they also recognize certain limits to its appropriateness. I have heard singers criticize one another for putting into a song so much ornamentation that the story has been obscured, and, more commonly, I have heard singers say that too much ornamentation is not good because it represents additions to the song which cannot be true since they were not in the story as it was learned by the singer. The first objection is from the point of view of artistic story-telling, the second from that of historicity, because the singers look upon their songs as historical and true." See further Benjamin A. Stolz, "Historicity in the Serbo-Croatian Heroic Epic: Salih Ugljanin's 'Grčki rat'," *SEEJ*, 11(1967), 423-32.

[30] (New York, 1951).

[31] *TAPA*, 84(1953), 124-34.

[32] I would add that there exists a brilliant example of creativity within the tradition in Avdo Medjedović's

striking reformulation of a common story pattern as described in Lord's "Tradition and the Oral Poet: Homer,
Huso, and Avdo Medjedović," pp. 20-21, an essay
discussed below (see note 59).

[33] Coll. by Milman Parry and Albert Lord, ed. and
trans. by Albert Lord. See below for discussion of
S-CHS III and IV; V, VI, and XIV are forthcoming.

[34] Trips made since 1933-35 by Lord and David Bynum,
as well as the latter's photoduplication of texts from
various Yugoslav archives, have added a diachronic axis
to the holdings of the Parry Collection (see further
note 19).

[35] A brief article, "Notes on *Digenis Akritas* and
Serbocroatian Epic," *HSS*, 2(1954), 375-83, probes correspondences among the Russian, Greek, Turkish, and
Serbo-Croatian traditions, particularly with respect to
the "birdless courtyard" (which is traced to Sanskrit
avarana), the ornamental figures of griffins, and weddings and rescues, in order to "demonstrate how fruitful
the comparative study of Byzantine Greek and Serbocroatian oral epic tradition can be" (383).

[36] "Avdo Medjedović, Guslar," *JAF*, 69(1956), 320-30.

[37] "The Wedding of Smailagić Meho" has been published
as *S-CHS* III and IV; "Osmanbey Delibegović and Pavičević
Luka," to appear as part of the same series, is now in
press.

[38] Lord furnishes a comparative analysis of these two
performances in *Singer*, pp. 102-5.

[39] In *For Roman Jakobson* (The Hague, 1956), pp. 301-
5.

[40] See espec. *TWW*, pp. 169-215.

[41] In *Comparative Literature: Proceedings of the
Second Congress of the International Comparative Literature Association*, ed. Werner P. Friederich (Chapel Hill,
1959), pp. 1-6.

[42] The dynamic character of the formula has often
been overlooked by scholars following out the principles
of *Singer* in other traditions. See, for example, the
confusion in Old English criticism (below, Part III).

[43] Note further: "The metrical convenience, or even
better, the metrical necessity, is probably a late phenomenon, indispensable for the growth of epic from what
must have been comparatively simple narrative incanta-
tions to more complex tales intended more and more for
entertainment. This was a change concomitant with the
gradual shift toward the heroic and eventually the his-

toric. It is quite likely that the later stages could
not have developed until the formula became a compositional device; yet because of its past it never could
become merely a compositional device. Its symbols, its
sounds, its patterns were born for magic productivity,
not for aesthetic satisfaction." (p. 67). See also "The
Role of Sound-Patterns in Serbo-Croatian Epic," discussed
above.

[44] See further "Tradition and the Oral Poet: Homer,
Huso, and Avdo Medjedović," discussed below; and my
"Narrativity in *Beowulf*, the *Odyssey*, and the Serbo-
Croatian Return Song," in *Proceedings of the Ninth Con-
gress of the International Comparative Literature Asso-
ciation*, forthcoming.

[45] *ZNŽO*, 40(1962), 313-20. See also his "Some Common
Themes in Balkan Slavic Epic," in *Actes du Premier Con-
grès des Études Balkaniques et Sud-Est Européennes*
(Sofia, 1971), pp. 653-62.

[46] "Midway, as it were, between the separate groups
of elements as we have found them in the *Odyssey* there is
an episode that combines the essentials of both groups.
It is, then, in essentials the closest parallel to the
episode in 'The Captivity of Šarac'." (319).

[47] In *CH*, pp. 179-214.

[48] On the Homeric epics as education, see also Eric
A. Havelock, *Preface to Plato* (1963; rpt. New York,
1967). I will not discuss here either Lord's "The Epic
Singers," *Atlantic*, 210(1962), 126-27, which is intended
for a popular audience; or his "Beowulf and Odysseus,"
in *Franciplegius*, pp. 86-91, included in the treatment of
the Old English theme in Part III; or his review article,
"Ivo Andrić in English Translation," *SR*, 23(1964), 563-
73.

[49] *HSCP*, 72(1967), 1-46.

[50] Review of G. S. Kirk, *The Songs of Homer*, in *JHS*,
83(1963), 157.

[51] "Have We Homer's *Iliad*?" 212.

[52] For true comparative work, a thorough knowledge of
the language, literature, and literary history of all
traditions directly involved is, of course, essential;
oral literature research has nonetheless, as in the two
cases just cited, suffered from the occasional disregard
of this simple principle. As Lord puts it (*ibid.*, 5, n.
13), "I am constantly amazed at the ease with which
scholars, meticulous in their own field, make *ex cathedra*
statements about poetries of whose language they know

nothing."

[53] Russo, "The Structural Formula in Homeric Verse,"
YCS, 20(1966), 219-40; Kirk, "Formular Language and Oral
Quality," *YCS*, 20(1966), 155-74.

[54] He does, however, caution that the size and kind
of referent (the Homeric poems also formed part of the
referent for the *Batrachomyomachia*) and the size of the
sample may have affected his results.

[55] He also believes that "it is important to work
from line break to line break rather than with simple
repetition of words and phrases by themselves, because
it is in terms of parts of a line, I believe, rather than
words in themselves, that the singer thinks" (26).
Though Lord is speaking here specifically of Homer (cp.
TWW, pp. 66-117), the context of his remarks could be
widened to take into account a number of oral poetries
whose lines are syllabically based, including Serbo-
Croatian.

[56] Kirk, *The Songs of Homer* and "Formular Language";
Parry, "The Gates of Horn and Ivory," *YCS*, 20(1966), 3-
57.

[57] For a bibliography of writings on the "story pattern," see my essay in this volume, note 5.

[58] *Prilozi*, 35(1969), 18-30.

[59] In *Atti del Convegno Internazionale sul Tema: La
Poesia epica e la sua formazione* (Rome, 1970), pp. 13-
28; "Discussione," pp. 29-30.

[60] Lord adds later on "the principle that oral tradition duplicates what is significant and meaningful, be it
episode, or detail, or a sequence of episodes" (26).

[61] *JFI*, 8(1971), 85-92.

[62] See Page, *History and the Homeric Iliad* (Berkeley,
1959); and Finley, J. L. Caskey, G. S. Kirk, and Page,
"The Trojan War," *JHS*, 84(1964), 1-9.

[63] In *Aspects of the Balkans: Continuity and Change*,
ed. by Henrik Birnbaum and Speros Vryonis, Jr. (The
Hague, 1972), pp. 298-318.

[64] *WF*, 31(1972), 53-60.

[65] See further Lord's "An Example of Homeric Qualities of Repetition in Medjedović's 'Smailagić Meho'," in
Serta Slavica: Gedenkschrift für Alois Schmaus (Munich,
1971), pp. 458-64, where he observes "a possible parallel with Telemachus' journey in the *Odyssey*" (464). See
also my review of *S-CHS* III and IV, in *SEEJ*, 20(1976),
203-6.

[66] *The Multinational Literature of Yugoslavia* (New

York, 1974); also issued as *RNL*, 5(1974). See also in
this volume Mary P. Coote, "Yugoslavia: Bibliographical
Spectrum," pp. 127-40.

[67] In *OLSE*, pp. 1-24.

[68] *Typical Battle Scenes in the Iliad: Studies in
the Narrative Techniques of Homeric Battle Description,
Hermes* Einzelschriften, no. 21 (Wiesbaden, 1968).

[69] That section of this article concerned with Old
English is taken up in Part III.

[70] In *Hellenism and the First Greek War of Liberation
(1821-1830): Continuity and Change*, no. 156 (Thessaloniki,
1976), pp. 79-94. Compare his "Folklore, 'Folklorism,'
and National Identity," in *Balkanistica: Occasional Papers in Southeast European Studies*, vol. 3(1976), ed. by
Kenneth E. Naylor (Columbus, Ohio, 1978), pp. 63-73.

[71] In *OL&F*, pp. 1-15; "Response" and "Discussion,"
pp. 17-29.

[72] *BMGS*, 3(1977), 71-80.

[73] In *The Relationships among the Gospels: an Interdisciplinary Dialogue*, ed. by William O. Walker, Jr.
(San Antonio, 1978), pp. 33-91.

[74] Forthcoming publications include "Interlocking
Mythic Patterns in *Beowulf*," in *Old English Literature
in Context: Ten Essays*, ed. by John D. Niles (London and
Totowa, 1980); and the essay in this volume.

[75] Because it has seemed to me more useful to provide one complete and annotated bibliographical history
than to make scattered remarks on many literatures, I
offer the following essay (Part III) as a thorough survey
of the oral theory's influence on an example literature.

[76] See *Singer*, espec. pp. 198-202; and Magoun, "The
Oral-Formulaic Character" (note 1).

[77] Thus John S. P. Tatlock's much later remark on the
lack of answers to such questions: "It is rather surprising that so concrete, interesting, and suggestive a matter of style has not been adequately treated...."
("Epic Formulas, Especially in Layamon," *PMLA*, 38
[1923], 494, n. 1).

[78] E.g., Otto Arndt, *Über die altgermanische epische
Sprache* (Tübingen, 1877).

[79] (Halle, 1878), pp. 391-496.

[80] *Anglia*, 2(1879), 265-308.

[81] He concluded "dass Guthl. B den Cynewulf als
verfasser hat, Guthl. A dagegen ganz fremd zu demselben
steht und irgend einem andern dichter zuzuschrieben ist.
Diese ansicht wird noch bestätigt durch mancherlei

einzelne versanklänge zwischen Guthl. B und den Cynewulf'schen gedichten, die ich ebenfalls im folgenden
zusammenstelle." (303-4).

[82] *Anglia*, 9(1886), 515-50. See also R. Simons, *Die
Wörter und Wortverbindungen Cynewulfs* (Bonn, 1898); and
"Cynewulfs Wortschatz," *BBA*, 3(1889), 47-79. Compare H.
Ziegler, *Der poetische Sprachgebrauch in den sogen.
Cædmonschen Dichtungen* (Münster, 1883); and, later, Alois
Brandl, "Englische Literatur," in *Grundriss der german-
ischen Philologie*, ed. by Hermann Paul, II. Band, I.
Abteilung (Strassburg, 1901-9), pp. 941-1134.

[83] Sarrazin summarized (550): "Wenn wir daher in
verschiedenen dichtungen dieselben sonst wenig üblichen
wortverbindungen, wendungen, stabreimformeln, verschlüsse
häufig widerkehren sehen, wie an den Kynewulfischen
dichtungen gegenüber dem Beowulf gezeigt ist, so sind wir
berechtigt, daraus auf identität der verfassers zu
schliessen."

[84] (Marburg, 1886). See also Richard Kistenmacher,
Die wörtlichen Wiederholungen im Beowulf (Greifswald,
1898).

[85] "Die Innere Geschichte des Beovulfs," *ZDA*, 14
(1869), 193-244; rpt. as Chapter 3 of his *Beovulf:
Untersuchungen über das angelsächsische Epos und die
älteste Geschichte der germanischen Seevölker* (Berlin,
1889), pp. 110-60. Müllenhof's structure (pp. 110ff.)
consisted of the *Einleitung* (1-193), *Das erste alte Lied*
(194-836), *Die erste Fortsetzung* (837-1628), *Die zweite
Fortsetzung* (1629-2199), and *Das zweite alte Lied* (2200-
3183), according to his lineation of the text.

[86] (Berlin, 1888).

[87] Sarrazin actually puts the problem in a form which
resembles the Homeric Question: "Die nächste Frage ist,
ob dem ags. Bearbeiter (Interpolator B), die Beowulf-
(Bǫðvar-) Dichtung schon als Ganzes vorgelegen, oder ob er
erst verschiedene Lieder zu einem Ganzen verbunden hat"
(p. 70).

[88] (Berlin, 1889). Compare F. Schulz, *Die Sprach-
formen des Hildebrands-Liedes im Beowulf* (Königsberg,
1882); A. Hoffmann, "Der bildliche Ausdruck im *Beowulf*
und in der *Edda*," *EnSt*, 6(1883), 163-216; O. Hoffmann,
Reimformeln im Westgermanischen (Darmstadt, 1885); Georg
Radke, *Die epische Formel im Nibelungenliede* (Kiel,
1890). Of related general interest is Walther Paetzel,
*Die Variationen in der altgermanischen Alliterations-
poesie* (Berlin, 1913).

[89] For example, he offers this explanation of the origin of "broken repetition": "Die unterbrochene Wort-wiederholung (man könnte sie auch 'intermittirende' nennen) hat ihre Ursache in der metrischen Technik. Wiederholt werden die Worte, die besonders wichtig sind; und eben die Worte, die besonders wichtig sind, bringt die Alliterationsdichtung an den Taktanfang oder noch lieber an den Versanfang." (p. 228).

[90] His definition of a "parallel verse" offers an example: "Verswiederholung mit Variation der Schlagworte ergiebt die wichtige Figur der Parallelverse" (p. 327). Compare this concept with the various definitions of the formula given below.

[91] "Über die Parallelstellen in der angelsächsischen Poesie," *Anglia*, 12(1889), 21-40.

[92] *Anglia*, 14(1892), 186-92.

[93] Further, he claimed, "es ist natürlich nicht gleich, ob sich 2-3 oder ob sich 2-3 dutzend anklänge nachweisen lassen. Und ebenso ist es unterschied, ob die parallelstellen allgemein übliche, ob sie seltener vorkommende, oder individuell charakteristische formeln sind." (192).

[94] "Neue Beowulf-Studien," *EnSt*, 23(1897), 221-67, espec. 259-64.

[95] *Studien über die Verfasserschaft des Andreas* (Heidelberg, 1899).

[96] *Typische Motive in dem weltlichen Epos der Angelsachsen* (Berlin, 1902).

[97] "Die Eigenschaften dieser vier Typen sind mehr oder weniger vollkommene Abstufungen des damaligen Menschenideals" (p. 98).

[98] "Epic Formulas, Especially in Layamon." His shorter, and relatively much less important, essay, "Layamon's Poetic Style and its Relations," in *The Manly Anniversary Studies in Language and Literature* (Chicago, 1923), pp. 3-11, will not be treated here.

[99] In addition, Tatlock felt that "the similarity of phrase grows out of similarity of situation" (510), and that formulas varied considerably in character and tone: "Some formulas are highly poetic and probably original; others as we shall see may have been traditional in po-etry; a few are colorless, commonplaces of daily speech" (511). As far as variation is concerned, "some formulas are nearly petrified, others vary much, some so much that they verge into mere stock rimes, with no consciousness of being formulas at all" (512). In relation to metrical

properties, "[the formulas] suit the alliterative verse, *staccato*, with its strongly marked units and rare *enjambement*, neither restless nor nimble" (514).

[100] In "Layamon's Poetic Style and its Relations," he remarks (p. 3): "But Anglo-Saxon poets, like modern, deliberately avoided [formulas], and cultivated variety and ingenuity of phrasing." Moreover, he **continued,** "this avoiding a natural epic usage is a sign of the artificial sophistication of Anglo-Saxon poetry." (*ibid*).

[101] See note 1; rpt. in *AnthBC*, pp. 189-221; in *EsAr*, pp. 319-51; and in *BP*, pp. 83-113. I use the pagination of *BP* throughout this section.

[102] In *KlMisc*, pp. 73-78. Compare A. Hoffmann, "Die bildliche Ausdruck im *Beowulf* und in der *Edda*"; and Otto Krackow, *Die Nominalcomposita als Kunstmittel im altenglischen Epos* (Berlin, 1903).

[103] In *KlMisc*, pp. 120-34.

[104] The conventional opinion is reported earliest by Karl Schemann, *Die Synonyma im Bēowulfslied mit Rücksicht auf Composition und Poetik des Gedichtes* (Münster, 1882), and later by Krackow. See also Fr. Klaeber, "Studies in the Textual Interpretation of *Beowulf*, A., Rhetorical Notes," *MP*, 3(1905-6), 241.

[105] C. W. M. Grein, *Sprachschatz der angelsächsischen Dichter*, rev. by F. Holthausen and J. Köhler (Heidelberg, 1912). Now see the Bessinger-Smith concordances, discussed below (see notes 163 and 164).

[106] See, in the following order, Parry, "The Traditional Metaphor in Homer," which first appeared in *CP*, 28 (1933), 30-43, rpt. in *MHV*, pp. 365-75, espec. pp. 372ff.; George M. Calhoun, "Homeric Repetitions," *UCPCP*, 12 (1933), 1-26; Calhoun, "The Art of the Formula: ἔπεα πτερόεντα," *CP*, 30(1935), 215-27; and Parry, "About Winged Words," which first appeared in *CP*, 32(1937), 59-63, rpt. in *MHV*, pp. 414-18.

[107] Mention should also be made of two works from the earlier period, both of which suggested methods of investigation which have continued to run parallel to formulaic criticism, as will be shown in the next section. These works are: John O. Beaty, "The Echo-Word in *Beowulf* with a Note on the Finnsburg Fragment," *PMLA*, 49(1934), 365-73; and Adeline C. Bartlett, *The Larger Rhetorical Patterns in Anglo-Saxon Poetry* (1935; rpt. New York, 1966). More recently, Eugene R. Kintgen has contributed studies along similar lines: "Echoic Repetition in Old English Poetry, Especially *The Dream of the Rood*," *NM*,

75(1974), 202-23; "Wordplay in *The Wanderer*," *Neophil*, 59
(1975), 119-27; and "*Lif*, *lof*, *leof*, *lufu*, and *geleafa* in
Old English Poetry," *NM*, 78(1977), 309-16. See also my
"*Christ* 164-213: a Structural Approach to the Speech
Boundaries," *Neophil*, 59(1975), 114-18; and J. R. Hall,
"Perspective and Wordplay in the Old English *Rune Poem*,"
Neophil, 61(1977), 453-60. A later application of
Bartlett's ideas may be found in Constance B. Hieatt's
"Envelope Patterns and the Structure of *Beowulf*," *ESC*, 1
(1975), 250-65.

[108] I do not, of course, mean to imply that these
units should be construed as separate entities, for their
interrelationship is one of the many intriguing questions
posed by the oral theory. Their individual treatment
here is simply a taxonomic convenience.

[109] About *Beowulf* he adds: "The formulaic character
of the Old English *Beowulf* has been proved beyond any
doubt by a series of analyses beginning with my own in
1949 ..., which Professor Magoun improved and elaborated
in 1953, and which Professor Creed has carried to its ultimate detailed conclusion. The documentation is complete, thorough, and accurate." (p. 198).

[110] In "Studies I," in *MHV*, p. 276, Parry explains
that "the thrift of a system lies in the degree in which
it is free of phrases which, having the same metrical
value and expressing the same idea, could replace one
another." In a later study, "Variation and Economy in
Beowulf," *MP*, 65(1968), 353-56, Donald K. Fry shows that
Homeric thrift is impossible in the alliterative verse
form of Old English. See further note 138.

[111] *Speculum*, 30(1955), 49-63.

[112] *BGDSL*, 80(1958), 214-18.

[113] Compare Robert Kellogg's argument in "The South
Germanic Oral Tradition," in *Franciplegius*, p. 72: "We
can safely assume that the many poetic elements common
to Anglo-Saxon, Old Icelandic, Old Saxon, and Old High
German alliterative poetry reflect the common usage of
a more or less unified and indisputably oral tradition
stretching back in time to the early centuries of the
Christian era, and perhaps much further." See also
Winfred Lehmann, *The Development of Germanic Verse Form*
(1956; rpt. New York, 1971), espec. pp. 88-123; Alain
Renoir, "Oral-Formulaic Theme Survival: a Possible Instance in the *Nibelungenlied*," *NM*, 65(1964), 70-74; "The
Armor of the 'Hildebrandslied': an Oral-Formulaic Point
of View," *NM*, 78(1977), 389-95; "The English Connection

Revisited: a Reading Context for the *Hildebrandslied*,"
Neophil, 63(1979), 84-87; "Germanic Quintessence: the
Theme of Isolation in the *Hildebrandslied*," in *Saints,
Scholars, and Heroes*, ed. by Margot King and Wesley M.
Stevens (St. John, 1979), pp. 143-78; "The Kassell
Manuscript and the Conclusion of the *Hildebrandslied*,"
Manuscripta, forthcoming; Edward R. Haymes, *Das
mündliche Epos: eine Einführung in die oral poetry
Forschung* (Stuttgart, 1964); "Oral Poetry and the
Germanic *Heldenlied*," *RUS*, 62(1976), 47-54; Franz H.
Bäuml and Edda Spielmann, "From Illiteracy to Literacy:
Prolegomena to a Study of the *Nibelungenlied*," in *OLSE*,
pp. 62-73; Bäuml, "Medieval Literacy and Illiteracy: an
Essay toward the Construction of a Model," in *Germanic
Studies in Honor of Otto Springer*, ed. by S. Kaplowitt
(Pittsburgh, 1978), pp. 41-54; and Holger Homann, "Die
Heldenkataloge in der historischen Dietrichsepik und die
Theorie des mündlichen Dichtung," *MLN*, 92(1977), 415-35,
which draws heavily on oral-formulaic studies in Old
English.

[114] "On a New Theory of Old English Poetic Diction,"
Neophil, 40(1956), 303.

[115] See also his *Critical Studies in the Cynewulf
Group* (1949; rpt. New York, 1967), *passim*.

[116] Storms, *Compounded Names of People in Beowulf, a
Study in the Diction of a Great Poet* (Utrecht-Nijmegen,
1957). Malone's untitled review appeared in *ES*, 41
(1960), 200-205.

[117] "Cædmon and English Poetry," *MLN*, 76(1961), 193-
95.

[118] "Studies in the Techniques of Composition of the
Beowulf Poetry in British Museum Cotton Vitellius A.
xv.," unpub. Ph.D. diss. (Harvard University, 1955).

[119] Creed's figure for whole-verse formulas is 19%
(see "Studies," p. 31).

[120] *Speculum*, 32(1957), 523-28. Compare Thomas C.
Rumble, "The Hyran-Gefrignan Formula in *Beowulf*," *AM*, 5
(1964), 13-20.

[121] *PQ*, 35(1956), 206-8.

[122] *MLN*, 73(1958), 321-25.

[123] *ELH*, 26(1959), 445-54, rpt. in *OEL*, pp. 52-61;
in *EsAr*, pp. 363-73; and in *BP*, with "Additional Remarks," pp. 141-53. I use the pagination of *BP*.

[124] See also Lewis Nicholson, "Oral Techniques in the
Composition of Expanded Anglo-Saxon Verses," *PMLA*, 78
(1963), 287-92. On the criterion of placement in the

poetic line, compare Eugene O'Neill, Jr., "The Localization of Metrical Word-types in the Greek Hexameter,"
YCS, 8(1942), 103-78, versus J. B. Hainsworth, *The Flexibility of the Homeric Formula* (Oxford, 1968); later *TWW*,
espec. pp. 66-117. On the question of syntax, see the
discussion of Cassidy, O'Neil, Gattiker, and Green below.

[125] *Speculum*, 37(1962), 382-89, rpt. in *EsAr*, pp.
393-403; and in *OEL*, pp. 62-72. I use the pagination of
EsAr.

[126] On the role of memorization in the performance of
Old English poetry, see Alan Jabbour, "Memorial Transmission in Old English Poetry," *ChauR*, 3(1969), 174-90;
and studies by Jeffrey Opland: "'Scop' and 'Imbongi'—
Anglo-Saxon and Bantu Oral Poets," *ESA*, 14(1971), 161-78;
and "African Phenomena Relevant to a Study of the European Middle Ages: Oral Tradition," *ESA*, 16(1973), 87-90;
see further notes 200 and 201. On the musical analogy,
see Roberta B. Bosse, "Aural Aesthetics and the Unity of
The Seafarer," *PLL*, 9(1973), 3-14.

[127] In *Essays on Style and Language*, ed. by Roger
Fowler (London and New York, 1966), pp. 166-83.

[128] In *OEP*, pp. 69-92.

[129] "The Diction of the Signed Poems of Cynewulf,"
unpub. Ph.D. diss. (Harvard University, 1953).

[130] *PQ*, 38(1959), 228-41.

[131] In *Studies in Honor of John Wilcox*, ed. by A. D.
Wallace and W. O. Ross (Detroit, 1958), pp. 3-7.

[132] Compare Carol J. Wolf's more detailed discussion
in "Christ as Hero in *The Dream of the Rood*," *NM*, 71
(1970), 202-10.

[133] Janua Linguarum, Series Practica, vol. 10 (The
Hague, 1963). See also Robert S. Breitzer, "A Stylistic
Study of the Old English Metrical Psalms," unpub. Ph.D.
diss. (University of Iowa, 1970), abstr. in *DAI*, 31:
2867A.

[134] In *A-SP*, pp. 301-11. On similar subjects, see
Reja-e Busailah, "Christian Themes in the Formulaic Tra-
dition of Old English Poetry," unpub. Ph.D. diss. (New
York University, 1972), abstr. in *DAI*, 33:720A; Sandra
J. Harmatiuk, "A Statistical Approach to Some Aspects of
Style in the Signed Poems of Cynewulf: a Computer-Assist-
ed Study," unpub. Ph.D. diss. (St. Louis University,
1973), abstr. in *DAI*, 36:1429A; and Sr. Jane Morrissey,
"The Old English *Advent*: a Convergence of Traditions and
Rituals," unpub. Ph.D. diss. (University of Massachu-
setts/Amherst, 1976), abstr. in *DAI*, 37:2202A.

[135] "The Homeric Epithets," *YCS*, 17(1961), 97-142;
"Formulaic Poetry in the Old Testament," *CL*, 15(1963), 1-
14; "The Shield of Ajax," *YCS*, 19(1966), 5-36; "Old
Testament Poetry and Homeric Epic," *CL*, 18(1966), 113-31;
and "Wrote Down the Formulaic Poem?" in *Actes du Ve Congrès de l'Association Internationale de Littérature Com-
parée*, ed. by Nikola Banašević (Belgrade, 1969), pp.
469-72. See also Gayle K. Byerly, "Compounds and Other
Elements of Poetic Diction Derived from an Oral-Formulaic
Poetic Tradition: a Comparison of Aeschylus and the *Beowulf* Poet," unpub. Ph.D. diss. (University of Pennsylvania, 1965), abstr. in *DAI*, 27:1333A.

[136] *PMLA*, 76(1961), 309-19.

[137] The principle of formulaic utility, stressed
throughout Parry's work, has often been understood to
preclude aesthetic judgments about composition, to rob
the poems it purports to explain of the truth and beauty
assigned to them by generations of literary critics.
Consider, for example, Frederick Combellack, "Milman
Parry and Homeric Artistry," *CL*, 11(1959), 193-208,
espec. 196; and Stanley B. Greenfield, "The Canons of
Old English Criticism," *ELH*, 34(1967), 141-55, espec.
141-44. Note that Parry himself foresaw this difficulty
as early as his M.A. thesis and argued against a simplis-
tic notion of the concept of utility in these terms: "We
realize that the traditional, the formulaic quality of
the diction was not a device for mere convenience, but
the highest possible development of the hexameter medium
to tell a race's heroic tales" ("A Comparative Study of
Diction as One of the Elements of Style in Early Greek
Epic Poetry," in *MHV*, p. 425).

[138] Fry, in "Variation and Economy in *Beowulf*,"
countered Whallon in denying the applicability of the
concept of thrift to Old English poetry. He claimed that
"every idea to be expressed required formulas, and for
each semantic need thus met, more formulas were required
to satisfy the alliterative demands of the prosody and
the variational needs of the traditional style. As long
as poets used the device of variation, thrift was impossible." (356). Similar conclusions are reached by Nora
B. Barry, "Formular and Thematic Composition in *Beowulf*:
an Index of Lament and Celebration Themes," unpub. Ph.D.
diss. (New York University, 1974), abstr. in *DAI*, 35:
1036A.

[139] *MP*, 63(1965), 95-104.

[140] *PMLA*, 80(1965), 19-23.

[141] He speaks specifically against Fr. Klaeber's "Die christlichen Elementen im *Beowulf*," *Anglia*, 35(1911), 111-36, 249-70, 453-83; and 36(1912), 169-99.

[142] (Washington and Cambridge, Mass., 1969).

[143] *MÆ*, 35(1966), 95-102.

[144] An interesting comparison could be made between the kinds of variation noted in these two poems and that observed in Serbo-Croatian epic. Once adjustments for prosody had been made, a relatively clear comparison might be drawn.

[145] Compare the "hard" and "soft Parryist" distinction made by Thomas G. Rosenmeyer in "The Formula in Early Greek Poetry," *Arion*, 4(1965), 295-311.

[146] "Oral-Formulaic Structure in Old English Elegiac Poetry," unpub. Ph.D. diss. (University of Wisconsin, 1960). Of related interest is O'Neil's "The Oral-Formulaic Structure of the Faroese *kvæði*," *Fróðskaparrit*, 18 (1970), 59-68. See also his "Another Look at Oral Poetry in *The Seafarer*," *Speculum*, 35(1960), 596-600, a reply to Jackson Campbell's "Oral Poetry in *The Seafarer*," *ibid.*, 87-96. Later articles by Campbell, "Learned Rhetoric in Old English Poetry," *MP*, 63(1966), 189-201, and "Knowledge of Rhetorical Figures in Anglo-Saxon England," *JEGP*, 66(1967), 1-20, assume a very literate poetics.

[147] "The Syntactic Basis of the Poetic Formula in *Beowulf*," unpub. Ph.D. diss. (University of Wisconsin, 1962), abstr.in *DAI* 23:2114-15.

[148] In *Franciplegius*, pp. 75-85.

[149] Compare Joseph Russo, "The Structural Formula in Homeric Verse," 234: "We have seen, then, that in certain Homeric passages structural formulas are not only obvious, but also exert a local influence on subsequent verses, so that the structures, or patterns, are the more easily recognized by virtue of their close recurrence. In other passages the structural patterns used may be 'repetitions' only in the broader sense that they are used again somewhere in the Homeric corpus. Both types of pattern repetition should be considered formulaic, since they are natural expressions of the schematization of language that makes possible a traditional, orally-evolved style." To Russo's article may be juxtaposed William W. Minton, "The Fallacy of the Structural Formula," *TAPA*, 96(1965), 241-53.

[150] Unpub. Ph.D. diss. (University of Wisconsin, 1967).

[151] *CHum*, 6(1971), 85-93.

[152] *NM*, 64(1963), 373-78, rpt. in *OEL*, pp. 82-86.

[153] In *OEP*, pp. 275-84.

[154] See further "Expectations and Implications in Diction and Formula," in his *The Interpretation of Old English Poems* (London and Boston, 1972), pp. 30-59.

[155] In *SmithSts*, pp. 150-71.

[156] On the role of the audience, compare James A. Notopoulos, "Parataxis in Homer," *TAPA*, 80(1949), 1-23; Lord, *Singer*, pp. 14-17; Tauno F. Mustanoja, "The Presentation of Ancient Germanic Poetry: Looking for Parallels," *NM*, 60(1959), 1-17; and John Miles Foley, "The Traditional Oral Audience," *BS*, 18(1977), 145-54. On collocations, see Winfred P. Lehmann and Takemitsu Tabusa, *The Alliterations of the Beowulf* (Austin, 1958); and Eileen Lynch, "A Statistical Study of the Collocations in *Beowulf*," unpub. Ph.D. diss. (University of Massachusetts/Amherst, 1972), abstr. in *DAI*, 33:2898A.

[157] *PMLA*, 81(1966), 334-41.

[158] (The Hague, 1973). See also his "On the Authorship and Originality of the *Meters of Boethius*," *NM*, 71 (1970), 185-87.

[159] "A Note on Verse Composition in the *Meters of Boethius*," *NM*, 71(1970), 576-85.

[160] "The Making of the Old English *Meters of Boethius*: Studies in Traditional Art and Aesthetics," unpub. Ph.D. diss. (University of Massachusetts/Amherst, 1975), abstr. in *DAI*, 36:6117A-18A. Naomi S. Myrvaagnes also focuses on formulaic structure in her "A Stylistic Study of the Old English *Meters of Boethius*," unpub. Ph.D. diss. (New York University, 1970), abstr. in *DAI*, 31:4131A. See further F. H. Whitman, "A Major Compositional Technique in Old English Verse," *ELN*, 11(1973), 81-86, who describes the method of adding a word or phrase to the literal translation of a Latin unit to yield an Old English poetic verse. In a later article, "The Meaning of 'Formulaic' in Old English Verse Composition," *NM*, 76(1975), 529-37, Whitman extends this idea to a virtual equation with the term "formula," in the sense of a much-used, verbatim tag. Compare Harvey Minkoff, "An Example of Latin Influence on Ælfric's Translation Style," *Neophil*, 61(1977), 127-42.

[161] (New Haven, 1969).

[162] Compare the somewhat similar objections of H. L. Rogers, in his "The Crypto-Psychological Character of the Oral Formula," *ES*, 47(1966), 89-102.

[163] Ed. by Jess B. Bessinger, Jr., programmed by

Philip H. Smith, Jr. (Ithaca, 1959).   Compare Joseph J.
Duggan, *Concordance to the Chanson de Roland* (Columbus,
1970); Guy Lushington Prendergast, *A Complete Concordance
to the Iliad of Homer*, rev. by Benedetto Marzullo
(Hildesheim, 1971); and Henry Dunbar, *A Complete Concordance to the Odyssey and Hymns of Homer*, rev. by Benedetto
Marzullo (Hildesheim, 1971).

[164] (Ithaca, 1978). See also Bessinger's "Oral to
Written: Some Implications of the Anglo-Saxon Transition," *Explorations*, 8(1957), 11-15; and note 175.

[165] *L&S*, 5(1972), 204-20.   Compare William C. Johnson, Jr., "'Deep Structure' and Old English Poetry: Notes
toward a Critical Model," in *In Geardagum: Essays on Old
English Language and Literature*, ed. by Loren C. Gruber
and Dean Loganbill (Denver, 1974), pp. 12-18; John W.
Schwetman, "The Formulaic Nature of Old English Poetry: a
Transformational Analysis of the Cynewulf Poems," unpub.
Ph.D. diss. (University of Kansas, 1974), abstr. in *DAI*,
35:6110A; and Genette D. Ashley, "A Generative Grammar of
the Formulaic Language in the Single Combat of the
Chanson de Roland," unpub. Ph.D. diss. (Columbia, 1976),
abstr. in *DAI*, 37:6470. On related subjects, see Joseph
J. Duggan, *The Song of Roland: Formulaic Style and Poetic
Craft*.

[166] *ES*, 48(1967), 193-204. See also Michael Nagler,
"Toward a Generative View of the Oral Formula," *TAPA*, 98
(1967), 269-311; and *S&T*.

[167] In addition, Fry sees "a slight semantic relation inherent in the system due to the constant meaning
of the non-variable words" (203).

[168] *NM*, 69(1968), 516-22.

[169] In *OLSE*, pp. 41-61. Another analysis of the same
problem, with a Christian emphasis, is D. W. Fritz,
"Cædmon: a Traditional Oral Poet," *MS*, 31(1969), 334-37.
For a survey of stories of the same type in other litera-
tures, See G. A. Lester, "The Cædmon Story and its
Analogues," *Neophil*, 58(1974), 225-37. See also Earl R.
Anderson, "Passing the Harp in Bede's Story of Cædmon: a
Twelfth Century Analogue," *ELN*, 15(1977), 1-4, who men-
tions a parallel in the twelfth century Latin prose, *De
Gestis Herwardi Saxonis*.

[170] "How Free Was the *Beowulf* Poet?" *MP*, 71(1973),
111-27.

[171] *Neophil*, 60(1976), 570-76.

[172] See Albert Lord's essay in this volume.

[173] *MP*, 74(1976), 111-23.

[174] In *OL&F*, pp. 207-32.

[175] These ideas took initial form in my "The Ritual Nature of Traditional Oral Poetry: Metrics, Music, and Matter in the Anglo-Saxon, Homeric Greek, and Serbo-Croatian Poetries," unpub. Ph.D. diss. (University of Massachusetts/Amherst, 1974), abstr. in *DAI*, 35:3676-77A. Compare Thomas Cable, *The Meter and Melody of Beowulf* (Urbana, 1974), pp. 106-8, who independently posits metrical or melodic formulas but does not relate them to composition; also his "Parallels to the Melodic Formulas of *Beowulf*," *MP*, 73(1975), 1-14. On related subjects, see Barbara J. Lawrence, "A Computerized Metrical Analysis of Cynewulfian Poetry," unpub. Ph.D. diss. (St. Louis University, 1973), abstr. in *DAI*, 34:5184-85A; and Evelyn Roma Ball, "Music and English Poetry in the Middle Ages," unpub. Ph.D. diss. (University of Missouri/Columbia, 1975), abstr. in *DAI*, 36:6666-67A, who argues that "*Beowulf*'s music was similar in method to the later *chanson de geste*, consisting of repeated musical formulas ..., that the poem was accompanied heterophonically; that is, the singer played on the harp the same basic melody that he sang, but he may have added a little instrumental ornamentation" (abstract, 6666-67A). On the instrument used for accompaniment, see Jess B. Bessinger, Jr., "*Beowulf* and the Harp at Sutton Hoo," *UTQ*, 27(1958), 148-68; "The Sutton Hoo Harp Replica and Old English Musical Verse," in *OEP*, pp. 3-26; John Nist, "Metrical Uses of the Harp in *Beowulf*," *ibid.*, pp. 27-43; Charles L. Wrenn, "Two Anglo-Saxon Harps," in *BrodeurSts*, pp. 118-28; Rupert and Myrtle Bruce-Mitford, "The Sutton Hoo Lyre, *Beowulf*, and the Origins of the Frame Harp," *Antiquity*, 44(1970), 7-13, rev. as Chapter 7 of *Aspects of Anglo-Saxon Archaeology: Sutton Hoo and Other Discoveries*, ed. by Rupert Bruce-Mitford (New York, 1974), pp. 188-98.

[176] *CHum*, 12(1978), 71-80.

[177] Robert P. Creed has extended our original joint analysis programs, formulated by David Woods, George Maiewski, and Dorothy Grannis, to automatic scansion routines. I take this opportunity to thank the computer facilities of Colgate University and the University of Massachusetts/Amherst for supporting our research.

[178] *SP*, 75(1978), 371-90.

[179] Lord, *Singer*; G. S. Kirk, *The Songs of Homer* (note 23); Whallon, *Formula, Character, and Context* (note 142); and Watts, *The Lyre and the Harp* (note 161).

[180] *CompC*, 2(1980), 71-92.   Compare also my "*Læcdom and Bajanje*: a Comparative Study of Old English and Serbo-Croatian Charms," *Centerpoint*, forthcoming; "The Power of the Word: Healing Charms as an Oral Genre," with Barbara K. Halpern, *JAF*, 91(1978), 903-24; and "*Bajanje*: Healing Magic in Rural Serbia," with Barbara K. Halpern, in *Culture and Curing*, ed. by Peter Morley and Roy Wallis (London and Pittsburgh, 1978), pp. 40-56.

[181] See Lord, "The Role of Sound-Patterns in Serbo-Croatian Epic" (note 39) and *Singer*, pp. 54-58; *TWW*, pp. 182-215; and Creed's essay in this volume.

[182] See also my "Hybrid Prosody: Single Half-lines in Old English and Serbo-Croatian Poetry," *Neophil*, 64 (1980), 284-89, in which the nature of responsion is discussed.

[183] On this field trip and the collection that re-sulted from it, as well as a description of the analyses to date, see my "Research on Oral Traditional Expression in Šumadija and its Relevance to the Study of Other Oral Traditions," in *Selected Papers on a Serbian Village: Social Structure as Reflected by History, Demography, and Oral Tradition*, ed. Joel M. and Barbara K. Halpern (Amherst, 1977), pp. 199-236; and "Field Research on Oral Literature and Culture in Serbia," *PacQ*, forthcoming 1982.

[184] In *In Geardagum III: Essays on Old and Middle English Language and Literature*, ed. by Loren C. Gruber and Dean Loganbill (Denver, forthcoming). See also Fry's "Formulaic Theory in Old English," *PIMA*, forthcoming.

[185] See my essay in this volume. See further Bynum, *The Daemon in the Wood: a Study of Oral Narrative Patterns* (Cambridge, Mass., 1978), espec. pp. 10-11: "Even a moderately strict constructionist of Parry's method must admit that work in Anglo-Saxon *has yet to be begun* in a mode acceptably faithful to the original model. And until Parry's own method (rather than the mechanistically imitative, unreasoning one devised by Magoun) has actual-ly been applied to the *one* text in Anglo-Saxon that is by its genre clearly appropriate to the Parry Test, namely *Beowulf*, and the results of that application are care-fully compared with Parry's results for Homer, there can be no basis for speculation about the orality of any other texts in Anglo-Saxon within the framework of the Parry theory."

[186] In *Old English Literature in Context: Ten Essays*, forthcoming; see also "The Viability of the Comparative

Method in Oral Literature Research," *CT*, forthcoming.

[187] Before his death in 1935 Milman Parry indicated some preliminary conceptions of a traditional unit larger than the formula; see "On Typical Scenes in Homer" and "Čor Huso."

[188] It should be noted that Lord recognized a difference between his idea of theme and that employed in the first analyses of Old English verse: "the concept of theme which Professor Magoun and others have been using differs to some extent from that presented in this book, although I feel that there is no basic conflict but rather a difference of emphasis. I should prefer to designate as motifs what they call themes and to reserve the term theme for a structural unit that has a semantic essence but can never be divorced from its form, even if its form be constantly variable and multiform." (p. 198). See further his "Perspectives on Recent Work on Oral Literature," the Old English section of which is treated below.

[189] *NM*, 56(1955), 81-90. Magoun uses definitions of the theme as they appear in two of Lord's early articles: (1) "a subject unit, a group of ideas, regularly employed by the singer, not merely in any given poem, but in the poetry as a whole" ("Homer and Huso II," 440); and (2) "a recurrent element of narration or description in traditional oral poetry" ("Composition by Theme in Homer and Southslavic Epos," 73). See further Hrafnhildur Bodvarsdottir, "The Function of the Beasts of Battle in Old English Poetry," unpub. Ph.D. diss. (State University of New York/Stony Brook, 1976), abstr. in *DAI*, 37: 7122A.

[190] In *Studies in Medieval Literature in Honor of Albert Croll Baugh*, ed. by MacEdward Leach (Philadelphia, 1962), pp. 272-83. See also Magoun's "*Beowulf* A': a Folk-Variant," *Arv*, 14(1958), 95-101, and the companion piece, "*Beowulf* B: a Folk-Poem on Beowulf's Death," in *SmithSts*, pp. 127-40. In these two articles he attempts to resolve certain textual inconsistencies by dividing *Beowulf* into a number of smaller poems, in a manner somewhat reminiscent of the *Lieder* and *Fortsetzungen* studies of nineteenth-century scholars. See Robert Creed's rejoinder, "'wel-hwelc ӡecwæþ...': the Singer as Architect," *TSL*, 11(1966), 131-43.

[191] *Speculum*, 30(1955), 200-206.

[192] See also Jackson J. Campbell, "Oral Poetry in *The Seafarer*" (note 146).

[193] *PMLA*, 72(1957), 563-73. See also his "Poésie héroique du moyen âge et critique littéraire," *Romania*, 78(1957), 243-55; and "*Beowulf* et l'épopée anglo-saxonne," *LTR*, 132(1958), 140-51.

[194] See especially Robert E. Diamond, "The Diction of the Signed Poems of Cynewulf" and "The Diction of the Old English *Christ*."

[195] *NM*, 61(1960), 362-72. Note that Crowne's exposition does not take into account Lord's criterion of verbal correspondence (see *Singer*, pp. 68-98, and "Perspectives," below). Many thematic studies in Old English were to follow Crowne's lead in concentrating on the "hero on the beach," but in directing attention away from the verbal aspect of the theme and toward its abstract pattern exclusively.

[196] See George P. Krapp, "Introduction," *The Vercelli Book*, Anglo-Saxon Poetic Records, vol. 2 (New York, 1932, rpt. 1969), p. lv. See further Leonard Peters, "The Relationship of the Old English *Andreas* to *Beowulf*," *PMLA*, 66(1951), 844-63.

[197] *TSLL*, 3(1961), 97-106.

[198] Compare Michael D. Cherniss, "*Beowulf*: Oral Presentation and the Criterion of Immediate Rhetorical Effect," *Genre*, 3(1970), 214-28, who argues that "poetry intended primarily, if not exclusively, for oral presentation, is like drama, composed with the auditor, not the reader, in mind. The poet, therefore, must first of all concern himself with the immediate effect of his words upon the audience which will be listening to the recitation of his poem." (214). He goes on to try to prove the poet's primary concern with the immediate narrative environment rather than larger and more complex structures within the poem. For a statement of the relationship between thematic occurrence and narrative time similar to Creed's, see Christopher Knipp, "*Beowulf* 2210b-2323: Repetition in the Description of the Dragon's Hoard," *NM*, 73(1972), 775-85.

[199] *CL*, 14(1962), 44-52.

[200] "*Beowulf* on the Poet," *MS*, 38(1976), 442-67.

[201] Though Opland's own comparative analysis of Old English and Xhosa material suffers from an incongruity in genre (the African songs are mostly panegyric), his comments are appropriately cautious. See also his "*Imbongi Nezibongo*: the Xhosa Tribal Poet and the Contemporary Poetic Tradition," *PMLA*, 90(1975), 185-208; "The Oral Origins of Early English Poetry," *UCTSE*, 1

(1970), 40-54; and his forthcoming book on *Beowulf* and oral poetry.

[202] *PMLA*, 76(1961), 461-68; rpt. in *EsAr*, pp. 374-93. I use the pagination of the reprint.

[203] *NM*, 63(1962), 154-67; rpt. in *BP*, pp. 154-66. I use the pagination of the reprint. Compare the similar method of his "*Judith* and the Limits of Poetry," *ES*, 43 (1962), 145-55, which also analyzes the reaction of a listening audience. Of related interest is his "The Self-Deception of Temptation: Boethian Psychology in *Genesis B*," in *OEP*, pp. 47-67.

[204] In *BrodeurSts*, pp. 237-66.

[205] *JEGP*, 64(1965), 645-59. See also his "Beowulf's Armor," *ELH*, 32(1965), 409-41, espec. 411-12 and 434, where themes detailing "the impact of a weapon upon some part of a warrior's armor or upon the man himself" and "the advancing army" are discussed, respectively. See further his "*Beowulf* and Njálssaga," in *Proceedings of the First International Saga Conference, University of Edinburgh, 1971* (London, 1973), pp. 66-87; and "Some Traditional Scenes and Situations in Anglo-Saxon Poetry," unpub. Ph.D. diss. (Harvard University, 1961).

[206] In *Franciplegius*, pp. 86-91.

[207] See my essay in this volume, note 5. Of related interest is Bruce A. Rosenberg, "Folktale Morphology and the Structure of *Beowulf*: a Counterproposal," *JFI*, 11 (1974), 199-209.

[208] *NM*, 67(1966), 27-31.

[209] *NM*, 68(1967), 168-84. See also Janet Thormann, "Variations on the Theme of 'The Hero on the Beach' in *The Phoenix*," *NM*, 71(1970), 187-90.

[210] Fry reacted specifically against Crowne's notion of "pure form" ("The Hero on the Beach: an Example of Composition by Theme in Anglo-Saxon Poetry," 368). Compare Lord's insistence on the integrity of individual performances: "Each performance is the specific song, and at the same time it is the generic song. The song we are listening to is 'the song'; for each performance is more than a performance; it is a re-creation.... In a sense each performance is 'an' original, if not 'the' original." (*Singer*, p. 101).

[211] *Neophil*, 52(1968), 48-53.

[212] Note that Fry's narrative-based "type-scene," rather than the cluster of details he calls the "theme," is the near equivalent of Lord's "theme." An important difference between the concepts of Lord and Fry is the

matter of verbal correspondences among occurrences of the narrative unit, a criterion which Fry dismisses.

[213] Fry cites as source material Lee C. Ramsey, "The Theme of Battle in Old English Poetry," unpub. Ph.D. diss. (Indiana, 1965), abstr. in *DAI*, 26:2758. Compare Hèdi Sioud, "Oral-Formulaic and Thematic Structure in the Old English Battle Passages," unpub. Ph.D diss. (University of Massachusetts/Amherst, 1973), abstr. in *DAI*, 34:2579A.

[214] *Speculum*, 44(1969), 35-45.

[215] Another article by the same author, "Type-Scene Composition in *Judith*," *AM*, 12(1972), 100-19, contains a second analysis of the "approach-to-battle" type-scene, with the stress on the traditional artist's manipulation of the aesthetic possibilities inherent in that pattern.

[216] In *OEP*, pp. 249-74.

[217] *NM*, 71(1970), 83-96.

[218] "Theme and Motif in Old English Poetry."

[219] *NM*, 72(1971), 51-59.

[220] This article is one example of a relatively new critical genre concerned with providing a truly traditional context for the poem or passage under consideration. Two fine additional examples are: Jess B. Bessinger, Jr., "Homage to Cædmon and Others: a Beowulfian Praise Song," in *Old English Studies in Honour of John C. Pope*, ed. by Robert B. Burlin and Edward B. Irving, Jr. (Toronto and Buffalo, 1974), pp. 91-106; and Alain Renoir, "A Reading Context for *The Wife's Lament*," in *A-SP*, pp. 224-41.

[221] G. C. Britton also assumes a written mode of composition for the Christian poems, directing attention to various kinds of narrative patterns; see his "Repetition and Contrast in the Old English *Later Genesis*," *Neophil*, 58(1974), 66-73.

[222] Lord quotes these comments from an unpublished paper, "The Marks of an Oral Style and their Significance," read at the meetings of the International Comparative Literature Association in Belgrade (1967), in "Perspectives," p. 20. Note Opland's emphasis on particular words as a thematic substrate in "*Beowulf* on the Poet," espec. 446-53; see also my "Formula and Theme in Old English Poetry," discussed below.

[223] *NM*, 77(1976), 337-46.

[224] On a similar subject, see his "The Terror of the Dark Waters: a Note on Virgilian and Beowulfian Techniques," *HES*, 5(1974), 147-60; and "Crist Ihesu's Beasts

of Battle: a Note on Oral-Formulaic Theme Survival,"
Neophil, 60(1976), 455-59. The particular cluster which
Renoir analyzed in "Oral Theme and Written Texts" may be
of much earlier origin and much more widespread occur-
rence than the three examples indicate; see Calvert
Watkins, "The Indo-European Family of Greek ὄρχις: Lin-
guistics, Poetics, and Mythology," in *Indo-European
Studies II* (Cambridge, Mass., 1975), pp. 44-63.

[225] A view of the same traditional process operating
in another context may be found in my "*Christ* 164-213: a
Structural Approach to the Speech Boundaries," *Neophil*,
59(1975), 114-18.

[226] *Neophil*, 61(1977), 443-52.

[227] W. A. van Otterlo, *Untersuchungen über Begriff,
Anwendung und Entstehung der griechischen Ringcomposition*
(Amsterdam, 1944); and *De ringcompositie als opbouwprin-
cipe in de epische gedichten van Homerus* (Amsterdam,
1948); James A. Notopoulos, "Continuity and Interconnec-
tion in Homeric Oral Composition," *TAPA*, 82(1951), 81-
101; and Cedric H. Whitman, *Homer and the Heroic Tradition* (Cambridge, Mass., 1958).

[228] *CASS*, 12(1978), 230-46.

[229] Certain additional studies which do not bear
directly and significantly on the history of the oral
theory, or which there was no opportunity to mention
above in relation to other works, appear here: Earl R.
Anderson, "*Sæmearh* and Like Compounds: a Theme in Old
English Poetry," *Comitatus*, 3(1972), 3-11; Walter H.
Beale, "Rhetoric in the Old English Verse-Paragraph,"
NM, 80(1979), 133-42; Janet Taylor Buck, "Aspects of
Thematic Organization in *Beowulf*," unpub. Ph.D. diss.
(Yale, 1959-60); Marcia Bullard, "Some Objections to the
Formulaic Theory of Composition of Anglo-Saxon Poetry,"
BRMMLA, 21(1969), 11-16; André Crépin, "Récentes études
sur le style formulaire de la poésie vieil-anglaise,"
EA, 23(1970), 274-81; "Tradition et innovation: Con-
texture de la poésie vieil-anglaise," in *Tradition et
innovation, littérature et paralittérature: Actes du
Congrès de Nancy (1972)* (Paris, 1973), pp. 25-31;
Michael Curschmann, "Oral Poetry in Medieval English,
French, and German Literature: Some Notes on Recent Re-
search," *Speculum*, 42(1967), 36-52; Raymond Eichmann,
"Oral Composition: a Recapitulatory View of its Nature
and Impact," *NM*, 80(1979), 97-109; Patricia Morford
Evans, "Oral Interpretation in Anglo-Saxon England,"
unpub. Ph.D. diss. (Northwestern, 1958), abstr. in *DAI*,

18:1145-46A; Stanley J. Kahrl, "Feuds in *Beowulf*: a Tragic Necessity?" *MP*, 69(1972), 189-98; J. Kerling, "Kunst
of kunstjes: De oral formula en Oudenglese poëzie," in
Literatuur en samenleving in de middeleeuwen (Wassenaar,
1976), pp. 33-62; Richard A. Lewis, "*Beowulf* 992a: Ironic
Use of the Formulaic," *PQ*, 54(1975), 663-64; Leena Löf-
stedt, "Formules de salutation au moyen âge," *NM*, 79
(1978), 193-215; John D. Niles, "Aspects of the Oral Art
of *Beowulf*: a Comparative Investigation," unpub. Ph.D.
diss. (University of California/Berkeley, 1972), abstr.
in *DAI*, 35:467A; G. R. Russom, "Sequential Repetition of
Similar Narrative Units as Proof of the Scop's Original-
ity," unpub. Ph.D. diss. (State University of New York/
Stony Brook, 1973); Elizabeth S. Sklar, "The Battle of
Maldon and the Popular Tradition: Some Rhymed Formulas,"
PQ, 54(1975), 409-18; Godfrid Storms, "The Author of
Beowulf," *NM*, 75(1974), 11-39; Hildegard L. C. Tristram,
"Stock Descriptions of Heaven and Hell in Old English
Prose and Poetry," *NM*, 79(1978), 102-13; Charles Witke,
"*Beowulf* 2069-2199: a Variant?" *NM*, 67(1966), 113-17.
Two very different attempts at reconciling the oral
theory with other methods of investigation are: Joshua
H. Bonner, "Toward a Unified Critical Approach to Old
English Poetic Composition," *MP*, 73(1976), 219-28, who
argues for a redefinition of grammar in the Anglo-Saxon
period and a consequent joining of grammatical (or
rhetorical) theory with formulaic theory; and Thomas E.
Hart, "Tectonic Design, Formulaic Craft, and Literary
Execution: the Episodes of Finn and Ingeld in 'Beowulf',"
ABäG, 2(1972), 1-61, whose focus is the illustration of
"the compatibility between formulaic style and intricate
literary structuring" (2).

The influence of the oral theory has also extended
to Middle English literature; see Albert C. Baugh, "Improvisation in the Middle English Romance," *PAPS*, 103
(1959), 418-54; "The Middle English Romance: Some Questions of Creation, Presentation, and Preservation,"
Speculum, 42(1967), 1-31; Jerome E. Coffey, "The Evolution of an Oral-Formulaic Tradition in Old and Middle
English Alliterative Verse," unpub. Ph.D. diss. (State
University of New York/Buffalo, 1969), abstr. in *DAI*,
30:2477-78A; Francis D. Covella, "Formulaic Second Half-
lines in Skeat's A-Text of *Piers Plowman*: Norms for a
Comparative Analysis of the A-, B-, and C-Texts," unpub.
Ph.D. diss. (New York University, 1972), abstr. in *DAI*,
33:2887A; Ruth Crosby, "Oral Delivery in the Middle

Ages," *Speculum*, 11(1936), 88-110; Dennis P. Donahue,
"Thematic and Formulaic Composition in Lawman's *Brut*,"
unpub. Ph.D. diss. (New York University, 1976), abstr.
in *DAI*, 37:5808-9A; Laila Gross, "The Meaning and Oral-
Formulaic Use of Riot in the Alliterative *Morte Arthure*,"
AM, 9(1968), 98-102; William E. Holland, "Formulaic Diction and the Descant of a Middle English Romance,"
Speculum, 48(1973), 89-109; James D. Johnson, "The Hero
on the Beach in the Alliterative *Morte Arthure*," *NM*, 76
(1975), 271-81; S. T. Knight, "The Oral Transmission of
Sir Launfal," *MAE*, 38(1969), 164-70; Bruce V. Roach, "A
Concordance to Layamon's *Brut* Lines 1-8020, with Introductory Essay Descriptive and Illustrative of the Structure and Uses of the Concordance for Literary Scholars,"
unpub. Ph.D. diss. (Washington University, 1972), abstr.
in *DAI*, 33:4361A; Ronald A. Waldron, "Oral-Formulaic
Technique and Middle English Alliterative Poetry,"
Speculum, 32(1957), 792-804; R. F. Lawrence, "Formula
and Rhythm in *The Wars of Alexander*," *ES*, 51(1970), 97-
112; Susan Wittig, "Formulaic Style in the Middle English
Romance," *NM*, 78(1977), 250-55; Edward J. Wolff, "Chaucer's Normalized Diction: a Comparison of Recurring
Phrases in Chaucer and *Beowulf* to Determine the Validity
of the Magoun Thesis," unpub. Ph.D. diss. (Michigan State
University, 1966).

As this volume goes to press, an important new bibliography has just appeared: James P. Holoka, "Homer
Studies 1971-1977," *CW*, 73(1979), 65-150; see also his
additions to the corrections of *Haymes* in *CW*, 68(1975),
385-86.

THE INTRICATE WEB: THEMATIC COHESION IN RUSSIAN ORAL TRADITIONAL VERSE NARRATIVE

Patricia Arant

Themes in the Russian tradition of oral verse narrative have a life of their own from singer to singer, from
performance to performance, and from song to song. They
readily combine with other themes when the need arises.
They are fluid. They are protean. Nevertheless, they
exhibit certain redundant formative features or patterns
which contribute to thematic cohesion.

Woven into the thematic fabric of all Russian oral
verse narrative is the thread of semantic cohesion, which
is based on a minimum core of tradition-dependent narrative material that is useful to the oral bard in composing his oral epic songs and that is acceptable to his
audience as well. But whether large or small, the themes
of Russian oral narrative poetry cohere in a variety of
other tangible ways. For example, in a single line of
verse, which can represent either a thematic component or
a theme in itself, cohesion depends on such redundant
features as sound repetition, repetition of roots, affixes, individual words and word phrases, and ordered
repetition of basic syntactic categories, in addition to
repeated rhythmical impulses. Cohesion among themes consisting of larger groupings of lines, and thematic clusters as well, depend on these same redundant features.
Thematic cohesion, however, is not to be equated with
thematic stability or inflexibility, but rather with
fluidity, the kind of fluidity that is associated with
movement, which in oral traditional narrative verse is
always forward—movement from line to line, movement from
act to act, movement from adventure to adventure.

In simple terms, a theme makes a logical statement
about something. An oral epic poem is comprised of a
collection of such statements or themes that relate to
one another in a logical sequential way to tell a story.
The problem of determining thematic parameters, however,
is a complex one; and although there is still disagreement among scholars concerning the nature of a theme—
how it should be determined and defined—I will nevertheless suggest certain organic structures that seem to
contribute to a perception of themes or clusters of
themes in Russian oral traditional narrative verse. These

suggestions will be bound, of course, by the constraints
imposed by the materials used for this study, namely
5,402 lines of oral epic poetry of Trofim Grigor'evič
Rjabinin, a 78-year-old unlettered singer from the Onega
region in northern European Russia whose narrative verse
was collected by A. F. Gil'ferding in the summer of
1871.[1]

In the brief discussion of Rjabinin's themes which
follows, I will attempt to demonstrate that the semantic
concepts expressed by the actions and descriptions of
Rjabinin's verse narratives are not the only essential
and identifiable aspects of his themes and thematic clusters. Rjabinin's verbal formulation of them exhibits
features so distinctive, due primarily to a multilevel
density of redundancy, that this aspect cannot be ignored. Only the most obvious repetitive devices connected with thematic generation will be discussed. My ultimate objective is not to present a comprehensive survey
of Rjabinin's techniques of making themes, but rather to
suggest with a few typical examples that thematic generation can be as dependent on repetitive structures as
the making of lines of oral "formulaic" verse, a fact
that we are well aware of even though scholars still
argue among themselves about the nature of this "formulaic" verse.[2]

My discussion of thematic generation will begin with
a brief examination of the internal form of a few frequently recurring types of single verse lines in isolation, focusing in particular on those features that seem
to function primarily as intralinear cohesive or binding
devices. The most obvious of these devices include repeated sounds, roots, affixes, words or word phrases, and
syntax. Take, for example, a whole-line prepositional
phrase with repetition of the same preposition at the
beginning of two or more cola, that is, at the beginning
of line segments which contain a principal rhythmical
stress (line-initial particles are excluded from consideration)[3]:

A *vo* tot *vo* slavnyj v stol'në-Kiev grad (83:59)
(In that famous capital city Kiev)

So svoeju *so* družinuškoj xorobroju (73:58)
(With his brave companions)

In the above examples, the repeated preposition binds

cola; but since prepositions are proclitic, there is the
additional dimension of the repeated preposition as a
device to bind cola through alliteration. Colon alliteration, however, is not a phenomenon that is restricted to
repeated prepositions. It obtains in words with the same
initial sounds occurring in colon-initial position:

>   *Po*rozvernuta *po*latka *po*lotnjanaja (78:34)
>   (The linen tent was raised)
>
>   Ty udalen'koj *do*rodnëj *do*broj molodec (79:94)
>   (Oh you stalwart brave young man)

Nor does colon alliteration exclude a combination of like
prepositions and word-initial sounds:

>   A *po* gorenke *P*ermin ën *po*xaživaet (81:65)
>   (Permin begins to pace in his chamber)

Or take, for example, the type of line that binds segments through the repetition of roots:

>   So*služi*-tko ètu *slúže*bku velikuju (79:333)
>   (Carry out that great task)

Another form of cohesion, particularly characteristic of
lines that break into two cola (hemistichs) rather than
three, is based on parallelism between the main syntactic
elements of the two cola, frequently reinforced by word-
repetition (e.g., *dvenadcat'*, 'twelve'):

>   A *dvenadcat' lebedej, dvenadcat' krečenej* (80:17)
>   (Twelve swans and twelve gyrfalcons)

Of note also is a more subtle type of binding based on
internal sound symmetry. The line type below consists
of two cola or hemistichs which cohere primarily on the
basis of the main vowels under stress:

>   U nëj *ru*saja kos*á* porosp*úščena*j*à* (84:140)
>   (She has let down her light-brown hair)

The symmetrical stress pattern can be illustrated as
follows:

>   *u   a   :   u   a*

    Just as there is something special about the inter-
relationship of discrete segments of a significant number of Rjabinin's lines of verse in isolation from other
verse lines, so there is something special about the relationship between a significant number of sequential
lines. Many of the cohesive features noted prove also
to be characteristic of the relationship that obtains
across line boundaries. A description of the most obvious types of interlinear cohesion will be restricted
at first to two sequential lines. Whether these sequential lines represent a thematic component or a theme
itself is not important to this description. The repeated word is one of the most easily identifiable features of interlinear cohesion. Hence, the examples below will focus primarily on this aspect of line-binding.
The reader will become aware quickly, however, that
certain other aspects of cohesion already mentioned also
are present. The colon will serve as the primary basis
for designating the location of repeated words or word-
phrases. Most lines break into three cola: initial, internal, and final. Repeated words will be underlined. The
important role of syntactic parallelism in the binding of
lines also will be called to the reader's attention.
Syntactic parallelism will be designated by parallel
bars ($\|$).[4] The following examples represent the most
obvious types of interlinear binding in two adjacent
lines:

1. Initial

    Ne slyxal li posvistu solov'jago,
                   $\|$ $\|$
    Ne slyxal li pokriku zverinogo? (74:75-76)
    (Have you not heard the nightingale whistling,
    Have you not heard the beast shouting?)

2. Internal

    Per'ico u vorona černym černo,
       $\|$ $\|$
    Kryl'ico u vorona belym belo. (87:64-65)
    (The feathers of the raven are black,
    The pinions of the raven are white.)

3. Final

Prjamoezžeju dorožkoj v <u>stol'nëj Kiev grad</u>.
Ën priexal-to vo slavnyj <u>stol'nëj Kiev grad</u>.
(74:135–136)
(By the direct way to the capital city Kiev.
He arrived in the famous capital city Kiev.)

4. Initial, internal

<u>I smotrel, čto v gramote</u> napisano,
                              ‖
<u>I smotrel, čto v gramote</u> da napečatano. (75:68–69)
(And [he] read what was spelled out in the letter,
And [he] read what was written in the letter.)

5. Internal, final

Natjanul <u>tetivočku šelkovuju</u>,
   ‖
Da spustil ètu <u>tetivocku šelkovuju</u>. (80:545–546)
([He] pulled the silken string,
Let loose the silken string.)

6. Initial, internal, final

<u>Starago kazaka Il'i Muromca</u>.
   ‖   ‖   ‖
<u>Staromu kazaku Il'e Muromcu</u>. (76:6–7)
(The old cossack Il'ja Muromec.
To the old cossack Il'ja Muromec.)

7. Initial to internal

<u>Ne mogu ja</u> zasvistat' da j po solóv'emu,
                              ‖
Zakryčat'-to <u>ne mogu ja</u> po zverinomu. (74:229–230)
(I cannot whistle like a nightingale,
I cannot shout like a beast.)

8. Internal to initial

Po kolenušku <u>v zemel'ku</u> ën ugrjazyval,
   ‖   ‖
<u>Iz zemel'ki</u> svoi nožen'ki vyxvatyval, (80:327–328)
([The horse] began to sink in the mud,

And when he freed his legs from the mud,)

9. Internal to final

   Nalil-to ja <u>rjumočku</u> kak knjazju Vladymiru,
   Pozvol' pódnesti mne ešče <u>rjumočku</u>. (80:946-947)
   (I have poured a cup for you, Prince Vladimir,
   Allow me to offer another cup.)

10. Final to internal

   Bil on palicej bulatnëj <u>po teremu</u>,

   Da po slavnomu <u>po teremu</u> zlatú verxu. (84:127-128)
   (He hit his club against the tower,
   Against the famous tower, the golden bower.)

11. Final to initial

   Ukažite mne dorožku <u>prjamoezžuju</u>,
   <u>Prjamoezžuju</u> da v stol'nij Kiev grad. (74:25-26)
   (Show me the direct way,
   The direct [way] to the capital city Kiev.)

12. Initial to final

   A j v <u>okošečkax</u> okolenki rossypalis'.
   Pogljanul korol' v kosjavčato <u>okošečko</u>. (86:23-24)
   (The window gratings were sundered.
   The king looked out of the latticed window.)

And certain sequential lines cohere primarily on the
basis of syntactic parallelism alone:

   Naložil on streločku kalenuju,

   Natjanul tetivočku šelkovuju. (80:544-545)
   ([He] laid on the string a tempered arrow,
   And pulled the silken string.)

Repetition of equivalent syntactic elements, however, is
not to be found only in corresponding colon positions.
Like repeated words or word phrases, equivalent syntactic elements also can occupy different colon positions
in adjacent lines. Example 7 above, for instance, could
be described as cohering as well on the basis of a

verbal infinitive which appears in internal colon position in the first line and in initial position in the
line which follows. Additional and more subtle types of
recurring intralinear cohesive patterns could be in-
stanced; however, I believe the types already cited to
be sufficient illustration of most of the basic binding
patterns that Rjabinin used again and again, with or
without variation.

 If we now turn our attention to larger groups of
lines, it should not surprise us to find identical or
similar cohesive techniques in use. On this expanded
scale, one of the more striking features of Rjabinin's
cohesive techniques is their distinctive use in the composition of his themes, a usage that keeps demanding my
attention when I attempt to define or identify the parameters of Rjabinin's themes. In Rjabinin's *bylina*
about Vol'ga and Mikula, when Vol'ga is asked where he
is going, he responds:

> A edu k gorodam ja za polučkoju,
> K pervomu ko gorodu ko Gùr'ёvcu,
> || ||
> K drúgomu-to gorodu k Orexovcu,
> || ||
> K tret'emu gorodu k Krest'janovcu. (73:60-63)
> (I am going to the [following] cities to collect
>   tribute:
> The first city is Gur'ёvec,
> The second city is Orexovec,
> And the third city is Krest'janovec.)

The line which precedes Vol'ga's answer (*Govoril Vol'ga
takovy slova*, 'Vol'ga said the following') labels the
speaker and signals as well that new information in the
form of a response is to come. This kind of line is
representative of most of Rjabinin's lines which introduce speech.[5] The limits of this thematic unit which
contains the "new information" telling where Vol'ga is
going can be defined primarily through repetition of a
"core" element (*gorodam/gorodu*, 'cities/city') in colon-
internal position and repetition of the colon-initial
preposition *k/ko* in all lines, and full syntactic parallelism among the last three lines (a prepositional phrase
consisting of a preposition, adjective, and two apposi-
tional nouns). Thematic cohesion through repetition of
of the same word in the same colon position can also be

illustrated by the first nine lines of a *bylina* about
Mixajlo Potyk:

> Da j xodil-to <u>molodec</u> da iz ordy v ordu,
>   ‖   ‖
> Zaguljal-to <u>molodec</u> da k korolju v Litvu,
> A j korol'-to <u>molodca</u> on ljubit žaluet,
> Korolevna <u>molodca</u> ёna v ljubí deržit.
> Da j xodil-to <u>molodec</u> da porosxvastalsja:
>   ‖
> Da j xodil-to <u>molodec</u> da iz ordy v ordu,
>   ‖   ‖
> Zaguljal-to <u>molodec</u> da k korolju v Litvu,
> A korol'-to <u>molodca</u> da ljubit žaluet,
>   ‖
> Korolevna <u>molodca</u> ona v ljubí deržit.   (82:1-9)
> (A young man traveled from country to country.
> The young man went to the King of Lithuania.
> The King was kind and gracious to the young man,
> And the queen was fond of the young man.
> The young man traveled and boasted
> That he had gone from country to country,
> That he had gone to the King of Lithuania
> That the King had been kind and gracious to him,
> And that the queen had been fond of him.)

These lines introduce us to a young hero named Mixajlo
who left home, probably for the first time, impressed
the king and queen of Lithuania, and then boasted of
these things. This boasting passage is comprised of two
parts: lines 1-4, Rjabinin's report of Mixajlo's reason
for boasting, and lines 6-9, the boasting itself, which
is almost letter-for-letter the same as lines 1-4, as
well as syntactically identical (lines 1-2 and 6-7: verb,
nominal subject, verbal complement; 3-4 and 8-9: nominal
subject, verbal complement, verb). But an equally
striking aspect of the above lines is that a "core" element (*molodec/molodca*, 'young man'; i.e., Mixajlo) is
repeated in each line in precisely the same colon position, regardless of its dual syntactic function as subject (*molodec*) and object (*molodca*). This passage indicates that colon repetition can serve as a powerful
theme-binding device. In spite of the fact, however,
that the structure of this boasting passage can be described as consisting primarily of colon-bound "core"
repetition and two sets of identical lines, I would like

to suggest that these kinds of redundancies can and probably should be understood as viable structural devices
for advancing a story, for progressing from the beginning
to the end of a theme, rather than as retarding devices,
as is so frequently stated.

From the above examples it is clear that a redundant
internal "core" element can function as a useful theme-
making technique. The example below will illustrate how
the lines of a thematic unit can be held together by an
initial position-bound "core" element. At the end of a
bylina about Il'ja and Solovej the robber, just after
cutting off the robber's head, Il'ja says farewell to
his slain monster:

> Tobi polno-tko svistat' da po solov'emu,
>
> Tobi polno-tko kryčat' da po zverinomu,
>
> Tobi polno-tko slezit' da otcej-máterej,
>
> Tobi polno-tko vdovit' da žen molodyix,
>
> Tobi polno-tko spuščat'-to sirotat' da malyx detušok.
> (74:266-270)
> (Long enough have you whistled like a nightingale,
> Long enough have you shouted like a beast,
> Long enough have you made fathers and mothers weep,
> Long enough have you widowed young wives,
> Long enough have you orphaned little children.)

The speaker Il'ja (*Govoril Il'ja takovy slova*, 'Il'ja
said the following') is identified in the line preceding
this farewell address, the dimensions of which are im-
pressively reinforced by the repeated colon-initial
"core" element. In this example, repetition of the
initial colon is regular enough and prolonged enough to
create an effect similar to that created by end rhyme.
Syntactic parallelism also plays an important role in
binding these lines. The repeated initial colon is
followed consistently by a verbal infinitive and complement (lines 266-67: prepositional phrase; lines
268-69 and 270: direct object).

But not all thematic units cohere on the basis of
word or phrasal repetition that is bound to specific
colon positions or by ordered repetition of grammatical
forms. A more complex cohesive pattern can be seen in

the following lines from Rjabinin's *bylina* about Vol'ga
and Mikula. The episode concerns strength, namely the
inability of young Vol'ga and his companions to move
Mikula's plow. This passage can be seen as consisting
of two parts: a) a difficult task is to be performed and
b) the task cannot be performed.

a) Molodj Vol'ga Svjatoslavgovič
   Posylaet tut dva da tri dobryx mŏlodca
   Şo svoej ş družinuški ş xorobroej
   Da ko̧ ètoj ko̧ soške klenoven'koj,

105   Ctoby sošku ş zemel'ki povydernulî,
      Iz omešikov zemel'ku povy̧trjaxnulî,
      Brosili by sošku za rakitov kust.

b) Edut tudy dva da tri dobryx molodca
   Ko̧ ètój ko̧ soški klenovoej;

110   Oni sošku za obži krugom vertjat,
      A im soški ot zémli podnjat' nel'zja,
      Da ne mogut oni sošku ş zemel'ki povydernutî,
      Iz omešikov zemel'ki   povytrjaxnut',
      Brositi soški za rakitov kust.   (73:101–114)

(Young Vol'ga Svjatoslavgovič
Sent three young men
From his group of brave companions
To the maple plow,
To pull the plow out of the earth,
To shake the earth from the plowshare,
To throw the plow behind a bramble bush.

Three young men went
To the maple plow
To turn the plow around;
But they could not lift the plow from the earth,

They could not pull the plow out of the earth,
Nor shake the earth from the plowshare
So that they might throw the plow behind the
bramble bush.)

Repetition is dense. The following line-binding techniques mentioned earlier are in use: internal colon
repetition (lines 105-106), internal to initial (lines
109-10), initial (lines 110-11), and initial to internal
(lines 111-12). But what is worth special note is the
way in which two words, *soška* ('plow') and *zemel'ka/*
zeml'ja ('earth'), are used. I have underlined these
words in order to focus the reader's attention on them,
and have used dotted lines to indicate other word and
phrasal repetition that occurs. *Soška* ('plow') and
zemel'ka/zeml'ja ('earth'), both separately and in combination, are woven into the thematic fabric in such a
way that one is left with the impression that Rjabinin
the theme-maker has stitched line to line, joining one
to another with these word-threads, until expression of
the thematic content is complete.

As indicated earlier, repeated sounds, roots, and
affixes in themselves can serve as strong binding devices.[6] In the passage below, which represents a negative answer, namely silence in response to someone's request, one act is added to another in rapid succession
with nothing intervening. Even though these lines are
complete syntactic units, a characteristic of Rjabinin's
verse lines, the binding techniques that he uses create,
nevertheless, a feeling of subtle enjambement as the
singer moves from one line to the next, constantly advancing the story.[7] I have indicated word repetition
with a single line and sound, root and affixed repetition with two lines.

Vse bogatyri za stolikom umolknuli,

20 Vse umolknuli i priutixnuli,

Kak bogatyri za stolikom-to prituljalisja,

A bol'šaja-to tulîtsja za serédnjuju,

A serednja túlitsja za men'šuju,

A ot men'šoëj ot túlicy otvetu net.   (80:19-24)

(All the warriors at table fell silent,
All fell silent, became quiet.
The warriors at table sought refuge:
The great hid behind the lesser,
The lesser hid behind the least,
And from the least in rank there was no response.)

Other types of binding repetition are anaphoric (*vse*,
lines 19-20; *a*, lines 22, 23 and 24); colon internal
(lines 22-23) and final to initial (lines 19-20, 22-23,
and 23-24); and nonadjacent whole-line syntactic parallelism (lines 19 and 21: nominal subject, prepositional
phrase, verb).
     A few lines from a *bylina* about Xoten Bludovič can
provide us with other examples of Rjabinin's thematic
formative elements within a larger narrative context.
This passage concerns the young hero Xoten's departure
from home, travel, arrival, and preparation for entry
into the chamber of his bride-to-be. In these lines I
have underlined those verbs directly associated with departure, travel, arrival, and preparation for entry
(primarily root repetition), the prepositions related to
these acts (frequently resulting in colon alliteration),
and the place which is the ultimate focal point of
everything, the maiden's chamber in the tower (internal
to final and final to internal colon repetition in lines
126-27 and 127-28):

To on poexal po rozdol'ju čistu polju,

125 A vo vsju ën exal v silu lošadinuju,

On pod"exal kak ko teremu k zlatú verxu.

Bil on palicej bulatněj po teremu,

Da po slavnomu po teremu zlatú verxu. (84:124-128)

(He set out across the wide and open plain,
He rode his horse at full speed,
He rode up to the tower, the golden bower.
He beat against the tower with his damask steel
cudgel,
Against the famous tower, the golden bower.)

In this passage we can determine a three-line unit (lines
124-26) which coheres on the basis of verbs which share
the same root: poexal/exal/pod"exal. But we can also
identify a second three-line unit (lines 126-28) based on
the repeated occurrence of teremu. The first line of
this second unit, however, is the last line of the first
unit. Hence, the first unit, which has been identified
through verbal repetition, and the last unit, which has
been identified through nominal repetition, merge into a
single cohesive compositional unit based on a shared
line which contains not only the crucial verbal root but
also the equally decisive noun.

My final and perhaps most complex illustration of
Rjabinin's theme-making techniques, which depend to a
significant degree on methods of moving from line to
line, is from his *bylina* about Dobrynja and Vasilij
Kazimirov. In the following passage Dobrynja (like
Odysseus) arrives home disguised as a stranger and re-
quests from Dobrynja's mother his minstrel garb so that
he might gain entry to the wedding feast celebrating the
marriage of his wife to someone else. After identifying
himself as a friend of Dobrynja, the stranger who is
Dobrynja in disguise then continues with his request of
Dobrynja's mother:

My s Dobryṇjuškoj včeras' da poroz"exalis',   verb

A j Dobrynjuško poexal ko Tsarjugradu,   verb   prep.

A menja poslal on k stol'në-Kievu,   verb   prep.

A j k tobi ved' on zajti velel da na širokoj dvor   verb   prep.

715 Da j sxodit' k tobi v polaty belokamenny,   verb   prep.

Da j velel tobi sxodit na pogreby glubokii,   verb

Prinesti velel so pogreba lapotiki šelkovenki,   verb

Da velel-to prinesti ešče-to plat'ice da skomorovčato,   verb

Da i prinesti velel guseluški jarovčaty,   verb   frame   no.°

720 Da v koi guseljyški-to s molodu Dobryṇjuška poigryval;   verb   no.°   no.*

Da j velel sxodit' Dobryṇja na počesten pir   verb   no.*

Ko tomu ko knjazju ko Vladymiru,   verb   prep.

Da sxodit' velel ko knjazju ko Olešenku k Popoviču   verb   prep.

Da ko toej ko knjagine ko molodoej,   prep.

725 Ko Nastas'juške da j ko Mikuličnoj. (80:711-725)   prep.

(Yesterday Dobrynja and I parted;

Dobrynja set out for Tsargrad

And sent me to the capital city Kiev,

And he ordered me to come to your wide courtyard,

To enter your palace of white store,

To order you to go down to the deep cellar,

To order you to bring his silken slippers from the cellar,

To order you to bring his minstrel's clothing,

To order you to bring his harp of maple wood,

The harp that Dobrynja has played since his youth.

And Dobrynja ordered me to go to the feast of honor,

To prince Vladimir,

And ordered me to go to prince Alësa Popovič

And to the young princess,

To Nastas'ja Mikulična.)

A sense of thematic beginning, middle, and end is conveyed in particular by frequent repetition of semantically and/or root-related verbs concerned with moving
someone or something from one location to another—
poroz"exat'sja/poexat'/zajti/sxodit'/prinesti—verbs
which co-occur often with *velel* ('ordered'). This
verbal inventory is complete. In addition, these lines
are even more tightly bound through repetition of the
preposition *k/ko* in four lines toward the beginning of
this passage and in the last four lines—yet another organic signal, subtle though it may be, of thematic beginning and end. These verbs and the prepositions *k/ko*
have been underlined. The final four-line unit is also
connected to the majority of the preceding lines through
the only verbal phrase in these final lines, *sxodit'*
velel. But this is only a partial answer to what makes
these lines cohere as a theme. Lines 711–12 as well as
720–21 are joined by *Dobrynjuškoj/Dobrynjuško/*
Dobrynjuška/Dobrynja, lines 714–16 by *tobi*, lines 716–
17 by *pogreby/pogreba*, lines 719–20 by *guseluški/*
guselyški-to, and lines 722, 723, and 724 by *knjazju/*
knjagine. Thus these additional repetitions, which I
have indicated in the text by dotted lines, also unite
adjacent lines as well as advance the theme. In the
schematic description that accompanies the Russian text,
in addition to the verbs and prepositions already mentioned, I also have indicated *guseluški/guselyški* (no°),
which unite lines 719 and 720 and advance the theme, as
well as *Dobrynjuška/Dobrynja* (no.*), which advance the
theme by uniting lines 720 and 721. Besides word repetition, the last four lines which name the main festal
participants, all of whom appear as objects of the
preposition *k/ko*, share the same basic syntax; i.e.,
they are whole-line prepositional phrases. I have ignored the verb phrase of line 723 in the syntactic description of the last four lines because I view it as
functioning primarily as a line filler or line-binding
device rather than as a significant syntactic unit. All
of these redundancies reinforce progressive movement from
the beginning to the end of this theme, an ending decisively marked by the line which follows, the type of
line that we already know signals a new speaker and new
information: *Govorila-to emu vdova da gor'ko plakala*
('The widow cried bitterly and said to him').

A theme is the sum of the devices which generate it,
the product of the principles by which small and large

formative elements are combined to make a statement about
something. Themes are dynamic; but the dynamics of
thematic structure in an oral verse narrative tradition
depend largely on how each oral bard perceives a theme
from its beginning to its end. Thematic perception seems
to be inextricably linked with the oral bard's conscious
or subconscious sense of thematic structure. It is the
actualization of this structure that I have attempted to
explore in a very limited way in the oral traditional
narrative of a nineteenth-century Russian epic bard. I
have attempted to identify and illustrate in action, as
it were, some of the most obvious and most frequently
recurring, hence most useful, types of discrete formative elements, as well as some of the intra- and inter-
line relationships among these elements.

     High frequency repetition of structural devices and
semantic content represents laconic style par excellence.
Rjabinin's theme-making techniques call again and again
upon the same small store of tradition-bound materials.
To some, repetition is synonymous with things static,
with things that retard or hinder forward movement. In
the hands of this traditional "singer of tales," however, repetition on a thematic level seems to serve an
altogether different purpose. It is a powerful compositional technique, one by which the singer is able to
move forward the "ear" of an "oral" audience as well as
the "eye" of a "surrogate" audience, the reader. It is
a dynamic technique used by an unlettered bard to put a
theme in motion, to sustain its forward progression,
and to bring it to an end, ready nevertheless, almost
instantaneously, to move on to the next one until the
story itself reaches closure.

Brown University

                          NOTES

     [1]A. F. Gil'ferding, *Onežskie byliny*, 4th ed. (Mos-
cow and Leningrad, 1950), vol. 2, 1-166. P. N. Rybnikov
collected oral epic poetry from Rjabinin about ten years
prior to Gil'ferding; see *Pesni, sobrannye P. N.
Rybnikovym*, 2nd ed. (Moscow, 1909), vol. 1, 3-141.
     [2]See in particular Milman Parry, "Studies in the
Epic Technique of Oral Verse-Making. I. Homer and Homeric Style," in *MHV*, pp. 266-324; Albert B. Lord, *Singer*;
and the many subsequent discussions of the oral formula

in *Haymes*.

[3]In a recent study of the language of Russian oral
poetry of the seventeenth through the twentieth centuries, A. P. Evgen'eva has given a detailed review of major
Russian works concerned with the problem of repeated
prepositions; see her *Očerki po jazyku russkoj ustnoj
poèzii v zapisjax XVII-XX vv.* (Moscow and Leningrad,
1963), espec. pp. 20-40. See also Felix J. Oinas, "Con-
cord in Balto-Finnic and Prepositional Repetition in
Russian," *ASUL*, 1(1960), 121-38; Roy G. Jones, *Language
and Prosody of the Russian Folk Epic* (The Hague and
Paris, 1972), pp. 55-63; and my "Repetition of Prepositions in the Russian Oral Traditional Lament," *SEEJ*, 16
(1972), 65-73.

[4]If the words or phrases of one line belong to the
same basic grammatical categories as the words or phrases
in an adjacent line, but differ in meaning, the words or
phrases of these two lines will be considered syntactically parallel to each other. Syntactically parallel
words and phrases occupy the same colon positions. See
Roman Jakobson, "Linguistics and Poetics," in *Style in
Language*, ed. by Thomas A. Sebeok (New York and London,
1960), pp. 369-70, for a discussion of those oral traditions which use grammatical parallelism to connect
consecutive lines, as well as his article "Poèzija gram-
matiki i grammatika poèzii," in *Poetics*, ed. by Roman
Jakobson *et al.* (Warsaw and The Hague, 1961), pp. 400-
402. See also Wolfgang Steinitz, *Der Parallelismus in
der finnisch-karelischen Volkdichtung*, FFC no. 115
(1934); and Robert Austerlitz, *Ob-Ugric Metrics: The
Metrical Structure of Vogul Folk-Poetry*, FFC no. 174
(1958), *passim*.

[5]See M. O. Gabel', "Forma dialoga v byline," *NZK*, 6
(1927), 315-28, for a detailed analysis of dialog in the
Russian *bylina*. For an English translation of this
study, see Felix J. Oinas and Stephen Soudakoff, eds.
and trans., *The Study of Russian Folklore* (The Hague and
Paris, 1975), pp. 187-205.

[6]See Lord, "The Role of Sound Patterns in Serbocroatian Epic," in *For Roman Jakobson* (The Hague, 1956),
pp. 301-5.

[7]In general, Rjabinin's ideas follow one another in
a paratactic way. Verse line follows verse line in logical order, rarely with the aid of a subordinate conjunction. This particular aspect of oral style, which
is frequently referred to as an incremental or adding

style, has been discussed at length. See, for example,
Milman Parry, "The Distinctive Character of Enjambement
in Homeric Verse," in *MHV*, pp. 251-65; Lord, "Homer and
Huso III: Enjambement in Greek and Southslavic Heroic
Song," *TAPA*, 79(1948), 113-24; James A. Notopoulos,
"Parataxis in Homer," *TAPA*, 80(1949), 1-23; and Erich
Auerbach, *Mimesis: The Representation of Reality in
Western Literature* (New York, 1957), Chapter 5.

MYTH AND RITUAL: TWO FACES OF TRADITION

David E. Bynum

Humanism, it seems to me, is an intrinsically funda-
mentalist profession. As a class, we have little else
entirely in common than our confidence in the supernal
inspiration and the revelative inerrancy of our several
scriptures. In varying degrees many of us share also a
determination—as one says—to "get to the root of the
matter"; the "matter" being always some tradition whose
source or sense we should in duty to our calling understand better than we do, and expound to each other. This
latter motivation must be especially strong in humanists
who find anything attractive in anthropology. To make
significant use of contemporary anthropology for other
than its own ends requires considerable inventiveness at
the least, and also close attention to matters of religion and ritual which the fathers of humanism would
surely have thought more appropriate to theology than to
humanistic learning. The theological odor of much modern
anthropology is reason enough for many to cry fie upon
it; and to fundamentalists such as I think we mostly are,
invention too is ever suspect, except when it can be
shown to enhance or to introduce some new purity of doctrine. The earnest doctrinal disputations and the evident concern for doctrinal purity in anthropology have
thus had some power of attraction for humanists, even
when the aspects of culture that have occasioned them
were topically rebarbative to us.

The anthropologist's programmatic ideal of detachment or "social scientific objectivity" has also seemed
a salubrious alternative to the long habit of Cartesian
subjectivity in literary criticism. And of course the
example of famous individual anthropologists, who may
have done more—or seem to have done more—than our profession has done in recent years to illuminate "the non-
genetically determined behaviour of man," this too has
given humanism a smart fillip toward imitation if not
outright adoption of anthropological methods.

Forceful as these causes have been, however, I do
not believe we could have moved so far so quickly or in
such numbers but for the effect of two additional determinants. One has been the relentless and right growth
of awareness in our profession that among all the tradi-

tions we value—the very fundaments of the humanist's
fundamentalism—oral traditions generally are more ancient and hence more traditional, and often very much
more traditional at that, than are any written traditions. Even though they are often more difficult or less
accessible to conventional understanding than are written
traditions, oral traditions have come to be more widely
respected as the tried, proven, and densely economical
conveyors of thought and ideology that they are. The
trouble Western humanists have had understanding them is
after all not chargeable to the witlessness of an unwashed, half-mad peasantry, or to the blithering of a
barely awakened, still inchoate power of reason in simple
savages, but rather to the narrowness, or perhaps even
the unsuitability, of literary learning to the real challenge of such more ancient and more truly *traditional*
traditions. To the uneducated, the fact that oral traditions belong in the first instance not to the library but
to the habits of living people has seemed reason enough
to consign them wholly to anthropology, although neither
the origination nor the continuing inspiration of literary traditions by oral tradition warrants it so. Thus
the fathering of responsibility for the collecting and
interpretation of oral traditions upon anthropology
arises not from any real right or even any actual interest in most oral traditions on the part of most anthropologists (whose real *métiers* are in fact physical man
and the organization of societies), but more often from
the default of humanists in this century, who if they
had any inkling of it, have mostly dreaded and shunned
what Edmund Leach has correctly described as the "extremely personal traumatic kind of experience and the
personal involvement" of fieldwork.[1] The uncomfortable
awareness of this on the one hand, and on the other hand
the eruption of Claude Lévi-Strauss' reflections on
Amazonian Indian and other New-World mythologies, have
given contemporary humanism an irresistable impetus toward new and different, if not actually altogether anthropological, approaches to literature, both oral and
written.

    One assigns singular influence to Lévi-Strauss not
because he is necessarily a good anthropologist or a
good mythologist—one need not judge that—but only because as an anthropologist he wrote egregiously and in-
terestingly about myth, whereas mythology was of old the
especial bailiwick of humanists. For that reason alone

he rapt the attention of humanists as other, perhaps more
strictly competent professional anthropologists never
had. Never before had myth seemed to be a main concern
of anthropology, and perhaps it still is not, but for a
time Lévi-Strauss made it appear so.

Not that anthropology was devoid of interest for
humanists before Lévi-Strauss. Kinship, the basic technical discipline of anthropology, never had much appeal
for the humanities in itself. But above all else, kinship has to do with marriage, and marriage is ritual, and
ritual in that connection bears directly and profoundly
on religion. More than kinship studies, the humanistic
interest of religion and ritual made humanists aware of
the gradual and fruitful commingling of French social
philosophy and British anthropology in the long descent
from Robertson-Smith through Frazer, Durkheim, Marcel
Mauss, Van Gennep, Malinowski, Radcliffe-Brown, Evans-
Pritchard, and even the American, Kroeber. But if kinship studies meant hardly anything to humanists, religious and ritual studies too seemed often to tantalize
without clearly fulfilling the needs of criticism in the
humanities. So anthropology with its increasing predilection for the trauma of objective experience "in the
field" became identified with ritual studies in the minds
of many humanists, while humanism with its increasing
predilection for the self-indulgence of critical subjectivity continued to dominate the study of myth. Put
simply, the tacit understanding arose that to comprehend
ritual, one turned to anthropology, but to humanistic
learning for mythology. Lévi-Strauss changed all that,
injecting a large dollop of subjective criticism into
what purported to be anthropology, and in so doing evok-
ing a great desire for more objectivity in humanists.

To see how that came about, one should, I think, discriminate certain developments in the anthropology of
ritual. The older and more ample stream of studies in
rite was religious in nature, concerned like Robertson-
Smith with ritual that connoted a large element of belief in preternatural or supernal beings in its cele-
brants. One of the most respected contemporary students
of ritual in this sense is Victor W. Turner, whose studies in indigenous Central African religion are theoretical landmarks, as, for example, his work on the Chihamba
cult of the Ndembu people of northern Zambia.[2] But the
criticism of any scholarship so accomplished as Turner's
may be as stimulating as the achievement itself. Another

admirer of Turner, Maurice Bloch, has commented that
Turner's self-expressed dissatisfaction with explanations
of religion that preceded his own work has led him into a
serious compromise if not actually a renunciation of
scientific detachment. As Bloch remarked,

> Professor Turner criticizes these approaches for
> "explaining away religion in naturalistic terms."
>   By this he means first of all that the stud-
> ies inspired by these theories gave an insuffi-
> cient account of religious belief, and conse-
> quently did not pay sufficient attention to its
> content. He himself, at first working within
> this tradition, later found it unable to account
> for the complexity of belief, for the emotional
> and intellectual richness and interconnectedness
> of symbols. By contrast, for him religion deals
> with truth not bounded by a particular social
> situation or a particular society, perhaps uni-
> versal psychological truth of a Freudian or
> Jungian nature, although he finally settles for
> the frankly religious view that these are re-
> vealed truth, more or less perfectly expressed....
>
>   The non-believers among us might well excuse
> this idiosyncrasy if, as Professor Turner sug-
> gests, the acceptance of religion is necessary
> for the best possible account of its nature. To
> a certain extent the excellence of detailed study
> we find in [Turner's book] *Revelation and Divina-
> tion in Ndembu Ritual* is due to this commitment
> to religion as such, but there is also a major
> drawback which can be attributed to the same
> cause. The problem is one of scale and it comes
> from studying symbolism primarily from the in-
> side—in other words as a believer. The refusal
> ultimately to *account* for religion means that we
> cannot understand what kind of phenomenon is
> being examined.... Without this perspective,
> without being given the scale that such a point
> of view would give, these wonderfully sensitive
> and accurate studies are a little reminiscent of
> the inside of the vacuum cleaner in *Our Man in
> Havana*. Every part meshes perfectly and mysteri-
> ously with every other, bringing to mind endless
> interlinked connotations; but without an external

reference point, without an attempt to know what
the whole thing is for, the mind of the anthropologist, like that of the believer, forever marvels but never gets anywhere.[3]

What Bloch describes as Turner's cast of mind is
quite simply mysticism. And when, speaking as a scholar,
Turner says "...if we would discover religious truths ...
we must be prepared to accept the fruits of simple wisdom
with gratitude and not try to reduce them to their chemi-
cal constituents, thereby destroying their essential
quality as fruits and their virtue as food" (Turner, p.
196), his attitude must at least be reckoned a material
retreat from the traditional anthropological ideal of
intellectual objectivity toward the more emotive, par-
ticipatory kind of interpretation already so familiar in
modern humanism generally, and so overworked in modern
literary criticism particularly. Nor is there anything
new for us in the realization that it gets us nowhere.
But if to culminate so brilliant a study of complex religious ritual as Turner's monograph on Ndembu Chihamba
the best an anthropologist can do is to allow himself a
few pages of highly personal critical rambling on Melville's *Moby-Dick* like the obbligato in some moderately
competent graduate paper in comparative literature, then
contemporary anthropology at the top of its form in the
field of ritual studies only just approaches the elementary condition of literary criticism, and it is that profession that should be seeking better approaches to literature rather than we looking to anthropology for something new.
     Turner digressed to contemplate the whiteness of
Melville's Moby-Dick because it suggested something of
more than merely African validity in the particular manifestations of African religion which he had chosen to
study. One may therefore agree with Turner to excuse the
digression on the grounds that the religion somehow required it. Yet a ritual life so fraught with belief in
preternatural and supernal persons and powers, and hence
so entangling to the sensitive anthropologist's own com-
mitments as the Ndembu is not everywhere typical of man-
kind. The steady expansion of ritual studies in modern
anthropology has, indeed, disclosed certain major cleav-
ages in *kinds* of ritual behavior in different ethnic
milieux. Much of it, like Robertson-Smith's or Victor
Turner's subjects, is gravid with religious belief, but

much also is not, or is only tangentially or associative-
ly so. Such ritual often involves important references
to belief, and although for that reason it is not always
strictly secular, it is nevertheless dominated rather by
motifs of *contest* or *gaming*. So, for example, the hoop-
and-pole gambling of the Apaches described by Morris
Opler, the Palio at Siena, the ancient Olympics, or modern Balinese cock-fighting as studied by Clifford Geertz
in his widely acclaimed article on that custom.[4] In such
ritual activity the element of contest or gaming is not
necessarily any more germane to the real referents of the
symbols manipulated in the rites than is the element of
belief in the more strictly religious kind of ritual. So
in both kinds of rite the burden of the evident symbolism
becomes the real object of scholarly investigation, no
matter how different the rites themselves may be. Geertz
on the Balinese sport of cock-fights consequently ends
his discussion in a posture indistinguishable to me from
that of Turner treating a Ndembu rite for the revelation
of deep religious mysteries:

> Enacted and reenacted, so far without end, the
> cockfight enables the Balinese, as read and re-
> read, *Macbeth* enables us, to see a dimension of
> his own subjectivity. As he watches fight after
> fight, with the active watching of an owner and a
> bettor (for cockfighting has no more interest as
> a pure spectator sport than croquet or dog rac-
> ing do), he grows familiar with it and what it
> has to say to him, much as the attentive listener
> to string quartets or the absorbed viewer of still
> life grows slowly more familiar with them in a way
> which opens his subjectivity to himself. (p. 28).

Thus Geertz and Turner alike hail ritual as works of art,
and finally achieve by their finest skills as anthropologists the attitude of novice literary and art critics.
And for the would-be critic of ritual, it must of course
follow from their own conclusions that because such
works of art as the rites and customs they study are ultimately only about ego, there can be no other explanation or interpretation of them than whatever ego elects
to think is right. All hail Descartes.

As I have already remarked, the ritual studies of
anthropologists have never greatly affected the humanities, though they have certainly attracted attention in

some quarters from time to time, especially when and if
those studies impinged somehow on the humanist's proper
province of mythology. Perhaps it was because in the end
anthropology would have little to offer humanism in that
field except a merger of its own highest theoretical
functions into literary criticism. This has been true at
least of anthropological studies on rituals of belief and
contests. But Claude Lévi-Strauss has been exceptional
because, in addition to the more obvious rituals of belief
and gaming, he has said there is a third major class of
rites. This third class one might call *rites of reasoning*, which according to Professor Lévi-Strauss include
all rites of primal myth-making, and hence the larger and
best part of the whole great, traditionally humanistic
field of mythology. Here was a claim humanism and anthropology would both have carefully to consider, and
which still intrigues and provokes them both. That the
proof of Lévi-Strauss's proposition is subjectivistic
none can well deny; even Clifford Geertz has called that
subjective kettle black. He wrote about his French colleague:

> He does not seek to understand symbolic forms
> in terms of how they function in concrete situ-
> ations to organize perceptions (meanings, emo-
> tions, concepts, attitudes); he seeks to under-
> stand them entirely in terms of their internal
> structure, *indépendent de tout sujet, de tout
> objet, et de toute contexte* ("Deep Play," p. 36).

He then uses the confession of an indiscrete moment to
finally defeat Lévi-Strauss' implied pretension to social
scientific objectivity:

> Today I sometimes wonder if I was not attracted
> to anthropology, however unwittingly, by a
> structural affinity between the civilizations
> which are its subject matter and my own thought
> processes. My intelligence is neolithic.
>   Claude Levi-Strauss, *Tristes Tropiques*[5]

If methodologically it can only return to a familiar
humanistic reliance upon the omnipotent wisdom of ego,
it may not matter much in theory whether Lévi-Strauss
has stolen myth for anthropology or not. Yet he has
raised the question in not merely an interesting way but

also in a vital way as to what the systematic relationship between myth and ritual actually is: whether at his
extreme they are really the same thing in alternative
forms, or whether it is still useful to keep some distinction between them, if indeed the diversity of ethnic
practices in the world will permit such generalization at
all.

Much of the confusion arises because most anthropologists are programmatically scholars of social organization and not artistic traditions, and because the cultural elaborations of myth and ritual everywhere occur
together at the *locus ethnographicus*, the location "in
the field" of the anthropologist's programmatic personal
trauma of concentrated exposure to alien ways. If myth
and rites are not the same things in different forms, it
is at least very easy to confound them since both are
obviously traditional in the consciousness of the anthropologist's subjects, and since both require to be
interpreted, not merely reported.

But at the minimum it seems to me that myth and
ritual present to the observer *in situ* two different
faces of tradition in every ethnic context I have been
able to learn about.

In any given place, for example, there is a right
way to be married, or christened, or initiated, or dis-
posed of after death, or healed, or to be conducted
through any other rite of passage. Differences in the
ritual procedures for these purposes correspond predict-
ably to other differences of a clearly utilitarian or
functional sort, whether of the ritual participant's
social class, the rite's perfection of performance, the
degree of symbolic transition meant to be accomplished
in the rite, and so forth. So too for games and contests; one plays "according to the rules," or institutes
some additional customary procedure for altering the
rules, and then plays by them. But contrastingly, narrative traditions in these same places will describe a
diversity of hypothetical rites, customs, and, more significantly, an even more extensive repertory of wholly
unreal or *fabulous* procedures and fictitious experiences,
some of which might work in a real world other than the
immediate one, but many also blatantly and instructively
quite incapable of ever being realized in any imaginable
real transformation of the ethnographic present. These
narratives especially bewilder the determinedly literal,
factually-minded observer, while subtly engaging the

mind of anyone, be he native or alien, who has the "imagination" to meet them on their own terms.

For my present purpose it will be useful explicitly
to recognize two senses of the polysemantic word "myth."

In the whole sum of a narrative tradition, only
certain tales are regarded by the influential or opinion-
making members of a community as stories of which all
mature and responsible people should be cognizant. So
among us, for example, despite the frequency of its incidence, the story of Strong John is in no sense compulsory
knowledge; but every properly educated man or woman
should know the story of Oedipus. Similarly the Garden
of Eden is mythic, but few remember the vineyard in the
fifth chapter of the biblical Book of Isaiah; there is
no compulsion to remember that vineyard, even though the
account of it is constantly reprinted and is among the
most accessible literature in our world. In this sense
Odysseus and Hamlet are mythic, but whether one likes it
or not, Tartuffe and Ulysses are not.

Typologically continuous with myths in that sense,
but always more numerous and varietal, the rest of a
narrative tradition in its totality may also be regarded
as the sum of the variants and multiforms of a more limited number of basic tale-types or narrative patterns
which, though embodied in a theoretically infinite number
of particular narrations, are themselves, however, relatively few in quantity. Thus one may never have heard
the story of Mally Whuppie from Aberdeenshire, but if
one knows the Cinderella tale, one still knows typologically all that he generally needs to know about Mally
Whuppie. These underlying typological schemes or structures of narrative tradition are also its myths in one
sense of the word, and arguably these too should be common knowledge among mature and responsible, or at least
educated, people, even if they know or can recall only a
tiny fraction of the individual narrations informed by
such "myth."

In this connection another irreducible and, I think,
very general distinction between myth and ritual comes to
the fore. The typology of rituals is locally and ethnically specific; rituals are idiosyncracies of the particular peoples to whom they distinctively belong. The
religious phenomena of shamanism, for instance, may have
been very widespread among the different peoples of central and north Asia, but no one would suggest that a
Buryat shamanic *séance* could under any circumstances be

substituted for its Chukchee counterpart in actual Chukchee practice. Contrastingly, the ability of oral narratives to cross language and ethnic frontiers, and to be
pandemic, universal, and largely interchangeable, is well
known.

A third, equally general difference between myth and
ritual as they have been seen in actual field-experience
concerns the nature of the links binding them to the
people who are their hosts. The more deeply one pene-
trates into the ideas enmeshed in the web of signification surrounding ritual symbols, the more local indoctrination and the more local data one needs to understand
what the ritual is about. Rituals are in this way typically esoteric in meaning, socially demanding of performers and onlookers alike, and expensive of economic
resources and energy. Myth on the other hand yields its
deeper layers of ideas the more one can appreciate its
independence of specific ethnic moments and the generality of its description of "how things are" in human experience anywhere. Professional anthropology's preoccupation with society to the contrary notwithstanding,
Professor Lévi-Strauss was right about that, and we must
perfect some scholarly method that will accord with that
fact, whether it be Lévi-Strauss's own or some other. In
keeping with that aspect of its character, myth unlike
ritual is typically undemanding of social support and
inexpensive of wealth and physical energy.

Synchronously regarded, ritual thus presents an aspect of tradition that is ideally fixed and in principle
invariable as to form, but also ethnically idiosyncratic,
and measurable as to its importance by the physical prominence and expense accorded it by its host people. Myth,
however, is varietal and multiform, independent of ethnic identity in its claim to truth, and measurable as to
its importance by the easy ubiquity and inexpensiveness
of its currency among its human hosts. Here, of course,
I speak of myth in my second sense, meaning the common
types, structures, or patterns, which, though they are
themselves relatively few in number, nevertheless inform
an endless succession of constantly self-renewing variants and multiforms of oral traditional narrative.

Viewed diachronously, however, these same two faces
of tradition take on aspects inversely different from
those they present to an observer at a given ethnographic moment. The fixed and theoretically unalterable
face of ritual cracks, crumbles, undergoes metamorphosis

or replacement, and in a few centuries or millennia
changes beyond recollection. Where are the rites of
Mithras or Eleusis, or even the holy mass as it once
was, not to speak of the American Indian Potlatch or the
rites of investiture for a Chinese emperor of the Han
dynasty? Ethnic identities fade, change, vanish, and
emerge anew, and their rites with them. But the face of
myth, seemingly so protean in its ambitus of form and expression at any given time and place, presents despite
its perpetual motility the same essential lineaments
wherever and whenever in history we glimpse it. On that
point Professor Lévi-Strauss is obscure, and on it will
stand or fall the inference that myth is only another
form of ritual.

     With its growing penchant for caudal—one hesitates
to call them terminal—excursions into literary criticism, backing into the humanities as it were tail first,
contemporary anthropology suggests that besides anthropological approaches to literature, a sober literary approach to anthropology might presently have fully as much
to offer as to receive from that discipline in some matters. Perhaps too ritual and religion are not the firm-
est of anthropological ground to support the combined
weight of so much two-way traffic between humanism and
social science. If anthropology and humanism truly have
something worth sharing with each other, I would prefer
to look for it nearer to the central, precise core of
anthropological discipline than religion and ritual studies seem to be, nearer to the heart that sustains that
apparently so set, but also so perishable, face of tradition that is ritual. And I would also shun the leaping
of such yawning chasms as that between the Balinese
cock-fight and *Macbeth*, or Chihamba and *Moby-Dick*, or
between the Bagre rites of the West African LoDagaa and
T. S. Eliot, to quote Jack Goody, another present-day
anthropologist with the same susceptibility to belle-
tristical analogies as Turner's and Geertz's.[6] To haz-
ard such great flights of subjective fancy as they do
over those chasms while ignoring the down-to-earth
abundance of local oral traditional story-telling right
at hand in their *loci ethnographici* among the Ndembu,
Balinese, and LoDagaa, where *real* parallels and mutually
explanatory cross-references between myth and ritual
ought objectively to be found, seems both reckless and
wasteful.

     I turn less daringly therefore to the fields of

kinship and oral tradition, the one anthropological and
the other humanistic in my conception of it, and to an
elementary question which I think opens up a real and
rather easy avenue of profitable commerce between the
two fields. My avenue—or perhaps less pretentiously I
should only call it my country lane—lies through the old
and yet recurring problem in anthropology of generalizing
a definition of human marriage. Upon definition of that
institution much depends, of course, for the whole understanding of kinship. Rethinking anthropology in 1961,
Edmund Leach reached the conclusion, which has not been
effectively challenged since then, that "all universal
definitions of marriage are vain" (Leach, p. 105). Borrowing a phrase from Sir Henry Maine, the father of
scholarship on oral traditions of law and jurisprudence
in Great Britain, Leach argued that the institution of
marriage in differently organized societies cannot be
more universally defined than as a "bundle of rights"
that comes into being between bride and bridegroom, and
through kinship with them, also among others in the
larger social fabric that contains them all. Although
Maine himself thought that the root of kinship was pa-
rental authority,[7] Leach reverses the priority and sees
the legal right of parenthood as springing from marriage,
together with such other rights in the variable "bundle"
of marital privilege as the right to monopolize or
otherwise wholly or partially to "own" a spouse's sexu-
ality, labor, property, benefits of affinal kinship beyond the spouse, and so forth. But, said Leach, "in no
single society can marriage serve to establish all these
types of right simultaneously; nor is there any of these
rights which is invariably established by marriage in
every known society" (Leach, p. 108). As an institution
at the base of social order everywhere, marriage thus
cannot be said to be any one thing to all men.

No doubt all this is good social science. Yet from
a humanistic point of view, it is also somehow obtusely
literal, as I feel sure Leach would not resent my saying. A more challenging and,I would think,more reward-
ing question than the obvious one about the capability
of all human marriages to submit to a single institutional definition would be whether there is any society anywhere that is actually organized exclusively upon the
principles empirically evident to an alien anthropological investigator of its working social institutions, or
rather upon the hopes and intentions which its members

repose in those institutions, or maybe better still, in
shared conceptions of those institutions of a more abstract and more perfect kind than the institutions themselves can ever be. Is it not so in regard even to the
variable bundle of rights which bride and bridegroom af-
ford each other and each other's kin in the institution
of marriage? And where might one look for empirical
evidence of that more perfect ideal beyond the practice
of actual marriages and the rituals of wedding that mark
their institutional inception? What rights in each
other do bride and bridegroom bring to each other *ideally*, and what generality or universality may attach to
such ideals?

In a paper which I read to the Folklore and Mythology Group at the University of California at Los Angeles
in 1977, I described as well as I can presently discern
it what in the eyes of oral narrative tradition a bridegroom is ideally expected to bring to marriage.[8] In the
space remaining here I shall consider the corresponding
facets of bridehood.

For a beginning, let me submit in evidence a piece
of oral narrative tradition which I have selected in an
utterly random fashion from the superabundance of pertinent material that I am aware of. It is the story of
"Mossycoat," a folk-tale from Lancashire collected in
January, 1955.[9] It represents a very common international type: *A mother spins a magic or "wishing" coat of
green moss and gold thread for her younger daughter, and
names the girl herself after it, "Mossycoat." The coat
bestows the power of translocation and bestioform shape-
shifting on its wearer, who has only to* assert *her will
to be anywhere or to become any animal she wishes.
While the mother spins, an itinerant hawker courts the
girl, giving her presents of a white satin dress with
decorations of gold, a silk dress of every color found
in the plumage of birds, and silver slippers. With this
trousseau, the girl wishes herself a hundred miles away,
leaving mother and the unsuccessful suitor behind for
ever.*

*She presents herself to the mistress of a fine
manor-house, saying she is a qualified cook. The mistress explains that she already has a good cook in her
employ, but will hire the girl as a cook's assistant.
Inferring that she is to be "under-cook," the girl
agrees. But when she appears in the kitchen to begin
work, the other women already in service there put her*

*solely to the meanest scullion-drudgery: "...soon she
was up to de ears in grease, and her face as black as
soot." This state of affairs persists for some time.*

*With the approach of a three-day festival and ball
in the shire, the mistress of the manor, who has noticed
how handsome a girl Mossycoat is, invites her to the
dance, but the girl refuses resolutely on the ground
that she has not the quality to be included in such
grand society as will attend the ball. She returns to
the kitchen, but boasts there of the splendid invitation
she has rejected, and her jealous workmates abuse her on
account of it. "Dat night, Mossycoat decided as she'd
go to de dance in right proper style, all on her own,
and wi' out nobody knowing it." She does, she dances
with the only son and heir of the master and mistress
of the very house where she is in service, and she capti-
vates the youth. He pines into sickness until her identity is discovered, then they marry. As for Mossycoat's
erstwhile fellows in the kitchen, "...de whole'n de kitchen sarvants was telt to go, and de dogs sent after 'em,
to drive de varmints right away from de place." The marriage is a success: "dey lived happy ever after, and had
a basketful o' children."*

Mossycoat attains and brings to her marriage four
general qualifications or equipments for bridehood.
Firstly, she is mistress of fabrics, the possessor and
sole female user of cloth and clothing which are in color
like the three seasons of winter, spring, and summer; she
both acquires and wears these things in the same sequence
as the seasons: first white satin laced with gold, then
silk of rainbow hues, i.e., "having the colour of all
birds," and finally the coat of "green moss and gold
thread." *Secondly*, Mossycoat is skilled in preparation
of food-substances, and qualified to be head-cook in a
grand manor even if that office is in fact already filled
by some other person who is perhaps equally as qualified
as she in cooking, although not perhaps so qualified in
all the other matters essential to a girl's achievement
of a perfect marriage. *Thirdly* (and in the most intimate
possible connection with her nutritive potential), Mossycoat learns to lustrate: to cleanse the filthiest of kitchen contaminations, to bathe herself, and to purge away
her rivals. These are all things of a kind which she and
she alone does in this rather plentifully populated tale.
Fourthly, she asserts and learns to assert her own will,
both in the use of her mossy coat which grants her the

power to be anywhere and do whatever she chooses if only
she will choose and will it so, and also in actively re-
solving to do for her own reasons what her social super-
iors offer her the opportunity to do for reasons separate
from her own. Her example in this regard teaches another
useful lesson: that the will to act in concert with the
policy of one's betters need not arise so much from any
great understanding or admiration of that policy, nor
from any specific ambition of one's own, but rather from
the general necessity in order to make the best of one's
own skills to escape the narrowing coercion of other less
able but nevertheless formidably organized people.

Although the details of her story are not interna-
tionally so commonplace as Mossycoat's, Mucketty Meg, the
girl of another Lancastrian traditional tale (*ibid.*, 481-
83), is also taught that a good marriage wants the exercise of her strong mind within a policy that serves larger and longer established interests than just her personal ones.

*"There was a pretty lass they called Jane, but she
was proud and greedy and very poor. She thought her
looks made a lady of her, and she wouldn't lift a finger
to sweep or dust or clean herself, or help on the farm,
or mind the sheep.*

*"She said they were dirty, and when they answered
her 'Dirty beast,' she didn't like it."*

*She has similarly uncomplimentary exchanges with
cows and pigs. Then she steals fine silk from the fairies and makes herself an elegant gown which she simply
puts on over her dirty rags without any ablution. The
fairies protest her larceny and her shabby pomp, and send
her to be hanged. She buys a stay of execution by lus-
trating herself in a river. Immediately pig, sheep, and
cow speak respectfully to her. She milks the cow, then
decides suddenly to run away home to avoid any further
to-do with the fairy folk. On the way she meets a young
farmer who is instantly smitten with her and asks on the
spot to marry her.*

From the first, Mucketty Meg resolutely goes where
and does, or does not do, what she will. Like Mossycat,
she also asserts rights of property and use in fancy and
magically potent fabric or cloth which she has not herself made. Thirdly, she lustrates, and fourthly (in direct consequence of her lustration), she prepares nourishment (milking the cow), which is however destined to
feed someone other than herself.

There is not space enough on this occasion fully to
explore the whole generality of this oral traditional
narrative pattern in all the many regions and localities
or among all the peoples where it evidently obtains.
Only because the types of their traditional tales are so
very unlike the tale-types of the Indo-European sphere
of cultural contact and influence, I turn now for a moment to a pair of stories collected just a few years ago
by a well-known anthropologist, Kenelm Burridge, from the
Tangu, an indigenous people of North-eastern New
Guinea.[10]   Both tales reflect on the nature of the institution of marriage.

The Tangu took delight in the chewing of areca-palm
nuts, a physically and socially stimulating activity not
unlike the social drinking, smoking, or chewing of other
vegetal substances more familiar to us in the West.
Sharing rights to and use of areca-nuts was patently
analogous to sharing the larger assets of marriage in
the Tangu view: *"Once upon a time long ago, the women of
the village went down to the stream to fish.   The men
stayed at home, chewing areca-nuts with ash.   Yet the
mixture of areca-nut and ash was not very appetizing.
And when the women returned to the village and started
to chew areca-nut with ash from their cooking fires,
their faces wrinkled in disgust.*

*On the morrow the men hunt and the women chew.   But
the women mix their nuts with lime rather than ashes
(the customary Tangu procedure), and thoroughly enjoy
themselves.   They conceal their gourd full of lime from
the men, however, and next day when again they go hunting
the men leave a boy behind hidden in the village to spy
out the women's secret of satisfactory nut-chewing.   That
evening the boy reports to them how he saw the women take
the lime-gourd from its place of concealment down to the
stream to make the lime, and how they then used it with
enjoyment in their chewing.*

*On the following day the women fish and the men re-
main in the village, where they take and use up the
women's câche of lime.   When the women return and learn
this, they are infuriated, but uncertain what to do about
it.   While they debate, the eldest of them spins a long
string of palm-fibre, and then throws one end of it high
in the air, where it remains suspended.   All but two of
the women then climb the string and disappear.   This is
why Tangu today never have women enough in their villages
for all the men, because in that village long ago only*

*the old crone who made the string and a single little
girl much too young to marry remained behind after the
general exodus of the women."(ibid., pp. 241-43).*

The concoction of an appetizing sauce for the areca-
nuts is a feminine achievement in this narrative; like
the Lancastrian English Mossycoat who is such a good
cook, or Mucketty Meg who milks for the consumption of
others, the Tangu women also excel in producing something
tasty, but it inures finally to others than themselves.
In the Tangu tale the preparation of the savory dish and
the act of washing are not just intimately proximate as
in the English tales, they are in fact the same act—that
of washing the lime at the stream (as compared with
Mossycoat's washing in the kitchen where she had expected
to cook, and the curious nonsequitur of Mucketty Meg's
milking the cow on the bank of the river where she has
just washed).

Next comes the old woman's manufacture of the palm-
fibre string, a fabric which the other, more nubile women
appropriate exclusively for their own use, however, even
though they had no more part in making it than did Mossycoat in weaving her namesake or Mucketty Meg in producing
the elven silk she stole for her tawdry gown. But once
they have it, the women display the resolute will to use
it to translate themselves physically, and by so doing,
also to metamorphose their social and kinship status. In
this narrative the very perfection simultaneously of all
the women's qualifications for marriage through these
four accomplishments is made to account for the short
supply of marriageable women in Tangu society.

Lest anyone suppose the correspondence in ideals of
married feminine competence as between this Tangu tale
and my two English examples (or the international tale-
types to which they belong) is merely coincidental, I
adduce one more of Burridge's Tangu stories. It tells
how *"once upon a time there were two villages. In the
first of these all the women had perished, leaving men
and boys only, and in the second there were no men or
boys, only women and girls."*

*The village of women holds a communal dance, a kind
of native ball. A youth in the men's village hears the
beating of their drums, and decides to go to their dance.
He labors for a day making himself a new breechclout,
then donning it and taking other ornaments with him in a
basket, he sets out toward the sound of the women's village.*

It is so far away, however, that he must travel all night, and does not arrive until dawn. By then the dance is over, and all the women have climbed the surrounding trees where they will sleep through the day in the form of unpicked, ripe areca-nuts. All the women, that is, except one grandmotherly old woman, who remains awake on the ground, being too old to dance or climb.

Tired, hungry, and disappointed, the youth turns to the old woman to learn where the other, invisible women are; but she puts a pot on the fire and invites him to rest and share a meal with her instead. Afterwards the crone suggests that the young man climb one of the areca-nut trees nearby, and "pick two small nuts. Don't pick the large ones—only two small ones. And be careful how you pick them. Take them eyes and all!" He does this, obeying her instructions carefully about the first nut, but the second he plucks incautiously and separates it from its eye.

Carrying these two nuts in his basket, the youth returns homeward through the woods. He comes to a stream of clear, cool water, where he removes his breechclout, folds it neatly, and places it atop his basket of nuts. He then goes nude into the water where he wades slowly upstream, washing away the soil and heat of his journey. (Burridge remarks that movement upstream is a common Tangu metaphor for maturation and creativity.) But this lustration occasions a remarkable change in his two nuts. Gay laughter rings out in the woods behind him, and when he returns toward his basket and breechclout on the bank, he finds two girls have taken possession of his breechclout and are using it as a sitting-mat. Crouching modestly behind a bush, he calls to them to get off his cloth and go away so that he may dress. They laughingly reply that if he wants it, he will have to come and get it as is. He does, and they do, and all is well with them except that one of the girls has only one eye due to the youth's careless picking of her from her native tree.

Thus happily married, the young man returns with his new wives to his own village. There he instructs another youth, a friend of his, in this procedure for marrying. The second youth exactly repeats the adventures of the first, except that he is more careful in plucking his nuts and so brings both his wives home unblemished. The sons and daughters of the two resultant lineages subsequently intermarry, and thus the institution of marriage arises anew where formerly it had died out. (*ibid.*, pp. 243-45).

The fabric in this tale, the two young men's new ceremonial breechclouts, is their own manufacture, but marriage comes only when the young women lay claim to it and use it for their own ends. As in the Lancastrian English myth, the purloined fabric is the instrument of the girls' translocation and social transformation from maids to wives. Secondly, their elder protectress, the old woman who remained on the ground in human form in the all-female village, prepares nourishment, but primarily for the benefit of another than herself and her female charges. But among the things she offers as nourishment are the areca-nuts, the brides-to-be, who, carried away in the young man's basket as provision for his future, are the very epitome of nutriment ready for the mouths of others than themselves.

None of the brides' four requisite qualifications or competences for marriage is sufficient in itself; the entire cluster of four elements is essential to the efficacy of each element severally. So in the present Tangu narrative, the emergence of a usable bride requires lustration. Only in conjunction with the act of cleansing can the girls assert themselves and by their willful determination catalyze their curiously lambent relationship with men and a larger society into the organized and durable institution of marriage.

If one now incorporates together with these four feminine preparations or competences for marriage the reciprocal four male virtues which I described in my previous paper—the demonstrated ability to provide and manage hewn wood and water, to kill, and to select or discriminate (i.e., to make wise and correct decisions of either/or, or "multiple choice"), one confronts I think an ideal institution of marriage of extremely wide currency among the peoples of the world to which bride and bridegroom contribute certain clearly delimited generic provisions for themselves, each other, and their respective kith and kin both present and future. The inherently complementary character of the provisions is self-evident, although there is no particular sequential order implied among the various elements. In the ideal sense, marriage is accordingly defined as the institution of spouses' reciprocal rights to the benefit of each other's qualifications in these specific matters:

FEMALE	*MALE*
1. Preparation of nutriments.	1. Control of hewn wood.
2. Lustration.	2. Control of water.
3. Fabric(ation).	3. Killing.
4. Assertion.	4. Decision.

Like the divergence in detail and form given differently to the myth of marriage in the English and Tangu traditions of oral narrative, other ethnic and regional traditions also present in sum an endless diversity of expression for a basically constant scheme. In dealing with the myth, one gazes upon an aspect or face of tradition that is constantly in motion and that constantly reaffirms by the very amplitude of its nominal divergences and local adaptations (as in Lancashire and New Guinea) the fixity and unchanging character of its central ideals. Thus the mythic face of tradition on the one hand; but on the other hand the local institutions of actual marriage and the rituals of wedding whereby it is entered into by real people. One may well concede to Edmund Leach that these myriad local, ethnically distinctive institutions of real flesh and blood are in any generally valid definition only a variable bundle of differently construed rights, by nature incapable of an uncompromised perfection in any actual social system. And whereas narrative tradition plays upon multiformity of expression to assert a central, unvarying ideal, the ritual of wedding tends rather to keep its singularity of form locally, and like the institution of marriage to display no great community of symbolism from people to people except that which it gets by the loan of imagery from the narrative tradition. In their nature, marriage and its liminal rites of wedding can only approach the realization of ideals as nearly as an individual's or a people's long- and short-term circumstances—their local formulas for compromise with life—will permit. Thus, in contemplating the social reality of wedding and marriage in any milieu, one looks upon a locally fixed and formally repetitive face of tradition—fixed because it represents a locally tried and proven adjustment between the ideal and the possible, fixed because it must be so as an established, workable model in imitation of which to shape the restive plastic of real experience as best one can.

Such an understanding of the relationship of myth to social institutions and their cognate rituals suggests a methodological conclusion too. The old allure of ritual studies to humanistic consideration of myth—the fundamental enticement to the humanist to try anthropological approaches to traditional literature at least—should perhaps be more resolutely acknowledged and our professional presence extended in that direction to include not only awareness of the conspicuous recent successes of anthropology in research on religion and ritual, but also basic competence in the stricter discipline of kinship studies that has been at the very kernel of anthropological science since its beginnings. For if a pair of minor oral fables from Lancashire or New Guinea can disclose something basic about the most basic of kinship institutions, one may reasonably inquire what mutual illumination to the humanities and to social science, to the science of kinship and the interpretation of literature, might come from examining kinship systems in national literatures. If Jane Austen, for instance, was (as her novels palpably are) much indebted to the premise of English kinship, may not an understanding of that kinship system that is not merely personal and subjective go far toward enhancing the objective value of the personal and subjective belletristic understanding and its academic interpretation? I leave the judgment of that potential to others, however; I myself can speak properly only in regard to oral traditions of narrative. In respect of them, the time I think has come for more and stricter attention to kith and kin.

Harvard University

NOTES

[1]*Rethinking Anthropology* (London, 1961), p. 1.
[2]*Revelation and Divination in Ndembu Ritual* (Ithaca, 1975), pp. 37-203.
       [3]*TLS*, no. 3872 (May 28, 1976), 653.
     [4]"Deep Play: Notes on the Balinese Cockfight," in *Myth, Symbol, and Culture* (New York, 1974), pp. 1-37.
     [5]Geertz, *The Interpretation of Cultures* (New York, 1973), p. 345.
     [6]Jack Goody, *The Myth of the Bagre* (Oxford, 1972), p. 4.
       [7]*Ancient Law* (1861; rpt. New York, 1972), p. 88.
     [8]:The Parry Test for Orality: Reason and Dogma."

[9] In Katherine M. Briggs, *A Dictionary of British Folk-Tales*, Pt. A, vol. 1 (Bloomington, 1970), 416-24.
[10] *Tangu Traditions* (Oxford, 1969).

FLYTING IN *BEOWULF* AND REBUKE IN *THE SONG OF BAGDAD*: THE QUESTION OF THEME

Francelia Clark

It is a noble paradox of scholarship that one benefits most from one's opposition. This paper and the
dissertation from which it comes attempt to refute Albert
B. Lord's application of the theory of the oral-formulaic
theme to *Beowulf*. But not only does it take its inception and vitality from Lord's work, it owes its existence
to his intellectual generosity. He encouraged me to go
ahead.

In *The Singer of Tales* as I read it there were two
overlapping and compatible conceptions of the term
"theme." One was that themes are "groups of ideas regularly used in telling a tale in the formulaic style of
traditional song" (p. 68). The second, which emerged primarily through discussions, was that themes are also recurring scenes (p. 71). These conceptions were solidly
grounded in Serbo-Croatian epic, recorded from oral performance and closely observed. One of the epics most
frequently cited was *The Song of Bagdad* sung by Salih
Ugljanin. It was in *Singer* too that Lord first published his application of the oral theory to *Beowulf*,
of unknown origin.

The two conceptions of the theme tended to split
distinctively in the Old English studies that followed.
First, certain patterns of ideas were identified by the
name of the *central idea*, such as "The Traveler Recognizes his Goal." Second, large visual scenes were
identified, such as the sea voyage, which are now frequently called *type-scenes*. [1]

Then in 1974 in "Perspectives on Recent Work on
Oral Literature," Lord brought to wider attention this
very specific definition of the oral-formulaic, or
"compositional," theme in comparative literatures:

> The theme as *subject* alone is too general for our
> very special purposes. But if by theme one means
> a repeated narrative element together with its
> verbal expression, that portion of a poem, an ag-
> gregate of specific verses, that tells a certain
> repeated part of the narrative, measurable in

terms of lines and even words and word combinations, then we find ourselves dealing with elements of a truly oral traditional narrative
style....[2]

This newer definition gives us a clear basis with which
to return to the discussion of *The Singer of Tales*. Now
what about *Beowulf*? To ground the definition we need to
see the contexts. We need to examine a theme in *The
Song of Bagdad* and apply its principles to an equivalent
entity in *Beowulf*. Of the several potentially shared
themes, the most intrinsically interesting surrounds a
personal insult.

Each of these epics contains a noticeable double
structure of statements which controvert; the statements are made by two characters about the same situation and culminate in personal insults. They are both
forms of dispute in the weakened sense of exhibiting
difference of opinion. In *Beowulf* this dispute is the
telling and retelling of a story. Here it is technically a flyting, "an extended and vigorous verbal exchange,"
mutual abuse in verse. The Scandinavian tradition of
the flyting, which contains these characteristics, has
been examined by Joseph Harris.[3]

The dispute in *The Song of Bagdad* can also be seen
as a flyting.[4] It is in the form of two letters. In
the first letter, the hero Alija asks his betrothed,
the heroine Fatima, for her permission to go to war. In
the second letter, Fatima challenges Alija's bravery
because he has asked her permission. The prominent distinction in kind between it and the *Beowulf* flyting is
that here only one letter carries insults. In the first
letter, Alija is soberly asking a question. All of the
insult and argumentation rests with Fatima's reply.
Thus the pair can most suitably be seen as a statement
and a rebuke. Finally, is this double structure an
oral-formulaic theme in *The Song of Bagdad*? There is
no question, I think, that it shows a theme.[5] It fits
Lord's definitions in *The Singer of Tales* as well as in
"Perspectives."

There is a secondary level of comparison between
the flyting and the rebuke. In both we can observe
something about the intent of the poets. (I am referring to both artists as poets, however much they may
inherit their traditions.) Both poets intend to show
difference of opinion; both create a war of words with

a winner.   In both epics the disputes contain repetitions in form, contradictions in content, and irony.

The present study makes its primary comparisons
only within the recurring subjects or scenes of an epic.
Thus the tables do not show a formula count, nor are the
markings based on the epic as a whole.   My operating
question is: When the poet rebuilds a subject, what
does he use from the original?   Thus, each table is
marked as identically as possible to show two things:
first, words significantly bearing the narrative, which
recur in the dispute.[6]   (These are underlined, and
half-lines which recur are double-underlined.)   Second,
each shows ideas recurring in the dispute.   (The dotted
bracket marks recurrent general ideas as identified by
the critic, and the solid bracket marks recurrent
specific ideas as expressed in the narrative.)

Table 1 shows the pair of letters from *The Song of
Bagdad*.[7]   The bracketed, recurring ideas in this table
are of two sources.   The first source of ideas is the
matching part of the disputing letter.   These ideas are
the address, and "wait" and "protect" in sequence.   Recurring sequence of ideas is a major method of construction in *The Song of Bagdad*.   Here the two specific ideas
are only a suggestion of the use of sequence.   Other recurrent scenes, such as ones showing the giving and following of advice, may be constructed by as many as
fifteen specific ideas in a sequence followed virtually
line by line.[8]

The second source of recurring ideas is a subject
that appears throughout the epic, and also recurs within
each of these letters.   This subject is marked Leitmotif
A and B.   It is Alija's call to war, the reason for the
correspondence, and also the basic problem which generates the epic.   It is told and retold in three fixed
parts of a story, A, B, and C, each of which is only a
few lines long.   It recurs; it is so frequent and so
perfectly repetitious that I identify it as a "leitmotif," in the Wagnerian sense of "a short figure of
melody . . . of marked character, used to illustrate
situations, personages, objects and ideas essential in
a story or drama to which music forms a counterpart."[9]
In *The Song of Bagdad*, the short figure of marked character is a poetic phrasing, and it accompanies the re-
appearance of an idea.

Leitmotif A, "The Futile Attack," gives the previous history of the war.   Only echoed here in Fatima's

Song, Table 1

Alija

318	"E, ću lj' me, Budimka Fatimo!	address from
	Ho' lj' me s hrzom pričekat', đevojko,	Leitmotif B wait
320	Da devljetu sljegnem u hizmetu	
	Da bijemo bijela Bagdata?	Leitmotif B
	Sa mnom vojske stotinu hiljada.	
	More biti tamo poginuti.	
	Znamo koljko u Bagdat će biti,	
325	Al' će mlogo alj' odviše malo.	
	Da lj' me moreš s hrzom pričekati?	wait
	Da lj' se moreš sa Budima branit?	protect
328	Hoću lj' caru ju hizmet otići?"	Leitmotif B

Song, Table 1

Fatima

Line	Text	Annotation
376	"Ej! Gazijo Đerđelez Alijijo!	address from Leitmotif B
	A što pitaš Budimku Fatimu?	
	Aj, devljetu sljegni u hizmetu!	Leitmotif B
	Ti pokupi Bosnu cip cijelu!	
380	Sljegni z Bosnom caru jod indata,	
	Pa prifati bijela Bagdata!	
	Fata će te s hrzom pričekati.	wait
	Da me skolju do tri kraljevine,	
	Braniću se sa Budima grada,	protect (Leitmotif A)
385	Niti odbit' vara od duvara,	
	A deljatim Budim prifatiti.	
	A ne boj' se, careva gazijo!	
	Ako ne šće tako juraditi,	
	Spremi mene kanalji dorata,	insult (I)
390	A spremi mi sablju dimiškinju,	
	A spremi mi siljah i oruže,	
	I spremi mi tvojega dorata!	

Fatima (Contd.)

Ja ću caru Bosnu pokupiti,
I devljetu od indata sići,
395 Z božom pomoj prifatit' Bagdata.   } Leitmotif B

Ja ću tebe đerđef opremiti,
Spremit' đerđef i kudelju moju,   } insult (II)
398 Pa ti predi s majkom u odaju!"

Song, Table 1

Alija

318 "Now, hear me, Fatima of Budim!   — address from
       Leitmotif B
Would you wait for me with honor, maiden,   — wait
320 As I go in force in service to the empire
As we attack white Bagdad?   Leitmotif B
With me an army of a hundred thousand men.
It may be that I shall die there.
We know how many men will be at Bagdad,
325 But not whether they will be too many or too few.
Could you wait for me with honor?   — wait
Could you defend yourself in Budim?   — protect
328 Should I go off to the emperor in service?"   Leitmotif B

Song, Table 1

Fatima

376 Ah! Hero, Ðerðelez Alija! | | address from |
And why do you ask Fatima of Budim? | | Leitmotif B |
Surely, go in force in service to the empire! | | |
You gather all Bosnia! | | |
380 With Bosnia go in force as a help to the emperor, | | Leitmotif B |
And then take white Bagdad! | | |
Fatima will wait for you with honor. | | wait |
Though the three kingdoms surround me, | | |
I shall defend myself in the city of Budim. | | |
385 They will not even chip off mortar from the walls, | | protect |
Not to speak of taking Budim. | | (Leitmotif A) |
And do not fear, emperor's hero! | | |
If you would not do thus, | | |
Send to me your blood-bay horse,* | | insult (I) |
390 And send me your Damascene saber, | | |
And send me your belt and weapons, | | |
And send me your bay horse! | | |

Fatima (Contd.)

I shall gather Bosnia for the emperor
And go as a help to the empire,
395 With God's aid to take Bagdad.   } Leitmotif B
I shall send my embroidery frame to you,
Send you my embroidery frame and my distaff,
398 And then you spin with your mother in her chamber!   } insult (II)

---

*Lord's note to this description shows his research on the possibility of "blood" as part of the color of the horse, *S-CHS*, p. 335, n. 11. I have taken the liberty to add "blood-," therefore, to represent the word *kanalji*.

reply, it appears in the epic six times in total. Leitmotif B is the most frequent grouping of ideas in the
epic, "Alija Gathers an Army." Shown here in a full
form three times, it appears in the epic in total twenty-
six times.[10] Each appearance of it draws on the same
fund of about six ideas. As Lord has pointed out, there
is no perfect form for a theme. Leitmotif B appears
cast as commands, explanations, and conditionals ("I
would go to war, but . . ."). This exchange of letters
contains it in a first-person question. Here it is at
lines 320-22, following "would you wait":

> . . . As I go in force in service to the empire
> As we attack white Bagdad?
> With me an army of a hundred thousand men.

And here, for comparison, is Fatima's first reply using
it at lines 378-81:

> Surely, go in force in service to the empire!
> You gather all Bosnia!
> With Bosnia go in force as a help to the emperor,
> And then take white Bagdad!

Fatima's references to Bosnia, though not heard in
Alija's letter, are present because the poet is building
these lines from the whole fund of the leitmotif.

In *The Singer of Tales* Lord identified this kind of
passage as a "cluster" of repeated lines and discussed
it under formulas. But these passages are also groupings of ideas, self-contained discrete subjects, recurrent subjects indeed. Lord's newer definition of the
theme includes them. "When we find a passage used over
and over again, we know it to be a theme, in the very
technical sense applicable only to oral literature"
("Perspectives," p. 21). Thus we have, appropriately
from what we have learned in *The Singer of Tales*, a
theme called "Alija Gathers an Army" inhabiting another
dimension of theme, an exchange of letters. As one cannot hear the letters in context without recognizing the
leitmotifs, the markings of the leitmotifs in this table
are made from the whole fund of them. These two kinds of
themes habitually merge in *The Song of Bagdad*: the leitmotif appears in a letter which conveys it.

How does the poet Salih Ugljanin set up the dispute? His technique is most characteristically to

reverse the personal pronouns, and thus reverse the referents of the ideas in the second letter. The statements remain almost identical in form. In the larger
sense he most noticeably places versions of Leitmotif B
in a corresponding order so that they answer each other.

Specifically, the first line in each letter is a
direct address, the second half-line of which holds the
recipient's name. This one-line direct address is the
standard opening of letters in a group, and also a
standard introduction to Leitmotif B. The second line,
or idea, in each letter gets to two different respective
points swiftly. Fatima's question, "And why do you ask
Fatima of Budim?" immediately tells us that something is
wrong. The third line, or idea, in each letter begins
to use Leitmotif B as was quoted above. Alija's line
320 begins "shall I go in force . . .?"; Fatima's same
line, 378, begins "Surely, go in force. . . ." It is
a substitution of *Aj* for *Da*. And so the leitmotif continues. In fact, the same exhortative form is used by
Alija's mother, indistinguishable from Fatima's form,
ninety-five lines earlier. At the same time this exhortative form here can be seen as beginning to work to
the advantage of characterization. Fatima's very fullness—her three exclamations, three commands—suggest an
answer of intensity.

Alija's next three contemplative lines (323-25) are
unique within this epic and fitting to a candid letter
about his future. Then his line 326 repeats his own
question of line 319, but makes a change of the auxiliary verb from *Ho' lj'* to *Da lj' moreš* that can be seen
as one toward intimacy and feelings. His line 327 expands the question to "Could you protect yourself?" So
far the effect of so many querying lines has given us
the feeling that the hero is overcautious, but the actual
queries have been whether Fatima is up to her task.
Finally, Alija's last line, 328, summarizes his letter
with the words of Leitmotif B once more: "Should I go
off to the emperor in service?" The effect of this last
line is apparently more than just a summary; with *Hoću
lji* it closes his letter in a doubtful tone, subtly making him seem progressively more uncertain. Now he is
asking her if *he* should go. Thus by shifting of tenses
and enclitics in familiar half-lines, the poet re-uses
the same distribution of the same vocabulary, yet
changes the effect upon the audience. One can question
here whether this oral performance would have the effect

on a listening audience that we can hypothesize by looking at it. The answer is: it has an effect upon
Fatima.[11]

The reaction of Fatima grows in this way. The poet
casts two of Alija's lines identically into her affirma-
tive, "wait" and "protect." But by adding line 326 he
makes Fatima's answer "Though the three kingdoms surround me / I will defend myself in the city of Budim."
It is the equivalent of "come hell or high water," and
the critic, and presumably the audience, begins to suspect that Fatima is more powerful and determined than
Alija thinks she is. This suspicion is confirmed by the
use of the fragment from Leitmotif A, lines 385-86.
Verbally, the adaptation is simple, and the recurring
phrases can be seen as *clichés*. But they can also be
seen fruitfully as an example of recurrence used for
special effect in oral composition, wherein the idea
receives a new irony. Elsewhere line 385, "They will
not even chip off mortar from the walls," repeatedly refers to the heroes attacking Bagdad. It means "how
futile is our attack." Here it refers to enemies attacking Fatima: it means "how impregnable is my for-
tress." With it Fatima shows willpower as well as military power. Two familiar lines from another context
have given the requested reassurance with unexpected
force. This letter is our first meeting with Fatima.
Every action she takes will bear out the promise here.
I submit that characterization is being shown with the
slightest changes in blocks of words and lines.

Fatima's last twelve lines are devoted to a new
idea and an open insult. She leads off with line 387,
"Do not fear, emperor's hero!" Do not be afraid? Is
this an idiom or an insult? We cannot be sure. The
singer and his audience would know which way it is intended. Immediately following this surprise is an extended ironic bargain. "If you will not go, send me
your equipment," she offers. Lines 389-92 are a repetitive construction depending upon the first-lines "Send
to me"; the second half-lines are words new only in
this context. They are a standard part of brief descriptions of armor elsewhere in the poem. The audience
does know this list of the battlegear of a hero and, by
this recognition, the irony of sending it to Fatima is
the keener.[12]

Lines 393-95 return again precisely to Leitmotif B.
Verbally, Fatima's irony enters here simply by the

first-person emphasis *Ja ću* (393). Ideationally, irony
enters by the placement of this block. The inference of
the block of details now becomes how completely the
maiden threatens to take over the hero's mission. It
appears to be another manipulation of the standard leitmotif for special effect. The total effect of the three
full passages from Leitmotif B reminds us of the refrain
of a song. Moreover, it is the effect of the recurring
fixed chorus of a progressing ballad, such as *Lord
Randall*. The intervening information has changed the
impact of the same set of words when the set reappears.

Finally, Fatima increases her emphasis on her own
abilities by a new "insult II": now she will send Alija
her womanly handicrafts so that he can embroider at
home with his mother. It is a humorous and devastating
ending. Verbally, it shows a repetitive construction by
Lord's concept of linking of phrases, and from another
viewpoint, by a clustering of nouns similar to those of
the first insult. Ideationally it is a reciprocal
second half of her insult, a kind of doubling of the
point.

Considering the ideas in total, Fatima's answer introduces one wholly new idea, "I will trade," which generates lines 387-98. This new idea will itself be reported in full, verbatim, by Alija to his mother within
thirty lines. That is, the section most original within
this rebuke will be brought under the custom of repetition at the next opportunity.

In summary, a count of all the echoing whole lines
in these two letters shows that seventeen of the thirty-
four total lines are built upon verbal duplication of
each other.[13] That is, half of the lines differ from
one another in words only by changes of pronouns or verb
tenses. Thus in idea they are simply direct reversal.
All the while, even the very directness and number of
pronouns can indicate intensity and through it characterization. The last doubtful line of Alija's letter
and the last outrageous line of Fatima's letter are
dramatic codas well beyond mere question and answer. An
equally impressive aspect of the poet's craft is that he
appears to manipulate standard ideas to evoke irony.
Fatima's adaptations of them in her anger give them new
connotations. Her use of the two lists of equipment is
an achievement in sarcasm.

There is no verbal or narrative complexity in the
dispute in *The Song of Bagdad*. It asks one basic ques-

tion and answers it dramatically. Yet the rebuke is
enormously effective. This sample shows a glimpse of an
art based on repetition. As Lord has pointed out, we
literate-oriented researchers have much to get used to
here. This art celebrates repetition on every level—
word, idea, scene. This is the discipline that features
seven nearly identical letters of invitation told in
full, the arrival of six heroes in six nearly identical
scenes of fifteen to thirty lines each, and a leitmotif
used twenty-six times. It is an art built on sameness:
its surprises and changes take place in the slight modifications of the sameness upon which the audience depends. Thus the rebuke is masterful. Here we discover
hesitancy in Alija and insubordination in Fatima.
Through it we seem to have the rare chance to observe a
self-consciousness of the poet as he works with this art
of repetition.

Table 2 shows the flyting from *Beowulf*.[14] Unferth's
speech is compared with most of Beowulf's long answer.
Space has necessitated omitting the undersea battle.
Here brackets mark ideas of three kinds: dispute, elements of the story that both men tell, and the rhetorical form of the whole speech.
First, the right-hand brackets show that another
kind of structure appears in this flyting—a structure
of rhetoric. In its larger shape each man's speech
breaks into distinct rhetorical divisions:

> an address
> an insult
> a story
> the significance of the story in the past
> a conclusion for the present

This common rhetorical form of the two speeches suggests
a whole dimension of formality and fixed delivery for
this flyting. It is not the form of classical public
argument, and it is not the form of the flyting in the
Nibelungenlied. It is not the form of Loki's flyting in
the *Lokasenna*. Since this study restricts itself to two
epics, it can only ask whether there may have been a
contemporary form for the *Beowulf* flyting; but it assumes
simply that, analogous to Fatima's answer to Alija, the
commentary upon Unferth's form determines Beowulf's
form.

Beowulf, Table 2

Unferth

Text	dispute	narrative elements	rhetorical form
506 'Eart þū sē Bēowulf, sē þe wið Brecan wunne,	A— understatement		address
on sīdne sǣ ymb sund flite,			
ðǣr git for wlence wada cunnedon	B you bragged		insult
ond for dolgilpe on dēop wæter	risked		
510 aldrum nēþdon? Nē inc ǣnig mon,			
nē lēof nē lāð, belēan mihte			
sorhfullne sīð, þā git on sund rēon;	C swim;		
þǣr git ēagorstrēam earmum þehton,	irony	preparations and summary	
mǣton merestrǣta, mundum brugdon,			
515 glidon ofer gārsecg; geofon ȳþum wēol,			
wintrys wylm[um]. Git on wæteres ǣht	D elements,	struggle, water, nights	story
seofon niht swuncon; hē þē æt sunde oferflāt,	irony		
hæfde māre mægen. Þā hine on morgentīd	E he was stronger	morning and landing	
on Heaþo-Rǣmes holm up ætbær;			
520 ðonon hē gesōhte swǣsne ēþel,		peace, ties, future	
lēof his lēodum, lond Brondinga,	[you lack these]		
freoðoburh fægere, þǣr hē folc āhte,			
burh ond bēagas. Bēot eal wið þē			
sunu Bēanstānes sōðe gelǣste.	F you failed contest		significance
525 Ðonne wēne ic tō þē wyrsan geþingea,			
ðēah þū heaðorǣsa gehwǣr dohte,	G your		conclusions for present
grimre gūðe, gif þū Grendles dearst	bodes defeat		
nihtlongne fyrst nēan bīdan.'			

Beowulf, Table 2

Beowulf	dispute	narrative elements	rhetorical form
530 'Hwæt, þū worn fela, wine mīn *Unferð*	A' understatement		} address
bēore druncen ymb Brecan sprǣce,			
sægdest from his sīðe! Sōð ic talige,	E' I was stronger		} insult
þæt ic merestrengo māran āhte,			
earfeþo on ȳþum, ðonne ǣnig ōþer man.			
535 Wit þæt gecwǣdon cnihtwesende	B' we vowed, risked	preparations and summary	
ond gebēotedon — wǣron bēgen þā gīt			
on geogoðfēore — þæt wit on gārsecg ūt			} story
aldrum nēðdon, ond þæt geæfndon swā.			
Hæfdon swurd nacod, þā wit on sund reōn,	C' swim, preparation		
540 heard on handa; wit unc wið hronfixas			
werian þōhton. Nō hē wiht fram mē	E' I was stronger		
flōdȳþum feor flēotan meahte,			
hraþor on holme, nō ic fram him wolde.			
Ðā wit ætsomne on sǣ wǣron			
545 fīf nihta fyrst, oþ þæt unc flōd tōdrāf,	D' the elements, challenge	struggle, water, nights	
wado weallende, wedera cealdost,			
nīpende niht, ond norþanwind			
heaðogrim ondhwearf; hrēo wǣron ȳþa.			
. . . [undersea battle] . . .			

significance

conclusions for present

[morning] landing

F' you and Breca fail to compare to me

[your ties, future]

G' Grendel is your defeat

G' my victory

morning, peace, ties, future

Ðā mec sǣ oþbær,

580 flōd æfter faroðe   on Finna land,
wadu weallendu.   Nō ic wiht fram þē
swylcra searoniða   secgan hȳrde,
billa brōgan.   Breca nǣfre gīt
æt heaðolāce,   nē gehwæþer incer,
585 swā dēorlīce   dǣd gefremede
fāgum sweordum   — nō ic þæs [fela] gylpe —,
þēah ðū þīnum brōðrum   tō banan wurde,
hēafodmǣgum;   þæs þū in helle scealt
werhðo drēogan,   þēah þīn wit duge.
590 Secge ic þē tō sōðe,   sunu Ecglāfes,
þæt nǣfre Gre[n]del swā fela   gryra gefremede,
atol ǣglǣca   ealdre þīnum,
hȳnðo on Heorote,   gif þīn hige wǣre,
sefa swā searogrim,   swā þū self talast;
595 ac hē hafað onfunden,   þæt hē þā fǣhðe ne þearf,
atole ecgþræce   ēower lēode
swīðe onsittan,   Sige-Scyldinga;
nymeð nȳdbāde,   nǣnegum ārað
lēode Deniga,   ac hē lust wigeð,
600 swefeð and snēdeþ,*   secce ne wēneþ
tō Gār-Denum.   Ac ic him Gēata sceal
eafoð ond ellen   ungeāra nū,
gūþe gebēodan.   Gǣþ eft sē þe mōt
tō medo mōdig,   siþþan morgenlēoht
605 ofer ylda bearn   ōþres dōgores,
sunne sweglwered   sūþan scīneð!'

* Emended in Klaeber from the original *snēdeþ*.

Beowulf, Table 2

Unferth

	Unferth	dispute	narrative elements	rhetorical form
506	"Are you that Beowulf, he who struggled with Breca	A understatement		address
	on the broad sea, contended about swimming;			
	where you two for pride tempted the waters			
	and for foolish bragging on deep water	B you bragged, risked		insult
510	you risked your lives? Nor might any man,			
	neither loved nor loathed, dissuade you from			
	the sorrowful journey, that you two swam on the sea;	C swim, irony	preparations and summary	
	there you enfolded the sea-stream with arms,			
	you measured the sea-road, you swung with hands,			
515	you glided over neptune; the ocean welled with waves,	D the elements, irony	struggle, waters, nights	story
	with winter's wellings. You two in the water's power			
	toiled seven nights; he overcame you at swimming,	E he was stronger		
	he had more main. Then in the morning		morning, landing	
	the water bore him up onto Ronerike;			
520	From there he sought his own dear homeland,		peace, ties, future	
	loved by his people, land of the Brondings,			
	fair fortification where he possessed folk,	[you lack these]		
	stronghold, and rings. The boast against you entirely			significance
	the son of Beanstan in truth fulfilled.	F you failed contest		
525	Therefore I for you expect worse things	G bodes your defeat		conclusions for present
	though you were strong everywhere in combat-rushes,			
	in grim war, if you for Grendel dare			
	to wait near at hand for a nightlong time."			

Beowulf, Table 2

Beowulf	dispute	narrative elements	rhetorical form
530 "Lo, very many things you, my friend Unferth, drunk with beer, have spoken about Breca, have said about his journey! The truth I maintain,	A' under-statement		} address
that I had more sea-strength, hardships on the waves, than any other man.	E' I was was stronger		} insult
535 We two agreed, being boys, and boasted — we were both then yet in our youth-period — that we two on neptune outward would risk our lives, and that we carried out so.	B' we vowed, risked		
We had naked swords, when we two swam on the sea,		preparations and summary	
540 hard in our hands; we two against whales thought to protect ourselves. Never he one whit from me	C' swim, preparation		} story
far in the flood-waves could float, more quickly on the water, nor would I from him.	E' I was stronger		
Then we two in company were on the sea			
545 five nights' time, until the flood drove us apart, the welling waters, coldest of weathers, darkening night, and the northwind	D' the elements, challenge	struggle, water, nights	
548 combat-grim, turned against us; savage were the waves. . . . . . [undersea battle]			

```
                    ... Then the sea bore me off,
580 flood according to the current onto the land of the Finns,
    the welling waters.  I never one whit about you
    heard say of such contests,
    horrors of swords.  Breca never yet
    at combat-sport, nor either of you two,
585 accomplished such a brave deed
    with variegated swords — I never brag of this much —
    though you became the slayer of your brothers,
    of near relatives; for this you shall in hell
    suffer damnation, though your wit be strong.
590 Say I to you in truth, son of Ecglaf,
    that never would Grendel have accomplished so many terrors,
    the horrid fighter, against your prince,
    humiliations in Heorot, if your spirit were
    a heart as armor-grim as you yourself maintain;
595 but he has discovered that there in feud he has no need,
    through a horrid blade-storm from your people,
    to dread very much the Victory-Scyldings;
    he takes enforced toll, he shows mercy to none of them,
    to the people of the Danes, but he feels joy,
600 puts to sleep and sends away; he does not expect a conflict
    from the Spear-Danes.  But I shall offer him Geatish - - -
    strength and courage before long now,
    at war.  Again he who may will go
    high-spirited to the mead, when the morning light
    of another day over the sons of men,
    the sun clothed in radiance, shines from the South!"
```

Marginal annotations:

[morning] landing

F' you and Breca fail to compare to me } significance

[your ties, future]

G' Grendel is your defeat } conclusions for present

G' my victory } morning, peace, ties, future

Next let us turn to the relation of words to levels
of ideas. Verbally the table shows a frequency of repeated words and half-lines that is high for a pair of
scenes in the *Beowulf* poem. A check of correspondence
of words to ideas yields a range of patterns. At one
extreme, some of the words of Beowulf's answer seem to
echo without significant correlation of ideas, such as
garsecg for ocean (lines 515, 537). At the other extreme, no words seem to echo in some of the important
recurring ideas of the second speech, such as "peace"
and "future." But most words relate tangentially.

To get at the relation, let us look at the insult.
At A and A', *þu* and the opponent's name, a noticeable
recurrence of form marked by the dotted underline, introduce a personal insult through a direct address
which becomes an understatement. By understatement here
I refer to "Are you that Beowulf. . .?" when Unferth
intends no doubt at all, and "Many things you have
spoken about Breca," when neither man is concerned with
Breca here. The insults themselves, B and B', are generally about the relationship between boasting and
reality; they are wholly different in grammar and
specific idea. They do share the quality of irony: both
imply the insult before openly stating it. Unferth suggests moral judgment through *wunne, flite,* and *wlence,*
but it is *dolgilpe* ("foolish bragging") at line 509 that
openly claims that Beowulf is a charlatan. Beowulf's
ironic references to Breca and drunkenness become a firm
claim that Unferth is a liar at line 532 with the words
sōð ic talige ("the truth I maintain"). The flags *þu*
and proper names have alerted us to a rhetorical relationship, and then have started two freely different
ironic ideas. The whole basis of the insult has changed:
Unferth's insult was on Beowulf's past boast. Beowulf's
insult is that Unferth's present insult is a lie. Now
he must prove it by the story, which will be about a
different conception of boasting. It will use *gebēotedon*
and *gecwǣdon* as terms of honor.

But before we look at the story, we should follow
what happens to the conception of boasting and its relationship to truth at the end of the flyting, in points
of dispute F and F' and G and G'. "Breca won his boast"
(*bēot*) is Unferth's idea at line 523b, referring back to
their original boast, making a different point. "I never
brag of this much" (*gylpe*), says Beowulf parenthetically
at line 586 while devastating Breca's reputation in con-

trast to his own. Finally, in G', Beowulf transforms
the idea, but not the word, of the empty boast to apply
to Unferth himself. *Sōð* and *talast* echo as he begins
his withering disclosure: "*in truth* . . . never would
Grendel have accomplished so many . . . humiliations in
Heorot, if your spirit were . . . as armor-grim as *you*
yourself *maintain*." So is a representative idea displayed verbally, and then transformed.

The story is changed by Beowulf's points of dispute,
which are made notably on the verbal level. The clearest and most telling of these changes are well known:
the change from *dolgilpe* to *gebēotedon*, boasted in the
sense of vowed, that establishes a partnership; the distinction between "he could not swim away from me, nor
would I from him" that establishes Beowulf's superior-
ity.[15] There is still room, I think, to focus on two
points of comparison to *The Song of Bagdad*.

1. *The isolated words*. The verbal echoes which
suggest contradiction almost never make an exact contradiction. One example is the opposition between seven
nights and five nights in lines 517 and 545. The contexts at D and D' change both the use and the basis of
the claims. Unferth is showing the extent of the boys'
foolishness; Beowulf is showing the extent of the boys'
strength, but only before they were separated. By the
implied contradiction we may be reminded that only his
version of the details is authentic. The audience seems
to hear a point-for-point refutation, in passing. Another implied contradiction is in the two stories of
landing after the storm, *Heaþo-Ræmes* at line 519 and
Finna land at 580. With the echoes *Ða mec* and *bær* and
a different country, Beowulf only implies that Unferth's
story is wrong. Again the tangential contradiction has
the effect, but not the letter, of discrediting Unferth's story point for point.

—Re-use of words, but for something other than a
direct contradiction? What is the principle here? The
principle appears to be a rhetorical strategy: "Turn
your opponent's words to your own favor." The strategy
appears to affect the vocabulary of the second speech.
Not in method, but in principle, it can be seen as
analogous to what Salih has done in Fatima's reply.

2. *The recurring half-lines*. Half-lines recurring
across the speeches show a significant change of context. The first recurring half-line, *aldrum neþdon*
("risked lives"), is at B and B' in that area where

Beowulf changes the "brag" to an agreement. At Unferth's line 510 it is the climax, the substantiation
that the boys were senseless. At Beowulf's line 538 it
has become part of the boys' vow, a calculation. The
second recurring half-line, *þā git on sund rēon* ("that
you two swam on the sea") makes the same kind of transformation. In C, Unferth's use of it is embedded in
open sarcasm. From the oral theory we have learned
that his preceding phrase *sorhfullne sīð* ("sorrowful
journey"), as used in this poem, connotes death: Grendel
and Grendel's mother took sorrowful journeys.[16] His
succeeding lines are derisive, and famous, words showing
the boys enfolding, measuring, swinging at the ocean.
They are also an extraordinary use of the Old English
variation to show irony. In his own sentence carrying
þā wit on sund rēon at C', Beowulf answers with this
picture: "we had naked swords, when we two swam on the
sea, hard in our hands." The hands that we just saw
swinging foolishly are now prepared with swords. Beowulf's authority of tone and detail seem to continually
remind the audience that only he was there. The passage
has no grammatical parallels beyond the one phrase. At
the level of the half-line there is no direct contradiction. There is a whole opposing idea. These half-lines
appear to be markers of ideational distinctions being
made, a working part of the war with words.[17]

But what about the recurring half-lines that seem
to have no significance? As far as I can see, the repetition of *Nō hē wiht fram mē* (lines 541, 581) has no
special significance: it is simply a recurrent phrase
building a different idea. So is *wado weallende* simply
a recurrent phrase building a different idea at lines
546 and 581. These two pairs recur only vertically,
that is, within Beowulf's speech, and are in context
separated by the undersea battle. These are the ones
that are typical of half-line recurrence in the poem.[18]
This pattern would reinforce the suggestion that the
poet was consciously reusing his phrases across the
flyting in order to make distinctions. But whether or
not he was doing this, the result across the flyting,
the changes of context of half-lines and the indirect
contradictions of words, remains.

Another way to learn about the construction of this
flyting is to look at the order of the parts. The order
within the large rhetorical form is the same. And the
order of the parts of the told story are essentially the

same. But the ordering within the points of dispute differs. Then we see that the relative focus on the points
also differs. After Unferth claims that Beowulf was
foolish at B, the insult, he moves into the story. It
is here that he exaggerates the picture of the two boys
swimming at C. C becomes his major focus. Having built
this derisive picture, at D Unferth intensifies it by
reference to the power of the ocean, and at E he makes
the clear climactic point: Breca won, "he had more
main."

The *Beowulf* speech by contrast jumps directly from
the insult at A to contradict Unferth's conclusion with
E'. It is the single direct contradiction of the flyting: "I had more sea-strength. . . ." Even this phrase,
however, is linked within the sentence to Beowulf's own
version of the story and his next major point: *earfeþo*
("hardships"). Beowulf's story then moves through the
vow at B', the preparation at C', and the explicitly
different confirmation of his strength at E'. E' is important, and it has been used twice, differently. Then
at D' Beowulf turns to his own flourish of variations.
It is the awesome power of an ocean storm (lines 546-
48), and he describes it only after he has reversed the
conception of what the contest really was. It begins to
involve us in his own main focus: details of the challenge of the undersea battle, the fact that by winning
it he made the sea safe for mariners. Thus Beowulf has
changed the effect of the story by attacking the conclusion, rearranging, and refocusing from swimming to
challenge. Hereby he has changed the image of himself
on the whole, though it is not explicitly verbalized,
from unsuitable to meet Grendel to precisely suitable
to meet Grendel.

More should be said about the transformation of
ideas—those of the adversaries' references to each
other and to Grendel, those of their indirect references
to each other's ability to achieve peace, ties, and
future happiness. In this last, Unferth's verbal weapon
that Breca's story ended happily becomes, after two negative uses, Beowulf's forecast of the happy ending he
will provide, in his own conclusion. In a word, there
is verbal and narrative complexity there.

But the poet's method is clear enough. He changes
the ideas. It is not easy to match the disputed points
A-G with the points A'-G'. The ideas are strikingly
freely rendered. But when they are aligned in a direct

comparison, they are stunning. It is the very changes
of the ideas that give this flyting its drama. The underlying concepts of boasting, strength, hardship, and
peace—these echo yet change, both across the arguments
and vertically within the arguments. Meanwhile the recurring vocabulary, which is relatively dense, may not
match, yet sometimes multiply matches the development
of the ideas. Contradictions are tangential. Contexts
change. Parts of the dispute are never openly stated.
The relationships of words and verses to ideas, and
ideas to each other, do not resemble those of *The Song
of Bagdad*. In *Song*, the repeated phrase is the repeated
idea. The reverse grammar is the reversed idea.

These observations in part lend themselves to statistical tabulation. In the thirty-four lines of the
letters of *The Song of Bagdad*, the percentage of repetitious whole lines including the leitmotif patterns is
26.5%. The percentage of repetition in the unit of composition, the half-line, is 47%. In method of construction, the rebuke is an emblem of those recurrent sections
which constitute about half of the epic. In percentage
of repetitions too it is emblematic: fourteen comparisons of recurrent scenes in *Song* show an average of
42.4% half-line repetition.[19]

Beowulf too is generally considered to be built of
half-line units of composition. Within the seventy-two
lines shown here of the *Beowulf* flyting, eight half-
lines, or 6%, are repetitious. This percentage is a
little over twice as high as the average percentage of
half-line repetition in fourteen comparisons of recurring scenes in *Beowulf*. That average is 2.7% half-line
repetition.[20] This higher than average percentage could
account for the reader's sense that in the flyting the
poet shows Beowulf manipulating Unferth's words.

The statistics give one more viewpoint on what is
appreciable. Those recurring half-lines in *Beowulf* do
not suffice as the method of composing the scene. They
do suffice as the method in *The Song of Bagdad*. Whatever determines the scattering of recurring words in
Beowulf, it is not the system of fixity of words to line
to idea that it is in *Song*. Lord continues in "Perspectives": "Themes are useful as an aid in composition because they can be employed in more than one place in a
song or in more than one song, and because the singer
has a ready-made form for them" (pp. 206-207). This
describes what we have seen in *The Song of Bagdad*. It

does not describe what we have seen in *Beowulf*. In light of Lord's definition of 1974, then, the oral-formulaic or compositional theme is a striking entity in *The Song of Bagdad*. It does not appear in *Beowulf*.

The theory does not fit. But it does lead us to new discoveries about *Beowulf*, and about artistic creation. For instance, here is what working with the oral theory uncovers as common devices in these two unrelated disputes:

1. *Set-up*. Immediately after the address, both poets show plainly in the answering speech that there is a dispute, and then proceed with their development.

2. *Vocabulary*. Both poets use vocabulary from the first speech to gain effect as they build the answering speech.

3. *Main idea twice*. Both poets use a main idea twice but differently within the answer to gain effect.

4. *Contradiction*. Both use direct contradiction and change of context. Once a contradiction in *Beowulf* can be seen as that exact reversal which appears throughout *Song*. Once a clear change of context appears in *Song*, though it is of a different order than those throughout *Beowulf*.

5. *Both may use an epithet ironically*: consider in context "Do not fear, emperor's hero!" and "he has no need . . . to dread very much the Victory-Scyldings."

6. On a *structural level*, both poets connect winning the dispute with saving the nation.
Are these then traditional elements in some disputes? They may be. They invite further connections.

The oral theory is expanding to show us that oral literatures are composed on different principles, that Serbo-Croatian epic is *a* model but not *the* model. If these two epics are both orally composed, *Beowulf* follows some other model. There are other oral models that show repetition analogous to that in *The Song of Bagdad*. Is there an oral model that is analogous to the *Beowulf* flyting? Is the *Beowulf* flyting oral traditional? We can see that tradition is in it. But can we see that tradition accounts for it?[21]

University of Michigan

NOTES

[1]The scholarship on the oral-formulaic theme is re-
viewed and this distinction is observed by Donald K. Fry
in "Old English Formulaic Themes and Type-Scenes,"
Neophil, 52(1968), 48-54. The scholarship is later re-
viewed by John Miles Foley in the Introduction to this
volume. A briefer summary may be found in Alain Renoir,
"Oral Theme and Written Texts," *NM*, 77(1976), 337-38.
The ideational theme cited is in George Clark, "The
Traveler Recognizes His Goal: A Theme in Anglo-Saxon
Poetry," *JEGP*, 64(1965), 645-59. For type-scenes, and
sea voyages as type-scenes, see especially Fry, 52; and
Lee Carter Ramsey, "The Sea Voyages in *Beowulf*," *NM*, 72
(1971), 51-59.

[2]In *OLSE*, p. 20, quoting from an unpublished paper,
"The Marks of an Oral Style and Their Significance,"
read at meetings of the International Comparative Literature Association, Belgrade, 1967.

[3]The definition quoted is from C. Hugh Holman, *A
Handbook to Literature*, 3rd ed. (Indianapolis, 1972).
On the *senna* and flyting, see Joseph Harris, "The *senna*:
From Description to Literary Theory,", *MGS*, 5(1979).

[4]"Scolding, rebuking. . ." (*Oxford English Dictionary*).

[5]Though it could also be seen as two parts of a
larger theme of the recurring letter; and Fatima's proposed bargain within it could also be joined with
Alija's repetition of that part to his mother. This rebuke might best be said to inclusively *represent* a
theme in *The Song of Bagdad*.

[6]In both languages the varying inflections are included in the conception of repetition. But in *Beowulf*
words of the same root but different parts of speech
are also counted, simply because they appear—e.g., *bēot*,
lines 523 and 536; *wēol*, lines 515 and 546. In the
passages from *The Song of Bagdad*, this question of root
forms does not occur: recurrent words appear as recurrent parts of speech.

[7]The text in Table I is from *S-CHS*, I, no. 1. My
translation is primarily an adaptation of Lord's translation in *S-CHS*, no. 1, to as literal a form as possible. For accuracy in changes, I am indebted to Gena
Fine and James O. Ferrell; errors are my own.

[8]See, e.g., *S-CHS*, II, no. 1, lines 1100-15 and
1118-31. For the general principle of recurring

sequence, see also lines 45-52 and 59-66 (advice opposed); 154-58 and 161-65 (directions followed); 238-46 and 285-90 (permission granted); 312-30, 331-34, 335-39, 340-63 (advice followed); 498-511 and 512-26 (feasting plan followed). This principle is discussed as the "sequential plan" in my "Theme in *Beowulf* and in the Oral Epic *The Song of Bagdad*," unpub. Ph.D. diss. (University of Michigan, 1978), espec. Chapter 1.

[9] *Grove's Dictionary of Music and Musicians*, 5th ed., ed. by Eric Blom (New York, 1960).

[10] These and other leitmotifs are cited in "Theme in *Beowulf*," tables 6, 10, and 22.

[11] An evidence that the passage may not characterize Alija is that the letter was dictated by his mother. Among the evidences that it does are the similar characterizations of him in the testing scenes before the sultan, especially in comparison to Fatima. See, in *S-CHS*, II, no. 1, lines 927-86; and lines 1297-1348 and 1391-1410.

[12] *Ibid.*, lines 940, 947, 951-52, and 1041-42, for example. At line 392 of Table 1 (above), the bay horse seems to be simply an extra rendition of the idea in line 389.

One can ask the same order of question here as that weighed in note 11. An evidence that Fatima's recurrent phrases are simply *clichés* is their use in other epics, e.g., *Halil Hrnjičić and Miloš the Highwayman*, lines 242-44, sung by Alija Fjuljanin, no. 31 in *S-CHS*. An evidence that the singer does show characterization through small changes are the humorous descriptions of Tale Budalin in comparison to other heroes, e.g., *The Song of Bagdad*, lines 528-655.

[13] They are lines 318-21, 326-28, 376, 378-82, 383, and 393-95.

[14] The text in Table 2 (below) is taken from Fr. Klaeber, *Beowulf and the Fight at Finnsburg*, 3rd ed. with 1st and 2nd suppls. (Boston, rpt. 1968). The translation is my own, with consultation from Sherman M. Kuhn; errors are my own.

Recurrent words and a single perfect grammatical substitution appear by the narrator in the introductory lines "Unferð maþelode. . ." and "Bēowulf maþelode. . ." (499,529), not included in this table. These relate equally to the other *maþelode* lines in the poem, which introduce, but are not included in, major speeches.

[15] As, for instance, in Arthur G. Brodeur, *The Art*

of Beowulf (Berkeley, rpt. 1971), pp. 142-57, espec. p. 143.   The distinction on boasting I owe to Sherman M. Kuhn.

[16] See Paul B. Taylor, "Themes of Death in *Beowulf*," in *OEP*, pp. 249-74.

[17] Another pair of half-lines, nearly repetitive, for which there is not room in the table, appear to have this same significant relationship; they are 518b and 565a.

[18] Other exceptional half-lines would appear to be those used negatively, approaching litotes, such as 1463b, "næs þæt forma sið. . . ."

[19] "Theme in *Beowulf*," pp. 607-610.

[20] *Ibid.*   In these percentages for *Beowulf* scenes, I am essentially reinforced by Ann C. Watts' observation that "over 400 verses (6%) are substantially repeated within the poem" (*The Lyre and the Harp* [New Haven, 1969], p. 101).   There is a potential equation here, a relationship of recurrent verses within scenes to those of the whole.

[21] During the discussion period after delivery of a shortened form of this paper at Kalamazoo, Professor Lord made the following comments, which I paraphrase here.

a. The definition of the theme in *The Singer of Tales* does include the statement that the theme is "verbal."   I agreed with his comment.

b. The larger context of Serbo-Croatian oral epic provides a different and sounder explanation for my hypotheses.   "Do not fear, emperor's hero" is not ironic, but a standard reassurance, here referring to the danger that General Lauš will capture Fatima.   Furthermore, Fatima is not being "original," nor is she disputing, nor even essentially "putting down," Alija; her passage is a stereotyped response.   My reply was to agree on the first example.   On whether Fatima's response is insulting, however, I countered that when Alija returns to his mother he says of this letter, "Shame!   Fatima has upbraided me!"   Subsequently in conversation, Professor Lord made the distinction that Fatima's letter is a *stereotyped ironic* response.

c. Whether or not there may be themes in *Beowulf*, these two *Beowulf* passages do not constitute a potential theme.   Only Beowulf himself tells a story.   I disagreed, offering from Table 2 that Unferth tells a narrative of preparations, struggle, the coming of morning, and the conclusion that Breca won, which is then retold. Professor Lord suggested that only these portions constitute a potential theme, and shortness of time prevented further discussion.

"THE *BEOWULF*-POET: MASTER OF SOUND-PATTERNING"*

Robert P. Creed

My working hypothesis in my studies of *Beowulf* is
this: the poem that has come down to us in Cotton
Vitellius A. XV[1] is a copy of a recording of a performance. The recording was made at a time when the traditional technique of singing tales was alive and vigorous. The composing, as opposed to the recording, of
what we call *Beowulf* depended in no way upon the use of
writing.

I began to think about *Beowulf* in this way a long
time ago, in time, as it turned out, to contribute in a
small way to the work of my mentor, Professor Francis
Peabody Magoun, Jr., whose "Oral-Formulaic Character of
Anglo-Saxon Narrative Poetry" appeared in *Speculum* just
twenty-five years ago.[2] Several years before that Professor Magoun had introduced his classes in Old English
poetry to the work of Milman Parry and to the person and
presentations of his colleague, Albert Lord. On several
occasions Professor Lord had brought some of his wire
recordings of Yugoslavian *guslari* to Magoun's classes;
it was hearing these recordings as much as reading
Parry's articles and Lord's recently completed dissertation that took me to the path I have since followed.
Since it is my lot to be the last speaker in the present
series,[3] I take this opportunity to name and celebrate
these guides.

I have found other guides along the way. Avdo
Medjedović, with whose performances I am acquainted
through my own slow working out of the transcribed text
in Professor Lord's fourth volume of the great series
(*S-CHS*, vol. 4; hereafter *Ženidba*), has taught me to
have confidence in the existence and importance of sound-
patterning. And finally, my paper today is a preliminary
report on my attempts to apply to *Beowulf* the tests for
traditional oral style as reformulated and added to by
Berkley Peabody.

Peabody's study of the Homeric-Hesiodic oral tradition in *The Winged Word* is a systematic approach to the
study of techniques of composition when words are *heard*,
not seen, *sounded*, not written. For us, this situation
suggests *loss*: for us, words are heard and then gone,
unless we write them down. But, Peabody relentlessly

forces us to ask, is our way of apprehending the situation that of traditional, of *aural* societies? Does speaking mean *loss* to these societies, or does it instead mean exactly the opposite: *keeping*? To speak in some memorable way in a traditional society means to keep, to conserve. What Parry, Lord, and Peabody do, what they teach us to do, is to study the records of past and present speakings in order to learn from them the techniques by which these speakings have been kept.

I have already suggested the first point I want to make about Peabody's approach to the study of oral traditions: that approach is *systematic* in two senses. Peabody perceives the traditions as homeostatic systems (*TWW*, p. 58), and he has devised a systematic method for studying these systems. The immense importance of these two points has been brought home to me by the discovery that I can characterize the meter of *Beowulf* as a system and can devise systematic ways of studying that metrical system.[4] But I am anticipating Peabody's first test for orality.

(1) The *phonemic test* requires consistency in the patterns of language-sounds used by a singer; this consistency should not only be present in a singer's own compositions, it should also appear in compositions of related provenance. This test examines redundancy in the use of sounds in a text. In oral styles, more redundancy is to be expected than in ordinary discourse; and it takes such forms as rhyme, alliteration, assonance, and much that is usually described as meter. The applicability of this test is limited by the phonetic accuracy of written texts, for writing systems (except those used by professional descriptive linguists) regularize the sounds of utterance to a considerable degree. While the sound patterns of many non-traditional compositions are unselfconsciously regular, the phonemic test immediately excludes any text that plays irregularly or quixotically with sound. (*TWW*, p. 3).

There is a regularity about what we call the lines of *Beowulf*. Every line is marked by the recurrence of a simple pattern: a HEAVY stress is succeeded by a *lighter* stress; then the pattern is repeated. The line emerges from this repeated pattern through the sensing of

isochroneity and a dominant alliteration. This is alliteration on stressed syllables: we sense at least two,
often three, more rarely four alliterations in the
measured flow, and sense that the line is complete when
the dominant alliteration has ended. There is little
or no irregularity in *Beowulf* at this level. There is a
great consistency at this level between *Beowulf* and
nearly every surviving Old English poem.

Other patterns can be heard in the flow of sound.
Assonance and rhyme occur and die away, not regularly,
but neither, I think, quixotically. These features create patterns, sometimes within the line, sometimes
through a series of lines. There is, for example, a
pattern of assonance in the first eight half-lines of
the exemplar text, that is, lines 1802b-6.[5] The assonance of the long *eo* diphthong within the last half-line
of this set, 1806b—*ceoles neosan*—reminds us that we
have heard sounded both the long and the short versions
of this diphthong in this brief passage: the long *eo* is
the end of 1804, *leodum*, and the short *eo* (+ *r*) are
placed at identical points in 1802b and 1805b. I shall
have more to say about the significance of this particular pattern when I get to Peabody's third test. But now
I want to comment upon two other patterns.

Line 1812 begins with the four-fold repetition of *e*,
long and short: *meces ecge*. The line ends with what I
hear as a *rhyme* with the second stress of the line:
þæt wæs *modig secg*. Another rhyme is contained *within*
the second half-line of 1813: *searwum gearwe*. And *then*
as we listen to the flow of sound our ears may catch another pattern: *searwum gearwe wigend wæron*. The *w*-sound
that appears in the final syllable of both words in line
1813 becomes the dominant alliteration of the next line.
The poet is a master of sound-patterning.[6]

Lest any Anglo-Saxonist think that such mastery is a
matter of sitting in a cell and working out with the aid
of stylus or pen a pattern of assonance or consonance or
rhyme, I quote a passage from Avdo Medjedović, whom no
one can accuse of literacy:

Sad nećemo begstvo preturati,
I u Stambol tebe opravljati,   990
No je emer doš'o od sultana,
U Budimu uštugli veziru;
Tu je ferman carski sa emerom;
Kad se šćene begstvo preturati, ... (*Ženidba*, 989-94)[7]

The first *preturati*, in 989, introduces a passage in
which the command, the *begstvo*, is to be passed on to
Mehmed by means of a decree, *emer*, from the Sultan in
Stambol. The next *preturati*, in 994, introduces a new
passage with other echoes of 989: *Kad* echoes *Sad* followed
by the further echo of *e*-sounds in the first colon, and
of course *begstvo* at the beginning of the second. But
what most delights my ear is the way in which the *emer*
gets from the Sultan to Mehmed: it is, I think, borne on
a pattern of *u*-sounds beginning with the very lightly
stressed *u* in *sultana*, 991, moving to the heavily
stressed *U*—which by the way means *to*—in 982, through a
succession of five more *u*'s in this line, to the trium-
phant *Tu* (*here!*) in the next line.

    This is not an unusual passage in Avdo Medjedović's
great performance. But then we have long heard of such
dazzling sound-play from reading Professor Lord's *The
Singer of Tales*. The trouble is—I speak for myself—
Lord's quotation and brilliant analysis of, for example,
the search for *Alija* (*Singer*, pp. 54-57), did not mean
nearly so much to me until I began to try to sound out
Avdo's *Ženidba* for myself. I read it haltingly, but
perhaps for that reason I find myself paying close attention to each sound. I have come to realize that Avdo
Medjedović, an illiterate peasant, was a great master of
sound-patterning. I celebrate his memory by thanking
him for teaching me to listen to *Beowulf* with a more re-
sponsive ear.

    As I listen and begin to catch patterns and then,
poor disadvantaged literate that I am, work them out on
paper, I find myself wondering why so many of my colleagues feel it necessary to imagine the *Beowulf*-poet as
a *writer*. Why is it necessary to think of one who was a
master of sound-patterning working *silently*—or mumbling
at most—over his wax tablets or parchment? The answer,
of course, is that this way of working is comfortably
familiar to us. It does not seem possible to us, on the
other hand, that anyone can *keep track* of an *eo*-run or
find the absolutely right association of sound and sense
over and over again *unless* we imagine him working out
these patterns with some sort of notation. But what an
inhibition notation would prove to be! And all this
fails to reckon with Avdo Medjedović and Salih Ugljanin
and the scores of masters of sound-patterning Milman
Parry and Albert Lord have begun to introduce us to.

    There are four more tests of traditional orality

proposed by Peabody. We all know the next one too well.
As Peabody says, we have paid too much attention to the
formulaic test. Nevertheless Peabody's formulation of
that test is worth attention:

(2) The *formulaic test* requires consistency in the pat-
    terns of word-forms used by a singer; this consist-
    ency should not only be present in a singer's own
    compositions, it should also appear in compositions
    of related provenance. This test examines the
    structure and distribution of morphemic clusters
    in a text. In oral styles, the frequent repetition
    of phrases is to be expected. Since Parry's day,
    the concept of formula has undergone more change
    and development than any other in the study of oral
    literature. It should be made very clear at this
    point that formula is a quantitative category of
    repeated morphemic clusters. To argue that two
    particular formulas (which may seem interchangeable
    to us) "mean" the same thing, and that therefore there
    are two different ways to say only one thing, is to
    create a confusion between morphemic and semantic
    aspects of language that causes endless difficul-
    ties and explains nothing. (*TWW*, p. 3).

In his third chapter, "The Form of Words," Peabody discusses composition by *cola* in the Greek epos. *Cola*
(singular *colon*) are "groups of closely associated syllables" (*TWW*, p. 70) that occur between "points of decision in the compositional process" (*TWW*, p. 349).
There are usually four *cola* in each of Homer's and
Hesiod's lines. A particular *colon* tends to occur in a
particular position in the line. Such "localization"
has been much studied in the Greek epos but not in Old
English poetry. Instead, then, of pointing out what is
obviously formula[8] or formulaic in the exemplary passage, I shall make only one observation about localization, choosing forms of inflected æþeling-, that is,
æþeling in the genitive and dative cases in the singular
and all cases in the plural.[9]
    A first glance at the seventeen instances of un-
compounded æþeling- in Bessinger and Smith's *A Concordance to Beowulf*[10] suggests little localization if any at
all. There are three instances in the *first* measure of
their lines, nine instances in the *second*, four in the
third, and one in the *fourth*. Apparently the Anglo-Saxon

poet has complete freedom to place inflected *æþeling*-
anywhere in his line he wishes to.

Yet a closer look reveals that two and possibly all
three *first*-measure instances of *æþeling*- are in the genitive case followed by the word, *bearn*. The four *third*
measure instances are these:

æþelinges	fær	33
æþelinga	gedriht	118
æþelinga	bearn	1408
æþelinga	gest[reon]	1920

All of the instances of inflected *æþeling*- in the *first*
and *third* measures are, then, in the *genitive*.

But not all instances of the genitive appear in the
odd measures. The remaining instances are all to be
found in the second measure of their lines:

hraðe heo æþelinga anne hæfde	1294
þ hig þæs æðelinges eft ne wendon	1596
feorh æþelinges flæsce [b]ewunden	2424

Before I can comment on the position of *æþelinga/*
æðelinges in lines 1294 and 1596, I must list the remaining instances of inflected *æþeling*- in *Beowulf*. Three
are in the dative:

eallum æþellingum to aldorceare.	906
ofer [æþ]elinge ýþgesene	1244
æt ðā æðelinge [æn]ige ðinga	2374

Four are in the nominative plural:

hu ða æþelingas elle[n] fremedon.	3
siþðan æþelingas eorles cræfte	982
[wæron] æþelingas eft to leodum	1804
idel hweorfan sýðða æðelingas	2888

All but one of these seven instances occupy the *second*
measure of the line. The usual position of inflected
æþeling-, then, seems to be the second measure. On the
other hand, the poet can employ the *set-phrase* consisting of *æþelinges/æþelinga* + noun to fill either half-
line. In other words, the poet uses the genitive forms
+ noun as *set-phrases*, but *not* the genitive + pronoun or
without a noun, and not other cases of the word. On the

evidence of inflected æþeling- it seems worth pursuing
the question of the localization of words and phrases
in the Old English poetic line.

Peabody's formulation of the third test for orality
is as follows:

(3) The *enjambment test* requires consistency in the patterns of syntactic periods used by a singer; this
consistency should not only be present in a singer's
own compositions, it should also appear in compositions of related provenance. This test examines the
complexity of syntactic periods in a text and the
frequency with which these periods extend across
metrical line breaks. In oral styles, such extensions are not expected to occur frequently; those
that do are often syntactically unessential. This
test is the simplest and most precisely defined of
the set; it is also the most neglected. The significance of the structure and organization characteristic of syntactic periods in oral styles has
not been adequately appreciated. (*TWW*, p. 4).

This test may in some sense be "the simplest of the
set," but that is not to say that it is simple. Peabody's fourth chapter, "The Extension of the Clause,"
the chapter that deals with this test, does not simply
present statistics about what he calls unessential and
essential enjambment. That chapter does nothing less
than lay the foundations for the construction of an
oral/aural grammar of the early Greek tradition.[11] It
seems to me, then, that, in order to apply this test to
Beowulf, one must try to do something similar for the
Old English tradition.

Early in Chapter Four Peabody distinguishes between
"clause" and "sentence," a distinction that will prove
useful in analyzing *Beowulf*: "By 'clause' is intended
'a syntactically closed period,' a quantum of structure.
By 'sentence' is intended 'a semantically closed period,'
a quantum of sense" (*TWW*, p. 118). I illustrate this
distinction with line 1819 in the exemplar text. The
last two words in that line, *we fundiaþ*, I take to be
a syntactically closed period. *we* is the entire noun
phrase at the left node under the domination of S;
fundiaþ is the entire verb phrase at the right node under the domination of S.[12] This clause ends with the
line break. We can demonstrate the completeness of this

clause by comparing[13] it first with *Beowulf* 1137—

> . . . fæger foldan bearm fundode wrecca   *Bwf* 1137
> gist of geardum he to gȳrnwræce . . .

—and then with *Seafarer*, line 47:

> ac he hafað longunge se þe on lagu fundað   *Sfr* 47;

we fundiaþ is, then, "a quantum of structure."

To this already complete clause the poet adds the first half-line of the next line: *higelac secan*. By using the infinitive *secan*, he can syntactically hook onto *fundiaþ* a specifying phrase. The *sentence*, then, consists of 1819b *plus* 1820a. The sentence, but *not* the clause, shows enjambment. Parry would have designated this enjambment *unperiodic*[14]; Peabody prefers to call it *unessential* (*TWW*, p. 4 and pp. 141–43). Whatever it is called, it is an example of the way in which the *Beowulf*-poet constructs his passages.

The *Beowulf*-poet now finds himself in midline with syntax and sense complete. Since his thought works by contrasts as well as similarities, and since he has just spoken of Hygelac over *there* in Geatland, he begins a new clause by speaking of things *here*, in Denmark. And this time he does *not* complete the clause at the line break, even though every other time he uses the last word in this line, *tela*, he uses it to close both line and clause.[15] So he produces the clause, *wæron her tela / willum bewende*, a clause that appears to be co-extensive with his sentence. Since the clause moves from midline to midline, it is an instance of Peabody's *essential* enjambment.

Again the poet finds himself in midline. This time he finishes the line with a half-line clause that is also a semantically closed period.

The final half-line in this passage does something else: it rounds off and defines a *stanza*. The stanza begins at line 1818 with the beginning of Beowulf's speech. The final word in that line hints that the stanza will play with the sounds of *w* and *l*, but we cannot appreciate these hints until we hear first *tela* in 1820 and then both *willum* and *wel* in 1821.

Let me say at this point that I did not expect to hear a stanza nor have I forced the passage into the stanzaic mold. I confess that I began to look, or rather

listen, for stanzas under the influence of Peabody, who
comments wisely on stanza-hunting: "The present study
sees the stanza neither as a Procrustean bed of prescriptive form, nor as an intentional form, but as a structural reflex generated by regular human behavior and subject
to variations in that behavior, which are in themselves
significant" (*TWW*, pp. 414-15, note 73). With this wise
caution in our minds, let us return to some of the sound
patterns that turned up earlier. Some while back I
noted that that last word in line 1804, with its long *eo*
diphthong, is twice echoed in 1806b. There is in these
lines, I think, a structuring of sound similar to that
in lines 1818-21: a pattern is stated late in the first
line of a passage, stated subtly within the passage, and
then stated twice at what thus comes to be the end of
the passage. In these two instances the final statement
ends at the line break.

A somewhat different structuring seems to govern
lines 1813-16. In this stanza, the pattern of assonance
(*searwum gearwe*) is stated first but not repeated, until
we go on to *bearn* in 1817. This stanza seems to me to
get under way *physically* with its second half-line: the
siðfrome begin to *march* with *searwum gearwe wigend
wæron*. With the long and short *eo* diphthongs of the
next half-line, *Eode weorð denum*, we hearken back to the
eo stanza that ended with 1806. We *should* hearken back
to that earlier stanza, since this one continues the
march that began with *eft to leodum* and *ceoles neosan*.
The present stanza comes to a halt with the series of
r's and *g*'s, and the final repeated *t* in *hroðgar grette*.

These are the sounds and movements we must learn to
listen for before we begin to compile statistics about
enjambment in *Beowulf*. Those statistics are likely to
show a high incidence of essential enjambment, even
higher than the 28.5% Parry found in the *Odyssey* (*MHV*,
p. 254). Parry's figures for the *Odyssey* are already
twice as high as the percentage Lord has determined
from 2400 lines of *guslar* poetry, 14.9% (*Singer*, p. 54).
What these different percentages show is what John Foley
has reminded us of: different traditions, even traditions within the Indo-European family, have had different developments.[16]

Peabody's fourth test is this:

(4) The *thematic test* requires consistency in the pat-
     terns of lexical clumps used by a singer; this

consistency should not only be present in a singer's own compositions, it should also appear in compositions of related provenance. This test examines the associations and attractions among lexical elements that organize paragraphs or sections in a text. In oral styles, similar lexical clumps can be expected to appear in separate contexts and compositions. Perhaps because many investigations important for thematic analysis have been made by scholars in nonlinguistic fields (folklore, religion, psychology, and so forth), more confusion has arisen between them and "idea" than between formula and "meaning." More work is needed to control theme as precisely as formula; but if this test is to operate adequately in the study of oral composition, it must, like the others, examine elements in the text that can be quantitatively defined. (*TWW*, p. 4).

The "lexical clump"—or rather *cluster* as I prefer to call such groupings, following John Foley's usage[17] — that I shall deal with here is sounded twice in this passage. It is the *feor*- + *cum*-cluster first heard in lines 1805 and 1806, and later in 1819:

ne wolde *feor* þanon	1805
cuma collenferhð . . .	
nu we sæliðend secgan wẏllað	1818
*feor*ran *cum*ene . . .	

At line 361 Wulfgar had announced to Hrothgar:

her sẏndon ge[fere]de *feor*ran *cum*ene	361
ofer geofenes [be]gang geata leode	

At line 430 Beowulf had asked Hrothgar not to refuse his royal permission for the hero to cleanse Heorot, *nu ic þus feorran com*. Seven lines later the far-comer says that he will not bear a sword in the fight—. . . *þæt ic sweord bere* (437a). The adjective *hearda* appears in line 433, as it does in 1807, as a subtle but definite link between the far-comer theme and the sword theme. Beowulf thinks of returning Hrunting to Hunferth—for this is what I think is going on in lines 1807-12—because of the association of the far-comer with a sword. *Sword*, *coming* (though not from afar), and *bright* (com-

pare 1802b) are all clustered in Beowulf's account—to
Hunferth!—of his swimming match with Breca. This cluster begins at 561 and continues through 574.[18]

I have not yet taken up all the associations of the
cluster *feor-* + *cum-*. I shall have to quote the next
passage at some length, beginning at 823b:

>   denum eallum wearð
> æfter þam wælræse willa gelumpen.
> hæfde þa gefælsod se þe ær *feor*ran *com*
> snotor 7 swyðferð sele hroðgares   823-26

I have not commented on the association of *wil-/wol-*
with the *feor-* + *cum-* cluster. That association occurs
with *willa* in 824 and *willum* in 1821. More importantly,
it occurs with *wolde* in 1805 and *wyllað* in 1818. These
words sound the note of *one who comes from afar and performs the will* of a beleaguered people.

Only a few minutes after hearing the two cluster-
ings of *feor-* and *cum-* at 1805-6 and 1819, you would
hear, in a performance of the poem, about the Geatish
coastguard who, *fus æt faroðe*, has been looking *feor* for
the hero. Three lines later you would hear *het þa* and
beran and *æþelinga* and then *feor þanon, to gesecanne,*
and then *higelac*, words that cluster around and between
the two clusters I have singled out for study.

What I think this clustering means is this: the
poem is like living tissue. The stanza running from
1804 (or 1802b) to 1806 is like a hand, or, better, a
leaf—complete, articulated, bounded at the joint or the
stem. The stanza running from 1818 to 1821 is like another leaf. We can bring these two leaves together,
compare them, perceive their differences. But the tissues that make them are the same tissues that will take
a different shape, a different completeness, a different articulation to form another part of this living
organism.

Peabody's fifth and final test is this:

(5) The *song test* requires consistency in the patterns
     of discourse generated by a singer; this consist-
     ency should not only be present in a singer's own
     compositions, it should also appear in compositions
     of related provenance. This test examines the
     structure and mode of large passages of text. In
     oral styles the close repetition of entire composi-

tions is to be expected. In the actual singing of
bards, this happens; but in material approachable
only through recorded texts, such close duplication is seldom apparent. At best, traces of this
appear only as inexplicably variant readings or
oblique indications like numerous attributions of
authorship and the number of cities that claimed to
be Homer's birthplace. (*TWW*, p. 4).

"Song is the remembrance of songs sung" (*TWW*, p.
216). With this gnomic utterance Peabody begins his
sixth and last chapter, "The Flight of Song." What
songs did the singer of *Beowulf* remember? We know a
few: the song about Sigmund's slaying the serpent; the
song about Finn's foolish attack on his guests; the song
about the death of Hygelac. We know of the events these
songs tell about from other sources, one of which seems
to be a song in the same tradition as *Beowulf*. But
though he sings these other songs, they do not seem to
interest the singer of *Beowulf* on this occasion as much
as the song about the hero who comes—or used to come—
from afar at men's need.

All of Peabody's tests have both a synchronic and a
diachronic dimension.[19]   But the song test may remind us
most sharply of the diachronic depth of the tradition.
The singer remembers having sung at other times; at moments during his performance he will try to remember and
be guided by other performances he has sung and heard.
But, as Peabody points out, the performer cannot focus
his mind too sharply on trying to recall what he has
heard or he will falter or stop. Anyone who has listened to the rate at which Yugoslavian *guslari* perform
once they get into their songs cannot take seriously the
notion that the performer is always exerting a fully
conscious control. In mid-song, the singer is the ves-
sel of the tradition, of the Muses. He is like a well-
trained athlete in mid-contest.

This comparison is apt to conjure for us the notion
of mindlessness. It should do just the opposite. The
notion of surrender to the Muses should convey a sense
of getting in touch with patterned sounds stored *as* patterns in the brain. Getting in touch with the Muses is,
in a modern metaphor, locking into a rapid retrieval
system. On occasion the system will retrieve something
the conscious mind would reject. Or the system will retrieve something from a pattern that makes the conscious

mind uneasy. Something of the latter sort seems to me
to be going on early in the poem, at the point where the
poet tells of the Danes' attempts to summon the *gastbona*.
The Anglo-Saxon poet consciously knows of Beowulf as the
immensely strong but quite human hero who comes from
afar, the hero of whose exploits he has no difficulty
singing. The Anglo-Saxon poet is a Christian, and for
him there are no other gods before—or beside—his God.
Yet the tradition he has absorbed seems to know something about Beowulf that would make the poet, if he focused consciously upon it, very uneasy. *Something* in
any case, in the "tension of essences" that is, in
Lord's beautiful phrase, this tradition, makes him uneasy. So we get the ten and a half lines of anathema
that has been dubbed the "Christian excursus."[20] What
makes the Anglo-Saxon poet uneasy is, I think, Beowulf's
ultimate origins, something the *tradition* distantly remembers.

In their need, the Danes summon an ancient god; the
poet, who emerges here as a good Christian, lashes out
at them for doing so. Then the singer sings five lines
of sympathy for the troubles of the Danes in a passage
that modulates to the introduction of the hero. But the
very syllables in which the Danes are said to summon the
gastbona—*geoce gefremede wið þeodþreaum*—cluster around,
and thus help to create, the *hero*, his weapons, and his
deeds, or his superhuman adversaries and *their* deeds,
time and again in this song.[21]

What seems to me to suggest most sharply the hero's
ultimate origin as a god, the god who came in answer to
prayer--*wordum bædon*—are both the placement and the
tone of the "excursus." There is a disturbance in the
performance and in the upper layers of the tradition
here, and the singer must deal with the disturbance consciously.

Now if the poem *Beowulf* were the work of a *writer*
working at a comfortable distance from the tradition, he
would, it seems to me, very likely have dealt differently with this reflex from the distant past. If he had
had time not only to *feel* uneasy, but to seek the cause
of his uneasiness in what he had *written*, he might well
have exorcized such ghosts of the past to replace them
with sound doctrine.[22] But the singer performing before our eyes recalls with us (*WE gefrunon*) the distant
past (*geardagum*) with the help of the tradition, to conjure that past as the living present.

If the tradition in which *Beowulf* has its place is as old as I believe it to be, it must have changed in many ways through its myriad performances. To our thinking, the greatest change must seem to be Christianity's adoption into the tradition. We have the story of Caedmon's discovery of the way to turn the tradition into Christian hymning and biblical narrative. The *Beowulf*-poet's way was different. He held more firmly to the ancient truth he had heard. But he was able to do so because the heroes he celebrated acted out and spoke of matters of deep importance to his society.[23] Indeed, the tradition—the voices of men and women keeping in memorable patterns the words and themes that keep and had helped to create human society and, ultimately, humanity—the tradition survived as long as it was needed because it was an adaptive mechanism. And it could itself adapt to a *truth*, as Christianity seemed to be, because it was itself the keeper of truth. One meeting-point of these two truths was the *god spell* of the hero who came from afar at men's need.

There is far more at stake over the question of the oral and traditional character of *Beowulf* than the discomfiting of one or another school of criticism.[24] What is at stake is *Beowulf's* relationship both to the past of the Indo-European linguistic community, and perhaps what lies even back beyond that, and also to us. The question is, with what *range*, what diachronic depth, can we ask of the poem this question: what has it kept of the patterns that keep man, those patterns that adapt him for survival by adapting him to a society that develops as much through *hearing* as through *hunting*? To settle for *Beowulf* as the work of a man who sat in his cell and used for Christian propaganda what he read or remembered of the traditions of his people is to settle for a certain kind of poem and a certain kind of poet, a poet with whom we might at first feel a certain familiarity. But I do not think we have to settle for such a poem or poet. I do not think we *can* settle for such a poem or poet. Avdo Medjedović, Albert Lord, and Berkley Peabody teach us how to place the song in a tradition, and traditions are the work of human kind through scores, perhaps hundreds, of generations. Traditions, the keepers of man's words, are the taproots that keep the societies that keep touch with them. They are survival mechanisms. If we do not try to understand them for what they are, the loss is ours.

University of Massachusetts
at Amherst

NOTES

*The working title of this paper, and the title by
which it was introduced in Kalamazoo on May 7, 1978,
was "The Excellence of the Traditional Oral Style of
Beowulf."
[1]See note 5.
[2]*Speculum*, 28(1953), 446-67; rpt. in *AnthBC*, pp.
189-221; in *EsAr*, pp. 319-51; and in *BP*, pp. 83-113 .
[3]For a description of the program at Kalamazoo, see
the "Preface" to this volume.
[4]Such a characterization of the meter of *Beowulf* is
the basis of a nearly complete book-length study with
John Miles Foley, "A Systematic Scansion of *Beowulf*."
[5]See Appendix I. Line references (digits only) and
half-line references (digits followed by either *a* or *b*)
are to the standard lineation of *Beowulf*, a lineation
into 3182 lines. I have used the standard lineation for
convenience, even though it does not take into account
the problems of non-alliterating passages, as, e.g., at
389a, which is followed immediately by 390a, or the
possibility of the triplet, as at 403a, which is followed
immediately by 404a. The text of *Beowulf* quoted in this
paper is, however, one that I prepared in consultation
with J. M. Foley and checked with the assistance of
Joanne Pratt. This is the text that is lineated and
scanned in "A Systematic Scansion of *Beowulf*" (see note
4 above). The text is based on only three kinds of
source: (1A) *Beowulf, Reproduced in Facsimile...*, transliteration and notes by Julius Zupitza, 2nd ed. by Norman Davis (London, 1959); (1B) *The Nowell Codex*, ed. by
Kemp Malone (Copenhagen, 1963); (2) *The Thorkelin Tran-
scripts of Beowulf in Facsimile*, ed. by Kemp Malone
(Copenhagen, 1951); and (3) H. Wanley's quotation of
lines 1-19 and 53-73 of Cotton Vitellius A. XV. in
Antiquae Literaturae Septentrionalis Liber Alter, seu
Humphredi Wanleii... Catalogus Historico-criticus (Oxford, 1705). In the quoted passages square brackets en-
close letters covered or illegible in the facsimiles that
are reported either by Wanley or Thorkelin A (not
Thorkelin himself—B—who is not one of our sources).

Capitalization, pointing, and all other marks are those
of our sources, *not* the editors.

[6] I do not make this claim solely on the basis of
the exemplary passage in Appendix I, nor do I need to.
I ask the reader to study carefully *any* portion of the
poem, to *listen* to it as well as observe the letters.
To add further support to my characterization of the
Beowulf-poet as a master of sound-patterning, I have
chosen two other examples, taken, as was the exemplary
passage, at random. The first is the passage from ll.
226-32:

    sæwudu sældon syrcan hrẏsedon.
    guðgewædo gode þancedon
    þæs þe him yþlade eaðe wurdon.
    [þa] of wealle gesea[h] weard scildinga   137r
    se þ[e holm]clifu healdan scolde   230
    beran ofer bolcan beorhte randas
    fẏrdsearu fuslicu hine fẏrwẏt bræc

Long æ sounds in two stressed and alliterating syllables
in 226a, and again in the second stressed (but not alliterating) syllable in 227a. Between these occurrences
comes the delightful onomatopoeic weaving of *s*, *y*, and *r*
in 226b. The *Ablaut*-play of *yþ*- and *eað*- in 228 suggests a charm against the dangers of the sea. Three of
the five stressed syllables in 229 contain the vocalization *ea*, which is sounded again in the first stress of
230b. The concatenation of *weall*-, *weard*, and *heald*- suggests the security of the coastguard's observation post.
These last two lines play with the consonant *l*, too,
which sound occurs twice in 229 and four times in 230.
The other liquid consonant, *r*, begins to sound insistent-
ly in 231 and acts as a sub-dominant in 232, in which *y*
emerges as the most important vocalization. Note also
the near-rhyme of *fẏrd*- at the beginning and *fẏr*- toward
the end of this line.
    The second passage runs from ll. 2788-93:

    he ða [mi]d þam maðmum mærne þioden
    drẏhten [si]nne driorigne fand
    ealdres æt ende he hine eft ongon   2790
    wæteres weorpan oð þæt [w]ordes ord
    breosthord þurhbræc.
    gomel on giogoðe gold sceawode.

The long low back sound of *a*, into which *þā* (elsewhere
usually *þæm*) is drawn, opens the passage. The vocalization then moves forward, rising up the "scale" from the
long æ of *mær*-, through the short final *e*, to the high

front of the first element of the long diphthong *io* in
þiod-. After retracting briefly to the second element
of the diphthong, the vocalization moves forward again
to the final *-e* of the line. It remains fronted almost
throughout 2789, repeating the long *io* diphthong in the
stressed syllable of *driorigne*. Does this succession of
sounds first mime Wiglaf's feelings of security with the
treasure (2788a), then his rising concern for his dying
lord, as well as miming his ascent from the barrow? The
three *r*-sounds of 2789 are echoed in the four *r*-sounds
of 2791. Then, in the two measures that make up 2792,
four more *r*-sounds seem to mime Beowulf's effort to
speak, as do the words themselves. The rhyming of the
word-, *ord*, and *-hord* carries the dying king's effort
from 2791 to 2792, in which, at last, the *ord þurhbræc*.
Stops, which make 2792 so powerfully expressive, are
again the dominant alliteration of 2793.

Most editors (e.g., Klaeber and Dobbie) emend 2793.
The text as it was recorded says, "The old one looked at
the gold on the youth." Beowulf's first words refer to
the *frætwa*, often something worn, perhaps a suggestion
that Wiglaf, having put on some of the armor from the
dragon's hoard, emerges from the barrow as a gold-
adorned successor to the dying hero. It might, then, be
these trappings that impel him, at 2784a, to present
himself to his lord. In any case, 2793 contains the contrast between youth and age in a whole-line clause, a
contrast destroyed and a clause broken by a century of
editors who assumed that the poem was the work of a
writer.

[7] I take this opportunity to thank David E. Bynum
for sending me a recording of Avdo Medjedović performing
to the *gusle* in the sung epic *Osmanbeg Delibegović i
Pavičević Luka*, as he does *not* do in the *Ženidba*, an
oral-dictated text (see Lord, "Homer's Originality: Oral
Dictated Texts," *TAPA*, 84 [1953], 124-34). In my recitation of this passage in Kalamazoo, I relied more on
stress than *guslari* generally do.

[8] J. M. Foley's brilliant definition of the formula
was not available to me when I was preparing this paper;
see, elsewhere in this volume, "Tradition-dependent and
-independent Features in Oral Literature: the Formula."

[9] See Appendix II.

[10] *A Concordance to* Beowulf, ed. by Jess B. Bessinger,
Jr., programmed by Philip H. Smith, Jr. (Ithaca, 1969).

[11] See *TWW*, p. 9: "The present study examines the *Works and Days* not only according to the criteria for oral style, it uses this text to provide information for a kind of grammar of ancient Greek oral compositional technique that can apply to all works of the Greek epos as well as to the exemplar text. This grammar is not a description of a surface—a synchronic analysis; rather, it is a description of traditional processes. A tradition generates phenomena that admit synchronic description, but its controlling habits are diachronic. The occasionally awkward attempt has been made in the present study, therefore, to describe textual patterns and historical causality in a single exposition, because this is the way an oral tradition works. The reader is asked to think of these aspects simultaneously; and an adequate understanding of the present study depends on a synthesized awareness of its whole, rather than on a grasp of its parts as a sequence."

[12] Simply diagrammed:

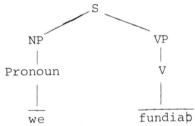

Note that the Chomskyan "S" equals Peabody's "clause."

[13] The comparative method lies at the heart of Peabody's work.

[14] "The Distinctive Character of Enjambement in Homeric Verse," in *MHV*, pp. 251-65; see, e.g., p. 253.

[15] See Bessinger-Smith, under *tela*.

[16] See J. M. Foley (note 8).

[17] See J. M. Foley, "The Ritual Nature of Traditional Oral Poetry: Metrics, Music, and Matter in the Anglo-Saxon, Homeric Greek, and Serbo-Croatian Poetries," unpub. Ph.D. diss. (University of Massachusetts/Amherst, 1974), pp. 232-79.

[18] Lines 561-74 have been singled out, first by David K. Crowne, in "The Hero on the Beach: an Example of Composition by Theme in Anglo-Saxon Poetry," *NM*, 61 (1960), 362-72, and by many scholars since, as an instance of a theme based on an "idea." (See *TWW*, p. 4, and Chapter 5, "The Responsions of Thought," pp. 168-215.) I cite the passage here because it contains

clusters that overlap the clusters that are sounded between 1802b and 1819a. But, since the crucial element
feor- is lacking in 561-74, the earlier clusters form a
theme related to but not identical with the themes clustering in the later passage.

[19] I take this opportunity to express my gratitude
to Joanne De Lavan Foley, an earlier draft of whose
paper, "Feasts and Anti-Feasts in *Beowulf* and the
Odyssey," included in this volume, led me to begin to
sense the diachronic depths to be glimpsed in *Beowulf*.
I contrast this approach, already visible earlier in J.M.
Foley's book in progress, *Studies in Oral Traditional
Literature*, with what I regard as the unfortunate implications of Kemp Malone's Chapter 3, "The Old Tradition:
Poetic Form," in his portion of *A Literary History of
England*, ed. by Albert C. Baugh (New York and London,
1948), pp. 20-31. I cite this thirty-year-old study not
only because it is still in print and certainly used by
many scholars and students, nor merely because of
Malone's authority, but more importantly because Malone
was always eager to relate poems surviving from the
Anglo-Saxon period to their Germanic origins. Yet he
leads the reader to believe that Old English poetic
styles went through a complete development during the
historical period, that is, from the seventh century on.
First comes "the short verse and line" (p. 23), then the
pairing through alliteration of two short verses to produce the "end-stopped style" (p. 26). Though there are
examples of the end-stopped style in *Beowulf* (p. 26),
that poem "may serve to illustrate the middle stage of
the [classical] run-on style" (p. 27).

I am not denying that such stylistic developments
took place, and probably in the order Malone supposes.
What I protest is the implication that such developments
affected almost every reflex of the tradition at about
the same time. At one moment Malone appears to paint a
picture of a smooth-surfaced, literary *Beowulf*; at another he portrays the *Beowulf*-poet as occasionally preserving an old-fashioned formula (p. 26). So we get the
literate antiquarian so much in fashion in the writings
of Anglo-Saxonists today. In contrast, I cite Lord's
brilliant denial that traditional oral poetry can "be
treated as a flat surface. All the elements in traditional poetry have depth," he continues in his "Homer as
Oral Poet," *HSCP*, 72(1968), 46. Then there is the man
Avdo Medjedović, master of sound-patterning, sound-

patterning that has developed through generations. Medjedović was neither literate nor literary, nor was he an antiquarian. He was a great singer.

[20] *Beowulf*, ll. 178b-88.

[21] My tentative, working definition of the cluster is this: a cluster consists of the stressed syllables within a certain range. Since more study must be done before that range can be as precisely defined for the Anglo-Saxon tradition as Peabody has defined it for the Greek epos, I have confined myself to tracking down other occurrences of the six stresses of the clause that forms the content of the Danes' prayer, ll. 177-78a: (1) *gast-/gæst-*, (2) *bona/bana*, (3) *geoc-*, (4) *frem-*, (5) *þeod-*, (6) *þrea*. The results of this exploration are intriguing. Numbers (4) and (5) cluster in lines 2-3, 1019, 2131-34a (where *þeod-* is replaced by *þeoden*), and 3003b-8. Beowulf himself is speaking in 2131-34a; the messenger speaks of Beowulf in the last passage. The formula *eorlscipe efnde* links the forms of *þeod-* and *frem-* in both of the last passages. Numbers (3) and (4) are sounded together in the same formula at 2674: *geongum garwigan geoce gefremman*. *gar-* in 2674a recalls the first line of the poem and suggests a different but closely related cluster consisting of (4), (5), and *gar-*. *gar-* is sounded again in association with (3) and (4) in 1832b-34. The clusters seem to suggest the language by which the divine *gastbona* was transformed into a human *garwiga*.

Forms of (4) can lead us to other signs of this transformation:

Hra[þe wæs] to bure beowulf fetod   1310
sigoreadig se[cg] samod ærdæge
eode eorla sum æþele cempa
self mid gesiðum þær se snot[e]ra bad·
hwæþre him alfwalda æfre wille
æfter weaspelle wyrpe gefremman   1315

Beowulf is summoned to serve as the agent of *alfwalda* in combatting the second Grendel threat. Since his relationship to God is the one sanctioned by the religious beliefs acceptable to Anglo-Saxon society at this time, there seems to be little linguistic disturbance as Hrothgar ponders whether God will be forward (*gefremman*) with a change for his people as Beowulf strides into his hall.

[22] A writer reading over what he written might simply have deleted lines 175-88.

[23] Students of *Beowulf* would do well to ponder the
significance of D. P. Kirby's statement: "Just as the
kindred was the basic social element in Anglo-Saxon society, so the folk-group was the fundamental unit in the
early kingdoms. A kingdom was but a conglomeration of
folk-groups over whom a folk-king reigned." (*The Making
of Early England* [London, 1967], p. 162).   William A.
Chaney, *The Cult of Kingship in Anglo-Saxon England:
the Transition from Paganism to Christianity* (Berkeley,
1970), provides a useful corrective to the easy assumption that Anglo-Saxon England shed all traces of paganism very soon after the king of each folk was baptized.

[24] The most important effect of *TWW* for students of
the Germanic oral tradition is to remind us how much remains to be done in the exploration of sound-patterning,
localization, syntax, clustering—indeed, everything
that Peabody has analyzed in his great study of the traditional epos of early Greece. The idea of the *Beowulf*-
poet as a *singer* can be tested in new ways. But, more
important, the processes of testing, carefully and
patiently undertaken, will deepen our knowledge of the
great poem and perhaps take us closer to those generations of men and women who, by shaping memorable sound-
patterns, shaped our very thought.

APPENDIX I

Dominant Alliter- ation	TEXT*	Folio/ Line	Supporting Alli- tera- tion
B	/ [beo]rht scacan	[172V]°	sc
SC	scaþan onetton		v
V	[wæron] æþelingas eft to leodum		
F	fuse to [are]ne ne wolde feor þanon	1805	
C	cuma col[enf]erhð ceoles neosan		-f
H	Heht þa se hear[da hr]unting beran		
S	sunu ecglafes heht [his s]weord niman		v, -l, h
L	leoflic iren sægde him [þæs] leanes þanc		v, s
G	cwæð he þone guðwine [god]ne tealde·	1810	c, -w
W	wigcræftigne nales [word]um log		-c
M	meces ecge þ wæs modig secg		s
S	[and þa] siðfrome searwū gearwe		
W	wigend wæron· [Eo]de weorð denum		v
V	æþeling to ẏppan [þæ]r se oþer wæs	1815	
H	helle hildedeor hroð[ga]r grette·		-g, g

xxvi.

B	[Beo]wulf maþelode bearn ecgþeowes		
S	nu [we] sæliðend secgan wẏllað		
F	feorran cu[m]ene þæt we fundiaþ		
H	higelac secan wæron [h]er tela	1820	
W	willū bewenede þu us wel dohtest·		
V	Gif ic þonne on eorþan owihte mæg		
M	þinre modlufan maran tilian·		
G	gumena drẏhten ðonne ic gẏt dẏde		d, d
G	guðgeweorca ic beo gearo sona·	1825	

*In this transcription *w* substitutes for Ms. *wynn*, *g* for the flat-topped insular *g*, *and* for the MS. abbreviation, and underlined þ for crossed thorn (which equals *þæt*).

APPENDIX II

The Localization of æþ*eling-* in *Beowulf*.

Genitive:

æþ*elinges* bearn ana geneðde	888
[æ]ð*elinga* bearn ẏmbe gestodon	2597
æþe *ini g* eal̇ra twelfa	3170
hraðe heo æþ*elinga* anna hæfde	1294
þ hig þæs æð*elinges* eft ne wendon	1596
feorh æþ*elinges* flæsce [b]ewunden·	2424
isig 7 útfus æþ*elinges* fær·	33
Fand þa ðær [i]nne æþ*elinga* gedriht	118
ofereode þa æþ*elinga* bearn	1408
het þa up beran æþ*elinga* gest[reon]	1920

Dative:

eallū̄ æþ*ellingum* to aldorceare·	906
ofer [æþ]*elinge* ẏþgesene	1244
æt ðā̄ æð*elinge* [æn]ige ðinga	2374

Nominative:

hu ða æþ*elingas* elle[n] fremedon.	3
siþðan æþ*elingas* eorles cræfte	982
[wæron] æþ*elingas* eft to leodum	1804
idel hweorfan sẏððan æð*elingas*	2888

LEGITIMATION AND THE HERO'S EXEMPLARY FUNCTION IN THE *CANTAR DE MIO CID* AND THE *CHANSON DE ROLAND*

Joseph J. Duggan

The *Chanson de Roland* and the *Cantar de mio Cid* are often compared, but usually for the wrong reasons. The Spanish poem has a documentary quality about it, and the single poetic version which has survived the Middle Ages, in a manuscript identified as the product of one Per Abbat, a scribe, was composed within a hundred and eight years of the hero's death. The *Cid* is thus much closer in narrative type to, say, *Garin le Loherain* or to the *Canso d'Antiocha* than it is to the *Roland*, which in its earliest extant form is at least three hundred years removed from the historical events it reflects and which is marked by notable geographical and temporal distortions. What justifies considering these two poems together is that they both incorporate myths looking back to a foundation, the *Cid* for the Spanish kingdom born of the union of Leon and Castile, and the *Roland* for the Carolingian Empire.

The relationship between literature and history underlies notions of the epic to a greater extent than it does conceptions of other genres. During the last hundred and fifty years certain models of that relationship have been dominant. For the Romantic critics, the people spoke by and large as if with one voice, and the role of individual poet-craftsmen who gave form to that voice was usually passed over. More than any other type of poetry, the epic embodied the people's sentiments, preserving the memory of heroes to whose model it had looked in the past for leadership in life and an exemplary way to die. Because of constant rivalry between modern France and Germany, two powers which were at least theoretically united in Charlemagne's empire, the question of whether the French populace was more closely linked to a Germanic or to a Roman ancestry preoccupied scholars who were concerned with the origins of the French epic. Even those who were cognizant of the Franco-Prussian War's distorting effects on French intellectual life may register surprise at the formulation found in the second edition of Léon Gautier's *Les Epopées françaises*: the French epic is surely of Germanic origin, Gautier tells us, because its leading female characters

are utterly without shame and their actions must thus be
based on Germanic models of womanhood.[1]   The myth of
origins itself—and here I use 'myth' in the pejorative
and popular sense of a belief which is not backed up by
verifiable facts—is a historical concept conditioned by
political and intellectual categories which are now out-
moded.   It is no secret that questions formerly asked
about origins are now more often framed in terms of manifestation or development.

     But all too often the issues posed by the giants of
nineteenth-century and early twentieth-century scholarship—Gautier, Gaston Paris, Joseph Bédier, Ramón
Menéndez Pidal, and others—are still being discussed in
the same terminology which they bequeathed to us.   In
particular the perception of history as a sequence of
striking events brought about by the potentates of this
earth has survived largely intact in the work of many
literary scholars concerned with the relationship between epic and history in western Romania.   In the
framework of their interpretations, great personages
manipulate the epic to support their own drive for he-
gemony.   Bédier's idea that the French epics were first
created in the eleventh century through a collaboration
between clerics and poets seeking to promote the fame of
certain shrines situated along the great pilgrimage
routes derives from a related view of history in that it
posits that the motivation and working habits of medieval poets did not differ from those of later and better
documented authors: witness Bédier's pronouncement that
a masterpiece begins and ends with its author, his comparison of the *Roland* with Racine's *Iphigénie*, and his
citation of La Bruyère's statement that making a book
is no less a feat of craftsmanship than making a clock.
But eleventh- and twelfth-century poets could not have
worked in the same ways as those of the seventeenth, because the processes of poetic creation are a function of
social, economic, and intellectual circumstances which
vary from period to period and from one type of society
to another.   The manner in which a poet creates is conditioned above all by what French historians of the
Annales school call *mentalités*, perceptual categories
which shape the way in which phenomena are viewed.   Substantial though they be, differences in educational
background and in political and social milieu are less
important than diversity in mental framework, a basic
and all-pervasive variance that prevents us from recon-

structing adequately the world view of medieval poets.

In studies on the *Cid*, a similar reliance on the concept of history as a sequence of noteworthy occurrences prevailed. While Menéndez Pidal appreciated the import of political events and the effects of Muslim pressure on the kingdoms of northern Spain, he gave less attention in *La España del Cid* to social and economic forces; although he took great pains to establish the geography of the epic Cid's progress from Burgos to Valencia, he seldom referred to medieval conceptions of time and space which contribute to the skewing of geographical reality. Pidal's achievements in filling in the backdrop against which the historical Cid acted are undeniable, and even his detractors make use of the data he collected. His discussion of the *Chanson de Roland*'s manuscripts is a masterful treatment of how medieval texts recorded from oral tradition differ radically from what we in the twentieth century normally mean when we speak of a text, and as such it contributes in a major way precisely to that history of mentalities which is so regretfully lacking in the *España del Cid*. In reading the *Cantar de mio Cid* with greater attention to its social aspects and to the relationship between political and economic history, I believe one can approach with greater hope of success a realization of the poem's significance.

Dealings between men as they are represented in the *Cid* cannot all be subsumed under the terms "vasselage" or "feudalism." Social relationships are marked by an economic give and take which mirrors a particular state of society best qualified as a "gift economy" in which exchanges of money and goods take place continually, but not under the conditions which one normally calls "economic" in the modern sense. The historian Georges Duby has drawn upon ideas developed by the socio-anthropologist Marcel Mauss to sketch out a description of exchanges in the early and high Middle Ages which can illuminate the meaning of gift-giving and other processes of the eleventh- and twelfth-century economy as they are reflected in the *Cantar de mio Cid*.[2] Conquests and the payment of various types of feudal dues and rents supplied political leaders and fighting men of that period with an abundance of wealth beyond what was needed for their sustenance. The economic workings of society required that such wealth be circulated to others, with the result that generosity in its distribution was not

merely an option open to the powerful, but an uncodified
obligation. Recipients of seignorial largess were not
all of a lower rank then benefactors: gifts from infer-
ior to superior were also immensely important. At the
top of the social pyramid the king was forced to have at
his disposal sources of wealth which he could dole out
to those who came to test his liberality, and while conquest and plunder provided much of this wealth, so did
the offerings of lesser men. The relationships whose
existence was fueled by these gifts were of a mutually
beneficial nature. Gift-giving was probably never considered to be disinterested. Between military men and
their followers, of course, service was commonly exchanged for largess; tributes guaranteed against attacks; even stipends and legacies made in favor of the
Church brought a return, in the form of divine favor.
The economic system sustained by this movement of com-
modities and coin in many cases had no relation to mer-
cantile trade, but nevertheless effected a flow of
goods which maintained the poor, supported significant
numbers of able-bodied if occasionally idle monks, provided motivation for the warrior class, and acted in
general as a cementing element in the social edifice.

        While the gift economy dominated in the early Mid-
dle Ages, its main traits were still present in the
period 1050 to 1207, that is during the Cid's career and
the time in which the poem in all probability took shape
in something close to the form in which we have it.
More than one observer has called the Cid a bourgeois
hero, the poem a bourgeois epic. Such a formulation
could only be based upon the conviction that obsession
with wealth is a monopoly of the city-dwelling, mercan-
tile class; as Duby has shown, this is manifestly un-
true for the eleventh and twelfth centuries. No hero in
all of epic literature is as concerned with money and
possessions of various kinds as is the Cid, but his insistence on the prerogatives of nobility is unmistakable.
Even the most cursory recital of the poem's themes confirms that economic interests dominate the *Cantar de mio
Cid* to an extent unmatched in the Romance epic, and yet
the outcome of the social process set in motion by the
hero's acquisition of wealth is attainment of the very
highest level of the aristocracy.

        In tracing the motivations for actions in the *Cid*,
one is forced to consult the prose version found in the
Crónica de Veinte Reyes, since the poetic text as found

in Per Abbat's manuscript lacks a beginning.[3] The
chronicle tells us that King Alfonso of Leon and Castile believed the accusations of evil counsellors to
the effect that his vassal Rodrigo Diaz of Vivar was
withholding from him tribute that was supposed to have
been delivered subsequent to a mission to Seville and
Cordova. While he was in Seville, Rodrigo had defended
Alfonso's tributary against an attack from Cordova, and
had earned by his prowess and magnanimity the honorific
"Cid Campeador." Whatever the historical Alfonso's motive for exiling the Cid, the poet responsible for the
Per Abbat text assumes that popular opinion lent cre-
dence to the accusation that the hero had profited at
his lord's expense. After receiving six hundred marks
from the Jewish money-lenders Rachel and Vidas in exchange for two chests which supposedly contain money
but are actually full of sand, the Cid is financed and
ready to face his exile which he will begin with a
series of raids.

        That an epic poem should devote any attention at
all to how a military campaign is funded is extraordinary, let alone that negotiations should occupy a
major scene. Why is the poem anomalous in this respect?
In placing the *Cid* in the context of medieval Romance
epic, one must refer primarily to the one hundred or so
French works which are extant, a preponderance of evidence against which the three fragmentary Spanish poems
and the half-dozen Provençal titles represent comparatively little. Allowance should be made, first of all,
for differing social conditions. Undoubtedly the landed
estate, the classic base for feudalism of the French variety,
played a lesser role in Spain than it did north of the
Pyrenees. In addition, whatever benefit might accrue
from possession of a territorial foothold was denied to
the Cid in his exile. A more important factor is also
at work, deriving both from the particular circumstances
of peninsular history and from the epic's role as a genre
which holds up models for emulation. In the expanding
world of northern Spanish Christendom, in which land was
available for capture by force from the Arabs and in
which one of the chief political problems was how to
motivate fighting men to leave familiar surroundings so
as to take advantage of the military inadequacies of
weak and fragmented Muslim principalities, the *Cantar
de mio Cid* furnishes the exemplary model of a noble of
relatively low rank rising to the highest level of the

social hierarchy without having at his disposal the power base of the landed estate. The poem is both an entertaining tale of military prowess and an economic and
social incentive for ambitious Castilian knights of low
rank and narrow means.

The acquisition of booty, its proper distribution
among the knights and soldiers, the appraisal of precious
objects, and the use to which wealth is put join together to form one of the poem's major thematic com-
plexes. The poetic Cid achieves his reintegration into
the social fabric directly through economic power, and
succeeds in proportion to his personal enrichment, beginning with the unhistorical raid on Castejón. Time
and again, the type and quantity of booty are enumerated:
coined money, shields, tents, clothing, slaves, camels,
horses, beasts of burden, and other livestock. At times
the amounts are stated to be beyond reckoning, but this
type of comment is only a figure of speech since the
poet also depicts the tallying up of loot by the
quiñoneros, officials whose job it was to divide and
count the spoils. Repeatedly and as early as the first
major engagement the fighting men are termed *ricos* (vv.
540, 800, 848, 1086). As lord, the Cid receives a fifth
of all plunder.

The relative worth of objects is of less interest
than what their possession connotes in social terms. In
the *Cid*, wealth and fame are closely linked, from the
hero's first proclamation inviting others to join him in
his exile, which frankly appeals to the desire for
rritad (v. 1189), through the marriage of his daughters
Elvira and Sol with the heirs of the house of Carrión,
to the climax at the court scene in Toledo where the Cid
is dressed in his most luxurious finery. Throughout the
poem he displays his wealth by bestowing gifts on those
who surround him, although he is never seen receiving
them. The outstanding examples of interested gift-giving are the three embassies which carry extravagant offerings to King Alfonso. In return the Cid receives
first the lifting of the king's official displeasure,
then that his wife and daughters be allowed to join him
in Valencia, and finally full pardon and, without his
having requested it, his daughters' marriage to the
heirs of Carrión.

The link between wealth and honor is nowhere more
apparent than in the hero's dealings with the heirs. The
villainous motives of this pair are epitomized when they

accept booty from the victory over King Búcar in spite
of having acted in a cowardly fashion on the battlefield.
The five thousand marks that come to them on this occasion lead them to the mistaken belief that they are now
rich enough to aspire to marriage with the daughters of
kings and emperors. Whereas for the Cid courage brings
material benefits in the form of possessions which can
then be exchanged for the prerogatives of birth and can
even, in a sense which I will discuss shortly, compensate for the inadequacies associated with doubtful
lineage, for the heirs of Carrión high birth conveys an
intrinsic value which makes it unnecessary for them to
put themselves to the test of battle. As they leave
Valencia supposedly to escort their wives to Carrión,
the Cid gives them more wealth in the form of a bride-
gift: three thousand marks and the precious swords
Colada and Tizón. That this contrast is essential
rather than coincidental is seen in the aftermath of the
incident at Corpes in which the brothers beat the Cid's
daughters and leave them for dead. Surprisingly for the
modern reader, the hero places loss of the wealth he has
distributed to the heirs of Carrión on the same level as
his daughters' dishonor: *"Mios averes se me an levado
que sobejanos son,/ esso me puede pesar con la otra
desonor"* (vv. 2912-3).[4] This preoccupation with worldly
goods as a symbol of intrinsic worth continues during
the court scene at Toledo. The Cid makes three legal
points against the heirs of Carrión, of which the first
two concern possessions: that they return the two swords,
and that they give back the bride-gift of three thousand
marks. The third point is a moral accusation, but it is
framed in an economic metaphor: the brothers are worth
less, since they struck their own wives. The key term
menosvaler sums up emblematically the relationship between wealth and honor, economic and moral "worth."

The poem ends in a curiously unhistorical fashion.
The Cid's daughters will become queens of two kingdoms,
according to the poet, who returns to this theme just
before he refers to the Cid's death:

Los primeros [casamientos] fueron grandes mas
   aquestos son mijores;
a mayor ondra las casa que lo que primero fue:
¡ved qual ondra creçe al que en buen ora naçio
quando señoras son sus fijas de Navarra e de Aragon!

Oy los reyes d'España sos parientes son.
                  (Vv. 3720-4.)

The Cid's historical daughters, Cristina and María,
married respectively Ramiro, lord of Monzón in Navarre,
and Ramón Berenguer III, Count of Barcelona. Thus
neither of his daughters became queen, and they did not
marry the infantes of Navarre and Aragon, although confusion on these points is conceivable in a poet composing in the mid-twelfth century or later since the son
of Cristina and Ramiro became King of Navarre in 1134
and Barcelona was united to Aragon in 1137. Questions
of title are not generally obscure to contemporaries, so
that it is likely the poem was composed in a form not
too far from the one in which we have these lines long
enough after 1137 for people's memories to have become
clouded regarding the chronology. In any event it is
more than surprising that a poet who knows the names of
the Cid's minor historical associates, such as Pero
Vermúdez, Muño Gustioz, Martin Muñoz, Alvar Salvadórez,
and Diego Téllez, should err on whether the hero's
daughters were queens, and of what political entities.
His inaccuracy on these points, although partly justified by later historical developments, at the very least
exaggerates the Cid's rise to respectability among the
very highest class of nobles. Why should a singer of
the twelfth or early thirteenth century be so intent on
depicting his hero's meteoric ascent as to represent the
Cid's immediate progeny as queens at the risk that some
members of the audience would recognize the error? The
answer to this question provides an explanation for the
poet's concern with the acquisition of wealth, gift-
giving, and other economic phenomena.

     Let us return to the court scene. There are two
heirs of Carrión, each of whom is challenged to single
combat by one of the Cid's men, who will use the swords
Colada and Tizón in their respective duels so that,
fittingly, the two brothers will be tested by the very
instruments which they received under the false pretense
of marriage-alliance with the Cid. But unexpectedly a
third duel is proposed, provoked by Asur Gonçález, elder
brother to the heirs of Carrión, who enters the palace
and flings an apparently gratuitous insult at the Cid:

     " ¡Hya varones!   ¿Quien vio nunca tal mal?
     ¡Quien nos darie nuevas de mio Çid el de Bivar!

¡Fuesse a Rio d'Ovirna los molinos picar
e prender maquilas commo lo suele far!
¿Quil darie con los de Carrion a casar?"
                    (Vv. 3377-81)

This curious intervention might at first seem to be only
an attack on the hero's position at the low end of the
noble hierarchy, since as an *infanzón* he was entitled to
collect feudal dues on the use of mills which came under
his jurisdiction. But as Menéndez Pidal points out,
mills were prized possessions of the seignorial class.[5]
Asur Gonçález is probably not simply assimilating the
Cid's possession of a mill to the actual operations performed by the miller, for as rude as such a quip might
be, it would hardly justify a challenge to mortal combat
such as Muño Gustioz subsequently proffers, nor is it
equal in weight to the outrage of Corpes which will be
avenged by the other two duels which are to be fought on
the same occasion. The *maquila* was a portion of wheat
given to the miller in return for his services, and the
Cid as an *infanzón* would hardly be expected to receive
recompense under that rubric, although he would take
other types of payment from a miller working under his
jurisdiction. Asur Gonçález's words convey a far greater
affront, an innuendo about the Cid's birth, suggesting
that he is descended from a miller and thus entitled to
a miller's pay. Verse 3379, scornfully exhorting the
Cid to go to his mill on the river Ubierna, the location
of Vivar, and roughen the millstones, can only mean that
for Asur Gonçález the Cid *is* a miller. A person of such
low rank would indeed be ill-advised to aspire to a
marriage tie with the powerful comtal family of the Vani-
Gómez.

An obscure legend, preserved primarily in the
romancero, has it that the Cid was the illegitimate son
of Diego Laínez, and one version reports that his mother
was a *molinera*.[6] The agreement between this detail and
Asur Gonçález's otherwise senseless insult can hardly be
coincidental. Acceptance of the Cid's daughters as
queens of Aragon and Navarre would be convincing proof
that his accomplishments transcended and annuled the dis-
advantages of his bastardy. Asur Gonçález's defeat at
the hands of the Cid's vassal shows that God approves of
the hero's deeds in spite of the fact that he was conceived out of wedlock, for the duel takes the form of
an ordeal.

The *Cantar de mio Cid* differs from the other extant
Romance epics in its author's obsession with the acquisition of wealth, then, not only on account of the differing social and political conditions of Reconquest Spain,
but because, unlike most of the heroes whose legends are
recounted in poems belonging to this genre, the Cid does
not enter the struggle with his honor intact. The
amassing of riches and their proper use allow him to
rise to the dignity and rank which great nobles of unblemished descent, such as the heirs of Carrión, could
claim by birth. He is a king by right of conquest, ex-
celling in knightly virtues that might well have been
called into doubt by his maternal ancestry. Seen in this
light, the *Cantar de mio Cid* is the story of how courage
and prowess are transmuted into economic power, and
wealth into lineage, the highest in Spain. As such it is
a message to the lesser nobles of Castile, because if the
Cid, whose line of descent was in question and whose king
exiled him from his land, could raise his kin to the
level of royalty through his participation in the Reconquest, then other nobles of his class could legitimately
aspire to the same heights of success in invading Arab-
controlled lands which enjoyed, despite their political
troubles, the most prosperous economy in medieval Europe
at this time.

The obscure allusion to Rodrigo of Vivar's bastardy
calls to mind a similarly fleeting reference in the
Carolingian foundation myth as it is found in the Oxford
manuscript of the *Chanson de Roland*. I refer, of course,
to Charlemagne's Sin. During his narration of the Battle
of Roncevaux, the Oxford poet invokes the authority of an
eye-witness to the events he is recounting:

> Ço dit la Geste e cil ki el camp fut:
> Li ber Gilie, por qui Deus fait vertuz,
> E fist la chartre el muster de Loüm.
> Ki tant ne set ne l'ad prod entendut. (Vv. 2095-8.)[7]

St. Giles of Provence was a hermit who lived in the late
sixth century, but whom legend has transformed into an
eighth-century contemporary of Charlemagne. The story
of the document God wrote for him is not found in the
Oxford *Roland* itself, but is confirmed by references in
a tenth-century Latin life of St. Giles, in the Old
Norse *Karlamagnússaga*, a compilation made for King Hákon

Hákonarson of Norway in the thirteenth century, in the
French life of Giles by Guillaume de Berneville, in the
chanson de geste Tristan de Nanteuil, and finally in the
Provençal version of the *Roland, Ronsasvals*.

The *Karlamagnússaga* is itself based largely on Old
French epic material and likely to preserve a form of
the legend close to what circulated in eleventh- and
twelfth-century France. Charlemagne, the saga tells us,
slept with his sister Gisla (Gisele). Going to church
afterward, he confessed his sin to St. Giles, but omitted mentioning the act of incest. As the saint was
singing mass, an angel descended and laid a letter on
the altar, the contents of which were: "Charlemagne has
lain with his sister, and she will bear a son who will
be called Roland. And he will give her in marriage to
Milon of Angres; she will give birth seven months after
they share their bed; and Charlemagne will know that the
boy is both his son and his nephew, and he should see to
it that the child is well looked after, because he will
need him."[8] When St. Giles read this letter to Charlemagne, the Emperor acknowledged having committed the
sin, promised not to repeat it, and begged forgiveness.
The presence of an allusion to St. Giles and to the document in Oxford can only signify that the poet knew the
legend of Charlemagne's Sin, and that for him Roland was
the Emperor's son as well as his nephew. With this in
mind, the long sequence of regrets which Charlemagne pro-
nounces over Roland's body on the battlefield, including
the wish that he himself might die, takes on a clearer
meaning: he is mourning the death of his own son.

As with the Cid, then, the question of Roland's
parentage is clouded. Neither the poet of the Oxford
Chanson de Roland nor the one who composed the extant
Cantar de mio Cid devotes more than a passing allusion
to the issue of the respective hero's birth[9]; it is nonetheless intriguing that in each case the problem of illegitimacy surfaces. In societies such as these where
kinship is a pervasive social bond, and in which a person is considered to be legally responsible for acts
committed by his kinsmen—above all in a genre in which
lineage, one of the two principal meanings of the term
geste, is one of the most important determinants of character—illegitimacy, whether it results from royal incest
or simply from a paternal liaison with a commoner, represents a most serious deficiency. Roland's case differs
from the Cid's in obvious ways. Nevertheless I believe

that as with the *Cantar de mio Cid*, the meaning of the
Oxford *Chanson de Roland* in its social context is
closely linked with the theme of the hero's birth.

The main reason for the Oxford *Roland*'s complexity
is that, as a song transmitted through oral tradition,
it has accumulated thematic elements between its earliest versions (whose existence and contents, when they
are discernible at all, are known to us only indirectly)
and the state in which it has survived in manuscript.
Taking a tenth-century element as evidence for one
point in a line of progression and the late eleventh-
century Oxford text as another, I would like to explore
the implications of interpreting the *Chanson de Roland*
as the myth of the death of the Frankish king's first-
born son.[10]

As the offspring of Charlemagne and Gisele, Pippin's
son and daughter, Roland's ancestry is dynastically pure
since he is the son of two members of the royal family.
The unusual circumstances of his conception are described
dryly in the *Karlamagnússaga*: "King Charlemagne went to
Aix-la-Chapelle, and there he found his sister Gisla.
He led her into the sleeping hall, and slept next to her,
so that he felt love for her, and they lay together."[11]
Obviously the only purpose of this scene is to provide
for Roland's birth, as Gisele's character is left unde-
veloped. That she and Charlemagne sin together only
once is made plain in the confession scene, where the
Emperor vows not to commit the act again.[12]

Many heroic figures, human and divine alike, are
said to have been the progeny of incestuous relations:
in antiquity Zeus, Apollo, Herakles, Romulus; among the
legendary Britons, King Arthur's and Morgan the Fay's
son Mordred; and among the Scandinavian peoples the god
Freyr, son of Njördr and his sister, and Sinfjotli, son
of king Sigmund and his sister Signy in the *Volsungasaga*.
Since we know that the historical Charlemagne could not
have conceived a son on his sister Gisele in time for
this boy to occupy a position in the Frankish army in
778, she being only twenty-two years old in that year,
it is certain that the relationship between Roland and
his uncle-father does not correspond to history. Unfortunately Frankish religious and mythic beliefs are
lost to us: in this case the closest analogue would be
in the archaizing mythology and folklore of the Scan-
dinavians where Sinfjotli is conceived through the extraordinary mating of a royal brother and sister, grows

into a vigorous young man because, in the words of the
Volsungasaga, "he is King Volsung's grandson on his
father's as well as on his mother's side,"[13] refuses to
call on his father for help in a fight against overwhelming odds, and dies young and without offspring through
his stepmother's treachery. I do not think that a
genetic relationship, in the sense in which that term is
normally used, is at stake between the two myths, although Sinfjotli is of pan-Germanic fame and it is more
than likely that his story was known to the Franks.[14]
The life story of a hero such as Roland, who is the very
embodiment of his people's ambitions, calls for an illustrious beginning. A traditional pattern of royal incestuous birth was perhaps imposed upon Roland because
of rumors, circulating as early as the ninth century,
that Charlemagne had committed some horrendous but un-
specified sin.

The positing of such a link with the mythic past
might appear groundless were it not for the occurrence
of an incident with unmistakable mythic overtones in the
Oxford version itself. Before Roland's death portents
are seen in nature:

> En France en ad mult merveillus turment:
> Orez i ad de tuneire e de vent,
> Pluies e gresilz desmesureement;
> Chiedent i fuildres e menut e suvent,
> E terremoete ço i ad veirement.
> De seint Michel (de Paris) [del Peril] josqu'as
>   Seinz,
> Des Besençun tresqu'as [port] de Guitsand,
> N'en ad recet dunt del mur ne cravent.
> Cuntre midi tenebres i ad granz;
> N'i ad clartet, se li ciels nen i fent.
> Hume nel veit ki mult ne s'essp[o]ant.[15]
>   (Vv. 1423-33.)

The historian Ferdinand Lot noted that the boundaries of
this earthquake, Mont-Saint-Michel, Wissant, Saintes,
and Besançon, correspond to the limits of tenth-century
Francia, so that the identification of the portents as a
Frankish element rests on strong philological grounds.[16]
As the son of two children of Pippin, Roland embodies
the Frankish land as no other hero could. The storm and
the earthquake show France itself anticipating the death
of its purest offspring, in union with him as the

Wasteland is united to the Fisher King.

Was the Oxford poet aware of this episode's mythic dimensions? I believe this is possible but not crucial, since the poet's intent is not a touchstone for significance in oral traditions, where songs take on the character of depositories of beliefs which, once they are concretized in the form of stylized plot elements, tend to endure despite their supersedure as beliefs. Hence the archaic aspect of many thematic elements in the *chansons de geste*. In line with this quality, the Oxford *Roland* reveals signs of previous stages in the tradition, with later developments tending to obscure but not eliminate earlier ones. Roland's ethical stance is an example of this process. His pronouncements prior to the Battle of Roncevaux, his conduct in the first horn scene, and the manner of his death all point to a conception of heroism much closer to that expressed in Germanic heroic poetry, such as the tenth-century *Battle of Maldon* in Old English, than to the attitudes reflected in French chronicles of the First Crusade. Controversy over whether the Oxford *Roland* is a Christian text or the expression of a primarily pagan set of ideals has become almost an institution because the poem contains passages which support both these interpretations. The contrast between Oliver's reproach of his companion's seemingly foolhardy conduct in refusing to summon help, and Roland's singular perspicacity in the first Frankish council scene when he alone among all the Christian knights sees through Marsile's feigned offer of peace, can only be explained by a process of historical accretion through which the old heroic virtues survive side by side with the new counsel of prudence. Other indications of historical layering are found: the persistence of the old term *Franc* with the newer *Franceis*, the survival of versions lacking the adventitious thousand-line Episode of Baligant, [17] and the extraordinary expansion of the Episode of Alda in the late twelfth century also bear witness to a process of continual change through the addition of new features. The revisions of plot and modernized nomenclature respond to a genuine need to adapt the poetic memory of Charlemagne to changing social and political circumstances. The poet has Roland's contemporaries comment on the possibility of an eschatological interpretation, but as with Charlemagne's Sin (*Ki tant ne set ne l'ad prod entendut*, v. 2098) he asserts his superior knowledge against the ignorance of the uninitiated:

> Dient plusor: "Ço est li definement,
> La fin del secle ki nus est en present."
> Il nel sevent, ne dient veir nient:
> Ço est li granz dulors por la mort de Rollant.
> (Vv. 1434-7.)

In a Christian context there can be no doubt about the connotations of Charlemagne's incest. Roland is the offspring conceived in a sinful moment, and even if God has forgiven the Emperor, penance still must be done for his transgression. This interpretation helps explain Charlemagne's perplexing attitude earlier in the poem when he expresses his powerlessness to help Roland even though he has learned from a dream that Ganelon has committed treason and that France will be destroyed. (France is not destroyed, of course, but Roland, France's personification, is.) It also illuminates the sudden change which the Emperor undergoes, from an accommodating sovereign allowing his chief vassals to make decisions for him, to the resolute champion of Christendom, victorious over Baligant. Grief at losing Roland has purged him of the last remnants of a weakness resulting from his sin against Christian morality, while angels have escorted the soul of his incestuous offspring directly to paradise.

While historians of the Romance epic, dominated by a concern for origins, formerly sought to isolate the historical kernel preserved in each work, a focussing of attention on *how singers have distorted history* and on the circumstances or purposes which have led them to do so will undoubtedly teach us more about the genre's function in society. Modern political forces tend in sometimes subtle ways to appropriate for themselves the "tale of the tribe," as Ezra Pound characterized epic. This deformation of the past is an interesting phenomenon in itself,[18] and its study will enable us to compensate in part for a collective wish to see the past in certain ways. The philologist's task is to appreciate medieval uses of epic legends, although at the same time he realizes that total awareness of them is unattainable. No one knew the Cid tradition as manifested in epic, chronicle, and *romancero* better than Menéndez Pidal, but he failed to see the meaning of a key element in the *Cantar de mio Cid*, one without which the poem's

ending is a puzzle. Bédier was aware of the motif of
Charlemagne's Sin, but, oblivious to the Oxford poet's
admonition against ignoring it, he did not consider it
to be an important theme. One cannot help thinking that
these giants of scholarship were little inclined to pursue clues leading to revelations which might be considered unflattering for the foundation myths of their respective nations. Not that either one was consciously
engaged in obfuscation. Rather in one instance the
political and intellectual climate fostered by the Generation of '98,[19] and in the other a propensity to identify Roland's Franks with the French,[20] may have left no
scope for the idea that the greatest of heroes were taint-
ed by the circumstances of their birth or that the
"national" epics, nos épopées as both Gautier and Bédier
preemptively referred to them, could have such a theme
among their key interpretive elements.

The different versions of the Chanson de Roland
have taken on various meanings for their singers and
audiences. To the late eleventh-century noble French
public, however, about to heed Urban II's exhortation
that it follow in the footsteps of the epic Charlemagne
to recover the Holy Land from the Arabs, Roland is an
exemplary hero because he was able to overcome the imped-
iments of his birth. To Castilian singers whose lords
had to resort to unique forms of land tenure in order to
encourage repopulation of border territory vacated by
the retreating Muslims, the Cid represented an ideal
model, achieving for his descendants access to the highest level of society although he may himself have been a
bastard. Both these heroes, deprived of the privileges
of irreproachable ancestry, acquired legitimacy in the
eyes of the epic public through their own actions.[21]

University of California, Berkeley

NOTES

[1] (Paris, 1878) vol. I, pp. 31-32. The first edition was published in 1868.

[2] *Guerriers et paysans* (Paris, 1973), translated as
*The Early Growth of the European Economy: Warriors and
Peasants from the Seventh to the Twelfth Century* by
Howard B. Clarke (Ithaca, 1974).

[3] See Nancy Joe Dyer, "*El Poema di mio Cid* in the
Crónica de Veinte Reyes Prosification," unpubl. Ph.D.

diss. (University of Pennsylvania, 1975).

[4] Quotations of the *Cid* are taken from Colin Smith, ed., *Poema de mio Cid* (Oxford, 1972).

[5] *España del Cid*, sixth ed., *versión abreviada*, third ed. (Madrid, 1967), p. 104.

[6] The elucidation of this passage is the work of Ian Michael, *Poema de mio Cid: Edición, introducción y notas* (Madrid, 1976), note to v. 3379. Slurs on the Cid's birth are recorded as far back as the *Tercera Crónica General*. Reference to the *molinera* is found in Francisco Santos's *La Verdad en el potro y el Cid resucitado* (Madrid, 1686).

[7] The *Roland* is cited according to the edition of Raoul Mortier, vol. I of *Les Textes de la Chanson de Roland* (Paris, 1940-44).

[8] Branch I, chapter 36. See Paul Aebischer, *Textes norrois et littérature française du moyen âge*, vol. II, *La première branche de la Karlamagnús saga*, Publications Romanes et Françaises, 118 (Geneva, 1972), and Constance B. Hieatt's English translation of the saga, *Karlamagnus Saga: the Saga of Charlemagne and His Heroes*, vol. I (Toronto, 1975).

[9] The Oxford poet, however, makes sure that his audience does not overlook the significance of the scene in Laon. Verse 2098 cited above stands as a reproach to those who proposed global interpretations of the poem without taking Charlemagne's Sin into account. Credit for the present interest in this theme goes to Baudouin de Gaiffier, "La Légende de Charlemagne: Le péché de l'empereur et son pardon," in *Recueil de travaux offerts à Clovis Brunel* (Paris, 1955), vol. I, pp. 490-503, and to Rita Lejeune, "Le Péché de Charlemagne et la *Chanson de Roland*," *Homenaje a Dámasco Alonso* (Madrid, 1960-63), vol. II, pp. 339-71.

[10] This interpretation has been proposed by René Louis in a wide-ranging synthesis published in *DArch*, 30(1978), as "Le Mystère de Roland, des réticences des annalistes officiels aux amplifications épiques des trouvères: Un entretien avec Sophie Leroy."

[11] Branch I, chapter 36.

[12] Conception from a single incestuous encounter characterizes the birth of heroes in Germanic tradition. See Franz-Rolf Schröder, *Germanische Heldendichtung, ein Vortrag nebst einer Studie zur Heroisirung des Mythos*, Philosophie und Geschichte, 55 (Berlin, 1935).

[13] R. G. Finch, *The Saga of the Volsungs* (London, 1965), p. 13.

[14] Sinfjotli is called Fitela in *Beowulf*, lines 879 and 889. The Old High German form is Sintarfizila. See Finch, *Saga of the Volsungs*, p. xii.

[15] Most editors correct the Oxford reading *de Paris* in v. 1428 to *del Peril*, that is "Mont-Saint-Michel au péril de la mer."

[16] "Etudes sur les légendes épiques françaises, V: *La Chanson de Roland*," *Romania*, 54(1928), 357-80, rpt. in Robert Bossuat, ed., Ferdinand Lot, *Etudes sur les légendes épiques françaises* (Paris, 1958), pp. 260-79.

[17] See "The Generation of the Episode of Baligant: Charlemagne's Dream and the Normans at Mantzikert," *RPh*, 30(1976-77), 59-82.

[18] A major contribution is Janine R. Dakyns, *The Middle Ages in French Literature, 1951-1900* (Oxford, 1973). See also the forthcoming article of John F. Benton, "'Nostre Franceis n'unt talent de fuïr': the *Song of Roland* and the Enculturation of a Warrior Class."

[19] Leo Spitzer read Mendéndez Pidal's *España del Cid* as an intellectual product of the Generation of '98: "Sobre el Carácter histórico del *Cantar de mio Cid*," *NRFH*, 2(1948), 105-17, esp. 111-12, although not with reference to this point, provoking a lively reply, "Poesía e Historia en el *Mio Cid*: el Problema de la épic española," *NRFH*, 3(1949), 113-29.

[20] See, for example, the lecture Bédier delivered at Oxford, *Roland à Roncevaux* (Oxford, 1921), which mixes allusions to the First World War with a presentation of the *Chanson de Roland*.

[21] An earlier version of this article was presented at a symposium on the hero in ancient and medieval epic held at Brown University, October 27, 1978, and again at Harvard University under the sponsorship of the Committee on Degrees in Folklore and Mythology, on October 30, 1978.

FEASTS AND ANTI-FEASTS IN *BEOWULF* AND THE *ODYSSEY**

Joanne De Lavan Foley

Since the appearance in 1928 of Milman Parry's first *thèse*,[1] and especially since the publication of Lord's seminal study, *The Singer of Tales*, oral theorists have been working to refine the critical apparatus of oral theory. A great deal of critical attention, much of it in the form of heated debate, has been devoted to defining and understanding the formula. The aim has been to make our definition of the formula[2] more applicable for stylistic analyses of oral poetry—to find a definition inclusive enough to account for the wide range of formulaic expressions found in oral poetry, but selective enough to distinguish between types of formulaic expressions, since it is upon such distinctions that we may found a methodology of formulaic analysis.[3] In this study, the method of formulaic analysis described and demonstrated by Donald K. Fry in his "Old English Formulas and Systems"[4] and "Cædmon as a Formulaic Poet"[5] will be rigorously applied to *Beowulf*, with the intention of demonstrating the existence of a *necessary* relationship between formulaic content and mythic, or ideational, content. The formula is much more than a mechanical device employed acontextually to fulfill certain metrical and narrative conditions. In *Beowulf*, the formula is indivisible from the meaning, structure, and archetypal rhythms of the entire work. In concluding, I will offer some tentative suggestions about formulaic meaning and aspects of myth in the *Odyssey*.

Among formulaic theorists in Old English, Fry has made perhaps the most considerable contribution to defining and understanding the Old English formula.[6] In OEFS he offers a definition which, while maintaining clearly defined and discernible boundaries, frees the formula from the prohibitive number of determinants accorded it by earlier critics. Fry defines the formula as a "group of words, one-half line in length, which shows evidence of being the direct product of a formulaic system" and the system as "a group of half-lines, usually loosely related metrically and semantically, which are related in form by the identical relative placement of two elements, one a variable word or ele-

ment of a compound usually supplying the alliteration,
and the other a constant word or element of a compound,
with approximately the same distribution of non-stressed
elements" (204, 203).[7] This paper will offer evidence
to support an extension of Fry's theory to include the
possibility of an even more highly organized systemic
organization than that which he describes,[8] where a number of what he would call systems—and I have found as
many as four—may be organized into a more comprehensive
superstructure: a unified group of *related* systems.

The "swefan æfter symble" formulas in *Beowulf* provide an example of a very complex, highly developed systemic organization. Following Fry's lead in analyzing
Cædmon's Hymn into systems, I am able to classify a
group of related formulas into four related systems or
"pool[s] of organized diction" (CAFP, 236), each presenting solutions to sometimes different metrical, alliterative, and narrative situations which the oral poet
will encounter while composing:

A. The following formulas imply the system, "(X)
symble":[9]

1. *Bwf* 81: sinc æt symle.   Sele hlifade
2. *Bwf* 119: swefan æfter symble;   sorge ne cuðon,
3. *Bwf* 489: Site nu to symle   ond onsæl meoto,
4. *Bwf* 1008: swefeþ æfter symle.   Ða wæs sæl ond mæl,
5. *Bwf* 2104: ond we to symble   geseten hæfdon.
6. *Bwf* 2431: geaf me sinc ond symbel,   sibbe gemunde;

The system may be described further in terms of position; all formulaic verses in this system appear in the
a-verse.

B. The following formulas imply the system, "(X) swefan":

1. *Bwf* 703: scriðan sceadugenga.   Sceotend swæfon,
2. *Bwf* 1280: geond þæt sæld swæfun.   þa ðær sona wearð
3. *Bwf* 1672: sorhleas swefan   mid þinra secga gedryht
4. *Bwf* 1741: weaxeð ond wridað;   þonne se weard swefeð,
5. *Bwf* 1800: geap ond goldfah;   gæst inne swæf,
6. *Bwf* 2060: æfter billes bite   blodfag swefeð,
7. *Bwf* 2256: fætum befeallen;   feormynd swefað
8. *Bwf* 2457: reohte berofene,--   ridend swefað,

There is a metrical tendency for the constant to bear an

alpha or delta configuration (75% of the time), both of which follow an alpha-prime variable configuration 63% of the time.[10]

C. The following formulas imply the system, "swefan/ swebban (X)":

1. *Bwf* 600: swefeð ond snedeþ,   secce ne weneþ
2. *Bwf* 679: forþan ic hine sweorde   swebban nelle,
3. *Bwf* 729: swefan sibbegedriht   samod ætgædere,
4. *Bwf* 2746: swefeð sare wund,   since bereafod.

D. And the following formulas imply the system, "symble (X)":

1. *Bwf* 564: symbel ymbsæton   sægrunde neah;
2. *Bwf* 619: symbel ond seleful,   sigerof kyning.
3. *Bwf* 1010: wolde self cyning   symbel þicgan,
4. *Bwf* 1782: Ga nu to setle,   symbelwynne dreoh

There are similarities between these systems just as there are similarities between the formulas composing each system. For example, in systems A and B, the variable precedes the constant, while C and D share the quality of having the constant precede the variable. The latter two systems may also be grouped under O'Neil's type II designation whereby the variable element is the "final word or final segment of a compound, necessarily stressed but not necessarily alliterating" (OEFS, 198). That which links the systems more convincingly, however, is *the idea of feasting and sleeping*. Each system type— if we consider A and B one type and C and D another—[11] expresses both the ideas implied by *symbel* and those implied by *swefan*; A and B share the configuration, "(X) *symbel/swefan*," and C and D share "*swefan/symbel* (X)," where (X) is the variable element. Linking of the concepts of feasting and sleeping occurs within the system grouping as well (see A, numbers 2 and 4, and C, number 1). The conceptual linking of feasting and sleeping implied by the above correspondences is carefully worked out in the text of the poem itself. Using a logic analogous to that by which Fry defines the formula, I would suggest that the four systems described above are related generically to one another because each bears the same relation to a central idea, described for now as feasting and sleeping. The systems and their formulas

are expressions of a central concept, and they are generated from this "essential idea," using Parry's phrase,
in a manner analogous to that by which a formula is—or
may be—generated from a system.

In his article, "Towards a Generative View of the
Oral Formula,"[12] Michael Nagler also suggests an ideational basis for formulaic expressions. The important
difference between Nagler's generative source, which he
calls the "Gestalt,"[13] and the "essential idea" proposed in this study is that the "essential idea," unlike
the "Gestalt," is part of the oral tradition inherited
by the poet rather than a mental template isolated somewhere in the preverbal consciousness of the poet. Although both lie below the immediate surface of the poem,
the "essential idea," again unlike the "Gestalt," may be
reconstructed through a process of abstraction. Nagler
considers the "family affiliations" of the "Gestalt" to
be "essentially continuous with the meanings and processes of myth" (S&T, p. 40), and myth is, in my opinion,
that which unifies the projection of formulas into a consistent and discernible pattern. It is common participation in the inherently logical myth implied by "feasting and sleeping" which links together all of the formulas described systemically above. It is with regard to
that "essential idea" that the four systems may be said
to be organized into a more comprehensive systemic complex. The mythic idea may be reconstructed by abstract-
ing generic similarities from the formulas which are
used to express it.

The first formula in the complex of systems and
formulas is "sinc æt symle" ("treasure at the feast")
at 81a[14]; here, the feast is the celebration of the creative activity of God celebrated with *hearpan sweg* ("the
song of the harp," 89b). This feast celebrates the cosmic order as well as the communal order of the comitatus,
the latter of which is cast into relief by the line preceding and governing the formula: "He beot ne aleh,
beagas dælde,/sinc æt symle" ("Nor did he fail to be
true to his vow; he distributed rings/and riches at the
feast," 80-81a). The world is, using Homer's phrase,
pánta katà kósmon—all things entirely in order. Cultural ceremony and ritual, represented respectively by
the *beot* motif and the feast, attest to a state of purity.[15] Rhetorically, the feasting passage marks the
transition from the *dream* ("joy") and daylight order of
Hrothgar to the dark, nighttime order of Grendel. The

next formula calls attention to the comitatus and the
cultural order which are about to be disturbed; Grendel
"fand þa ðær inne æþelinga gedriht/ swefan æfter
symble" (Grendel "found there within a band of nobles
sleeping after the feast," 118-19a). The members of the
comitatus sleep after the feast, as is physiologically
appropriate. The force of the formula and the passage
surrounding it is to contrast this near-mythic appropriateness and that of the creation feast (81ff.) with the
disorderly rule of Grendel, who does not sleep as members of the comitatus do, but who *gewat* ("depart[s]")
and threatens to rupture the natural and mythic rhythm
of sleeping after feasting. The feast of Grendel celebrates a disruption of the ritual of the feast, the order
of the comitatus, and the physiological rhythm; the
dream of feasting is converted to the *wop* ("weeping") of
Grendel's blood-feast, and natural sleep is converted to
funeral-less death.

     The next formula, "Site nu to symle" ("Sit, now, at
the feast," 489a), marks the transition from the night-
feasting passage to the day feast of Hrothgar which Beowulf attends. Again, the *scop* sings, and there is joy
of feasting in Heorot. Unferth's challenge, however,
suggests that the ritual of the feast has indeed been
disrupted; the communal manifestation of order implied
by the comitatus is ruptured. Rhetorically, the formula
and its surroundings mark a transition from Hrothgar's
story of "Grendles gryre" ("Grendel's terror," 478a) to
the Unferth-Beowulf confrontation. The *dream* of feasting is preceded and succeeded by scenes suggesting cosmic disorder on the one hand and communal disorder on
the other.

     The next formulaic expressions of the sleeping
after feasting concept occur in Beowulf's answer to Unferth; he says "Næs hie ðære fylle gefean hæfdon,/
manfordædlan, þæt hie me þegon,/ symbel ymbsæton
sægrunde neah" ("Nor did they have the joy of eating
their fill, the wicked evil-doers, that they would take
me for their food, sitting at a feast at the bottom of
the sea," 562-64). The feast described by Beowulf is a
dark-world celebration, which he counters with the action
implied by "sweo[r]dum aswefede" (he "put them to sleep
with a sword," 567a). He replaces the perverse feast
with the sleep of death and restores meaning to the ritual of feasting while restoring the cosmic daylight rule
of "beorht beacen Godes" ("the bright beacon of God,"

570a). Beowulf describes himself as one who can purge
the ritual of feasting and the rhythm of feasting and
sleeping, thereby restoring the cosmic and communal order described at 81a and surroundings; this description
is consistent with his initial promise, "Heorot fælsian"
("to cleanse Heorot," 432b). By putting the night-goer
into the sleep of death, Beowulf will act out the mythical restoration of life forces—and rhythms—over death,
order over disorder.

He balances this implicit promise with a formulaic
description of Grendel, his opponent: "ac he lust wigeð,/
swefeð ond snedeþ" ("but he takes his pleasure, puts to
sleep and sends to death," 599b-600a). Grendel is also
one who brings about the sleep which is death—*swefeð*—
and, as such, is a good match for Beowulf, who has spok-
en of his ability to do the same (567a). The disorder
implied in Grendel's perversion of the ritual feast—
snedeþ—[16] echoes the blood feast described at and
around line 119. Beowulf's restoration of life and order to Heorot promises to be a restoration of the daylight order of Hrothgar, of the cosmic order, and of the
communal order: "Gæþ eft se þe mot/ to medo modig,
siþþan morgenleoht/ ofer ylda bearn oþres dogores,/
sunne sweglwered suþan scineð!" ("Tomorrow morning, when
the morning light shines over the sons of men, and the
sun, clad in brightness, shines from the south, he who
wishes will again be able to go to the mead-drinking
with a brave heart," 603b-6). His promise again brings
joy to the feasting in Heorot and a temporary restoration of the ritual of feasting and of the order of the
comitatus: "he on lust geþeah/ symbel ond seleful,
sigerof kyning" ("The king, famed for victory, gladly
partook of the feast and the hall-goblet," 618b-19).
Hrothgar's pleasure of feasting, his *lust*, is contrasted to Grendel's *lust* of feasting (599b). The ban-
quet scene ends with the fall of night and acts as a
transition from Hrothgar's day-feast to Grendel's night-
feast.

Before assuming his night watch, Beowulf reiter-
ates his equality in battle with Grendel, who, as we
will recall, is able to "put [his enemy] to sleep"
("swefeð," 600a). Explaining his preference not to use
a weapon, Beowulf says, "ic hine sweorde swebban nelle"
("I do not wish to put him to sleep by means of a
sword," 679). By not sleeping as the others do at
night, Beowulf places himself out of the physiological

and communal rhythm; by countering the anti-rhythmic
activity of the "shadow-goer," Beowulf will restore the
disrupted order: "Came in the dark night, stalking, the
shadow-goer. The warriors were asleep, all except one,"
(702b-5). The sleep of the comitatus is then disrupted
by Grendel's feast: "Geseah he in recede rinca manige,/
swefan sibbegedriht samod ætgædere" ("He saw inside the
hall many a warrior, sleeping all together in a company," 728-29). The joy of heroes ("hæleða dream," 497b)
shared by members of the comitatus is contrasted to
Grendel's joyless feasting; he is "dreamum bedæled"
("bereft of joys," 721a). Again, the formula works
poetically to contrast the two dispensations at Heorot:
that of Hrothgar—daylight, order, ritual, and rhythm
versus that of Grendel—night, disorder, anti-ritual,
and anti-rhythm.[17]

The restoration of the mythic physiological and
communal rhythms is the result of Beowulf's defeat of
Grendel. The episode after the fight is emphasized by
the nearly back-to-back appearance of two feasting-
sleeping formulas and by the gnomic projection of the
first formula: "þær his lichoma legerbedde fæst/ swefeþ
æfter symle" ("There his body-house fast in the narrow
bed sleeps after the feast," 1007a-8a). The formula is
cast into relief by its placement at the end of the
gnome and by its virtually exact echoing of an earlier
formula, "swefan æfter symble" ("sleeping after the
feast," 119a). The meaning implied by the formula is an
expansion of its little more than literal, though suggestive, use at 119a. The gnomic perspective brings into
order the sleep which is death and the feast which is
life; with that perspective is brought the reinstitution
of the cyclic rhythm which requires the succession of the
one upon the other. The feast, then, becomes a metaphor
for life, which, quite in accord with physiological and
mythic rhythms, is succeeded by the sleep of death. Although continuous with one another, the feast and sleep
are separated, as day and night and as life and death
are separated. Appropriately, the sleep which is death
is not accompanied this time with ritualistic defilement; the dead will now sleep in the *legerbedde*—the bed
of death; they will depart with the ritual of the
funeral. The formula which follows this affirmation of
order describes the restoration of the day feast at
Heorot with its resonances of *dream*, singing, creativity, and communality: "wolde self cyning symbel þicgan"

("The king himself wished to partake of the feast,"
1010). The pre-Grendelean order is restored; ritual is
purified, and communal and mythic rhythms are set right:
"Heorot innan wæs/freondum afylled" ("Heorot within was/
filled with friends," 1017b-18a).

The revenge of Grendel's mother causes another
lapse into anti-ritual and anti-rhythm; the sleep of the
comitatus is again disturbed by a night-feaster: "Com
þa to Heorote, ðær Hring-Dene/ geond þæt sæld swæfun"
(She "came then to Heorot, where the Ring-Danes were
sleeping throughout that hall," 1279-80a). Her removal
of Æschere is significant as another disruption of the
funeral rite and, in general, the disruption of ritual
and natural rhythm in Heorot. Beowulf promises to restore "sorrowless" sleep to Heorot: "Ic hit þe þonne
gehate, þæt þu on Heorote most/ sorhleas swefan mid
þinra secga gedryht" ("This I promise you, that you will
be able to sleep in Heorot without sorrow with your
troop of men," 1671-72). The killing of Grendel's
mother fulfills his promise by removing the new threat
to ritual and rhythm in Heorot. By fulfilling his *beot*,
Beowulf demonstrates the restoration of communal ritual.
Hrothgar fulfills his promise by dispensing gifts and
words to Beowulf, and the feast which takes place is
once again a celebration of the creative order in Heorot
and in the cosmos.

Thus far, the rhythm which has been suggested by
the formulas of feasting and sleeping is order/rhythm/
ritual—disorder/anti-rhythm/anti-ritual—and order/
rhythm/ritual, hereafter described as R-A-R. The rhythm
implied by "swefan æfter symble" has been disrupted by
Grendel's converting the time for sleep to a time for
anti-rhythmic and anti-ritualistic feasting. To reassert the rhythm upset by Grendel, Beowulf places himself out of rhythm. He watches and wages warfare during
the time for sleep. It is by imitating Grendel's anti-
rhythmic activity that Beowulf restores rhythm in Heorot
and restores the rituals associated with feasting and
sleeping. The same may be said of his defeat of
Grendel's mother. In *Nature and Culture in the Iliad*,
Redfield describes the heroic ethic as "a pervasive
drive for order, a need to rescue form from the formlessness of the world," and he describes heroic activity
as the restoration of ritual in the community. Beowulf's actions may be understood as attempts to combat
impurity, which Redfield defines as "the formless, the

deformed, and that which threatens the forms" (pp. 162,
160). From his first to his last moments in the land of
the Danes, Beowulf's task is, as he put it earlier,
"Heorot fælsian" ("to cleanse Heorot," 432b).

Hrothgar celebrates the restoration of ritual and
rhythm performed by Beowulf with a feast and a speech,
in which he discusses spiritual death, a condition
which, whether individual or communal, makes the sacrificial feast or consumption of the body by the funeral
fire ineffective as a ritual of passage from physical
death to spiritual life: "þonne se weard swefeð/ sawele
hyrde; bið se slæp to fæst" ("Then the guardian sleeps,
the watchman of the soul; that sleep is too sound," 1741b-
42). The feast which follows Hrothgar's speech contrasts his domain, which has been restored by the hero,
with the unrestored domain of the proud king he has just
described. When Hrothgar sends Beowulf "to setle,
symbelwynne dreoh" ("to the bench, [to] take part in the
feasting joy," 1782),[18] he is performing an act of community purification. The hero, who has been estranged
from the rhythms and rituals of the community by virtue
of his heroic activity, is integrated into the communal
identity; he is adopted into the lineage of Danish
heroes, a gesture objectified by the passing of war
garments and equipment from Hrothgar to Beowulf. Appropriately, the hero feasts with the comitatus and, for
the first time since his arrival, participates in the
rhythm of "swefan æfter symble": "Reste hine þa
rumheort; reced hliuade/ geap ond goldfah; gæst inne
swæf,/ oþ þæt hrefn blaca heofones wynne/ bliðheort
bodode" ("Then the great-hearted one took his rest. The
towering hall stood, wide-gabled and gold-adorned; the
guest slept within until the black raven announced the
joy of heaven with a joyful heart," 1799-1802a). The
sleep is at last *sorhleas*; the rhythm of sleeping after
feasting is restored, and the ritual of the feast is
expanded to cosmic participation. It is now not only
hearpan wyn ("the harp's joy") heard at dawn but also
heofones wyn ("the joy of heaven"). All is, again,
pánta katà kósmon. Order is so complete that the raven,
usually a scavenger of battle and representative of ritualistic defilement in the poem,[19] is a messenger of
dawn.

The contrast between Heorot as it was in the anti-
rhythmic and anti-ritualistic stage of the R-A-R cycle
and as it is in this, the restoration stage, is deepened

by the use of verbal echoes. The clustering of *neosan*
at lines 1786, 1791, and 1806, which encloses the formula "gæst inne swæf" (1800b), recalls the clustering of
neosan at lines 115 and 125, which also encloses a formula from the feasting-sleeping complex. It was in the
earlier *neosan* passage that Grendel entered Heorot and
disrupted the rhythm of sleeping after feasting. Like
the rhythm and the rituals associated with feasting and
sleeping, the diction itself seems to have undergone
some sort of purification. It is now the Geat *glædmod*
("glad at heart," 1785a), not Grendel "grim ond grædig"
("savage and greedy," 121a), who is doing the action of
neosan. And the feast Beowulf is visiting is very different from the feast Grendel plans to hold in Heorot.
It is Hrothgar, afterwards, who is going to *neosan* his
beddes (1791b) in order to sleep, and it is the *cuma*
(1806a)—the hero this time and not Grendel—[20] who
wishes to *neosan* the *ceoles* ("to seek out his ship,"
1807b). We are at the end of an R-A-R cycle; the
cleansing of Heorot has been performed. It is no longer
dreorfah ("bespattered with gore," 485a) and "blode
bestymed" ("steeped in blood," 486b), but "geap ond
goldfah" ("wide-gabled and gold-adorned," 1800a), just as
it was "heah ond horngeap" ("high and wide-gabled,"
82a) at the beginning of the cycle. The order established at the creation of Heorot has been restored.[21]
The hero returns home and another cycle is begun, one in
which the hero is again called upon to restore rhythm
and ritual to a world brought out of order by a night-
goer.

In the land of the Danes, Beowulf accomplished the
purification of ritual and the restoration of the sleeping after feasting rhythm. Before performing the same
in the land of the Geats, the hero tells about the
Froda-Freawaru marriage and his own past accomplishments
at Heorot. By articulating both tales in terms of the
feasting-sleeping idea, Beowulf is, in effect, extending
the mythic ethos he sustained at Heorot at the land of
the Geats, thereby establishing a context in which to
perform the heroic activities of cleansing and restitution.

The first feasting-sleeping formula used in this
way occurs in Beowulf's digression on the fates of
Freawaru and Froda. Beowulf foresees an upset of the
peace between Hrothgar and Ingeld established by that
marriage. The feast will be disrupted by an "eald

æscwiga" ("spear-warrior," 2042) who is not joyful while
feasting but *grim sefa* ("savage [in] mind," 2043b) and
geomormod ("sorrowful," 2044a). The sleep which follows
the joyless feast will not be restful but full of strife:
"...se fæmnan þegn fore fæder dædum / æfter billes bite
blodfag swefeð/ ealdres scyldig" ("the bride's thane, on
account of her father's deeds, sleeps, stained with
blood after the sword's sting," 2059-60a). The sleep
which follows the perverse feast of the sword[23] is
blodfag ("stained with blood"), just as Heorot, after
Grendel's night-feast, was *blode fah* (934b) and "blode
bestymed" ("steeped in blood," 486b). Beowulf's digression suggests that the cycle which he has just brought
to completion with the purification of Heorot will begin
again. Another lapse into anti-rhythm and anti-ritual
will take place, and there will again be a need for the
heroic activities of cleansing and restitution.

Beowulf continues the account of his adventures and
tells the story of Grendel's night dispensation at
Heorot and of his demise. After the perverse feast and
subsequent defeat of Grendel, the "bona blodigtoð"
("bloody-toothed slayer," 2082a), who "lic eall
forswealg" ("swallowed the whole body," 2080b) of the
beloved Hondscio, comes a day of joyful, ritualistic
feasting:

Me þone wælræs	wine Scildunga	
fættan golde	fela leanode,	
manegum maðmum,	syððan mergen com,	
ond we to symble	geseten hæfdon.	
Þær wæs gidd ond gleo;	gomela Scilding,	2105
felafricgende	feorran rehte;	
hwilum hildedeor	hearpan wynne,	
gomenwudu grette,	hwilum gyd awræc	
soð ond sarlic,	hwilum syllic spell	
rehte æfter rihte	rumheort cyning;	2110

("When morning came, and we had sat down to the
feast, the friend of the Scyldings rewarded me
well for the deadly war-rush with beaten gold,
with many treasures. There was singing and glee.
A wise old Scylding told tales of long ago; at
times one brave in battle touched the mirth-wood,
the joy of the harp; at times drove out a song,
true and sad; at times the great-hearted king told
a wonderful tale according to right.")

The day-rule of Hrothgar where feasting is a time
for joy and song lasts only until night (2116). The invasion of Heorot by Grendel's mother marks a return to
anti-ritual: "Noðer hy hine ne moston, syððan mergen
cwom/ deaðwerigne Denia leode/ bronde forbærnan, ne on
bel hladan,/ leofne mannan" ("Nor, when morning came,
could the men of the Danes burn up the death-weary one
with fire, nor lay the beloved man on the funeral pyre,"
2124-27a). Beowulf goes on to tell about his defeat of
Grendel's mother and his reward at the hands of Hrothgar,
a gesture which signifies the restitution of the feasting
ritual where dispensation takes place and of the communal
ritual implied by the fulfillment of the *beot* (80a).

The R-A-R cycle, which now has been both performed
and articulated by the hero, immediately begins anew.
The "weard winegeomor" ("watchman mourning for his
friends," 2239a) tells of a reversal which occurred long
ago among the Geats; he says that whereas once his
people "gesawon seledream" ("saw joy in the hall,"
2252a), now "feormynd swefað,/ þa ðe beadogriman bywan
sceoldon" ("the polishers sleep, they who must polish
the war-masks," 2256b-57b). Klaeber glosses *feormynd*
as the present participle of the verb *feormian*, meaning
to "cleanse, polish" (p. 328). The loss of one who
cleanses is important here. Beowulf's cleansing of
Heorot and the fen (*fælsian*: ll. 432, 825, 1176, and
1620) has been a purification of ritual and a restitution of the feasting-sleeping rhythm. The Geats' lapse
into joylessness—"Næs hearpan wyn,/ gomen gleobeames,
ne god hafoc/ geond sæl swingeð, ne se swifta mearh/
burhstede beateð" ("There is no joy of the harp, mirth
of the glee-wood, nor does the good hawk sweep throughout that hall, nor the swift steed stamp in the castle
court," 2262b-65a)—is associated with the absence of
the one who cleanses, the hero.[23] The verse "Næs
hearpan wyn" recalls the "hearpan wynne" (2107b) of the
Danish feast celebrating Beowulf's defeat of Grendel,
which in turn echoes the *hearpan sweg* (89b) of the original creation feast. The negation of the joy of the harp
implies as well the disruption of the feasting ritual
where the harp's joy has been sounded. Likewise, the
absence of the *god hafoc* is contrasted to the appearance
of the *hrefn blaca* (1801a), which before announced
"heofones wynne" (1801b) and which marked the hero's
restitution of the rhythm and rituals at Heorot.

The *weard* of the Geatish hoard is telling about the

untimely sleeping of the *feormynd*; by now, the mythic
significance of the lapse into sleep should be clear.
There is no hero to restore rhythm and ritual to a community experiencing the anti-rhythmic and anti-ritualistic stage of the R-A-R cycle. The association of the
lapse at Heorot and the lapse in the land of the Geats
is reinforced by the echo in *feormynd* of the verb
gefeormian, used only once in *Beowulf* and then to refer
to Grendel's bloody night-feast, by which he had disrupted the rhythm of feasting and sleeping and had ne-
gated the rituals of the feast and the funeral at Heorot:

> Ne þæt se aglæca   yldan þohte,
> ac he gefeng hraðe   forman siðe   740
> slæpendne rinc,   slat unwearnum,
> bat banlocan,   blod edrum dranc,
> synsnædum swealh;   sona hæfde
> unlyfigendes   eal *gefeormod*,
> fet ond folma.   745

("Nor did the monster think to delay, but first he
quickly seized a sleeping warrior, greedily tore
him up, chewed the bone-locker, drank the blood in
his veins, swallowed him in huge morsels; soon he
had *consumed* all of the unliving one, feet and
hands.")

It is Beowulf, the cleanser of Heorot, who will be called
upon to restore purity to ritual and rhythm to feasting
and sleeping in the land of the Geats.

In his speech to his hearth companions, Beowulf
uses two of the feasting-sleeping formulas. The first
is used to tell about his joyful childhood when "Hreðel
cyning,/ geaf me sinc ond symbel, sibbe gemunde" ("King
Hrethel gave me treasure and feasting, remembered kinship," 2430b-31). Beowulf's early state is associated
with Heorot's early state, during which, as we were told
formulaically at 81a, Hrothgar also distributed riches
at a feast. The correspondence between Heorot before
its *edwenden* ("reversal," 1774b) in the first R-A-R
cycle and Beowulf before his reversal in the second
cycle precedes in importance the metrical regularity of
the verse at 2431a.[24]

Comparing his present state with that of an old man
mourning his dead son, Beowulf contrasts his early, joyful days of feasting with his later days of anti-ritual

and anti-rhythm. The anti-feast described at lines
2444-59 may be contrasted to the joyful feasts described
earlier in the poem: here, the *hrefn* is no messenger of
dawn as he was at 1801b, but a Beast of Battle feasting
on the corpse of the ritualistically defiled son (2448);
the feasting *gyd* ("song" or "tale," 2446b) is a "sarigne
sang" (a "mournful song," 2447a), not the "...gyd awræc/
soð ond sarlic" (the "song [driven out], true and sad,"
2108b-9a) which Beowulf described to Hrethel, and the
hall is no resting place for thanes as Heorot was after
the defeat of the monsters, but a "windge reste/ reote
berofene" (a "resting-place for winds, bereft of joy,"
2456b-57a). There is no *hearpan sweg* (2458b), laments
the old man, as there once was, and there are no heroes
to set things right: "ridend swefað,/ hæleð in hoðman"
("the riders slept, the heroes in the grave," 2457b-58a).
The hall described, then, is one in which anti-ritual and
anti-rhythm prevail: the son is without a proper funeral,
the only feast is the anti-ritualistic feast of the
Beast of Battle, and the heroes, who could restore order
to the old man's world, are all sleeping in the grave.
Beowulf's hall is reminiscent of the hall described
earlier by the "weard winegeomor" (2239a); there, too,
there is neither *hearpan wyn* (2262b) nor *god hafoc*
(2263b) announcing dawn. The Beast of Battle has replaced the joyful messenger of morning (1801-2). Beowulf's story of the defiled hall, like that of the old
guardian's, implies a need for purification like that
which he performed in the Danish hall. The *hearpan
sweg* and "gomen in geardum, swylce þær iu wæron" (the
"harp's song, mirth in the dwelling, as there were before," 2458b-59) need to be restored, just as the joy of
feasting at Heorot needed to be restored.

    The final use of a feasting-sleeping formula
(2303b) describes the sleeping of another night-goer,
the dragon, and the restitution of the treasure to its
proper guardian, a gesture which suggests the restoration of ritual in the community; Beowulf says, "Wiglaf
leofa, nu se wyrm ligeð,/ swefeð sare wund, since
bereafod" ("Wiglaf, beloved, now the dragon lies/ sleeping sorely wounded, bereft of the treasure," 2745a-46).
The restoration stage in the second R-A-R cycle is
celebrated with a sacrificial feast, the funeral of the
hero, which, like the feast initiated by Hrothgar at the
end of the first R-A-R cycle, is a ritual of purification.[25]   Redfield discusses the funeral of the hero in

terms of the heroic ethic, which he has described as "a
pervasive drive for order, a need to rescue form from
the formlessness of the world" (p. 162). The funeral
is a communal affirmation of this drive for order and
form: "the threat of deformation, formlessness, and impurity. . . is not local to the dead man; it affects all
bound to him in ties of community. . . . The funeral pyre
cauterizes and heals this wound. At the same time,
through mourning and memorial, the social fabric is reconstructed in a new form which takes account of the
absence of this member. In the funeral the community
acts on its own behalf to reassert its own continuity in
spite of the disorderly forces which assail it. By the
funeral, the community purifies itself. . . ." (p. 182).
At the individual level, the funeral of Beowulf is an
adoption into the heroic tradition first established in
the poem with the description of Scyld's funeral. At
the communal level, Beowulf's funeral is both the reconstruction of the social fabric ruptured by the loss of
the hero-king and the restoration of ritual in general.
The drive for order and form which has been expressed
individually by Beowulf's determination in restoring the
rhythm implied by "swefan æfter symble" ("sleeping
after the feast") is transferred to the community as it
seeks to impose order by ritualizing the passage of the
hero from the feast of life to the sleep of death
through the funeral.

It should be clear that the formulas comprising the
feasting-sleeping complex bear not only a relationship
to the "essential idea" which this study has tried to
reconstruct, but also poetically to one another. Each
formula expresses the idea of feasting and sleeping
and is generically related to every other formula of the
complex by virtue of its participation with them in that
"essential idea." It is by the formulas, then, that the
idea is developed at many levels of meaning. Saying
that these formulas are formulas because they originate
in a system and saying *only* that fails to capture the
poetically and mythically significant relationships
which the systems may share with one another and which
formulas may share with the larger systemic complex.
Formulas such as the ones I have examined above are not
acontextual entities devoid of expressive content. They
function aesthetically, that is, in the context of story
and meaning.

Although the Old English and the Homeric formulas

differ enough to make an exact transference of definition unprofitable, it is possible to apply the method
of formulaic analysis demonstrated above to the *Odyssey*.
The phrase *katà moîran* ("according to lot or share") and
its formulaic variations occur throughout the feasting
scenes in the *Odyssey* to express an idea which may be
close to the center of the Homeric feast.[26]   The idea
inferred from the formulas which express it may be para-
phrased as "appropriate share."   At the literal level,
the level of the feast, appropriate share is the individual's portion of the communal feast; at the meta-
phoric level, it is his cosmic portion—his lot or
fate—distributed by the immortals at the cosmic feast.
Except where there is unfailing store, the distribution
of appropriate shares, the task of the host, entails both
the ability to discern the common share, the fixed portion out of which individual shares will be distributed,
and the ability to proportion the individual share to
it.   The ethic implied here is straightforward.   What is
given to or, as in the cases of Aegisthus and the suitors, *taken* by one person cannot be given to another.
Reaching beyond appropriate share, "*hupèr móron*"[27] (1.35),
as Zeus says Aegisthus has done, entails denial of that
usurped portion to another.   It is according to this
principle that we should understand the anti-feast vis-
ited upon the suitors by Oddyseus in Book 22 of the
Odyssey.   He is reclaiming not simply his share of the
equal feast, but his cosmic portion or lot, which the
suitors, feasting in his hall and wooing his wife, have
sought to actualize for themselves.   It is entirely appropriate that his requital be presented as a feast; on
his return, Odysseus is the host, the arbiter who must
restore appropriate share where it has been denied, and
he is the hero who by so doing restores the ritual of
the equal feast.

The feast of Nestor is an equal feast; portions are
distributed as they should be, and all enjoy an
"*erikudéa daîta*" (3.66)—glorious feast.   Alcinous, too,
maintains the equal feast; not only does he see that
portions are distributed *katà moîran*, but he enforces
the principle implied by that formula at the communal
level.   He orders Euryalus to requite the stranger for
words spoken not "*katà moîran*" (8.397) with words and a
gift, restoring the order which had been disrupted by
challenges to the stranger.   Notably, Odysseus, too, re-
bukes one of his challengers, Laodamus, for speaking

"*ou katà kôsmon*" (8.179)— ("not according to order").
Although he will not come into his own as the host, up-
holder and restorer of appropriate share, until Book 22,
he undertakes the activity of distribution, the host's
activity, here and elsewhere. It is Odysseus who distributes a portion of the feast to the minstrel,
Demodocus, who, in return, distributes to Odysseus his
share of *kléos* by singing of the fate of the Achaeans
"*katà kôsmon*" (8.489)—according to order, that is,
rightly or truthfully. The singer's ability to tell a
tale "*katà moîran*" (8.496), we are told, is proof that
his is the gift of divine song. At the Aeolian feast
and elsewhere in the Phaeacian inset, Odysseus is himself the singer, commended for telling his tale "*pánta
katà moîran*" ("all things according to truth or portion," 10.16).

In Book 22, Odysseus is the host, the hero, and the
singer, invoking at all three levels the values of a
world *pánta katà moîran*. Before looking at that feast,
or, more appropriately, that anti-feast, I wish to look
briefly at Book 9 and the anti-feast hosted by Polyphemus. Consistent with his general spirit of "*athemístia*"
("lawlessness or godlessness," 9.189), the Cyclops invokes an unequal feast, one not *katà moîran*—an anti-
feast. Although he performs his milking "*pánta katà
moîran*," as we are reminded formulaically three times
in the space of less than one hundred lines (9.245, 309,
342), he is completely "*ou katà moîran*" (9.352) in his
distribution of the feasting portions. The portion he
distributes to his guests consists of undeserved death
and fate, a denial of their appropriate cosmic shares.
For the feasting ritual, so fully actualized in the
third, seventh, and eighth books of the *Odyssey*,
Polyphemus substitutes the anti-ritualistic blood-feast,
where the guest is himself the sacrifice and the host
the godless receiver of his own offering. He, like
Aegisthus, has reached *hupèr móron*—beyond that which
is ordained, beyond his share. To rectify the imbal-
ance, Odysseus, as host, distributes to the "host" an
equal share of his own blood-feast, the glut of the
spear, restoring the equal feast by re-establishing the
law of distribution and the retribution upon which it
is based.

In Book 22, Odysseus restores *kósmos* to the
Ithacan feast, a ritual long disordered by the reaching
hupèr móron of the suitors. The feast he invokes is

likewise an anti-ritualistic blood-feast:

> "νῦν δ'ὥρη καὶ δόρπον Ἀχαιοῖσιν τετυκέσθαι
> ἐν φάει, αὐτὰρ ἔπειτα καὶ ἄλλως ἐφιάασθαι
> μολπῇ καὶ φόρμιγγι· τὰ γάρ τ'ἀναθήματα δαιτός."

("Now it is time that the evening meal be prepared
for the Achaeans, while there is still light, and
afterwards other merriment be made with singing
and the lyre; for these things are the accompani-
ments of the feast." [21.428-30])

He is here performing what we have come to expect of a
host: he has called the feast. Although radically different from the others of its kind, it is an equal
feast. The portions or lots distributed by the bow,
ironically called his lyre, are death and fate. The
de-ritualization of the feast begins after Odysseus'
ironic call to the feast. While feasting on his undeserved portion, Antinous receives his deserved $moîr[a]$
("lot," 22.54), in effect exchanging his own cosmic portion, his lot in life, for the cosmic portion he had denied Odysseus. The host serves him his portion of the
anti-feast, the glut of the arrow. The food is spilled
onto the floor, and the bread and roast meat are
"*phorúneto*" ("befouled," 22.21), just as Polyphemus was
"*pephurménon*" (9.397) at Odysseus' earlier blood-feast.
De-ritualization reaches its conclusion when the guests
become the sacrifice; they become, we are told, like a
herd of cattle, and, a few lines later, like small birds
feasted upon by vultures, signifiers of ritualistic defilement (22.299-303). The ritual, the hall, and the
host have been rendered impure.

As host, Odysseus has distributed appropriate
shares. As hero, he must cleanse, purify, restore form
to the formlessness which he himself has invoked.
Odysseus brings about a restoration of *kósmos*, re-enact-
ing the original act of creation. He calls for everyone
in the house to "*pánta dómon katakosmésēsthe*" ("set the
house entirely in order," 22.440). The host prepares a
new feast. His bath and anointing, both of which we have
come to expect as preparations for the equal feast,[28]
accomplish at the individual level what the cleansing of
the hall accomplishes at the communal level. Like his
world, the hero is purified; he is invested with new
form and is, at last, prepared to participate "*theôn en*

daitì" ("in the feast of the gods," 3.336):

"ὥς μὲν τῷ περίχευε χάριν κεφαλῇ τε καὶ ὤμοις
ἐκ δ'ἀσαμίνθου βῆ δέμας ἀθανάτοισιν ὁμοῖος·"

("even so, the goddess shed grace on his head and
shoulders and forth from the bath he came, in form
like unto the immortals." [23.162-63])

At last, the host has been restored to his long-delayed
share of the communal feast and the hero has been restored to his cosmic share, his participation in a world
of form and order.[29]   It is left to the minstrel, the
singer of tales, to distribute to him his portion of
kléos, to confer upon him his share of glory from a traditional, unfailing store.[30]

University of Missouri

NOTES

*I wish to thank John Miles Foley of the University
of Missouri for his excellent and unfailing guidance in
the study of language and oral literature and for making
the Oral Literature program of the 1978 meeting of The
Medieval Institute possible. I am deeply grateful to
Robert P. Creed of the University of Massachusetts/
Amherst for his creative scholarship, including his
thoughtful and detailed comments on an earlier draft of
this paper. I also wish to thank Donald K. Fry of the
State University of New York/Stony Brook, who was another reader of this essay in an earlier form, and who
contributed significantly to its present shape. [A version of this paper was awarded first place in the annual
competition sponsored by the Ohio Medieval and Renais-
sance Conference, Cleveland, October 1976—Ed.]

[1]*L'Épithète traditionnelle dans Homère: Essai Sur
un problème de style homérique (The Traditional Epithet
in Homer)*, in *MHV*, pp. 1-190.

[2]As J. M. Foley's essay in this volume, "Tradition-
dependent and -independent Features in Oral Literature:
the Formula," makes clear, the formula is a tradition-
dependent construct. A primary fallacy, then, in an approach which seeks a cross-traditional definition of the
formula, is the assumption that a single definition may
serve ancient Greek, Serbo-Croatian, Anglo-Saxon, and

other oral traditions equally well. Strictly speaking,
no such definition may exist.

[3]In "Homer as Oral Poet," *HSCP*, 72(1967), 1-46,
Lord emphasizes the importance of maintaining a distinction between exact repetition and partial repetition
(what he calls a "formulaic expression"): "The distinction between the two is an important one, useful and
necessary, I believe, in practical analysis. By studying the relationship of formulas to formulaic expressions in a text we can distinguish between a purely oral
style, a conventional style, and a purely written
style. . . . Because these two categories are useful
they should be kept apart." (15-16). This distinction
will be more or less clear, depending upon the tradition.
The morphemic focus which sets apart the Anglo-Saxon
formula, for example, would lead us to expect the Anglo-
Saxon formula, unlike its counterparts in Greek and
Serbo-Croatian, to be definable in terms of partial,
rather than exact, repetition (see further J. M. Foley's
essay in this volume).

[4]*ES*, 68(1967), 193-204, hereafter cited as OEFS.

[5]In *OLSE*, pp. 41-61, hereafter cited as CAFP.

[6]For a complete survey of critical thought on the
Old English formula and theme since 1949, see J. M.
Foley's introduction to this volume and Fry, OEFS, 193-
99.

[7]I take "elements" to refer to both the variable and
constant parts of the formula; the variable element differs from the variable word only in that the former is
of an undetermined number of words. Thus, in the systemic description "(X) C," where (X) is the variable element and C is the constant element, (X) may be composed
of an undetermined number of words so long as it maintains, as a unit, an identical placement relative to the
constant element.

[8]After applying Fry's definitions of formula and
system in a close analysis of *Beowulf*, I have discovered
that in some cases the formula may indeed be said to
have been generated from a formulaic system, but not
necessarily in all cases. The system is a *sufficient*
condition for defining the Anglo-Saxon formula, but not
a *necessary* condition. At one end of the developmental
spectrum, formulas may be described not simply as parts
of a system, but as parts of an even more highly organized complex of systems, where a number of systems are
organized into a more comprehensive superstructure,

such as the feasting-sleeping complex dealt within this
study. Systematization, however, is not a uniformly occurring phenomenon. There are formulas, for example,
which break down into less highly developed systemic com-
plexes than the feasting-sleeping complex. The *gomen/
gamen* complex, for example, is composed of only two systems: "(X) *gomen/gamen*," composed of only two formulas
(*Bwf* 1775 and 2941); and "*gomen/gamen* (X)," composed of
four formulas (1160, 2263, 2459, and 3021). The frequency of formulas and the degree to which fossilization
or hypostasis may be said to have taken place both metrically and poetically are far lower than in the feasting-
sleeping complex. Furthermore, the inversion link binding these two systems is not nearly as complex as the
conceptual matrix binding the four systems of the more
highly developed complex. I take these differences in
frequency, hypostasis, and complexity of organization to
indicate a basic difference between the developmental
status of the *gomen* complex and that of the feasting-
sleeping complex. To call them both simply groups of
systems is to neglect these differences and, further, to
neglect the multi-developmental or diachronic texture of
the oral poem.

At the other end of the developmental spectrum are
what I call "verbal clusters." It is my opinion that
these clusters are formulas-in-the-making, lacking even
the low degree of frequency, hypostasis, and organiza-
tional complexity of the *gomen* complex. An interesting
example of this occurs in line 1581 of *Beowulf* (see note
11):

þonne he Hroðgares   heorðgeneatas
sloh on sweofote,   slæpende fræt   1581
folces Denigea   fyftyne men,

The idea of sleeping expressed in 1581a by *sweofote* is
immediately followed by the sleeping-feasting idea expressed in the b-verse by *slæpende fræt*. There is no
way to be certain that mention of sleeping in the *a*-
verse actually precipitated mention of sleeping and
feasting in the *b*-verse, or even that the singer was at
this moment associating the two ideas under the pressure
of the feasting-sleeping complex. The possibility,
though, is worth considering. Could this expression of
the concept of feasting and sleeping be an early stage
of a feasting-sleeping formula or a formula conceptually
related to it? The metrical configuration of the line
is similar to the metrical language of the feasting-

sleeping formulas. Is it only a coincidence that the
poet is expressing both the idea and the metrical language of the feasting-sleeping complex? To explore the
possibility is to explore the living art of the oral
poem.

    My point is this: if we accept the hypothesis that
the oral composition is indeed composed of formulaic
phenomena at different developmental levels—and evidence from the text of *Beowulf* calls for such an acceptance—then we must refine our critical apparatus in
order to make it effective as a means of exploring every
stage in the developmental continuum. Revision of the
definition of system from a necessary to a sufficient
condition of formularity makes it a useful critical tool
for determining some formulas and a sensitive gauge for
determining the developmental status of formulaic expressions. After finding and describing a system by Fry's
method, one may then look at such parameters as the frequency of formulas described by the system, the level of
systematization or organization of the system itself,
and the degree to which hypostasis has taken place both
metrically and poetically. By considering these qualities, one may determine the degree of development of any
formulaic expression with respect to any other.

    [9] All references to *Beowulf* are from Fr. Klaeber,
ed., *Beowulf and the Fight at Finnsburg*, 3rd ed. with
1st and 2nd suppls. (Boston, rpt. 1968), with macra
deleted.

    [10] An effective solution to the problem of metrical
analysis in Old English poetry has been advanced by
Robert P. Creed and John Miles Foley. A detailed explanation of their system and its symbolic language may be
found in Creed, "A New Approach to the Rhythm of *Beowulf*," *PMLA*, 81(1966), 23-33; Foley, "Formula and Theme
in Old English Poetry," in *OL&F*, pp. 207-32; Foley, "A
Computer Analysis of Metrical Patterns in *Beowulf*," *CHum*,
12(1978), 71-80; and Creed and Foley's forthcoming book-
length study, "A Systematic Scansion of *Beowulf*." According to this system, the alliterative line is scanned
in four measures; there are seven basic measure types:
alpha (/x), alpha+ (/\), beta (/x\), gamma (/\x), delta
(/<x>), epsilon (</>x) and eta (</>\x), where / = primary
stress, \ = secondary stress, and x = minimal stress;
and elements in small brackets (<>) indicate stresses
taken on the lyre. By syllabic ramification and resolution of stresses, these measure types produce over 130

configurations, accounting for all of *Beowulf*. The
Creed-Foley system of metrical scansion will be used
throughout this study.

[11] Here we must make choices and, to some extent,
our choice will be arbitrary, as Robert P. Creed has
reminded me (*per litteras*). How, for example, may we
capture the pair of links between lines 489 and 564?

Síte nu to *symle*   *Bwf 489*

symbel ymbsæton   *Bwf 564*

I do not wish to ignore such links and intend my descriptions of the relationships which exist between systems and formulas within the systems to be descriptive,
not prescriptive.

[12] *TAPA*, 98(1967), 269-311, hereafter cited as GV.

[13] Speaking of formulaic phrases, Nagler says that
these "phrases would be considered not a closed 'system' but an open-ended 'family,' and each phrase in the
group would be considered an allomorph, *not of any other
existing phrase*, but of some central Gestalt—for want
of a better term—which is the real mental template underlying the production of all such phrases. The
Gestalt itself, in our case, would seem to exist on a
preverbal level of the poet's mind, since we have found
it impossible to define other than as a comprehensive
list of all of the allomorphs which happen to exist in
the recorded corpus." (GV, 281).

[14] Except where my own translations seem more faithful to the original, I use those of R. K. Gordon, *Anglo-
Saxon Poetry* (1929; rpt. New York, 1970).

[15] In his *Nature and Culture in the Iliad: the
Tragedy of Hector* (Chicago, 1975), James M. Redfield
discusses the cultural and poetic significance of purification: "Purity is form; the impure is the formless,
the deformed, and that which threatens the forms. . . .
Physical cleansing is in itself a kind of ethical purification. The epic does not make a contrast between the
physical and the spiritual or between the personal and
the social. Rather, it is expected that disorder on one
level will be reflected in all and that when things are
in order—*en kosmoi*—the order will be pervasive." (pp.
160-61). The epic contrast is between the pure and the
impure.

[16] According to Klaeber, *sendan* "has been suspected
of being a relic of old heathen sacrificial terminology"
(152), linked to the idea of "feasting" and "to send to

death." Klaeber accepts Imelmann's emendation, snedeþ.
See further Anatoly Liberman, "Germanic sendan 'to make
a sacrifice,'" *JEGP*, 77(1978), 473-88.

[17] Redfield links purity and impurity with the funeral and the anti-funeral, respectively (pp. 167-71): "From
the very beginning of the [*Iliad*] we have heard that
birds and dogs eat the dead. . . . To be eaten as carrion has been a fate threatened in a general way to the
enemy or to the cowards on one's own side. . . . But
here for the first time a warrior promises to feed his
victim to the scavengers; the funeral is no longer the
common share of the dead but the special privilege of
the victor, who boasts that he can withhold it from the
vanquished. . . . The question of purity and impurity is
dramatized at the end of the *Iliad* as the question of
the funeral of Hector—dramatized, that is, through the
proprieties owed to the dead and through the willful im-
propriety of leaving a dead enemy to the dogs. . . . The
willful defilement . . . we shall call the antifuneral."

[18] The opposing connotations of *dreogan* characterize
the joy of feasting as something to be performed or
worked (as Beowulf has shown it to be), to be enjoyed
(as it was before the usurpation of Heorot), and to be
suffered (since the perfection of that joy, according to
Hrothgar, is contingent upon the feaster's remembering
his own mortality so as to avert the pride that kills
all joy of feasting and all life of the spirit). The
hypermetric configuration of the verse at 1782b, caused
by the maintenance of the alpha-alpha rhythm for the
symbel- compound, calls attention to the primary significance, the non-separability, of the compound itself
and to the inviolability of the ritual suggested by
symbelwynne.

[19] Nagler links the "Beasts of Battle" motif and the
feasting motif under the Gestalt of sacrifice (*S&T*, pp.
42-43), an association reinforced by the meanings of
sendan (see note 16 above). A comparison between
Grendel's blood-feast and the feast of the funeral fire
is very suggestive in this connection (see espec. ll.
631-45, 1119-24, and 3155b; as well as note 25 below).
See also James L. Rosier, "The Uses of Association:
Hands and Feasts in *Beowulf*," *PMLA*, 78(1963), 8-14, for
a brief discussion of the feasts, battles, and Beasts
of Battle in *Beowulf*; Francis P. Magoun, Jr., "The Theme
of the Beasts of Battle in Anglo-Saxon Poetry," *NM*, 56
(1955), 81-90, together with a response by Adrien

Bonjour, "*Beowulf* and the Beasts of Battle," *PMLA*, 72
(1957), 563-73.

[20] The manipulation of *cuman* in lines 702b-21a dram-
atizes Grendel's approach to Hrothgar's hall and characterizes him as a man-like *cuma*; see Stanley B. Greenfield, "Grendel's Approach to Heorot: Syntax and Poetry," in *OEP*, pp. 275-84.

[21] In a lecture delivered in May of 1974 at Johns
Hopkins University, entitled "The Origins of Epic,"
Albert Lord described the monster-battling activity of
Herakles as a continuation of the work of his father,
Zeus, orderer and preserver of the cosmos. It appears to
be the hero's task to make sure the order established
at the Creation is maintained and, when it is threatened
or temporarily disordered, to set it right again—to re-
create it.

[22] Nagler classes the feast, the Beasts of Battle
motif, and "the typical animistic metaphor of the weapon
seeking to glut itself on the life fluid of a man"
(*S&T*, p. 42) under the Gestalt of sacrifice.

[23] Lord examines the theme of the absented hero in
the Serbo-Croatian songs in "The Theme of the Withdrawn
Hero in Serbo-Croatian Epic," *Prilozi*, 35(1969), 18-30.

[24] The alpha-alpha measure which characterizes the
formula "sinc æt symle" (81a) is preserved in the similar expression "sinc ond symbel" (2431a), in spite of
the fact that maintenance of the metrical idiom creates
a hypermetric condition in the entire verse at 2431a.

[25] The table below demonstrates verbal correspondence in terms of stressed root morphemes between passages describing Beowulf's funeral (3143a-77b),
Grendel's feast (730b-90b), Hildeburh's son's funeral
(1107a-24b), and the old man's son's funeral (2419b-62a).
On the root morph as the unit of verbal correspondence,
see J. M. Foley, "Formula and Theme in Old English
Poetry," espec. pp. 220-32; "Tradition-dependent and
-independent Features," in this volume; and "*Beowulf*
and Traditional Narrative Song: the Potential and Limits
of Comparison," in *Old English Literature in Context:
Ten Essays*, ed. by John D. Niles (London and Totowa,
New Jersey, 1980), forthcoming.

Beowulf's Funeral	Grendel's Feast	Hildeburh's son's Funeral	Old man's son's Funeral
bælfyra mæst 3143b		1109b, 1116b, 1119b	
wud(u)rec astah 3144b	782b	1118b, 1160b	
sweart ofer swioðole 3145a	782a	1115b	
swogende leg 3145b	781b		
wope bewunden 3146a	763a, 785b	1119a	2424b
banhus 3147a	780a, 742a	1116a	
gebrocen 3147b	780b		
Higum unrote 3148b			2457a
modceare mændon 3149a	730b		
mondryhtnes cw(e)alm 3149b	767a		
swylce giomorgyd 3150a		1118a	2419b, 2444a
(b)undenheorde 3151b	774b		
(song) sorgcearig 3152a	787a		2447a, 2455a
sæde geneahhe 3152b	783a		
(hearmda)gas 3153a	766a		
hearde (ondre)de 3153b		1112a	
wælfylla worn 3154a	734a	1119b	2420a
(wigen)des egesan 3154b	784a		
h(æftny)d 3155a	788a		
Heofon rece swe(a)lg 3155b	743a, 782a	1122b	
genumen 3165b			2429b
gold 3167a		1111b	
lifað 3167b	733a, 744a		2423a, 2432a
hlæw riodan 3169a		1120a	2445b, 2457b
hildedeore 3169b	772a		
æþelinga bearn 3170a		1112b	2443a, 2433b, 2424a
ealre twelfe 3170b	744b, 767b	1111b, 1122b	2461b
wordgyd wrecan 3172a		1118a	2446b
sprecan 3172b	759a		
eorlscipe 3173a	769a		
gede(fe) 3174b			2435b
winedryhten 3175a	767a		

ferhðum freoge 3176a	754a		
of líchaman 3177a	733a	1122a	2423a

[26] There are a number of systems involving the word *moîra*; formulas in these systems occur in a number of colonic positions and colonic shapes (see *TWW*, pp. 66-117).

[27] All *Odyssey* quotations are taken from W. B. Stanford, ed., *The Odyssey of Homer*, 2 vols. (New York, rpt. 1967).

[28] See 3.466ff., 4.49ff., 6.96ff., 6.227ff., 8.454ff., 10.364ff., 10.450ff., and 24.366ff.

[29] In his "Sharing, Dividing, Depriving—the Verbal Ironies of Grendel's Last Visit to Heorot," *TSLL*, 15 (1973), 203-14, Robert W. Hanning explores the conceptual matrix established by repetition of the root *dæl*, glossed by Klaeber as "part, portion, share, measure" (Klaeber, p. 315). The *dæl* matrix provides for *Beowulf* what the *moîra* complex provides for the *Odyssey*: the cosmic order of "appropriate share" at the creation of Heorot is disrupted by a monster who has been *deprived of* his share ("dreamum bedæled," 721). Grendel robs Hondscio of his cosmic share, and it becomes the hero's task to respond by restoring the order of the creation.

[30] See Gregory Nagy's discussion of "The Hidden Meaning of κλέος ἄφθιτον and *śráva(s) ákṣitam*" in his *Comparative Studies in Greek and Indic Meter* (Cambridge, Mass., 1974), pp. 229-61.

TRADITION-DEPENDENT AND -INDEPENDENT FEATURES IN ORAL LITERATURE: A COMPARATIVE VIEW OF THE FORMULA*

John Miles Foley

In 1960 Albert Lord's landmark study, *The Singer of Tales*, presented the scholarly world with an opportunity to make great strides in the understanding of many ancient, medieval, and contemporary literatures. Now, almost twenty years later, a very large number of books and articles has derived from Professor Lord's work, testifying to its central importance in the history of literary, linguistic, and anthropological research.[1] Indeed, the wide range of interests represented by this group gathered to honor him with a *Festschrift* is evidence of how seminal the Parry-Lord theory—and particularly those comparative insights made by Professor Lord himself—has become. At the same time, lively controversies (most of them productive) have helped to characterize the developing field of oral literature. Schools, cliques, and countercliques have formed and dissolved, and various critical metaphors in vogue at various times have been applied to, or forced upon, the theory; in short, polemics have too often ruled the scholarly roost. This paper will try to be less polemical than suggestive: its main thrust is to exemplify in modest scope what I take to be a reasonable caveat—that in comparing oral literatures for the purpose of mutual elucidation, we must take care to truly *compare* rather than simply *reduce*. The time for unreserved, heady exhilaration over real and apparent *similarities* is past; we must now be just as concerned with *differences* among traditions, and with what these differences can tell us both about the individual traditions involved and about oral literature as a whole.[2]

Toward that end I will offer some comparative observations on the traditional unit identified as the formula.[3] My assumption in bringing together materials from the Serbo-Croatian, Old English, and ancient Greek literatures is that all of these texts are the products of oral traditions. To put it more exactly, we know that the Yugoslav songs are oral traditional; I will be treating only real, "non-bowderlized" *pjesme* from the Milman Parry Collection, songs which I have edited for the present purpose. And I take it as demonstrated, especially

by the recent works of Gregory Nagy, Michael Nagler, and
Berkley Peabody,[4] that the Homeric epics and at least
part of the Hesiodic corpus are also oral traditional.
The Old English *Beowulf* remains somewhat of a problem, so
I will at this point be content with understanding its
well-attested traditional character and hope that some
of my comments will point toward its close connection
with an oral tradition. The present format precludes extending the argument to the levels of theme and story
pattern,[5] but in both cases the situation is roughly the
same; indeed, all three levels taken together imply a
more inclusive, overarching dynamic, an interlocking system of multiformities which amounts to a way of thinking.
As fine and elaborate an instrument as such a system is,
however, it depends ultimately on natural language characteristics for its expression, especially at the fundamental level of formula.   In sum, our major concern here
will be the nature of formularity at the level of the
line—on its own terms in each of the three poetic traditions.[6]

      When Milman Parry developed his definition of the
formula, "a group of words which is regularly employed
under the same metrical conditions to express a given
essential idea" (*MHV*, p. 272), he meant it to serve for
one traditional compositional unit and one only—the
Homeric formula. As Parry understood the process of
formula generation, the verbal utterance took its shape
from the hexameter. Nagy has since that time argued convincingly that, from a diachronic point of view, formula
generates meter and not vice versa,[7] and other studies
have with mixed results refined the ideas explicit and
implicit in Parry's original writings. Whatever the exact balance diachronically and synchronically, however,
there remains an intimate relationship between meter
and formula. Even if the habitual groupings originally
generated the abstract pattern over time, later on (as
Nagy suggests) the abstract pattern came to govern the
deployment of phraseology, particularly at the level of
performance. To understand formulaic structure, then,
we must still consider its "chicken-or-the-egg" relative, metrical structure. To take the premise one step
further, we must understand the Homeric formula in terms
of the Homeric hexameter. This much is surely obvious
enough, but the next step is apparently not so simple,
for it has been violated over and over again in oral
literature studies. It is fundamentally this: to under-

stand the formula in any other traditional oral poetry,
we must look to the metrical structure of that tradition
and that tradition alone. Trying to construe the Old
English multiform phrase in terms of the Greek line is a
Pyrrhic task; all we can prove is that Old English is,
is not, or is to a certain degree, Greek. But unless we
are willing to take the particular, tradition-dependent
characteristics of each prosody into account, carefully
noting the features most important to formula generation, we are doomed to such tautologies.

Let us then attempt at least an overview of the metrical foundations in ancient Greek, Serbo-Croatian, and
Old English, concentrating for the present purpose on
making two simple measurements which I identify as *syllabicity* and *internal structure*. We will be trying to
assess comparatively, in other words, the extent to which
each poetic line is (1) syllabically regular and (2)
structured by demarcations (caesurae, bridges, diaeresis)
within the line. The hexameter may be schematized as indicated below.[8]

$$\mid\underline{\quad}\ \smallsmile\smallsmile\mid\underline{\quad}\ \smallsmile\smallsmile\mid\underline{\quad}\ \smallsmile\smallsmile\mid\underline{\quad}\ \smallsmile\smallsmile\mid\underline{\quad}\ \smallsmile\smallsmile\mid\underline{\quad}\ \smallsmile\mid$$

$$\ \ 1\qquad 2\qquad 3\qquad 4\qquad 5\qquad 6$$

The first five metra may be dactylic ($\underline{\quad}$ $\smallsmile\smallsmile$) or spondaic
($\underline{\quad}$ $\underline{\quad}$), though a spondee in position $\overline{5}$ is rare. The
sixth metron is disyllabic, its second element being con-
sidered long by position if not by nature (*brevis in
longo*). Though the line may therefore theoretically consist of from twelve to seventeen syllables, in practice
the vast majority are fifteen or sixteen syllables in
length.[9] A host of additional metrical constraints govern the internal structure of the hexameter. Caesura
must always occur in at least one of three loci:

  (1) between the elements of the third metron,
      called the "masculine" caesura,

      e.g. πλάγχϑη, ἐπεὶ Τροίης ǀ ἱερὸν πτολίεϑρον
      ἔπερσε   *Od.* 1.2
  (2) between elements two and three in a third-
      metron dactyl, called the "feminine" caesura,

      e.g. ῎Ανδρα μοι ἔννεπε, Μοῦσα, ǀ πολύτροπον,
      ὅς μάλα πολλὰ   *Od.* 1.1

or (3), much more rarely, between elements one and
two of the fourth metron,

e.g. εἴμ᾽ Ὀδυσεὺς Λαερτιάδης,| ὅς πᾶσι
δόλοισιν   *Od.* 9.19

Another very common word-division comes after a dactyl in
the fourth position and is called the "bucolic diaeresis":

e.g. πολλῶν δ᾽ἀνθρώπων ἴδεν ἄστεα | καὶ νόον ἔγνω
Od. 1.3

There also exist many "bridges," at which word-break is
seldom tolerated, as well as other rules and tendencies
too numerous to recount here. For our purpose is not to
describe comprehensively the make-up of the hexameter,
but to adumbrate its internal complexity and syllabic
definition. To summarize, fifteen- and sixteen-syllable
lines predominate and line-internal structures make a
great many demands upon the arrangement of those syllables. The highly patterned cola formed by the caesurae
are, as Peabody has shown in detail (*TWW*, pp. 66-117),
crucial word-units in poetic composition. This is not to
say, of course, that a poet working in the hexameter
tradition had any special gift or had to overcome any
particular difficulty; we must grant Homer's consummate
mastery of a medium which, after all, emerged from natural language characteristics. It is to say that the
hexameter was a complex and precise metrical filter which
tended to hypostatize or fossilize its verbal component
to an appreciable degree. [10]
    Our brief examination of the intricacies of Homer's
line gains perspective from a comparative look at the
guslar's epic decasyllable (*epski deseterac*). [11] It may
be schematized as follows:

1	2	3	4		5	6	7	8	9	10
s	s	s	s	|	s	s	s	s	s	s
				MC						

As the name indicates, the Serbo-Croatian line is yet
more demanding than the hexameter in regard to the first
of our criteria: more or less than ten syllables constitute an imperfect line. [12] Jakobson denominates five
additional "metrical constants," features "which admit of

no, or only occasional, deviation" (25):

(1) a compulsory syntactic break between lines,
(2) a main caesura (labeled MC on the diagram above)
    between the fourth and fifth syllables,
    e.g. Podraniše | od Kladuše Mujo
(3) a bridge between syllables 3 and 4 and between
    syllables 9 and 10,
    e.g. Pa od tȃla na noge skočijo
(4) one of the boundaries of each line-internal word-
    unit must occur before an odd syllable, so that
    word-units with an even number of syllables must
    begin with an odd syllable,
    e.g. Eh, zavika knjigonoša mladi
                5   9
(5) a "quantitative close" in syllables 7, 8, and
    9, with an accented long avoided in 7 and
    8 and an accented short avoided in position 9,[13]
    e.g. Dȃvno bȋlo, sàda pomȉnjēmo.

Of Jakobson's six "metrical tendencies," less regularly
observed but also of importance in determining the shape
of utterance, I note at this point only the third: "Taken
as a whole, some 75 per cent of all word-accents fall on
the odd syllables. Thus, in terms of the epic *deseterac*,
each even syllable functions as an up-beat (*temps faible*)
and each odd one as a down-beat. The verse inclines toward a trochaic pentameter pattern." (26). In any given
line, this tendency may or may not find full expression
in the five "feet," for, as Professor Lord puts it,
"there is a tension between the normal accent and the meter. The accent of the meter does not always fall on the
normal prose accent, nor are all five stresses of the
same intensity. The ninth syllable is the most prominent, has the strongest beat, and is held the longest;
the seventh and eighth are the weakest. The tenth may
be lost entirely, completely swallowed, or hopelessly
deformed." (*Singer*, pp. 37-38).

As in the case of the Homeric hexameter, a thorough
description of the decasyllable would require a much
more extensive explanation than is possible here, but we
do have enough data in hand to sketch a meaningful comparison of these two meters. First, both lines are syllabically quite regular, the *deseterac* absolutely so.[14]
This constraint helps to insure that the subdivisions of
the line (or cola) will themselves have regular syllabic

definition. The converse of this observation is also
worth stating: whatever the metrical texture of cola,
they will not admit much (or any) deviation in syllable
count. To take the simpler case first, the main caesura
of the decasyllable divides the line into one colon of
four and one of six syllables; these are therefore the
optimum phrase lengths. Noun-epithet formulas, for example, occur without exception in the more spacious
second colon, and their vocative inflection can substitute syntactically for the nominative to accomplish the
fit exactly:

      nominative (5 sylls.)   silan Mustajbeg
      vocative (6 sylls.)   silan Mustajbeže[15]

These and similar matters are discussed at length in the
third chapter of *The Singer of Tales*, so there is no
need to attempt a necessarily partial recapitulation
here. The important point is that the line and its cola
have regular definition by syllabic count.

    The studies of Parry, O'Neill, Porter, Peabody, and
others[16] have made clear the significance and function
of cola in the hexameter. Each line contains four of
these sub-units, bounded by caesurae, diaeresis, line-
end, and line-beginning. I have marked an example for
illustration:

         A   B   C
"Ἄνδρα μοι | ἔννεπε, Μοῦσα, | πολύτροπον, | ὅς μάλα πολλὰ
                                   Od. 1.1[17]

The hexameter can divide in other ways, depending on
which caesurae obtain, but there is a limited number of
possibilities. Though a discussion of all of them is
impossible here, we can note the relative intricacy of
colonic composition and its strictly observed parameters
of syllabicity and internal structure.

    Beyond the fact of segmentation lies the metrical
shape of each of the segments. Jakobson's metrical constants 3, 4, and 5—having to do with bridges, line-
internal word boundaries, and the "quantitative close"—
reflect the constraints on word and syllable groupings
within the cola of the *deseterac*. The dactylic-spondaic
rhythm of the hexameter and its great many caesurae,
bridges, and other rules of exclusivity govern the metrical scheme and, in large part, the formation of Homeric

diction. Both lines, in short, impose rather severe re-
strictions on the utterances they shape, allowing little
variance in syllable count or internal structure.

Under such conditions we may justifiably search for
the formula as originally defined, "a group of words
which is regularly employed *under the same metrical conditions* to express a given essential idea" (my italics),
confident that there exist both verbatim and formulaic
repetitions throughout the text. [18] While I am not suggesting a facile equivalence of hexameter and *deseterac*
(their comparison deserves an extended treatment of its
own), I am urging the recognition that their conservatism
encourages a high consistency of verbalization from occurrence to occurrence. Not only are the Homeric and
Serbo-Croatian lines exclusive and demanding from a synchronic point of view, but they would also tend strongly
toward a hypostasis of diction over time, so that a
phrase once made could by virtue of its metrical appropriateness and narrative usefulness gain a life of its
own. [19] As we shall see in a moment, however, the metrical foundation of Old English poetry differs remarkably
from those so far discussed, and the study of traditional structure in that corpus will require a different
perspective.

The metrics of Old English verse, specifically of
Beowulf, depend much less on the criteria of syllabicity
and internal structure than do the hexameter and the
deseterac. Partially because of the irregularities in
these two areas, the exact dynamics of the alliterative
line have puzzled scholars for many years, and a large
number of explanations has been advanced. [20] While some
of these are obviously more credible than others, there
remains a good deal of controversy over the finer points
of scansion. For the purpose of this brief comparative
analysis, I will therefore acknowledge only those metrical features upon which there is at least general agreement. There is a consensus on enough basic features to
permit some suggestions about the Old English formula,
and that is our primary goal.

First, we observe in *Beowulf* a very large variation
in count from 8 to 15 syllables per line. There seems
to be no special restriction on when a certain length is
to be used, so that the poet may juxtapose such lines as
51-54 [21] :

secgan tō sōðe,   seleradende,
hæleð under heofenum,   hwā þæm hlæste onfēng.
   Ðā wæs on burgum   Bēowulf Scyldinga,
lēof lēodcyning   longe þrāge

This sequence includes in succession lines of 10, 13, 10,
and 8 syllables. In addition, editors have long recognized a half-line (or "verse") subdivision, indicated in
the passage above by spaces.[22] These verses, like the
line they compose, have very little syllabic definition,
varying from four to eight in count. Nor are the half-
line units necessarily symmetrical in length or structure; they seem to have a semi-independent metrical life
of their own.[23] Alliteration of an initial consonant,
consonant cluster, or any vowel binds the two verses together.[24] Each line must contain at least two alliterating elements, but, as in the examples above, three may
occur.
     Unlike the hexameter and *deseterac*, then, the allit-
erative line and its subdivisions are highly variable
syllabically. We cannot speak of a syllabotonically
based colon in anything approaching the sense intended in
describing the Greek and Yugoslav poetic units. We would
do better to shift focus and determine what *does* remain
constant in the Old English line. Besides alliteration
the verse form requires four heaviest stresses per line,
or two per half-line. The metrical skeleton may be
represented as follows:

$$\acute{s} \qquad \acute{s} \qquad | \qquad \acute{s} \qquad \acute{s}$$

where s = a syllable or syllables bearing heaviest stress
($\acute{\ }$) and the rest of the line consists of a varying number
of secondary ($\grave{\ }$) and minimal stresses (x).[25] Beyond the
regular occurrence of four "stress maxima," or SM's, as I
will call them, any attempt to catalog line structure
must resort to a generative series or pattern. And whatever system of patterns one enlists to explain the hundreds of line combinations observed in *Beowulf*, he must
contend with two metrical properties which expand that
system.
     One of these expansive properties, "resolution,"
consists of the grouping of two syllables, the first of
which must be short by nature and by position, at a single SM. For example, we may compare the more usual in-

stance of

$$\text{sécgǎn or sóðe,}$$

where single syllables (long by position and nature, respectively) occupy SM positions, to the resolved

$$\text{hæleð,}$$

where a short initial syllable merges with the second element at an SM. Either one or two syllables can occur at each SM, a cumulative variance of from four to eight in count. The second factor leading to syllabic irregularity is the inclusion of from one to six syllables at various unstressed positions (or stress minima, SN's). This property, which may be called "ramification," permits a great variety of line actualizations. Taking resolution and ramification together, we derive a surprising number of variations on a single intra-line pattern. The table below, for example, is a partial list of the possibilities generated from the skelton ś š or SM-SN, a simple trochaic base.

Example	Schema	Bwf Reference
lónge	ś š	54b
scéawian	ś šš	840b
wígge under	ś ššš	1656b
léomum ond	śš š	97a
Méotud for þy	śš šš	110a
wésan, þenden íc	śš ššš	1859a

This table illustrates the syllabic variance caused by the metrical properties of resolution and ramification. Whatever system one uses to describe the rhythmic texture of *Beowulf*, he is left with a number of patterns, each one a multiform which generates many possibilities differing in syllable count and flexible in internal structure.[26]

    If from a comparative viewpoint the alliterative line shows significant variation from both the hexameter and the *deseterac* in both syllabicity and internal structure, can we realistically expect all three verbal components to answer to the same definition? The answer must be in the negative, since each verbal component derives its identity from the metrical underlay. And yet, from the appearance of Francis P. Magoun's work onward,[27] many scholars have simply "translated" into Old English the principles of traditional oral composition derived from the study of the Homeric and Serbo-Croatian traditions. When supposedly universal axioms proved faulty or ambiguous for the analysis of Anglo-Saxon verse, critics saw fit to question the nature of the poetry rather than the axioms. But the simple fact of the matter is that the Old English formula cannot be as consistently actualized from occurrence to occurrence as its counterparts *under the metrical conditions which prevail*. Judging the orality of a text in tradition A by applying a test developed through analysis of texts from tradition B without making the necessary adjustments is impossible: all that results is the tautological affirmation that A ≠ B. Perhaps we can now see that Larry Benson's clever argument in "The Literary Character of Anglo-Saxon Formulaic Poetry"[28] is both valid and invalid. What he was saying was that Old English has a certain number of Greek formulas—about the same number in possibly oral and probably written texts. He is quite right in claiming that *this formula* is therefore an ambiguous kind of measure in Old English, but he is wrong in questioning the possible orality of all Anglo-Saxon texts on the same basis. A faulty test no more disproves orality than proves it; what we need is a tradition-dependent diagnosis that takes note of the correct symptoms.

More positively, we need to attempt a faithful translation of the ancient Greek formula, which adapted extremely well to the Serbo-Croatian tradition,[29] into Old English, to find an idiomatic rendering that acknowledges the realities of the alliterative line. We can make a start by taking account of the recurrence of the four SM's per line, despite the irregularities shown above to proceed from resolution and ramification. These stressed positions and the alliterative constraint form the outline of an otherwise highly variable metrical filter. It is primarily these two features, along with the much less stable positions of secondary (but still heavy) stress and the substitutable rhythmic patterns, which act as the "selector" mechanism. According to these criteria, certain verbal configurations are admitted and others are deleted, and a number of phrases are to varying degrees hypostatized over time. These same features must also be mainly responsible for whatever consistency of verbalization obtains from one instance of a theme to the next. But note that these SM's, at least two of which are further focused by alliteration,[30] and the secondarily stressed positions (SSM's) are by definition not metrical molds in the sense that both the Homeric and Serbo-Croatian cola are, but rather occur as maximal points relative to what surrounds them.[31] The conclusion is inescapable: the fundamental site for consistency and patterning is in Old English not the colon of syllabic extent and internal structure, but rather the *stress maximum position* and *secondary stress maximum position* in the alliterative context. The SM and SSM have a finite length; they can be either a single, uncompounded word or an element of a compound—in other words, usually a single root morpheme.[32] Any longer, more complex utterance immediately becomes subject to the generative system of metrical variation, and cannot maintain the consistency of verbalization typical of colonic composition.

This is not to say that verse and even whole-line formulas do not exist in Old English poetry; the research of many scholars has shown that they do. It is, however, to assert that we must expect both a lower percentage of classically defined formulas and a higher index of variability among systems in the Anglo-Saxon poetic texts. With the primary prosodic emphasis on the SM and SSM and on the structural and syllabic flexibility of the line, we should expect a certain repetitive focus or density at the stress point and a looser aggregation of elements around that point. Without the enclosing function of the colon, an Old English formula should demonstrate a stressed core or kernel and a much less tightly organized (and therefore much more variable) shell.

There is also another factor to be taken into account. As I have shown elsewhere,[33] *Beowulf* displays a level of purely *metrical formula*, that is, a group of stress patterns which comprise a subset of all of the metrical possibilities in the alliterative line. Fully 94 percent of *Beowulf* is founded upon one of three metrical templates which I have identified and analyzed by computer techniques.[34] The template may be defined as a "rhythmic underlay, one whole poetic line in length with

verse (half-line) substitution, which predetermines the
structure of its verbal counterpart the formula" ("Formula and Theme," p. 219; italics deleted). Below the
level of verbalization, then, there lies a suprasegmental
latticework, a set of rhythmical predispositions from
which the lexical reality of the verbal formula takes
its shape. These patterns are syllabically very flexible, as in view of the generative properties of resolution and ramification they must be, and prescribe only
the relative position of SM's and SSM's. In other words,
they sharpen the morphemic focus at stressed positions
and help to define the much looser surrounding structure
as well. But their contribution is to *sequence* and to
relative position rather than to bound phraseology[35];
they *align* rather than *encapsulate*. They are also, of
course, much more generalized and generalizable than formulas at the verbal level. In fact, the formulaic situation in Old English is best viewed as a generative process which begins (at least synchronically and later on
in the diachronic scheme) with the metrical template and
which extends upward to a lexical component. The diagram following illustrates the levels and process of
formula in *Beowulf*.[36]

Verbal issue

$$
\begin{cases}
\text{gégnúm gángán (314a)} \\
\text{Gréndel góngán (711a) þrým gefrúnon(2b)} \\
\text{góld gégángán (2536a)}
\end{cases}
$$

↑ ↑ ↑ ↑   ↑ ↑ ↑ ↑ ↑ ↑ ↑ ↑ ↑ ↑ ↑

Metrical template   ś   x̌s   ś   x̌s

    While there is certainly some value in concentrating
on the verbal issue and determining variance in phraseology, from the point of view that Thomas Rosenmeyer has
called "hard Parryism,"[37] we must realize that such taxonomy represents only one aspect of formula generation.
To be faithful to tradition-dependent characteristics,
we should begin by asking the question of just what the
formula is in *Beowulf*. As demonstrated above, it is
clearly not the colonic encapsulation of Homeric and
Serbo-Croatian *provenance*. Its trace is a consistency
in phraseology which we have heretofore chosen to isolate
as a one-dimensional *product*, but more importantly its

real identity is that of a multi-dimensional *process*
which is best understood by considering both its metrical
and verbal levels and the interplay between them.[38]   In
future studies it will be useful to examine this process
from a number of perspectives; for the moment we need a
functional definition which relates the Old English verbal formula in a general way to its counterparts in the
Greek and Yugoslav traditions and yet preserves its
tradition-dependence.   I offer the following as a first
approximation: *a verbal formula in Old English poetry is
a recurrent substitutable phrase one half-line in length
which results from the intersection of two compositional
parameters—a morphemic focus at positions of metrical
stress and a limited number of metrical formulas.*[39] This
first parameter denominates an emphasis on the stressed
core of the phrase, while the second speaks to the relative position of stressed elements.   This conception has
the advantages of (1) indicating in general terms the
way in which the diction is generated and maintained;
(2) being quite specific about the stressed position as
the fundamental site for repetition and at the same time
directing attention away from the "bound phrase" assumption; and (3) eliminating the need for the unwieldy and
often inexact distinction between formula and system.   A
verbal formula is part of a process—at times the process
yields one product and at times another, according to the
SM/SSM focus, the influence of the underlying metrical
formula, and the demands of the narrative.   At no time
does the formula become an artifact; at no time does it
lose its identity as a multiform.   While the poet may recall certain verses verbatim from one instance to the
next, this apparent memorization does not compromise
formula generation.   Metrical and verbal relatives of
the memorized verse will still appear, and even the verbatim phrase itself owes its diachronic identity to the
multiform process.   In studying oral traditional form,
in short, we must cease being tyrannized by the written
word (that which we see), that is, by the individualized
instances of the formula.

The implications of a tradition-dependent formula
reach beyond the level of the line.   The traditional
unit which Professor Lord has called the "theme,"[40] an
exact description of which lies outside the scope of this
discussion, manifests in Old English both an abstract
idea-pattern and a degree of verbal correspondence among
occurrences.   Given the criteria developed above, we

might expect this verbal correspondence to appear mainly
in stressed positions, and this is precisely what happens.[41]   In narrative units such as the Beowulfian "sea
voyage," for example, the verbal redundancy occurs as a
morphemic rather than as a classical formulaic substrate.[42]   The verses containing key morphemes can vary
extensively, much more extensively than in the Homeric
or Serbo-Croatian oral poems. The relative freedom of
the SM/SSM elements even allows nonnarrative echo or
"responsion" among morphemes in a passage, a level of
traditional structure which lies somewhere between formula and theme.

In summary, then, we must discard the implicit assumption that the formula is a concept fully applicable
in a single form from one tradition to another. Understanding multiformity at the level of the line—for that
matter, at any level—means recognizing differences as
well as similarities in poetic structure. The metrical
foundation of Old English poetry, so different from those
of Homeric Greek and Serbo-Croatian, demands a conception
of formula which de-emphasizes the roles of syllabicity
and internal structure in favor of the tradition-dependent parameters of stressed position and metrical formula.
In addition, the verbal formula in Old English must be
viewed as a process which has as its products the
repetitive-seeming verses which we locate in the manuscript texts, rather than as those products themselves.
We must give the idiosyncratic aspects of each tradition their due, for only when we perceive sameness
against the background of rigorously examined individualized traits can we claim a true comparison of oral
traditions.

University of Missouri

NOTES

*The substance of this paper grew out of a presenta-
tion made to Professor Lord's graduate seminar on oral
literature at Harvard University on March 14, 1977. I
wish to thank the American Council of Learned Societies
for a 1976-77 fellowship to carry on research at the
Milman Parry Collection and, in particular, Albert Lord
and David Bynum for their invaluable counsel and generous assistance.

[1]See *Haymes*, supplemented by Samuel G. Armistead's review, *MLN*, 90(1975), 296-99.

[2]Though Ruth Finnegan professes to be interested in differences in her recent *Oral Poetry: Its Nature, Significance, and Social Context* (Cambridge, 1977), she confuses the issue by grouping all types of orally performed song into a single category (at one point juxtaposing Homer and the Beatles!) and then, tautologically, demonstrating the variety of her sample. Another serious weakness is Finnegan's lack of philological sophistication; she comments on almost all of her texts only in translation and with little attention to linguistic aspects.

[3]See *Haymes*; James P. Holoka, "Homeric Originality: A Survey," *CW*, 66(1973), 257-93; my "Introduction" to this volume; and my "The Oral-Formulaic Approach to Old English Poetry: A Historical Bibliography," *OPMPC*, forthcoming.

[4]Nagy, *Comparative Studies in Greek and Indic Meter* (Cambridge, Mass., 1974); Nagler, *S&T*; and Peabody, *TWW*.

[5]The bibliography on the theme is well enough known (see notes 1, 3, and 4). On the less studied level of "story pattern," see Lord, "Composition by Theme in Homer and Southslavic Epos," *TAPA*, 82(1951), 71-80; *Singer*, pp. 186-97; "Homer as Oral Poet," *HSCP*, 72(1967), 1-46; "The Theme of the Withdrawn Hero in Serbo-Croatian Oral Epic," *Prilozi*, 35(1969), 18-30; "The Traditional Song," in *OL&F*, pp. 1-16; Mary Louise Lord, "Withdrawal and Return: an Epic Story Pattern in the Homeric Hymn to Demeter and in the Homeric Poems," *CJ*, 62(1967), 241-48; Nagler, "The 'Eternal Return' in the Plot Structure of *The Iliad*," in *S&T*, pp. 131-66; Peabody, "The Flight of Song," in *TWW*, pp. 216-72; Nagler, "'Dread Goddess Endowed with Speech'." *ArchN*, 6(1977), 77-85; and my "The Traditional Structure of Ibro Bašić's 'Alagić Alija and Velagić Selim'," *SEEJ*, 22(1978), 1-14; "Education before Letters: Oral Epic Paideia," *DQ*, 13(1978), 94-117; and "Tradicionalna zgrada izrečinja na pesmom 'Alagić Alija i Velagić Selim'," *FP*, forthcoming.

[6]It is of course impossible to present more than a fraction of the available evidence in this format. A longer study, now in preparation, *Studies in Oral Traditional Literature*, treats these problems in the length and complexity they deserve.

[7]Nagy sees the diachronic process as a series of steps: "At first, the reasoning goes, traditional

phraseology simply contains built-in rhythms. Later, the
factor of tradition leads to the preference of phrases
with some rhythms over phrases with other rhythms. Still
later, the preferred rhythms have their own dynamics and
become regulators of any incoming nontraditional phraseology. By becoming a viable structure in its own right,
meter may evolve independently of traditional phraseology." (*Comparative Studies*, p. 145).

[8] My brief description of the hexameter is based
primarily upon Paul Maas, *Greek Metre*, trans. by Hugh
Lloyd-Jones (Oxford, rpt. 1966).

[9] As Peabody points out, all hexameter lines are
fundamentally equivalent in mora count (*TWW*, pp. 45-58).

[10] Thus Parry's insistence, from the time of *The
Traditional Epithet in Homer* (in *MHV*, pp. 1-190) onward,
on the crucial shaping influence of meter on the Homeric
formula.

[11] My brief description of the *deseterac* is based
largely on Roman Jakobson, "Studies in Comparative
Slavic Metrics," *OSP*, 3(1952), 21-66.

[12] Example lines of Serbo-Croatian epic are taken
from songs recorded by Milman Parry, Albert Lord, and
David Bynum, preserved in the Milman Parry Collection
of Oral Literature.

[13] The "quantitative close" and other rules lead to
Jakobson's statement that "it is consequently reasonable
to suppose that the Slavic epic decasyllable is traceable
to an Indo-European prototype" (63). That the quantitative close might better be considered a tendency than a
rule is suggested in John Miles Foley and Barbara
Kerewsky Halpern, "'Udovica Jana': a Case Study of an
Oral Performance," *SEER*, 54(1976), 19, n. 36.

Metrical constant (5) describes the sequence of
pitch-accent values on syllables 7, 8, and 9. In the
system of diacritics used in the example line, circum-
flex (ˆ) = long falling, acute (ˊ) = long rising, grave
(ˋ) = short rising, and double grave (ˏ) = short falling;
the macron (ˉ) implies simple length. See further Thomas
F. Magner and Ladislav Matejka, *Word Accent in Modern
Serbo-Croatian* (University Park, 1971); and Asim Peco,
Osnovi akcentologie srpskohrvatskog jezika (Belgrade,
1971).

[14] Long and short lines do, however, occur in the
epic songs (see, for example, the *Ženidba Čejvanoviča
Meha*, in *S-CHS*, II, no. 12). This kind of syllabic in-
felicity should be distinguished from the extrametrical

interjections which occasionally precede the line (more
rarely the second colon), most often at the beginning of
a performance. See Lord's caveat on isosyllabism and
singers' habits (*Singer*, pp. 282-83, n. 8).

[15] This type of accommodation was noted as long ago
as 1909 by Tomo Maretić in his *Naša narodna epika* (Belgrade, rpt. 1966), pp. 63-69.

[16] Parry, espec. *The Traditional Epithet in Homer*
and "Studies in the Epic Technique of Oral Verse-Making.
I. Homer and Homeric Style," in *MHV*, pp. 1-190 and 266-
324, respectively; Eugene O'Neill, Jr., "The Localization of Metrical Word-Types in the Greek Hexameter,"
YCS, 8(1942), 105-78; Howard N. Porter, "The Early Greek
Hexameter," *YCS*, 12(1951), 1-63; Joseph A. Russo, "The
Structural Formula in Homeric Verse," *YCS*, 20(1966),
217-40; and Peabody, *TWW*, espec. pp. 66-117 and 348,
n. 5.

[17] Colon 1, Ἄνδρα μοι, reaches from the beginning
of the line to A (the trochaic caesura); colon 2,
ἔννεπε Μοῦσα, from A to B (the feminine caesura); colon
3, πολύτροπον, from B to C (the bucolic diaeresis); and
colon 4, ὅς μάλα πολλά , from C to the end of the line.

[18] On Parry's notion of the formulaic system, see
"Studies I," in *MHV*, pp. 275ff.

[19] See Nagy's hypothesized sequence of metrical-
dictional events (note 7). As we shall see later on,
Donald Fry was right in denying the applicability of
Parry's criterion of "economy" to Old English verse; see
his "Variation and Economy in *Beowulf*," *MP*, 65(1968),
353-56.

[20] Major works on Old English metrics include: Eduard
Sievers, *Altgermanische Metrik* (Halle, 1893); M. Kaluza,
Der altenglische Vers: eine metrische Untersuchung (Ber-
lin, 1894); Andreas Heusler, *Deutsche Versgeschichte,
mit Einschluss des altenglischen und altnordischen
Stabreimverses* (Berlin, 1925-29); John C. Pope, *The
Rhythm of Beowulf*, rev. ed. (New Haven, 1966); Robert P.
Creed, "A New Approach to the Rhythm of *Beowulf*," *PMLA*,
81(1966), 23-33; A. J. Bliss, *The Metre of Beowulf*, rev.
ed. (Oxford, 1967); Morris Halle and Samuel J. Keyser,
*English Stress: Its Form, Its Growth, and Its Role in
Verse* (New York, 1971); and Thomas Cable, *The Meter and
Melody of Beowulf* (Urbana, 1974). The uncertainty at-
tending Anglo-Saxon metrics and associated philological
matters has been paralleled by controversy over the Russian *bylina* line (perhaps for some of the same reasons,

such as the lack of syllabic definition); see Patricia
Arant, "Formulaic Style and the Russian Bylina," *ISS*, 4
(1967), 7-51. See also John S. Miletich, "The Quest for
the 'Formula': a Comparative Reappraisal," *MP*, 74(1976),
111-23.

[21] All quotations from *Beowulf* are taken from Fr.
Klaeber, ed., *Beowulf and the Fight at Finnsburg*, 3rd
ed. with 1st and 2nd suppls. (Boston, rpt. 1968).

[22] Robert P. Creed has developed a series of ordered
rules for establishing the lineation and scansion of Old
English from the manuscript; these rules will appear in
our joint book, "A Systematic Scansion of *Beowulf*."

[23] This half-line model of metrical organization accounts for the attempt of most metrists to formulate a
theory of rhythm in terms of the verse unit. It also
accounts for most investigators' focus on the verse as
the length of the Old English formula. The so-called
"single verses"—many of these combine with whole lines
to form "triplets"—are evidence of a hybrid line
structure that exhibits both whole-line and half-line
identity. See further Bliss, "Single Half-lines in Old
English Poetry," *N&Q*, 18(1971), 442-49; and my "Hybrid
Prosody: Single Half-lines in Old English and Serbo-
Croatian Poetry," *Neophil*, 64(1980), 284-89.

[24] In lines 51-54, the alliterations are in "s,"
"h," "b," and "l," respectively.

[25] I set aside for the moment the question of whether
these four stresses are all uniformly taken on syllables
or whether one or more might be taken on the instrument
with a vocal rest. See especially Pope and Creed; for
information on the instrument which the Anglo-Saxons
called *se hearpa*, see Rupert and Myrtle Bruce-Mitford,
"The Sutton Hoo Lyre, *Beowulf*, and the Origins of the
Frame Harp," *Antiquity*, 44(1970), 7-13.

[26] If, for example, one chooses to accept Pope's system of scansion, he must reckon with 107 versions of
"Type A" in the first half-line alone.

[27] "The Oral-Formulaic Character of Anglo-Saxon Narrative Poetry," *Speculum*, 28(1953), 446-67.

[28] *PMLA*, 81(1966), 334-41. He remarks, 340: "That
the Old English oral singers used a heavily formulaic
style is only an attractive theory—probably true but
necessarily unproven; that lettered poets, such as the
author of the Boethian *Meters*, did use such a style is a
demonstrable fact. Therefore, we must use the greatest
caution in assuming the oral composition of any surviving

Old English poem." We should be at least equally cautious about two assumptions implicit in Benson's reasoning, namely, (1) that the translator is necessarily the
poet, and (2) that a demonstration based on such marginal poetry as the *Meters* also applies to *Beowulf*.

[29] The history of the oral theory will show that, in
moving from the Homeric hexameter to the Serbo-Croatian
deseterac, Parry was fortunate in finding another traditional line which depends heavily on syllabicity and internal structure, in other words on the colon. There
was no apparent reason to suspect that the Greek formula
was not a sure symptom of oral composition in all poetic
traditions.

[30] On the interplay of alliterative staves, see
Randolph Quirk, "Poetic Language and Old English Meter,"
in *SmithSts*, pp. 150-71; and Eileen D. Lynch, "A Statistical Study of the Collocations in *Beowulf*," unpub.
Ph.D. diss. (University of Massachusetts/Amherst, 1972),
abstract in *DAI*, 33(1972), 2898-A.

[31] Though it is beyond the scope of this essay to
explore the issue in the detail it deserves, I mention
in passing that we might include the Old French epic
decasyllable with the more conservative meters of Homeric
Greek and Serbo-Croatian oral song, thus distinguishing
it from the less syllabically regular Anglo-Saxon meter.
This should in turn bear on both the relative density and
relative generativity of Old French formulas. See Joseph
J. Duggan, *The Song of Roland: Formulaic Style and Poetic
Craft* (Berkeley, 1973).

[32] The essential criterion here is that the morpheme
bear one of the four heaviest stresses (SM's) per line
(any of which may be more than a single syllable in extent, as the laws of resolution dictate), or that it bear
a secondary but still heavy stress (SSM), as in the case
of compounds whose first element is an SM and second
element an SSM. Note also that inflection may fall under
a stress if the root syllable is short, though the inflection is clearly not part of the formulaic core.

[33] "Formula and Theme in Old English Poetry," in
OL&F, pp. 207-32.

[34] Compare Nagler's ideas of "template" and "Gestalt" (*S&T*, pp. 1-63).

[35] See Paul Kiparsky, "Oral Poetry: Some Linguistic
and Typological Considerations," in *OL&F*, pp. 73-106.

[36] There is of course no opportunity here to discuss
the metrical template at length (see note 33). Note,

however, that the simple trochaic pattern sketched in the example can take a large number of forms syllabically; up to three syllables can occupy either position.

[37] "The Formula in Early Greek Poetry," *Arion*, 4 (1965), 295-311.

[38] This topic demands a painstaking analysis of the *Beowulf* text, a task beyond the scope of the present essay.

[39] In "Formula and Theme in Old English Poetry," I showed that "we may set formula length by the standard of the template: a whole line with verse (half-line) substitution" (p. 213). Thus the real answer to the question of the formula's length is that it forms a half-line unit but also has a whole-line dimension. Compare Peabody's discussion of the "hybrid" nature of the Homeric line (*TWW*, pp. 143-67). See further note 23.

[40] See espec. *Singer*, pp. 68-98; Fry, "Old English Formulaic Themes and Type-Scenes," *Neophil*, 52(1968), 516-22; and the introduction to this volume.

[41] See further my "Formula and Theme," espec. pp. 220-32, and "*Beowulf* and Traditional Narrative Song: the Potential and Limits of Comparison," in *Old English Literature in Context: Ten Essays,* ed. by John D. Niles (London and Totowa, New Jersey, 1980), forthcoming.

[42] Even in Serbo-Croatian oral epic song, themes do not necessarily have a regular formulaic content; see Mary P. Coote, "The Singer's Use of Theme in Composing Oral Narrative Song in the Serbo-Croatian Tradition," unpub. Ph.D. diss. (Harvard University, 1964), espec. pp. 107-14; a shorter version is forthcoming in *CalSS*. See also my "The Oral Singer in Context: Halil Bajgorić, *Guslar*," *CASS*, 12(1978), 230-46.

THE MEMORY OF CÆDMON*

Donald K. Fry

    I am honored to contribute to a *Festschrift* for Professor Albert Lord, whose scholarship has influenced my thinking for the last fifteen years. This paper builds on the seminal insights of Lord, Milman Parry, and F. P. Magoun, attempting to propose a new model for Old English literary history on a formulaic basis. What do we mean by "formulaic"? I think we mean the typical traditionally expressed. We mean that traditional poets sound like the poets of their past, like their contemporaries, and like their own previous performances. They tell stories familiar to their audiences, organized in narrative and imagistic patterns familiar to their audiences, and expressed in diction familiar to their audiences. Even when they incorporate new stories and concepts requiring new vocabulary, they manipulate the old formal patterns to preserve the impression of traditional and familiar continuity. In short, they constantly play against their audiences' memory of poetry.

    We all think we know how memory works: like a computer, of course, storing bits of data and recalling them in original form whenever we need them. In fact, psychologists generally reject that model, preferring instead a reconstructive theory along lines suggested by F. C. Bartlett in his classic book, *Remembering, A Study in Experimental and Social Psychology*.[1] Bartlett divides memory into perception and recall, proposing that the process of perception itself organizes material to be memorized into general impressions accompanied by a few striking details, both then stored. Such perception patterns vary according to the individual, but with a counter-tendency toward standardized patterns determined by social groups. Memorizing proves quite simple when the memorizer's perception patterns fit the material closely, and difficult when they do not. Bartlett observes:

> In certain cases of great structural simplicity,
> or of structural regularity, or of extreme famil-
> iarity, the immediate data are at once fitted to,
> or matched with, a perceptual pattern which ap-
> pears to be pre-existent so far as the particular

perceptual act is concerned. This pre-formed setting, scheme, or pattern is utilised in a completely unreflecting, unanalytical and unwitting
manner. Because it is utilised the immediate perceptual data have meaning, can be dealt with, and
are assimilated. In many other cases no such immediate match can be effected. Nevertheless, the
subject . . . casts about for analogies with which
to subdue the intractibility of the perceptual
data.(p.   45).

Bartlett also found that these perceptual grids group together through associations drawn from past experience:

A study of the actual facts of perceiving and
recognizing suggests strongly that, in all relatively simple cases of determination by past experiences and reactions, the past operates as an
organised mass rather than as a group of elements
each of which retains its specific character.(p.
197).

In recall, we reconstruct the perceived material by com-
bining the stored general patterns and some details, although we may not recognize the discrepancies between
the original and this reconstruction. Bartlett comments:

Human remembering is normally exceedingly subject
to error. It looks as if what is said to be reproduced is . . . really a construction, serving
to justify whatever impression may have been left
by the original. It is this "impression," rarely
defined with much exactitude, which most readily
persists. So long as the details which can be
built up around it are such that they would give
it a "reasonable" setting, most of us are fairly
content,and are apt to think that what we build
we have literally retained.(pp. 175-76).

And Bartlett summarizes:

Remembering is not the re-excitation of innumer-
able fixed, lifeless and fragmentary traces. It
is an imaginative reconstruction, built out of the
relation of our attitude towards a whole active

mass of organized past reactions or experience, and
to a little outstanding detail which commonly appears in image or in language form. It is thus
hardly ever really exact, even in the most rudimen-
tary cases of rote recapitulation. (p. 213).[2]

The mind, according to Bartlett, consists of intercon-
nected patterns of organization, which control perception and recall. We might express his theory in a visual
metaphor: the mind organizes itself in certain associated
shapes. Perception is a screen pierced by holes shaped
like the mind's forms, a screen we hold up to outside
material. Data which fits enters easily through a hole;
data which does not fit must be altered to the shape of
an opening. In recall, we reconstruct the original
material by means of these shapes. Put another way, we
could say that perception compresses material into abstract patterns containing selected details; in recall,
we supplement those selected details with reconstructed
details sufficient to re-inflate the abstraction back
into the full-blown shapes of external experience. If
you are skeptical about this model, try a little experiment. Recall something you see every day: your own face.
Got the picture? Did you forget the ears? Put them in.
Are all the bumps and moles in place? Put them in. Did
you remember to color the eyes? You see, Bartlett is
right. We recall generalities and congratulate ourselves
on our precise memory, and we can reconstruct the details
if we want to. But the key word is "reconstruct."

Bartlett's model sounds familiar, for it parallels
current notions of formulaic poetry. The stereotyped
phrases we call formulas cluster into families, whose
abstract structures we label "systems." These substitution systems are analogous to the grids of perception,
abstract shells filled out with other words. At the narrative level, type-scenes function as the abstract patterns with plot details fleshing them out. Stories and
themes tend toward the typical, toward general patterns
of behavior modified for specific applications. These
traditional organizations of formulaic material fit
Bartlett's standards for easy memorizing: "great structural simplicity, . . . structural regularity, . . . extreme familiarity" (p. 45), allowing a simplified perception stage. The mind does not have to abstract perceived formulaic material because such material is already organized into familiar abstract patterns. To

return to my visual metaphor, the formulaic phrases are already shaped like the holes in the perceptual grid.[3] Furthermore, just as material stored in the memory has an internal structure of associations, so do the formulaic wordhoard and scenehoard and storyhoard structure themselves around ties of association. Certain formulas and systems cluster thematically with others, certain ideas and images cohere, certain scenes tend to include certain details, etc. Material formulaically organized is easily memorized, and easily recalled for members of a traditionally-oriented culture. Hence traditional poets can recall millions of formulaic phrases and thousands of systems and hundreds of scenes and stories. And so can their audiences.

We profess astonishment at such memory feats, but in fact powerful memories characterize nonliterate societies, indeed usually function as the primary device for education of the young and for ethical reinforcement in adults. Early Greek civilization proves a case in point.

The best evidence points toward the introduction of the Greek alphabet about 700 B.C.; Homer, who lived about this time or a generation earlier perhaps, probably composed his epic poems without the aid of writing, by formulaic means. Marcel Jousse characterizes Homeric man as a "mnemotechnician,"[4] whose practical and intellectual life turned on memorized cultural values, defined and reinforced by oral poetry. James Notopoulos puts it this way:

> The oral poet as a mnemotechnican preserved the useful by binding it in verse, by forging a metrical pattern which facilitated and guarded against mistake the information to be preserved. Memory therefore is equally important in conserving the useful as well as perpetuating the immortal in oral literature; the poet is the incarnate book of oral peoples.[5]

In a daring hypothetical reconstruction of early Greek culture, Eric Havelock differentiates the social function of oral verse from modern notions of art:

> Greek society before 700 B.C. was non-literate. In all such societies experience is stored in the individual memories of the members of the society

and the remembered experience constitutes a verbal
culture. The verbal forms utilized for this purpose have to be rhythmic to ensure accurate repetition, and the verbal syntax has to be such that
statements, reports, and prescriptions are cast in
the forms of events or acts. The Homeric poems,
and to an equal degree the Hesiodic, exhibit these
symptoms. They constitute not literature in the
modern sense, but orally stored experience, the
content of which incorporates the traditions of a
culture group and the syntax of which obeys the
mnemonic laws by which this kind of tradition is
orally preserved and transmitted.[6]

The introduction of writing about 700 B.C. brought
about changes, but probably not so drastic as we might
expect. Writing remained a difficult art to master, a
craft skill for the few, with widespread popular reading
far in the future.[7] In fact, this transition period
probably lasted until Socrates's lifetime (died 399
B.C.). Havelock believes that the first Greek texts
written down were *The Iliad* and *The Odyssey*, as one of

the measures taken by a non-literate culture to
preserve its corporate tradition in an enclave
of language existing apart from the vernacular,
metrically contrived to preserve an extensive
statement in the memories of the members of the
culture. To transcribe this enclave became the
first business to which the alphabet was put.
And so we reach in the first instance the poems
that pass under the name of Homer.[8]

The transition period involved authors such as Pindar,
Hesiod, and even the Athenian dramatists, writing for
essentially nonliterate audiences. Again, Havelock
proposes:

For a long time after the resources of transcription became available, they would be used still to
transcribe what had previously been orally composed, . . . the transcription would be made in the
first instance for the benefit of the composers
themselves rather than their public, and . . .
the products of the Greek poets who followed Homer
would be devised for memorization by listening

audiences, not for readership by literates ("Prologue," p. 362).

Conservative tendencies would prevail, both in style and
social functions of poetry; as Havelock puts it,

> Composers of the contrived word originally . . .
> allowed their compositions to be taken down by a
> listener. Later they took to writing them down
> themselves at dates which cannot easily be set-
> tled. But whichever they did, their initial pro-
> clivity would be to use the script now available
> only to record what was already previously com-
> posed according to oral principles. That is, the
> oral habit would persist and would remain effective
> to a varying degree, even in the case of composers
> whom we would style writers. This habit, after all,
> had not been personally chosen by themselves; it
> was a conditioned response to the needs of an audi-
> ence who still demanded of the compositions of-
> fered that they be memorisable. ("Prologue," p. 388).

Although these literate poets took advantage of the new
writing techniques to modify their own compositional
methods, they still lacked any significant reading public. So the authors probably produced only one copy of
their works, or at most just a few; families and author-
ities stored such copies in archives, even sometimes en-
graved the poems on temple walls.[9] Transmission and dif-
fusion of the texts depended almost completely on memory
and public recitation.

The Greeks memorized the early poets as a part of
their education, and Homer emerged as "the Hellenic educational manual *par excellence*" (*Preface*, p. 28). Tutors
recited Homer for their pupils to memorize. Poetry held
a position, says Havelock,

> central in the educational theory . . . a position
> held apparently not on the grounds that we would
> offer, namely poetry's inspirational and imaginative
> effects, but on the ground that it provided a mas-
> sive repository of useful knowledge, a sort of en-
> cyclopedia of ethics, politics, history and tech-
> nology which the effective citizen was required to
> learn as the core of his educational equipment.
> Poetry represented not something we call by that

name, but an indoctrination which today would be
comprised in a shelf of text books and works of
reference. (*Preface*, p. 27).

Memory and performance dominated education, both public
and private:

> A purely poetic *paideia*, to be effectively trans-
> mitted, requires only regular occasions for per-
> formance, whether professional or amateur. The
> youth would be required to repeat and to match
> their memories against each other and against their
> elders. Everything that was to be absorbed and
> remembered was communicated to them as the deeds
> and thoughts of their great ancestors. (*Preface*,
> p. 124).

In summary, after 700 B.C., Homer's poems were written
down and memorized for educational purposes, and later
writers composed in a form suitable for recitation and
memorization. Thus oral poetry continued to exert its
influence as a device for preserving cultural values
throughout the semi-literate era of Greek history.

The Anglo-Saxons remained semi-literate, or more
accurately nonliterate, both in English and in Latin,
throughout their history, at all levels of society. For
example, V. H. Galbraith counts exactly four literate
Old English kings (Sigbert, Aldfrith, Alfred, and perhaps Ceolwulf)[10]; Cædmon, although he became a monk,
never seems to have learned to read or write. Even after Christian missionaries introduced writing in England in 597, no popular reading audience ever developed.
Yet the Church faced the difficult twin problems of attaining and strengthening converts. I propose here that,
after about 680, the English church used written poetry
as an educational device, transmitted largely in memorized form.[11] And Cædmon and his memory began the whole
process.

Cædmon extemporizes exactly once, creating the original hymn in his dream; after that moment, he becomes exclusively a memorial poet. In his *Ecclesiastical History*, IV, 24, Bede tells us:

> When [Cædmon] awoke, he remembered [*memoriter
> retenuit*] all that he had sung while asleep and
> soon added more verses in the same manner,

praising God in fitting style. [12]

He recites these verses from memory the next morning to
Abbess Hild and "a number of the more learned men." They
read him "a passage of sacred history or doctrine, bid-
ding him make a song out of it, if he could, in metrical
form. He undertook the task and went away; on returning
the next morning he repeated the passage he had been
given, which he had put into excellent verse." [13] Cædmon
memorized what the scholars read to him and also memorized his own resultant poem in order to recite it the
following day. Later, Bede describes the poet's procedure explicitly:

> He learned all he could by listening to them and
> then, memorizing [*rememorando*] it and ruminating
> over it, like some clean animal chewing the cud,
> he turned it into the most melodious verse: and it
> sounded so sweet as he recited it that his teachers
> became in turn his audience. (Colgrave and Mynors,
> p. 419).

The Old English translator expands that last clause:

> and his song and his leoð wæron swa wynsume to
> gehyranne, þætte seolfan his lareowas æt his
> muðe wreoton and leornodon.
> [and his song and his music were so delightful
> to hear, that even his teachers wrote down the
> words from his lips and learnt them (Miller,
> pp. 346-47)].

The scholars did not memorize the poems and then write
them down. Rather they wrote them down from Cædmon's
memory in order to memorize them for themselves. Abbess
Hild, I believe, recognized immediately that Cædmon's
invention of Christian vernacular verse had broad applications as an educational device. In Bede's narrative,
before our very eyes, we see her turn Cædmon, as it
were, into a teaching machine. The scholars feed Cædmon
sacred narrative and/or doctrine, and he manufactures
palatable verse, which they record and memorize. Bede
tells us two subsequent effects of Cædmon's invention:

> By his songs the minds of many were often inspired
> to despise the world and to long for the heavenly

> life. It is true that after him other Englishmen
> attempted to compose [*facere*] religious poems, but
> none could compare with him. (Colgrave and Mynors,
> p. 415).

Cædmon's songs brought about conversions and started
others writing such verse, including Bede himself. Elsewhere I have suggested that later Anglo-Saxon poets,
whether they composed in writing or orally, used the
forms of the inherited oral poetry, simply because no
other poetic existed for them.[14] Now I wish to propose
another reason for such conservative loyalty to tradition: Old English poets used formulaic techniques because, as I argued in the first section of this paper,
formulaic poetry is easy to memorize. The pre-formed
units (formula, type-scene, known story), already organized for easy memorization by poets, also aid the
memory of the audience. I suggest that, as in early
Greece, memorized poetry formed a large part of the education of an essentially nonliterate populace. Such
poetry easily moved about, penetrating all classes of
society, lay and clerical, spreading by word of mouth
to remote areas. It promoted proper behavior, conveyed
the basic Christian message for conversion, and
strengthened the faith of new converts and old, all in
entertaining, familiar form, requiring no elaborate
training in Latin or theology. Such poetry also had the
latitude to absorb new subject matter while making it
sound like old familiar poetry; thus Christ becomes a
warrior with a *comitatus* of apostles,[15] Adam talks like
a thane, etc. So churchmen could inject doctrine into
narrative, raising the theological sophistication not
only of the laymen, but also of clerics, whose average
formal learning never reached very high. Indeed, the
Anglo-Saxon poetry we possess ranges from the simple
paraphrase of the *Lord's Prayer* to the rich density of
Christ I, from the flat piety of *Juliana* to the whirling
allegories of *Phoenix*, from the astonishing Patristic
virtuosity of *Exodus* to the inexpressible genius of *Beowulf*, a mirror for princes and Christians alike.
     Much evidence exists for this memorial transmission
and its educative function, but I shall confine myself
here to a brief discussion of King Alfred. His contemporary biographer Asser tells us:

> Alas, by the unworthy carelessness of his parents

and tutors, he remained ignorant of letters until
his twelfth year, or even longer. But he listened
attentively to Saxon poems day and night, and hearing them often recited by others committed them to
his retentive memory. . . .

 When, therefore, his mother one day was showing him and his brothers a certain book of Saxon
poetry which she held in her hand, she said: "I will
give this book to whichever of you can learn it most
quickly." And moved by these words, or rather by
divine inspiration, and attracted by the beauty of
the initial letter of the book, Alfred said in reply
to his mother, forestalling his brothers, his elders
in years though not in grace: "Will you really give
this book to one of us, to the one who can soonest
understand and repeat it to you?" And, smiling and
rejoicing, she confirmed it, saying: "To him will I
give it." Then taking the book from her hand he immediately went to his master, who read it. And when
it was read, he went back to his mother and repeated
it.[16]

Illiterate Alfred memorizes vernacular poems "recited by
others" constantly. Alfred must have the book read to
him by a tutor in order to memorize it. Since he did not
learn to read until about the age of forty, he continued
learning by memorizing vernacular books. Asser continues:

 Meanwhile the king, in the midst of wars and frequent hindrances of this present life, and also of
the raids of the pagans and his daily infirmities
of body, did not cease . . . to recite Saxon books,
and especially to learn by heart Saxon poems, and
command others to do so (Asser, chapter 76, p. 267).

Alfred took the church's educational technique, used it
for his own continuing education, and later applied it
to secular education as well.

 In summary, the formulaic techniques explored by
Parry, Lord, and Magoun allow us to account for the
phenomena of the surviving Old English poetic material.
Anglo-Saxon Christian poets, inspired by Cædmon, wrote
in the inherited formulaic style, whose familiarity and
formal properties made the poems easy to memorize.
Christian learning spread through an illiterate popula-

tion by means of memory and recitation, all radiating
from an author's original manuscript. The Vikings and
Henry the Eighth no longer need to shoulder all the
blame for our present scarcity of surviving Anglo-Saxon
poetic manuscripts. There simply were not very many in
the first place. Indeed, the manuscript of a traditional society, of the nonliterate Anglo-Saxons, was memory.

State University of New York at Stony Brook

NOTES

*This paper serves as a prospectus for a book in
progress, entitled *Cædmon's Memory*. My argument responds to the seminal work of Jeff Opland, published and
unpublished, and I wish to express my appreciation here
for his impressive scholarship. I also wish to thank
John Foley, Bruce Rosenberg, Walter Scheps, and Leo
Treitler for their helpful comments on this essay.

[1] (Cambridge, 1932).

[2] He admits the presence of rote recall as well (pp.
203, 264).

[3] For similar imagery, see, for example, John Miles
Foley, "Formula and Theme in Old English Poetry," in
OL&F, pp. 207-32; and Michael Nagler, *S&T*.

[4] *Le Style oral rhythmique et mnémotechnique chez
les Verbo-moteurs* (Paris, 1925).

[5] "Mnemosyne in Oral Literature," *TAPA*, 69(1938),
469.

[6] "Pre-literacy and the Pre-Socratics," *ULCSB*, 13
(1966), 50.

[7] *Preface to Plato* (rpt. New York, 1967), p. ix,
hereafter cited as *Preface*.

[8] "Prologue to Greek Literacy," in *UCCS*, II (Norman,
1973), p. 361, hereafter cited as "Prologue."

[9] J. A. Davison, "Literature and Literacy in Ancient
Greece," Chapter 4 of his *From Archilochus to Pindar*
(New York, 1968), pp. 86-128.

[10] Galbraith, "The Literacy of the Medieval English
Kings," in L. S. Sutherland, ed., *Studies in History*
(London, 1966), pp. 78-111; Rosalind Hill, "Bede and the
Boors," in G. Bonner, ed., *Famulus Christi* (London,
1976), pp. 93-105; C. P. Wormald, "The Uses of Literacy
in Anglo-Saxon England and Its Neighbours," *TRHS*, 5th
series, 27(1977), 95-114.

[11] Alan Jabbour, "Memorial Transmission in Old English Poetry," *ChauR*, 3(1969), 174-90.

[12] All references to Bede's Latin version cite *Bede's Ecclesiastical History of the English People*, ed. and trans. by B. Colgrave and R. A. B. Mynors (Oxford, 1969). For the ninth-century Alfredian translation, I cite T. Miller, ed. and trans., *The Old English Version of Bede's Ecclesiastical History of the English People*, EETS 95-96 (London, rpt. 1959). This quotation appears on p. 417.

[13] Colgrave and Mynors, p. 419. Cp. "sacrae historiae *sive* doctrinae sermonem" with "sum halig spell *and* godcundre lare word" ("a holy narrative *and* some word of divine doctrine," my italics; Miller, pp. 344-45). The Old English translator substitutes "and" for "or," suggesting that Cædmon melded history and doctrine; see my "Cædmon as a Formulaic Poet," in *OLSE*, p. 43.

[14] See my "Cædmon as a Formulaic Poet" and "Themes and Type-Scenes in *Elene* 1-113," *Speculum*, 44(1969), 35-44.

[15] See C. J. Wolf, "Christ as Hero in *The Dream of the Rood*," *NM*, 71(1970), 202-10.

[16] *Asser's Life of King Alfred*, trans. by Dorothy Whitelock, in her *English Historical Documents c. 500-1042* (New York, 1955), p. 266; quoted from W. H. Stevenson, ed., *Asser's Life of King Alfred* (Oxford, 1904), Chapters 22-23.

THE RELIGIOUS BALLAD OF NEW MEXICO AND THE CANARY ISLANDS: A COMPARATIVE STUDY OF TRADITIONAL FEATURES

William González

During the first part of this century Ramón
Menéndez Pidal began his search throughout the Spanish
peninsula for the *romancero* (Hispanic traditional balladry). Upon finding that this tradition continued to
exist in the villages, his interest increased to the
point that he undertook the task of organizing the study
and search for the *romancero* in all of those areas which
at one time had formed part of the Spanish Empire and
among those people who had lived on the Spanish mainland.
At the invitation of Menéndez Pidal, Antonio Espinosa
continued the search for the ballads in the Canary Islands, a task which was completed years later by Diego
Catalán with the publication of *La flor de la marañuela*
in 1969. In New Mexico, Aurelio Espinosa began the
search for ballads, publishing the results of his work
first in 1915 and then, after further investigation, in
1953 under the title *Romancero de Nuevo México*. One of
the salient characteristics of both collections is the
existence of the sacred, or religious, ballad and, since
a comparative study of ballads of this type had not been
made, they became the object of our study.

It is important to note that the areas where these
collections were gathered have several features in common, mainly that of isolation: the Canary Islands are
far removed from the Spanish mainland, and New Mexico is
separated from Mexico City by a great distance and by an
international border. Another point of interest is the
period of conquest and colonization in each area. In
the Canary Islands this period began during the first
part of the fifteenth century, and in New Mexico it began at the end of the sixteenth century. Yet, in spite
of this two-hundred-year time difference between the
settling of the areas, we can notice some marked similarities between traditions.

In the New World, once the task of colonization began, the religious orders and their institutions played
the primary role in the effective assimilation of the
new culture by the Indians. To achieve this result, the
religious orders utilized many different means to teach

the new religion, such as catechetical instruction,
theatre to explain the different doctrines,[1] singing,
and the memorization of prayers and hymns.[2]   The evan-
gelization of the Province of New Mexico followed the
same pattern that was developed in Mexico or New Spain.
However, due to the great distance between Mexico and
Santa Fe in northern New Mexico, the process was much
slower.

   In Mexico, during the first part of the seventeenth
century, a new term was developed in the catechetical
process—the *alabado*. This was a hymn sung by the na-
tives to express their belief in the newly accepted faith
as they went to the fields in the morning or returned to
their homes in the evening.[3]   It was through the efforts
of a zealous friar, Margil de Jesús, that it spread from
Central America to Northern Mexico.[4]   Later on in its
evolution, the term came to include the *alabanzas* which
the night watchmen would sing during the night in the
form of ballads. Many of these refer to the passion and
death of Christ (*ibid.*, p. 123).   The Mexican musicolo-
gist, Gabriel Saldívar, believed that the original
alabado had its origin in hymns that were sung during the
religious processions   in Mexico (*ibid.*, p. 126), a
practice which was and still is one of the fundamental
religious manifestations of the Brotherhood of Peni-
tents.[5]   The latter group has been instrumental in preserving the religious ballad in New Mexico up to the
present, designating it by the general term *alabado*.

   Since our study is mainly concerned with the *alabado*
rather than with the religious ballad of the Canary
Islands, we will not deal with the history of the latter
but merely use these European songs as a basis for iso-
lating similar traditional features which may appear in
the New Mexican balladry. The purpose of our analysis
of the two religious ballad traditions is to describe the
characteristics of each tradition separately and then
those which are common to both, and thus to establish
the relationship between the religious ballad of New
Mexico and the Hispanic ballad tradition.

   The materials used for the analysis consisted of
eleven ballads from the collection *La flor de la
marañuela* totaling 690 octosyllables, and seven ballads
from the *Romancero de Nuevo México* constituting 297
octosyllables. The ballads from the first collection
were chosen at random because of the large number available, and in the New Mexico collection only the most

complete versions of seven ballads were used. This sample was all of the *alabado* material available with the
exception of two very short ballads.

The limited number of New Mexican ballads and the
anonymity of all the ballads analyzed ruled out the possibility of a viable study making use of a "quantitative
formula(ic) analysis" in Parry-Lord terms.[6] Instead,
the analysis was conducted in the following three phases.
First, a search was made through both traditions for the
"formulas" and "formulaic expressions" as these terms are
defined in the Parry-Lord theory.[7] This analysis was
done by examining each tradition separately. The results in each tradition were organized into syntactic
categories and then into semantic categories according
to the patterns established by Ruth H. Webber.[8] In this
way general patterns existing in both traditions became
evident.

The second phase was the comparison of "formulas"
and "formulaic expressions" by matching the New Mexican
octosyllable against the Canary Island metrical unit. In
this way "formulas" and "formulaic expressions" existing
in both traditions became evident. The third phase involved a comparison of the themes of the ballads by basing the divisions on the different chronological periods
in the life of Christ: Nativity, Infancy, Public Life,
Passion and Death, and Resurrection. This sequence is
complemented by the devotion to Mary and to the Saints.[9]

To find all of the "formulas" and "formulaic expressions," the following procedure was followed in
phase one. The ballads were organized numerically within
each tradition; then, beginning with the ballads of the
Canary Islands, the first octosyllable of the first ballad was compared to the remaining octosyllables of that
collection. The same procedure was followed with each
remaining octosyllable consecutively until each line of
that collection had been compared against all of the
others in the same collection. In this examination we
were able to find 55 formulas and 104 formulaic expressions. The process was repeated with the New Mexico
ballads, yielding 10 formulas and 58 formulaic expressions.

Next, the formulas and formulaic expressions were
divided into two different types of categories. The
first category involved the following syntactical con-
structions:

1) Complete sentences or independent clauses,
2) Proper names,
3) Adverbial clauses,
4) Relative clauses, and
5) Miscellaneous.

The second category involved the different semantic
patterns established by Ruth Webber. For the formula
they are as follows:

1) Dialogue;
2) Exhortation;
3) Narrative in complete sentences;
4) Adverbial narrative: place, time, manner;
5) Narrative in relative clauses; and
6) Designation.

For the formulaic expression we were able to establish
the following categories:

1) Introduction to dialogue;
2) Dialogue: a) Imperative,
              b) Interrogative,
              c) Invocation,
              d) Exclamation,
              e) Narration;
3) Introduction to action; and
4) Narrative: a) Action,
              b) Description.

The semantic categories established for the Canary
Island material were more extensive than those of the
American collection; however, there were parallels for
all of the latter in the more numerous categories of the
Canary Island collection.

In phase two of the study, like features in formulary diction were established by comparing each octosyllable of the New Mexico ballads to all of the octosyllables of the ballads taken from the *La flor de la
marañuela*. Once this step was completed, the results
were divided into three categories: a) formulas which
were found in both traditions, b) formulas matched with
formulaic expressions from the tradition of the Canary
Islands, and c) formulaic expressions in both traditions.

In the first category of formulas common to both
traditions, we found that the New Mexico ballad number

153, "Por el rastro de la sangre," has nine formulas
which are found twelve times in three ballads of the *La
flor de la marañuela*: four times in the ballad number
304, "La Virgen camino del Calvario"; five times in ballad 479, "La Virgen camino del Calvario," a ballad with
the same title as the previous one but different in
story line; and three times in ballad 197, "El discípulo
amado y las tres Marías." The following are several examples of these formulas:

1. R.N.M.[10] 153:1   Por el rastro de la sangre
                        R.F.M. 304:1
2. R.N.M. 153:12   Al hijo de mis entrañas
                        R.F.M. 197:22; 479:8
3. R.N.M. 153:32   Cayó al suelo desmayada
                        R.F.M. 197:30; 479:20

In the second category, comparing formulas from the
New Mexico tradition to the formulaic expressions in the
Canary Island tradition, we discovered that five formulas from ballad 153 had seven formulaic expressions in
five ballads of the Canary Islands: two in ballad 197,
two in ballad 304, and one each in ballads 190, 478, and
475. The following are several examples of this category:

1. R.N.M. 153:13   Por aquí pasó, señora
        R.F.M. 304:17, 479:9
        R.F.M. 190:16 Por aquí pasó ayer tarde
                197:23 Por aquí pasó el Señor
                304:18 Por aquí Cristo ha pasado
2. R.N.M. 153:24   de madera muy pesada
        R.F.M. 479:10
        R.F.M. 197:24   con una cruz muy pesada
3. R.N.M. 153:43   San José y la Magdalena
        R.F.M. 304:31
        R.F.M. 425:6   San José y Santa María

The last category involves the formulaic expressions of both traditions. In the New Mexico tradition
thirty-six formulaic expressions compared to sixty-six
formulaic expressions in the ballads of the Canary Islands. The breakdown of these is as follows, beginning
with the New Mexico ballads: nineteen in ballad 153,
fourteen in ballad 179, two in ballad 139, and two in
ballad 186. In the ballads of the Canary Islands there

were seventeen in ballad 197, twelve in ballad 304, nine
in ballad 479, eight in ballad 478, five each in ballads
425 and 190, four each in ballads 297 and 66, and one in
ballad 643. Some of the examples of these formulaic expressions are the following:

1. R.N.M. 153:10 Ya de esta manera le habla
   R.F.M. 197:6 De esta manera le hablaba
           435:8 De esta manera decían
           478:6 Le dijo de esta manera
           478:11 Os diré de esta manera

The final aspect of the two ballad traditions to be
compared was the thematic content of the ballads studied. In the six thematic categories outlined above, the
chronological periods of the life of Christ and the
devotion to Mary and the Saints, we were able to place
all of the ballads from both traditions into these categories with the exception of the two hagiographies from
the Canary Island tradition.

In conclusion, it is evident, due to the similarities which appear in the semantic analysis, in the comparative study of the formulas and formulaic expressions,
and in the themes of the ballads, that both of the collections analyzed belong to the same tradition and that the
ballad has flourished in two totally different geographical areas far removed one from the other during several
centuries. These conclusions bear out Ramón Menéndez
Pidal's theory on the traditional continuity of the Hispanic ballad in space and time.

University of Utah

NOTES

[1]Carlos González Peña, *Historia de la literatura
mexicana* (México, 1972), p. 60.
[2]Jose María Kobayashi, *La educación como conquista*
(México, 1974), p. 197.
[3]Ann Livermore, *A Short History of Spanish Music*
(New York, 1942), p. 245.
[4]Gabriel Saldívar, *Historia de la música en México*
(México, 1934), p. 123.
[5]Dorothy Woodward, "The Penitentes of New Mexico,"
DAI, 28(1967), 136A.
[6]See *MHV*, *Singer*, and *Haymes*.

[7]Parry's "formula" is "a group of words which is regularly employed under the same metrical conditions to express a given essential idea" (*MHV*, p. 272); his "formulaic system" is "a group of phrases which have the same metrical value and which are enough alike in thought and words to leave no doubt that the poet who used them knew them not only as single formulas, but also as formulas of a certain type" (*ibid.*, p. 275).

[8]"Formulistic Diction in the Spanish Ballad," *UCPMP*, 34(1951), 175-253.

[9]H. W. Cowie and John S. Gummer, *The Christian Calendar* (Springfield, 1974).

[10] R.N.M. = *Romancero de Nuevo México*, ed. by Aurelio M. Espinosa (Madrid, 1953); R.F.M. = *La flor de la marañuela*, 2 vols., ed. by Diego Catalán (Valencia, 1969).

GENEALOGY AS ORAL GENRE IN A
SERBIAN VILLAGE*

Barbara Kerewsky Halpern

Background Remarks

Remnants of a versatile and once highly developed
traditional oral culture persist in many South Slav
areas. Heroic epics, as the apex of oral expression,
have been collected and analyzed intensively, notably
by Matthias Murko in the early 20th century, then to
prove Milman Parry's innovative hypothesis that the
Iliad and *Odyssey* were not written but were oral literature, a stunning theory he tested by recording Serbian
bards and analyzing their songs, and later by Albert
Lord's outstanding contributions.[1] Of particular importance to linguistics and to structural analysis of
poetry has been Roman Jakobson's work on the comparative
metrics of Slavic epic verse.[2]

The present paper draws on this background of impressive scholarship and the work that continues on oral
theory and process. But it is not the heroic epic, per
se, upon which our concern is focused. Based on these
works and others, and on original field data, I wish here
to present evidence for an oral genre not previously isolated or described: recitation of genealogy (*rodo-
slovlje*). By reproducing part of a real genealogy, ab-
stracting the underlying metrics, and analyzing its
structure, I will demonstrate how complex data can be
recollected[3] and will suggest that the prosodic characteristics of the recitation (the South Slav epic decasyllable), in consonance with the socio-cultural values of
the society in which it occurs, make possible the preservation and oral transmission of detailed and complicated genealogy in Serbian peasant society.[4]

My data are from Šumadija, a strongly patriarchal,
patrilocal, and culturally homogeneous area in central
Serbia. The population is Christian (Serbian Orthodox)[5];
their language is the *štokavski* dialect of Serbo-
Croatian (based on a lexical determinant, use of the in-
terrogative pronoun *što* [what?]) and is further identified as the *ekavski* sub-dialect, a phonological variant.[6]

Serbo-Croatian distinguishes by length two falling
and two rising tones. This tonal system is related to

stress (long vowels usually carry stress, but a short
stressed syllable may precede a long unstressed one).
Stress never occurs on a final syllable; the first syllable in a disyllabic word therefore takes stress. In
polysyllabic words stress is on the antepenultimate.
This information is pertinent to detail here because,
while the metrics of epic verse incline toward trochaic
pentameter, it is clear that, given the common occurrence of trisyllabic proper names in genealogical reci-
tations, dactyls will also appear frequently. Therefore, the tone-length-stress rules do not coincide invariably with what Jakobson calls the rhythmical impulse
of the epic metrics.

In the course of the initial field research (1953-
54), considerable information was elicited on kinship
and social structure. Many older village men had a remarkable ability to orally recall their ancestry back
eight or nine generations, to the founder of the clan
from which the lineage took its name.[7] In 1968, after
most of the social structure data had been worked up and
published,[8] I returned to Šumadija specifically to check
certain aspects of the genealogical materials. The
focus was still on kinship data, not on oral transmission. That time, however, equipped with printed dia-
grams of previously elicited data, and without the "in-
terference" of open-ended interviewing, I was able to
initiate genealogical recollections and then to concen-
trate on receiving the responses aurally.[9]

Later, proceeding to match kinship data, I checked
the new orally transmitted information from Grandfather
Mileta Stojanović (#47 on the original kinship diagram[10])
against data he had given orally fourteen years earlier.
Some 105 male individuals had been named. To avoid confusion and as an aid in keeping the generational levels
in order, I found myself repeating the data aloud, thereby unconsciously re-creating (or in effect performing) a
version of the oral presentation.

Two striking facts began to emerge: first, the data
from 1954 and 1968, spanning seven generations and covering more than 100 men, were essentially identical; second, clearly Grandfather Mileta was recollecting the
history of his lineage in poetic stichs.

Analysis of the Serbo-Croatian Epic Decasyllable

Before presenting evidence that the recitation of

genealogy, in conducive contexts and when performed by
particular elders, may be a special manifestation of
South Slav epic tradition, it will be useful to define
the characteristics of the *epski deseterac*, the traditional Serbian epic ten-syllable line.

Jakobson called attention to the features of this
tradition, maintaining that an abstraction of the underlying metrics must deal with certain rhythmic tendencies
as well as with formal metrical constants (29-30)

(1) Each line contains ten syllables.

XXXXXXXXXX

(2) There is a compulsory syntactic break between
lines.

[| |]

(3) There is a compulsory word boundary between the
fourth and fifth syllables.

XXXX XXXXXX

(4) Syllables three and four belong to one "word
unit," as do syllables nine and ten.

XX XX   XXXX XX

or

XX XX   XX XXXX, etc.

(5) Disyllabic word units ideally occur in syllables
one-two, three-four, five-six, seven-eight or nine-ten.

(6) Syllables seven-eight-nine bring the line to
what Jakobson called a "quantitative close," with syllables seven and eight ideally avoiding vowel length (and
therefore usually stress), in order to build up to stress
in the ninth syllable (here ideally avoiding a stressed
short vowel).

Within a stich both stress and alliteration of initial sounds favor odd-numbered syllables.[11] What is important here is that the metrical constants as well as
the tendencies correspond to phonological features inherent in the language itself. Moreover, while we may
talk about word, word boundary, and word unit, the
peasant-narrator is not conscious of syllabification,

word boundaries, or stress. Within the constraints of
the ten-syllable line, the village elder employs intui-
tive knowledge of the workings of his language to put
together strings which follow the traditional epic pattern. When necessary he freely uses elision, drops an
auxiliary verb, takes a nongrammatical inflectional ending, or borrows a needed extra syllable from the *ijekavski*
sub-dialect.[12] As he recollects his genealogy orally, he
is not aware that he is composing a narrative *u stiho-*
vima, in lines of verse. The sense of epic verse, self-
motivated, is generated at some deeper level. The impetus for this traditional mode of creativity appears to
be related to regard for his genealogy as his own personal epic, and thus he intuitively selects the appropriate
form for the re-telling. In turn, this epic form, both
metrically and structurally, enhances his ability to reconstruct and relate that which is so important to him.

The Stojanović Genealogy

Presented below is the first part of the genealogy
recollected orally by Grandfather Mileta, with a translation faithful to the original word order.[13]

> *Blago dedi, ti ćeš tuna sedi!*
> *Sedi dole da ti sve mu pričam.*
> *Davno došli oni naši preci;*
> *Doš'o Stojan čak i pre ustanka.*
> * * *
> *Ej! Stari Stojan im'o tri sinova:*   5
> *Ti su Petar, Miloje, Mihajlo.*
> *Od sinova im'o Petar čet'ri:*
> *Miloš, Uroš, Nikola i Stefan*
> *Znaš ti, ćero, Nikola moj deda?*
> *Od sinova im'o tri Miloje:*   10
> *Ti su Vučić, Matija i Lazar.*
> *Isto tako im'o tri Mihajlo:*
> *Radivoje, Radovan, Radoje.*
> *Onaj Miloš, im'o on dva sina:*
> *Ti su bili Milutin i Andrija.*   15
> *Potom Uroš, im'o sina troji:*
> *Tanasija, Vladimir, Djordje.*
> *Eto, ćero, najstari' je Djordje,*
> *A najmladji' nije ost'o živ . . . .*
> *Moj Nikola, im'o on četiri:*   20
> *Antonija, Svetozar i Miloš,*

A trećega, Ljubomir moj otac
(Neka mu Bog dušu prosti).
Stefan, pazi, od sinova nema.
Adj' sad Vučić; on je im'o troji: 25
Radojica, Andrija, Ljubomir.
A Matija samo jedan imao,
Koji zv'o se Blagoje . . . .
Ej, Radovan, taj od trećeg brata,
Im'o Petar, Miloje, Radimir.   30
Sad Radoje: Dragomir jednoga;
Radivoje: Velimir i Branko.
Pazi sada, brojim moja braća!
Te trojica im'o stric Milutin:
Živomir, Pavle i Velimir.   35
Nema od njih potomaka ništa!
Sad Andrija: Svetozar, Velisav.
Pa kod Djordja i Tanasije
Samo Veljko ost'o k'o maturan.
Dragoljub, Svetislav i Dragoslav,   40
Svi su bili poginul' u ratu.
Kod Svetozara isto nema sreću:
Ni Živomir, ni Miloš, ni Vitomir;
Kod njih uopšte muška deca nema.
Al' Dragiša, hvala Bogu, ima.   45
Adje sada, tu sam ja, Mileta!
Potom moj brat, Milosav rodjeni.
                          * * *
I ja, k'o stari, pijem malo rakije
I polako, eto, čekam smrt . . . .

Grandpa's dear, you will sit there!
Sit down so I can relate everything to you.
Long ago came they our ancestors;
Came Stojan even before the Uprising.
                          * * *
Ej! Old Stojan had three sons: 5
    These were Petar, Miloje, Mihajlo.
    Of sons had Petar four:
    Miloš, Uroš, Nikola and Stefan.
    Know you, daughter, Nikola my grandfather?
    Of sons had three Miloje: 10
    These were Vučić, Matija and Lazar.
    The same had three Mihajlo:
    Radivoje, Radovan, Radoje.
    That Miloš, had he two sons:
    These were Milutin and Andrija.   15

Then Uroš had sons three:
Tanasija, Vladimir, Djordje.
Like so, daughter, the eldest is Djordje,
And the youngest did not remain living . . . .
My Nikola had he four: 20
Antonija, Svetozar and Miloš,
And the third, Ljubomir my father
(May God forgive his soul).
Stefan, look here, of sons had none.
Come now, Vučić; he had three: 25
Radojica, Andrija, Ljubomir.
And Matija had only one,
Who was called Blagoje . . . .
Ej, Radovan, that one from the third brother
Had Petar, Miloje, Radomir.   30
Now Radoje: Dragomir only one;
Radivoje: Velimir and Branko.
Pay attention now, I'm counting my brothers!
Well, a trio had Uncle Milutin:
Živomir, Pavle and Velimir.   35
There are no descendants from them!
Now Andrija: Svetozar, Velisav.
And by Djordje and Tanasija
Only Veljko remained as a mature man.
Dragoljub, Svetislav, and Dragoslav,   40
All were killed in the war.
By Svetozar also there is no luck;
Nor Živomir, nor Miloš, nor Vitomir;
By them in general there are no male children.
But Dragiša, thank God, has.   45
Come now, here am I, Mileta!
Then my brother, Milosav [biological brother].
                    * * *
And I, as the old man, drink a little brandy
And slowly, so, wait for death . . . .

Analysis of the Language and Structure of this Genealogy

The existence of a *pripev* (lines 1-4), a prologue
to the narrative, is of much interest. Linguistically
it is not bound by the content restraints inherent in
transmitting genealogical information. As in traditional
oral epic recitation, it functions as a means of establishing a bond between narrator and listener. This is a
crucial condition; speaker and hearer(s) form a collec-

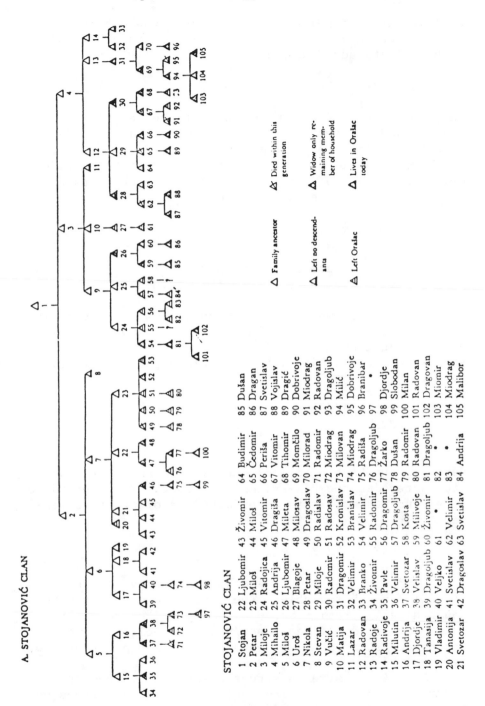

A. STOJANOVIĆ CLAN

STOJANOVIĆ CLAN

1 Stojan	22 Ljubomir	43 Živomir	64 Budimir	85 Dušan
2 Petar	23 Miloš	44 Miloš	65 Čedomir	86 Dragan
3 Miloje	24 Radojica	45 Vitomir	66 Periša	87 Svetislav
4 Mihailo	25 Andrija	46 Dragiša	67 Vitomir	88 Vojislav
5 Miloš	26 Ljubomir	47 Mileta	68 Tihomir	89 Dragić
6 Uroš	27 Blagoje	48 Milosav	69 Momčilo	90 Dobrivoje
7 Nikola	28 Petar	49 Dragoslav	70 Milorad	91 Miodrag
8 Stevan	29 Miloje	50 Radislav	71 Radomir	92 Radovan
9 Vučić	30 Radomir	51 Radosav	72 Miodrag	93 Dragoljub
10 Matija	31 Dragomir	52 Kronislav	73 Milovan	94 Milić
11 Lazar	32 Velimir	53 Branislav	74 Miodrag	95 Dobrivoje
12 Radovan	33 Branko	54 Velimir	75 Radiša	96 Branibar
13 Radoje	34 Živomir	55 Radomir	76 Dragoljub	97 •
14 Radivoje	35 Pavle	56 Dragomir	77 Žarko	98 Djordje
15 Milutin	36 Velimir	57 Dragoljub	78 Dušan	99 Slobodan
16 Andrija	37 Svetozar	58 Kosta	79 Radomir	100 Milan
17 Djordje	38 Veislav	59 Milivoje	80 Radovan	101 Radovan
18 Tanasija	39 Dragoljub	60 Živomir	81 Dragoljub	102 Dragovan
19 Vladimir	40 Veljko	61 •	82 •	103 Miomir
20 Antonija	41 Svetislav	62 Velimir	83 •	104 Miodrag
21 Svetozar	42 Dragoslav	63 Svetislav	84 Andrija	105 Malibor

△ Family ancestor

⚔ Died within this generation

△ Left no descendants

△ Widow only remaining member of household

△ Left Orašac

△ Lives in Orašac today

tivity, one responding to stimuli from the other.[14]

A fictive kin tie is posited immediately. Grandfather Mileta addresses the listener as

Blago dedi ("Grandpa's dear")

The tie is reinforced in the body of the recitation, in
lines 9 and 18: *znaš ti, ćero* ("know you, daughter") and
eto, ćero ("like so, daughter").

Another epic function of the *pripev* is to provide a
temporal frame and initiate the action of the personal
narrative which is about to unfold:

Davno došli oni naši preci;	3
Doš'o Stojan čak i pre ustanka.	4

Long ago came they our ancestors;
Came Stojan even before the Uprising.[15]

These lines were uttered spontaneously. Certainly
they were never before spoken by the narrator. Yet line
3 is an ideal epic decasyllable line in every way.
Structurally it exhibits the exemplary pattern of VP,
caesura, NP:

Davno došli	*oni naši preci*
XXXX	XXXXXX
VP	NP

Here, in the best epic mode, the VP, advancing the action, precedes the six-syllable epithet. With regard to
meter and stress, it is a perfect line of trochaic pentameter:

x́x x́x x́x x́x x́x

In accord with Jakobson's analysis, the heaviest stress
is on the ninth syllable. The line also displays con-
sonantal alliteration word-initially and -internally
(*davno/došli; došli/naši; oni/naši*) as well as vowel
assonance, succeeding segments bearing the patterns a-o,
o-i, a-i, i-i.

Line 4 illustrates stress shift when a proclitic
occurs before a noun. Nominative *ustanak* has stress on
the antepenultimate. Adding a proclitic results in

pre + ústanak ⟶ pré ustánka,

thereby rendering the entire string to the right of the caesura trochaic and again creating an ideal quantitative close on the ninth syllable, with stress and vowel lengthening:

$$\acute{5} \quad 6 \quad \acute{7} \quad 8 \quad \acute{9} \quad 10$$
čak i pre u-stan-ka

It is interesting to note that the opening two lines of this spontaneous prologue compare favorably to the opening lines of a 'real' *pripev*:

> *Blago dedi, ti ćeš tuna sedi!*   1
> *Sedi dole da ti sve mu pričam*   2

Grandpa's dear, you will sit there!
Sit down so I can relate everything to you.

Compare

> *Braćo moja, sokolovi moji,*
> *Čujte pesmu da vam čiča broji.*[16]

My brothers, my falcons,
Listen to the song that Uncle is recounting to you.

Each uses fictive kin to establish a tie with the listeners. Each displays rhyme, the former internally (*dedi/sedi*) and the latter interlinearly (*moji/broji*). Syntactically the two second lines are parallel, opening with an imperative verb (*Sedi/Čujte*), followed after the break by a *da* (connective) clause and ending with an imperfective verb, indicating that the process of narration is to be ongoing (*pričam/broji*).

The local example therefore is strong evidence that for Grandfather Mileta and many ordinary village men like him a subliminal epic pulse must be generating the epic mode so clearly marked in various manifestations at the surface. He "knows how" to do it.

Turning now to the genealogy proper, I note below some of the more salient linguistic features (although almost every line invites comment):

(1) Line 5 is not grammatical. In Serbo-Croatian, numbers two through four are inflected with genitive singular endings, and numbers five and over take genitive plural:

Ej! Stari Stojan im'o tri sinova: 5
Ej! Old Stojan had three sons

* *tri sinova*   (gen. pl.)
   tri sina   (gen. sing.)

But here the genitive plural fits the metrical requirements.

(2) Lines 7 and 9 demonstrate selective elision and
word order switching:

im'o Petar cet'ri   7
had Petar four

im'o tri Miloje   9
had three Miloje

Each of these procedures results in achievement of the
required six syllables and rhythm (word switching also
results in rhyme at the end of lines 9 and 13 [Miloje/
Radoje]; is this by intent or chance?). Now compare the
last segments of lines 7 and 20,

im'o Petar čet'ri

im'o on četiri
had he four

where use of the monosyllable pronoun *on* generates use
of the fully expressed form *četiri*.

(3) Lines 5, 16, and 34 illustrate alternate ways of
saying "three": *tri, troji,* and *trojica,* again selected
according to need (the first is "three," the second form
is a colloquial modifier for three males, and the third
a collective numeral meaning "trio of males").

(4) Line 28 is three syllables short of the decasyllable. Even so, the verb is elided and the auxiliary
dropped, thereby forming a perfect predicate string before the break:

Koji sv'o se Blagoje
Who was called Blagoje

The individual's name, Blagoje, completes the line minus

half the required syllables; there is nothing more to
say. There is, however, marked phonological compensa-
tion, with stress on the antepenultimate and highly
exaggerated length on the (unstressed) final syllable.

(5) In lines 13, 17, 21, and 26, all lines composed
of series of names, the strings before the caesura are
occupied by four-syllable proper names—Radivoje,
Tanasija, Antonija, and Radojica. "Radivoje" happens to
have main stress on syllable one and secondary stress on
syllable three, thus fitting the trochaic pattern. The
other names provide an example of what happens when
reality conflicts with the ideal: in these cases stress
is on the antepenultimate, and pronunciation is not
contrived to accommodate to the pattern.

With the name "Ljubomir" two situations can be observed: in lines 22 and 26 the name appears to the right
of the break (referring in each case to a different man
named Ljubomir).

A trećega, Ljubomir moj otac   22

Radojica, Andrija, Ljubomir   26

In the first instance stress is acceptable, since it
falls on the antepenultimate, with secondary stress on
the final syllable of the name, a compound proper name
meaning "he who loves peace," thereby permitting the
line to work itself out normally. In the second case,
the same pronunciation is used, thus giving stress to
the eighth syllable and causing syllables nine and ten
to be "wrong." This is balanced, however, by the utterance "Ljubomir" being a metrical repetition of the dactyl
"Andrija."

Now turning to a consideration of the structure of
the recitation of genealogy, I note that a grammar with
these ordered rules can be abstracted:

(1) The base point is the naming of the lineage
founder.

S

(S = Stojan)

(2) Each generational level is recollected collaterally, that is, chronologically from the first-born male
along the line to the last-born.[17]

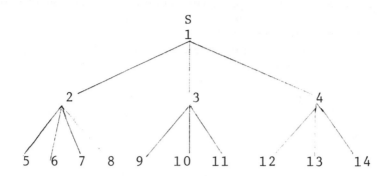

(3) Only after the entire generational level has
been recollected does the narrator proceed lineally to
the succeeding generation.[18]

(4) With the exception of the clan's founder, every
individual is mentioned twice, first as a son of his
father and then as a father of sons.

(5) In this manner the narration reaches the generational level of the narrator and proceeds regularly along
it.

(6) The narration then moves collaterally and lineally through all successive generations, concluding with
the line at which there are no further descendants.

An optional rule is employed by Grandfather Mileta
in his recitation:

(7) Data retrieval terms are employed for the second
recollection of an individual. This may be in the form
of opening segments: *Onaj Miloš* ("That Miloš," line 14)
or *Potom Uroš* ("Then Uroš," line 16), or an entire line
can be a retrieval string:

> *Ej, Radovan, taj od trećeg brata*   29
> Ej, Radovan, that one from the third brother

(8) Gapping or horizontal progression terms, which
advance the action along the generational level, from the
descendants of one brother to the descendants of the next

brother—*Ajd' sad* ("Come now," line 26)—indicate that
the recitation has gone through all the four sons (#'s
5, 6, 7 and 8) of Petar (#2 on the kinship diagram) and
is now moving across to the sons of Miloje (#3) starting
with his first-born, Vučić (#9).

(9) Affirmation of identity and direct descent within the larger structural frame is achieved by personal
reference:

> *Nikola moj deda*   9
> Nikola my grandfather
>
> *Ljubomir moj otac*   22
> Ljubomir my father
>
> *Pazi sada, brojim moja braća*[19]   33
> Pay attention now, I'm counting my brothers
>
> *Ajde sada, tu sam ja, Mileta!*   47
> Come now, here am I, Mileta!

In the last example, the gapping term moves the action
from the sons of Svetozar (#21), who left no living male
descendants (*Kod Svetozara isto nema sreću*[20] ["By Svetozar also there is no luck"]) to the sons of Ljubomir
(#22), the first-born of whom is the narrator, Grandfather Mileta (#47). The term also serves to call attention to the fact that the narration has now come to
his particular niche in it.

This entire recitation was marked paralinguistically
by paced smoking and facially expressive pauses, during
which bounded strings were recollected silently before
being transmitted orally. As presented in this paper, it
concludes with the narrator and his brother, but in
actual performance it concluded with the seventh generation descended from Stojan, that is, with the narrator's
grandson Milan (#100) and the grandson's generation-
mates (not included here for reasons given in note 13).

When Grandfather Mileta reached the end, there was
a silent interlude. Had the narration been accompanied
by the playing of the *gusle*, the single-stringed instrument which traditionally paces the chanting of epic
verse, there would no doubt have been several lines of
music here. He drew on his now stubby cigarette, ground
it out with the heel of his pigskin sandal, sighed and
appended an epilogue:

I ja, k'o stari, pijem malo rakije   48
I polako, eto, čekam smrt . . . .

And I, as the old man, drink a little brandy
And slowly, so, wait for death . . . .

These closing lines are interesting as poetry, as
linguistics, and for what they divulge about epic tradition and the culture. The narrator refers to himself
as *stari* ("the old man"), the same adjective he applies
to the founding ancestor in line 5. This is not acci-
dental; had he wanted to say "an old man" he would have
used the indefinite adjective *star* (which would have
been better metrically).
What Grandfather Mileta is doing, in fact, is showing how the cycle goes on: men are born, they produce
sons, they grow old, they die. The scheme of which he
is part will not end with his death, and there will be
other men to recollect the history of the lineage and to
keep the tradition alive.
The powerful cultural motivation in this society,
combined with a structural tree in the narrator's head
and a metrical model readily available from oral epic
tradition, all incline toward the conclusion that the
ability to recollect and transmit genealogy orally is
indeed, for some village men, a true oral genre.[21]

Afterword

A Serbian literary critic, upon discussing the foregoing with me, remarked, "The old man must have read it
in a *pesmarica* ("songbook")—peasants don't talk that
way!" Contrary to his expectation, this reaction de-
lighted me: it corroborates the point of this paper.
I take this opportunity, therefore, to present additional evidence that Grandfather Mileta is not unique;
villagers *do* "talk that way." In fact, sometimes even
the most ordinary conversations may display oral epic
features. This powerful pulse appears to manifest and
maintain itself over time, over the switch from oral to
literary modes, over changing life styles, across ethnic
and national boundaries and, poignantly (because identity
and perpetuation of self are so important in this culture), even when the informant is forced to recognize
himself as the last of his line.
A family history prepared in the 1920s by a prom-

inent Yugoslav diplomat begins with what he perceives as
his logical beginnings, in 1613! Written records were
used for this detailed compilation by a distinguished
intelektualac. Two factors are immediately salient: the
account reads like an oral recitation, and it starts
with the highly culturally significant opening line—

> *Svi su Smodlake seljačkog porijekla,*
> All the Smodlakas are of peasant origin,

The contemporary urban statesmen, lawyers, and
physicians of this lineage immediately acknowledge direct kin ties to a common rural ancestry and strongly
feel the collective pull of such ties. The line quoted
is clearly epic in mode. The fact that the cola each
bear an extra syllable is merely the result of the particular family name and, in the second colon, use of the
ijekavski dialect.[22]

In another case, a Slavicist taped his uncle's recollections shortly before the old man's death. That oral
account goes back to 1719 and it, too, begins at the
"beginning":

> *Naši stari potiču iz sela Gare,*
> Our ancestors spring from Gara village,

Again, from the very outset, one senses the power
of "we," of origins. The epic rhythm is nearly perfect,
and although the transcription happens to be typed in
run-on format, it was undisputedly transmitted by the informant in stichs. For example,

> . . .

> *I tamo je bio neki naš prvi predak,*
> *Zvao se Janko, imao sina Nikolu.*

> *A taj Nikola imao tri sina:*
> *Milovana, Miloša i Momira.*

> . . .

> *Miloš je imao posle čet'ri sina:*
> *Živana, Simu, Luku, i Jovana.*

And there was one of our first ancestors,
He was called Janko, [he] had a son Nikola.

> And this Nikola had three sons:
> Milovan, Miloš and Momir.
>
> . . .
>
> Miloš then had four sons:
> Živan, Sima, Luka, and Jovan.

The similarities to Grandfather Mileta's grammar of
kin are obvious. The old uncle, however, a retired law-
yer, chose to consistently and correctly inflect proper
names. Of interest is a line where the informant is
anxious to get on to the Lukič sub-lineage, founded by
their direct ancestor Luka, and he asks,

> *Ej sad! Je l' ti hočeš od deda Luke da počnemo,*
> *da znamo?*
>
> Well now! Do you want to start from Grandfather
> Luka, so we know [along which branch to recon-
> struct]?[23]

The line is in epic mode, although it does contain more
than ten syllables plus extrametrical expressions preceding and following it.
     Finally, I will close this exposition of genealogy
as oral genre with another example from Orašac. In this
instance the informant, an elderly villager, saddened at
having had no surviving sons, begins his recollection
with the bitter line,

> *Nema ko' da primi to od mene.*
> There's no one to receive this from me.

He then commences to recall his direct ancestor five
generations back and recollects the ascending generations lineally by proper names. Then he pauses, reverses the process, and, starting with himself, moves
back through the descent line, this time using kinship
terms in place of the already named individuals: a sigh,
an extrametrical expletive, and then the final line, a
repeat of the first.

> *Ej sad, nema ko' da primi to od mene.*
> Eh now, there's no one to receive this from
> me.[24]

If represented diagrammatically, this particular genealogy, in effect a beautifully balanced poem, looks like this:

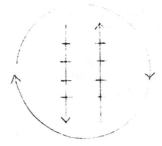

The account has come full circle.[25]   There is no further tale to tell.

University of Massachusetts at Amherst

NOTES

*I wish to express particular appreciation to my colleague Robert P. Creed, who first suggested to me the notion that analysis of the recitation of genealogies in contemporary rural Serbia might yield interesting structural and metrical features. Indeed, the present paper was motivated by this challenge.

[1]Murko, *La poésie populaire épique en Yougoslavie au début de XXe siècle* (Paris, 1929); *S-CHS*, I-IV; *MHV*; and *Singer*. For additional bibliography, see *Haymes*.

[2]"Studies in Comparative Slavic Metrics," *OSP*, 3 (1952), 21-66.

[3]The content of genealogies is not memorized; data are rather retrieved and recollected according to abstract rules in the head of the narrator. I am grateful to John Foley for calling my attention to the distinctions in Old English and ancient Greek similar to modern English "remember/recall" and Serbo-Croatian *pamtiti/ spomenuti*.

[4]Examples of somewhat analogous "preserved" genealogies in traditional poetry come to mind, such as the "Catalog of Ships" in the *Iliad* (II.483-93, prologue; and 494-877, catalog).

[5]The ancestors of Grandfather Mileta settled in then-wooded Šumadija as pioneers in Turkish-held territory. I suggest that the epic tradition, operating on a subliminal as well as surface level, was instrumental in

keeping alive both ethnic and personal identity.

[6]There are regional sub-dialectal distinctions, particularly phonological ones related to pitch. These are not directly pertinent here.

[7]Although perceiving some sort of structure to the recitation, the investigators were (unfortunately) at all times in the earlier field work period more interested in the data than in the manner of presentation. Joel Halpern stimulated the flow of information while I transposed the oral material to paper in conventional social anthropological kinship notation.

[8]Joel M. Halpern, *A Serbian Village* (New York, 1958, rev. ed. 1967). See also Joel M. and Barbara K. Halpern, *A Serbian Village in Historical Perspective* (New York, 1972).

[9]Such aural perceptions were not yet sensitive enough to encourage taping complete genealogies (see further note 21), or to focus on aural retention of orally transmitted material. Fortunately, small battery-operated tape recorders were by then coming into common use as field tools, and I do have fragments of several genealogies on tape which reinforce the evidence presented in this paper. Other informants, however, even those taped, did not display the epic impulse of Grandfather Mileta.

For the genealogy presented here, I rapidly jotted verbatim what I received aurally. My notebook shows the informant's utterances separated by regularized pauses which I marked as dashes between strings. Despite preoccupation with content, therefore, I was clearly conscious of metrical pattern and rhythm.

[10] Here reproduced on p. 307.

[11] See Lord, *Singer*, pp. 55-57, for an analysis of alliteration and assonance.

[12] The strings he generates, therefore, often are not those of the Chomskyan so-called "ideal speaker" (who functions in a communicative vacuum).

[13] I choose to end this exposition with the informant himself (actually with his younger brother [*rodjeni brat*, or "biological brother"]; cf. *brat*, "cousin"), this being a unit boundary which Grandfather Mileta himself recognized. Along the narrator's generational level the recitation begins to become encumbered, detailing in-marrying brides, wartime service, illness, out-migration from the village, and other data nongenealogical in nature. Metrics and structure appear to be preserved

throughout, but the material becomes more difficult to extrapolate for the purposes of exposition here. Readers of Serbian background or speakers of Serbo-Croatian may note syntactical or lexical inconsistencies or other "incorrect" usages; for example, often informants, when naming the sons of a given father, inflect the names in the grammatically more appropriate genitive, but Grandfather Mileta does not do this. We are not confronting an "ideal speaker" in a language laboratory, but a real man in a real situation.

[14] Compare J. M. Foley, "The Traditional Oral Audience," *BS*, 18(1977), 145-54.

[15] The reference here is to the First Revolt against the Turks (1804), a significant turning point in Serbian history. It took place in the precise region of the field work. Stojan was in fact a participant, having arrived in the area about 1790.

[16] These are the opening lines of many versions of the well-known epic *Kosovska djevojka*.

[17] This rule is broken in line 17, where the eldest son is mentioned last (because of meter?); however, this is compensated for in line 18. Line 21 has another structural violation, amended in line 22, where the narrator wishes to signal his own father.

[18] A genealogical tree is obviously similar to a syntactic structure tree. The concept of node is the exact equivalent of the Serbo-Croatian term *kolena*, or "generation," also meaning "knee, joint, node."

[19] That is, "generational level brothers," in other words, "cousins"; see also note 13.

[20] This is another example of "incorrect" usage. The correct form at the end of the line would be the partitive *sreče*; the narrator, however, said *sreću*, motivated perhaps by the vowels ending the preceding line (*u ratu*). See further note 13 and Lord, "The Role of Sound Patterns in Serbo-Croatian Epic," in *For Roman Jakobson* (The Hague, 1956), pp. 301-5.

[21] I must repeat that this particular genealogy is not preserved on tape; Grandfather Mileta unfortunately died before this could be done. A provocative question then poses itself: did the investigator really hear, for example, the subtle aural distinctions *tri/troji, čet'ri/četiri*? At the time of transcribing I was still more concerned with the data than with its form, as I have been careful to point out. Would it not have been logical to note number words by their symbols? The inevita-

ble answer is yes.   But the written field notes are as
presented; despite the recitation's having been filtered
aurally through a nonnative speaker, it remains intact.

[22] For generously sharing this long and fascinating
genealogy, currently undergoing kinship and prosodic
analysis by the author, I am indebted to Vojin N.
Smodlaka, M.D., of New York City.

[23] This is excerpted from an equally detailed genealogical recollection taped on the occasion of a 1969
visit to an 81-year-old uncle in the Old Country.   The
tape is labeled "*Razgovor sa Čika Žikom*" ("Conversation
with Uncle Žika").   I am grateful to Professor George
Lukić of the University of Pittsburgh for making it
available to me.

[24] Recorded by Joel Halpern and John Foley in Orašac
in 1975, on a day when the informant was feeling especially deprived of his cultural due as household patri-
arch.   The complete text of the account he gave that
day follows:

	Nema ko' da primi to od mene.	
Slušaj!	Maksim je im'o tri sina:	
	Mihajla, Miloša, i Živojina.	
	Ja sam Mihajlov potomak.	
	Mihajlo je im'o tri sina:	5
	Stefana, Milana, i Milivoja.	
	Milan im'o čet'ri sina:	
	Ljubomira, Sima, Miloša, i Dragutina.	
	Ja sam Milošov.	
	Dakle, meni je Milan deda,	10
	Mihajlo mi je pradeda,	
	A mojega oca, Maksim bio pradeda.	
Ej sad,	Nema ko' da primi to od mene.	

	There's no one to receive this from me.	
Listen!	Maksim had three sons:	
	Mihajlo, Miloš, and Živojin.	
	I am Mihajlo's descendant.	
	Mihajlo had three sons:	5
	Stefan, Milan, and Milivoje.	
	Milan had four sons:	
	Ljubomir, Sima, Miloš, and Dragutin.	
	I am [descended from] Miloš.	
	Therefore, Milan is my grandfather,	10
	Mihajlo is my great-grandfather,	
	And to my father Maksim was great-grand-father.	

Eh now, There's no one to receive this from me.

This text was collected during a joint field investigation, "Aspects of Serbian Oral Expression," funded by the National Endowment for the Humanities, in 1975-77, for which the researchers (Robert P. Creed, John M. Foley, Barbara K. Halpern, and Joel M. Halpern) wish to acknowledge their appreciation. See further J. M. Foley, "Research on Oral Traditional Expression in Šumadija and its Relevance to the Study of Other Oral Traditions," in *Selected Papers on a Serbian Village: Social Structure as Reflected by History, Demography, and Oral Tradition*, ed. by Joel M. and Barbara K. Halpern (Amherst, 1977), pp. 199-236.

[25] This structure is identical to the phenomenon which Homerists have designated as "ring composition." See further James P. Holoka, "Homeric Originality: a Survey," *CW*, 66(1973), 257-93.

SATIRE AND THE HEROIC LIFE: TWO STUDIES
(*Helgakviða Hundingsbana* I, 18 and Bjǫrn Hítdœlakappi's *Grámagaflím*)

Joseph Harris

Scholars like Otto Rank, Lord Raglan, and Jan de
Vries have pointed out a remarkably rigid patterning in
the lives of many legendary "heroes,"[1] and one of the
most interesting recent tendencies in the study of heroic
legend pursues such patterns to the influence of myth or
ritual or, at least, to tradition in an oral culture.[2]
Another route to what might be called "heroic conformity"
begins with the elusive background in a heroic ethos, and
George Fenwick Jones' *The Ethos of the Song of Roland* can
stand as a good representative of this more sociological
(and hence less exact) scholarly direction.[3] Strangely
the two approaches—the one from traditional narrative
structures and the other from the real-life ideological
matrix supporting such structures—are never combined.
As a general assignment the task would be too large for
the present small contribution to the honor of Professor
Lord; but if I focus here on a single neglected feature
common to both approaches, perhaps the results, though
minor, will be suggestive.

The connection of satire with the hero-life, its
role in a *Heldenleben*, may not appear obvious at first
glance. We are accustomed to thinking of our heroes as
shining figures, glowing with a generous inner passion
for heroic accomplishment; in this we are still seeing
through idealistic nineteenth-century eyes, eyes like
those of a Carlyle who could make even the treacherous,
contradictory, and, arguably, neurotic Odin an object of
"hero-worship." But there is evidence that heroic society embodied a strong dash of paranoia, that conformity
to social ideals was achieved partly through fear of
criticism and, especially, of satire—criticism in comic
form. In such a "shame culture," which Jones contrasts
with the predominant modern "guilt culture," a Roland's
quintessentially "heroic" act, his refusal to blow his
horn for help, arises largely in his fear of "male
chançun," satirical songs that might be composed to his
shame.[4] At the Battle of Maldon in 991 Earl Byrhtnoth's
men voiced a number of varied reasons, some as old as
Tacitus, for fighting on to the last man; among them was

Leofsunu, who promised not to flee but to advance because the "steadfast heroes around Sturmere" were not to be given cause to "criticize [him] with words," alleging that he turned from battle now that his lord lay dead.[5] Leofsunu's *wordum ætwitan* may or may not imply verse satire, but his probable pun on *stedefæste hælæð*, where "steadfast" could mean "unswerving" or "stay-at-home," certainly looks like a satirical preemptive strike.[6] No formal satire has survived in Old English, but in early Old English times the major word for poet, *scop*, must have carried connotations of its origin in "scoffing" and derision. In the closely related Old Frisian, *skof* meant "mockery," and Old High German *scof* embraced both "poet" and "derision."[7] A favored etymology for Old Norse *skáld* "poet" relates the word to these unromantic concepts, and English *scold* ("to abuse verbally," etc., or "an abusive person, especially a woman") is probably borrowed from Old Norse. The Scandinavian institution of *níð* (roughly: "legally culpable insults") is closely linked with poets and poetry.[8] Many of the heroes of the realistic family sagas are intimately involved with various forms of satire, either as its victims or its perpetrators, and such mudslinging extends more often than one would expect to the heroes of tradition, the "heroes" *par excellence.*

I. *Óneiss sem kattar sonr: Helgakviða Hundingsbana I*, 18

Notable for their satirical components are the first and third Helgi poems in the *Poetic Edda*; called *Helgakviða Hundingsbana I* and *II*, they tell different but overlapping segments of the same heroic biography.[9] The most likely explanation of the historical relationship between the two poems is that both derive chiefly from an "Old Lay of the Vǫlsungs" (*Vǫlsungakviða in forna*).[10] Both poems (along with the more distantly related *Helgakviða Hjǫrvarðzsonar*) contain long *sennur*, formal exchanges of abuse equivalent to the English and Scottish flytings, between the antagonist and Helgi's representative Sinfjǫtli, a certified specialist in billingsgate. Helgi himself intervenes only to put an end to the flyting, but other heroes, including the sterling Beowulf,[11] speak for themselves. Helgi's valkyrie heroine unleashes her sharp tongue in a curse directed at her brother, Helgi's slayer (*HHII*, 31-33); her first words to Helgi have a sarcastic edge (*HH*, 17); and in *HHII*, 25 she has the poor taste to jeer at Helgi's dying rival.

Helgi himself bluntly blames Sigrún for the death of her
father and brother (*HHII*, 26-29) and is even presented as
jibing unsportingly at his enemy Hundingr when they meet
in Valhöll after death (*HHII*, 39)—this last passage has
seemed so offensive that many commentators brand it a
late interpolation.

The remarks I wish to examine here are of this kind
but more cryptically satirical. In *Helgakviða
Hundingsbana I* Sigrún, accompanied by other valkyries
and dramatic celestial lighting effects, has sought out
the victorious young Helgi on a battlefield to complain
that she has been betrothed against her will to
Hoðbroddr; it is up to Helgi to save her, and the rest of
the poem narrates the preparations for and approach to
battle, the insults before battle, and the enemy's preparations; the concluding stanzas describe Helgi's victory in the words of his valkyrie consort.

In the problematical stanza 18, Sigrún protests:

> Hefir minn faðir   meyio sinni
> grimmon heitit   Granmars syni;
> enn ec hefi, Helgi,   Hoðbrodd qveðinn,
> konung óneisan,   sem kattar son.
> (My father has pledged   his daughter fair
> As bride to Granmar's   son so grim;
> But, Helgi, I   once Hothbrodd called
> As fine a king   as the son of a cat.) [12]

The groundwork for a full understanding of this debated
passage has been laid by Anne Holtsmark's definitive establishment of the basic meaning of *óneiss* and her discussion of *kattar sonr*, [13] and Bjarne Fidjestøl has added
an interesting further ramification. [14] It remains to
offer a clear statement of the primary meaning of the
last line and to suggest a number of more problematic
refinements.

The difficulty in fully capturing the primary sense
of the second helming or half-stanza has apparently been
caused by the lack of a close parallel, having the structure: adjective + *sem* + an animal, where the adjective is
complimentary and the comparison derogatory. In other
words, something like "as fierce as a lion" or "timid as
a mouse" is of no use as a parallel since there must be
an ironic discrepancy between the adjective and the comparison; the apparent absence of anything like "as fierce
as a mouse" elsewhere in Old Norse poetry has made

scholars very cautious about accepting the fairly obvious irony here.   An analogue that fulfills these
conditions and should remove the remaining skepticism
about the irony is to be found in Bjǫrn Hitdœlakappi's
satire *Grámagaflím*, where Bjǫrn claims that his enemy
Þórðr is *jafnsnjallr sem geit* "just as bold as a she-
goat."[15]   Here there can be no doubt about the scornful
intention and the ironic discrepancy between the adjective and the term for comparison since at least one
well-attested traditional quality of the she-goat was
cowardice.[16]   The parallel confirms, in essentials at
least, results to which Anne Holtsmark seems to have
come with a sense of surprise and also Sijmons' much
earlier guess that *óneiss* was ironically intended.[17]

Sigrún's scorn, then, is explicit, damaging, and
couched in a wittily memorable phrase, and it seems at
least possible that it was imagined as having been expressed as verse since there seems to be a special formality and prominence in *qveðinn* here.   This is arguable
not only from the frequent technically poetic meanings
of the verb and its derivatives[18] but also from the
structure of the stanza, where the main elements in the
first helming answer to elements in the second: *faðir/ek,
hefir heitit/hefi qveðinn, grimmr/óneiss, Granmars
sonr/kattar sonr*.   The parallelism is sufficient to establish the expectation that *qveðinn* must answer in precision and weight to *heitit* ("engaged").   The point cannot be proved; but I suspect that if *kveða* here does not
mean "I have stated in a *kviðling* (satirical verse)," it
must be at least as formal as "I have pronounced."   However, the *Vǫlsunga saga*, quoted below, supports this deduction only to the extent that its paraphrase presents
Sigrún as making a formal vow ("*heitit*") in contradiction
to her father.[19]

Anne Holtsmark established the meaning of *óneiss*
through the formally positive *neiss* which, however, is
shown to have the negative meaning "defen eless," especially in the (proverbial?) phrase *neiss ok nøkkviðr*,
"defenseless and naked."   The formally negative (semantically positive), then, would be "not defenseless."
The implication of Holtsmark's discussion is that from
this point the meanings generalized to "afraid" and
"fearless"; but since she also showed that *neiss* is especially found in contexts of clothing, including particularly war-gear, it seems worthwhile to point out that
the cruder "not defenseless" has the advantage of carry-

ing the sense of its opposite "defenseless" close to the
surface as *óneiss* apparently does in its five Eddic occurrences.

This is most obvious in *óneiss sem kattar sonr* "as
'un-defenseless' as a kitten," which suggests rather "defenseless as a kitten," while "fearless" or other generalized interpretations would mask this reference to the
base *neiss*. After all, a kitten may well be fearless; the
point seems to be that, fearless or not, it is weak and
helpless.   There is a second occurrence of *óneiss* in *HH*;
when Helgi's forces are gathering for the assault on
Hoðbroddr, Helgi asks his ally Hjǫrleifr: "Hefir þú
kannaða   koni óneisa?" (23, 7/8)   ("Hast thou counted
the gallant host?" 24).   The *konir* are Helgi's own
men; their numbers and arms make them *óneisir* "not defenseless," i.e., litotes for "well-defended." But *konr*
is also a "son," and *óneiss* has just before appeared in
a pregnant sense collocated with *kattar sonr*; it seems
almost certain that the reference (with litotes) in stanza 23 to *konir óneisir* is intended to recall the reference (with irony) in stanza 18 to the enemy who is *óneiss*
sem kattar sonr, i.e. *neiss*.

In *Atlakviða* 17 *óneiss* again has this quality of
suggesting its opposite:

langt er at leita   lýða sinnis til,
  of rosmofjǫll Rínar,   recca óneissa (17, 3/6).

Ursula Dronke translates: "it is a long way to seek/ for
an escort of men/ from the hills of Worms on the Rhine,/
for *valiant* fighters,"[20] but in this interpretation "valiant" becomes otiose since there is no question of
Gunnarr and his companions being unvaliant or having left
just the valiant men at home.   However, if we substitute
the ungeneralized, more primary sense of *óneiss* as established from *neiss (ok nǫkkviðr)* the passage gains in precision and depth.   Indeed, the meaning "unprotected,"
specifically by adequate arms, ought to be clear from the
preceding stanza where Guðrún says: "Betr hefðir þú,
bróðir,   at þú í brynio fœrir, / sem hiálmom aringrey-
pom,   at siá heim Atla" (16, 1/4)   ("You would have
done better, brother,   if you had come in coat of mail /
and hearth-encircling helmets   to see Atli's home,"
Dronke, p. 6).   That Gunnarr and his party come relatively unarmed (Hǫgni uses his sword in stanza 19) is
further suggested by stanza 14 where the Hunnish
guards were "to watch for Gunnarr and his men, lest they
should come here seeking with shrill spear to make war

against the tyrant" (Dronke's translation); in other
words, the guards' task was to determine whether they
were coming equipped for peace or for war; and since they
are subsequently received with a hypocritical show of
friendship (the implicit narrative underlying st. 15),
Atli and his guards must have determined that Gunnarr's
men came with peaceful intentions and equipage. So by
saying in stanza 17 to his sister that "it is a long way
to seek . . . for warriors who are not defenseless,"
Gunnarr is implying that he and his followers at Atli's
court are *neiss* "defenseless," specifically lacking the
arms mentioned in stanza 16. The *Atlakviða* poet, a consummate artist, seems also to be recalling his other,
earlier use of *óneiss* in stanza 12 of the poem:

> Leiddo landrǫgni   lýðar óneisir,
> grátendr, gunnhvata,   ór garði húna (12, 1/4).[21]
> (They led the prince of the land,   valiant people
> weeping led the war-keen men   from their chil-
> > dren's courts.)

At home the Burgundians were *óneisir* with reference perhaps to the storehouses of swords mentioned in stanza 7;
the stay-at-homes are, therefore, "not defenseless," yet
weeping, just at this point probably to imply that the
departing party are *neisir*. Certainly that is one's impression on rereading stanza 12 after careful attention
to the context of the adjective in 16-17.

A fifth occurrence of *óneiss* (as *óneisinn*) in
Guðrúnarkviða in þriðja, stanza 4, agrees fairly well
with the four usages just examined. Guðrún has been
falsely accused of adultery with þjóðrekr (Theodorich,
Dietrich). Speaking to her husband Atli she offers
oaths and an ordeal and denies the charge "except that I
embraced the governor of hosts (þjóðrekr), the prince
óneisinn, a single time."[22] Even here some version of
the primary sense "not defenseless" seems preferable to
Holtsmark's generalized "fearless," for the point in this
passage seems to be that Guðrún admits to having embraced
þjóðrekr once *in armor* and not in bed. I pointed out the
connections of *óneiss* with armor in *Atlakviða*, and
Holtsmark's discussion established a special connection
with clothing. Here the specific form of the accusation
is:

at þit þjóðrecr   undir þaki svæfit
oc léttliga   líni verðiz (2, 5/8).
(. . . that you and þjóðrekr   slept under cover
and tenderly   wrapped yourselves in linen.)

In bed lovers are *neiss ok nøkkviðr* "defenseless and
naked"; thus Guðrún denies the charge of having been in
bed with þjóðrekr by admitting that she once embraced
him *óneisinn*, in a not-defenseless condition, that is,
wearing armor and, of course, not *nøkkviðr*. Thus all
five occurrences of *óneiss* seem to conform to a common
pattern of usage; and this seems to be shared by Bjǫrn's
jafnsnjallr since in the collocation with *sem geit* it
surely suggests *ósnjallr*, a grave insult ranging in meaning from "cowardly" and "inarticulate" to "impotent."

    In view of the rather specific associations of *neiss*
and *óneiss* it appears that *kattar sonr* should be regarded
not as equivalent to "cat" (so Holtsmark[23]) but to "kitten." This interpretation is supported by the paraphrase
in *Volsunga saga*: "Hogni konungr hefir heitit mik
Hoddbroddi, syni Granmars konungs, en ek hefi því heitit,
at ek vil eigi eiga hann heldr en einn krákuunga."
("King Hogni . . . has promised me in marriage to
Hoddrodd, King Granmar's son, but I have vowed to have
him no more than I'd have a fledgling crow as a husband.") It seems that the paraphraser found the second
helming obscure or too complex; in any case, he substituted a simple promise and a more obvious comparison for
the parts of the helming under discussion, *qveðinn* and
óneiss sem kattar sonr. However, the new comparison
makes clear his understanding of the original; a
krákuungi "fledgling crow" is undesirable as a mate not
because it is, for example, ugly but because it is con-
temptibly weak and defenseless. This is perfectly clear
in the only other citation of the word in Fritzner:
"siðan tók Erlingr 2 brœðr mína ok festi annan upp sem
krákuunga en lét hǫggva annan."[24] ("Then E. took my two
brothers and strung the one up like a fledgling crow and
had the other killed.")

    Bjarne Fidjestøl has, further, suggested that *kattar
sonr* is an allusion to Hǫðbroddr's father: *Gran-marr* was
interpreted as a kenning "bewhiskered horse," i.e. cat.
At first glance this seems unlikely since it would compare Hǫðbroddr with himself ("Hǫðbroddr is as *óneiss* as
the son of Granmarr"); but wordplay cannot be reduced to
simple paraphrase, and double reference—having one's

semantic cake and eating it too—is the essence of para-
nomasia.[25] The phrase could mean "son of a cat, kitten"
and at the same time constitute an allusion to Granmarr;
but if so, the only evidence is in the passage itself
since the *Volsunga saga* paraphraser simplified the wordplay—if he recognized it as such—out of existence, and
Fidjestøl has not offered any supporting parallel.[26]   A
further bit of support for Fidjestøl's proposition can,
however, be extracted from the passage itself. I have
pointed out above how a certain symmetry informs the
stanza; the second helming, linked by the adversative
sense of *enn*, partly replicates the first, contrasting
the actions of father and daughter in a framework of parallelism. The syntactic symmetry ends with the different
types of object after each verb, but in place of a grammatical parallelism we find a combination of lexical repetition and symmetrical placing in the last line of each
helming: l. 4 *Granmars syni*: l. 8 *sem kattar son*. Though
final proof is impossible, I think Fidjestøl is correct
in perceiving wordplay here.

    The possibility has been raised by Holtsmark that
the Icelandic poet and storyteller Stúfr blindi was
alluding to *Helgakviða Hundingsbana I*, 18 when he told
King Haraldr harðráði: "Kattar son em ek" (I am [a]
kattar sonr).[27] Like the paraphraser of *Volsunga saga*,
Stúfr could simply have by-passed the putative pun,
which would have been irrelevant to his situation.
However, the evidence for Stúfr's acquaintance with the
poem is not strong, depending entirely on this phrase
and being tempered by the facts that Stúfr's father
really was called *kǫttr* "cat," his nickname, and that a
sufficient motive for calling himself *kattar sonr* instead of *þórðar sonr* is supplied, in the context of
Stúfr's story, by Stúfr's wish to touch very obliquely
on King Haraldr's father's nickname *sýr* ("sow"). It
seems unlikely that this part of Holtsmark's discussion
can profitably be taken further. Nevertheless, I cannot
resist the speculation that *if* Stúfr was playing on the
passage from *Helgakviða Hundingsbana I* and the king's
knowledge of it, then he may also have been expecting
Haraldr to remember the adjective *óneiss* "not defenseless"; for the purpose in Stúfr's story of the witty
hero's naming himself *kattar sonr* is to indicate subtly
to Haraldr, whom tradition characterized as given to
lampooning the people around him, that the Icelander's
tongue could be dangerous, that he was not without de-
fenses.[28] Thus this very indirect and finally quite

doubtful allusion to *óneiss* would fall in line with that
of *Helgakviða Hundingsbana I*, 23, 7/8 where a litotic
sense of *óneiss* ("undefenseless" = very well defended)
is evoked by reference to an ironic use (*HH* 18: "undefenseless as a kitten" = defenseless).

   II. *Grámagaflím*

   The saga about Bjǫrn Champion-of-the-Hítdalers tells
how Bjǫrn and his life-long *bête noire* Þórðr engaged in a
series of mutual provocations and attacks that at last
culminated in Bjǫrn's death, and many of the hostile acts
are satirical sallies, especially in verse, since both
men were adept skalds of the "serpent-tongued" variety.
In fact the structure of the saga itself resembles an
acting out of the alternating dramatic exchanges of a
flyting. At one point Bjǫrn had composed a lampoon . . .

> And not long before Bjǫrn had composed a lampoon
> (*flím*) about Þórðr; and it was at that time rather
> well-known to certain men. But its contents were
> to the effect that Arnóra, Þórðr's mother, had eaten
> the kind of fish he called a *grámagi*; and he
> claimed that it had been found on the shore and
> that from eating it she had become pregnant with
> Þórðr, and so he was not entirely of human origin on
> both sides of his family. And this is in the
> lampoon:
>   1. The flood went up on the sand, and a fish went
>   up on the land. Like to a lump-sucker, slime was
>   on its flesh. The wolf-bitch-of-the-gown (=
>   Arnóra, the mother) ate the "gray-belly," carrion
>   blended with poison. There is much that's evil
>   in the sea.[29]
>   2. The bride's belly rose down from her breast, so
>   that that oak-of-the-scarf (= Arnóra, the mother)
>   would walk bent quite backward and painful in her
>   gut. She became much too fat.[30]
>   3. A boy came to light. The lady said to her
>   collector-of-wealth (her husband) that she wished
>   to raise it up. As he lay there he seemed to her
>   a dog-biter, just as bold as a she-goat, when she
>   looked in his eyes.[31]

   The *Grámagaflím* is best understood as a parodistic
version of the kind of hero-life we find in the Helgi

poems or at least in *Helgakviða Hundingsbana I*, for several of the conventions of the life of the hero of tradition are exploited here in satirical form. In stanza 1 there are the topoi of supernatural conception and the riddle of fatherhood. Readers of Rank, Raglan, and de Vries will remember that the paternity of many heroes is ambiguous since there may be a divine father and a human husband; or the god's intervention may be rationalized as an adulterous or incestuous relationship.[32] The "hero" þórðr, however, is not the putative son of, say, an Óðinn or a Zeus; rather the supernatural conception here takes the comic form of a well-worn motif in which a woman conceives through eating some special food (T511, Conception from eating; cf. J1532.1, The Snow Child). In fact Bjǫrn may well have had in mind a particular version of this motif, the myth of how Loki became pregnant by eating the half-burned heart of an evil woman:

> A heart ate Loki,—   in the embers it lay,
> And half-cooked found he   the woman's heart;—
> With child from the woman   Lopt soon was,
> And thence among men   came the monsters all.[33]

Strengthening this possible alusion to Loki (or Lopt) is the similarity of *meinblandit (hræ)*, "poison-mixed (carrion)" to the *lævi blandit*, "poison-mixed (heavens)" of *Vǫluspá* 25, 6, another Loki reference.

Stanza 2 is a comic description of the resulting pregnancy, a phase which is decently passed over in most serious heroic legend. However, heroes occasionally cry out in the womb (cf. T570-579, Pregnancy); þórðr apparently lay there like a lump. Stanza 3 gives the birth itself. The doting mother's decision to rear the boy ("sagt hafði drós . . . at hon ala vildi") must be understood as a decision *not* to expose the infant; but such a decision was properly that of the father. And by specifying the decision at all Bjǫrn manages to imply that þórðr's was one of those poor families for which the possibility of exposing its infants, a practice frowned on even during the pagan period, was a real alternative; the phrasing further suggests that þórðr was actually a marginal case—the decision could have gone either way![34] Perhaps these lines also remind us that traditional heroes were often exposed at birth (typically by the father or maternal grandfather, according to Raglan).

The birth of the hero of tradition is often attended by prophecies of future greatness, and our Þórðr is no exception, for his mother could see at once that he would be a *hundbítr*. The editors differ on the exact sense of the word; Nordal and Guðni Jónsson give "someone who kills dogs (and eats them)," while R. C. Boer interpreted "wer, wie ein hund, von hinten angreift und beisst, ein feigling."[35] In any case, "dog-biter" is no flattery, and this prophecy is expanded by the phrase discussed above, "just as brave as a she-goat." This heroic prophecy is based on baby Þórðr's eyes in parody at the convention of "funkelnde augen . . . als das kennzeichen edler geburt" which Gering and Sijmons demonstrate from prose and verse.[36]

Beyond these general features of a satirical treatment of the "myth of the birth of the hero," the *Grámagaflím* bears some special resemblances to *Helgakviða Hundingsbana I*. Both are partial hero-lives; *HH* ends with Helgi's youthful deeds while the *Grámagaflím* does not progress beyond Þórðr's birth. Whether the poem is a fragment, as is usually assumed, is unclear; the saga author knew only the preserved three stanzas, but does he imply that there were once more stanzas ("en þetta er í flíminu" ["and this is in the lampoon"])? The simile makes a rather satisfactory conclusion, but one would like to think the poem originally went on to a satirical *Heldenjugend*, perhaps working out the consequences of the piscine paternity.[37] Apart from the ultimate origin of all the Volsungs, according to *Vǫlsunga saga*, in a fertility-bringing apple, nothing explicitly supernatural is reported about the conception of Helgi Hundingsbani, though Sigrlinn, mother of Helgi Hjǫrvarðzson, appears originally to have been a valkyrie, and the confused paternity of the Hundingsbani is a late development occasioned by his integration into the Vǫlsung line.[38]

However, the other points of a hero-life are present in *HH*. Helgi's birth is accompanied by impressive supernatural attendants, meteorological effects, and prophecies or blessings (2, 5/8; prophecy of the raven in 5-6, including 6, 7/8 "sá er varga vinr,   við scolom teitir": "He is friend of the wolves;   full glad are we"). The prophecy is partly based on Helgi's heroic eyes (6, 5/6 "hvessir augo   sem hildingar": "His eyes flash sharp   as the heroes' are"). Both *Grámagaflím* and *HH* focus special attention on the hero's mother (*HH* 5, 1/4, a difficult passage that may refer to a premonition of Helgi's tragic greatness and so resemble, *mutatis mutandis*, the insight of þórðr's mother); and both associate the birth of the hero with light (*HH* 6, 4). Finally, two rather far-fetched points of comparison: Helgi was given gifts at birth, apparently by his father (7, 5/8-8),[39] while þórðr's "father" is mentioned as *auðar gildir* ("collector-of-wealth") at the corresponding moment but gives nothing. With Thompson motif T585.7 ("Precocious hero leaves cradle to go to war, etc."), the raven says of Helgi: "*Stendr í brynio   burr Sigmundar / dœgrs eins gamall*" ("In mail-coat *stands*   the son of Sigmund, / a half-day old"). Can the recumbent and unprecocious þórðr be compared: "*henni þótti sá / hundbítr, þars lá*" ("he seemed to her a dog-biter there where he *lay*")?

The focus on the mother, the light, and the heroic eyes are impressive similarities, and one might be tempted to see the prophecy *hundbítr* as an ironic inversion of the prophecy *varga vinr*. However, these parallels probably should only be taken as evidence that Bjǫrn's satire is also a parodistic treatment of elements of a certain *kind* of poem, not as a direct dependence on *Helgakviða Hundingsbana I*. Many of the relevant elements are also present in the conception and birth of Karl and Jarl in *Rígsþula*, including the divine and human father, pregnancy, and the *accouchement* itself. *Rígþula* also conjoins the topos of heroic eyes in the infant with an animal simile: "*ǫtul vóro augu   sem yrmlingi*" (34, 7/8). ("Grim as a snake's   were his glowing eyes.")[40] The parallel here with "*jafnsnjallr sem geit,/ as í augu leit*" ("as bold as a goat when she looked in his eyes") is striking, and we can add that the list of the young Jarl's boyish skills includes *hundom verpa* (35, 10: probably "to egg on the dogs")[41] while the anti-hero þórðr will become a *hundbítr*. These almost equally impressive similarities to *Rígþula* confirm our suspicion against the postulation of a direct dependence or allusion by Bjǫrn to the Helgi poem.

* * *

The "heroes" of the two studies presented here have little more than their connection with satire in common. Helgi is a hero of tradition comparable to Sigurðr, Moses, Arthur, and the others; with a little ingenuity he might score fairly high in Raglan's scale. Formal satire and free-form insults echo around him at several points,

and in the passage examined here Sigrún's caustic characterization of the rival Hǫðbroddr is also her declar-
ation of alliance with her chosen hero Helgi. Bjǫrn
and þórðr were historical figures, Icelandic farmer-folk
who were never far from the nitty-gritty facts of ordinary
life. Yet for them poetry is largely a "martial art,"
and satire plays a part in shaping their life and death.
Despite the differences between Helgi and Bjǫrn our two
studies present complementary aspects of a single problem. For the Sigrún passage comprises an incursion
through satire of the homely detail of daily life into
the lofty career of a semi-mythic hero, while in the
satire *Grámagaflím* motifs associated with gods and
legendary heroes intrude into the prosaic pattern of
real life.

Stanford University

NOTES

[1] Otto Rank, *The Myth of the Birth of the Hero: a
Psychological Interpretation of Mythology*, tr. by F. Rob-
bins and S. E. Jelliffe (New York, 1955); Lord Raglan, *The
Hero: a Study in Tradition, Myth, and Drama* (London,
1936); Jan de Vries, *Betrachtungen zum Märchen* . . .,
FFC 150 (Helsinki, 1954) and in more popular form in
Heroic Song and Heroic Legend, tr. B. J. Timmer (London,
1963), ch. 11.
[2] A few examples: Otto Höfler, "Das Opfer im
Semnonenhain und die Edda," in *Edda, Skalden, Saga:
Festschrift zum 70. Geburtstag von Felix Genzmer*, ed.
by Hermann Schneider (Heidelberg, 1952), pp. 1-67; Franz
Rolf Schröder, "Mythos und Heldensage," *GRM*, 36(1955),
1-21 and revised in *Zur germanisch-deutschen Heldensage*,
ed. by Karl Hauck (Bad Homburg, 1961), pp. 285-
317; Jan de Vries, "Das Motiv des Vater-Son-Kampfes im
Hildebrandslied," *GRM*, 34(1953), 257-74 and expanded in
Hauck, pp. 248-84; Georges Dumézil, *From Myth to Fiction:
the Saga of Hadingus*, tr. by D. Coltman (Chicago, 1973).
[3] (Baltimore, 1963); another good example: George
Clark, "*The Battle of Maldon*: A Heroic Poem," *Speculum*
43(1968), 52-71.
[4] Jones, pp. 89, 96-98, and *passim*.
[5] *The Battle of Maldon*, ll. 246-53a, esp. 249-50, in
The Anglo-Saxon Poetic Records, VI, ed. by E. van Kirk
Dobbie (New York, 1942).

[6] I have not seen this (probable) pun pointed out, but on the topic generally cf. Roberta Frank, "Some Uses of Paronomasia in Old English Scriptural Verse," *Speculum* 47(1972), 207-26.

[7] Cf. further MDu *schop*, ON *skop*, *skaup*, Dan. *skuf*, and MHG *schelte*, and see C. T. Onions, *The Oxford Dictionary of English Etymology* (Oxford, 1966), s.v. *scop*, *scold*; F. Holthausen, *Altenglisches etymologisches Wörterbuch* (Heidelberg, 1963), s.v. *scop*; Jan de Vries, *Altnordisches etymologisches Wörterbuch*, 2nd ed. rev. (Leiden, 1962), s.v. *skald*; and Klaus von See, "Skop und Skald. Zur Auffassung des Dichters bei den Germanen," *GRM*, 14(1964), 1-14.

[8] The great study of *nið* is Bo Almqvist, *Norrön niddiktning: traditionshistoriska studier i versmagi*, vol. 1: *Nid mot furstar* (Uppsala, 1965) and vol. 2: *Nid mot missionärer. Senmedeltida nidtraditioner* (Uppsala, 1974) (= Nordiska texter och undersökningar, 21 and 23).

[9] Eddic poems are quoted from Gustav Neckel, ed., *Edda: die Lieder des Codex Regius nebst verwandten Denkmälern*, 3rd ed. rev. by Hans Kuhn (Heidelberg, 1962); the major Helgi poems are abbreviated *HH* and *HHII*.

[10] The best study nevertheless presents an unclear picture of these relationships: Jan de Vries, "Die Helgilieder," *ANF*, 72(1957), 123-54.

[11] Two recent articles study the "Unferth-Intermezzo" as a flyting: Carol Clover (forthcoming) and J. Harris, "The *senna*: From Description to Literary Theory," *MGS*, 5 (1979), 65-74.

[12] Unless otherwise noted, translations are those of Henry Adams Bellows, *The Poetic Edda* (New York, 1923); Bellows' stanza numbers often differ from the standard Neckel-Kuhn; this is Bellows' st. 19.

[13] "Kattar sonr," *Saga-Book*, 16(1962-65), 144-55. Older references are given in full by Holtsmark; translations and commentaries appearing since her article seem to have taken little note of it: Hans Kuhn, *Edda . . .*, II. Kurzes Wörterbuch (Heidelberg, 1968): "óneiss: ohne tadel"; Ólafur Briem, ed., *Eddukvæði*, Íslenzk úrvalsrit 5 (Skálholt, 1968), p. 269: "óneis: sem ekki þarf að blygðast sín, frægur, ágætur"; Patricia Terry, tr., *Poems of the Vikings: the Elder Edda* (Indianapolis and New York, 1969), p. 111: "but I, Helgi, have said that Hodbrodd, famed for his courage, is a feeble kitten." Terry seems to have been following F. Detter and R.

Heinzel (*Sæmundar Edda mit einem Anhang*, II. *Anmerkungen*
[Leipzig, 1903]) who, while not defining *óneiss*, says
plausibly enough that it is to be taken as "concessive"
here. L. M. Hollander, tr., *The Poetic Edda*, 2nd ed.
rev. (Austin, 1962) goes his own way with "callow like a
kitten" (p. 183) and equally arbitrary translations at
Atlakviða 12 ("faithful"), 18 [=19] ("brave and bold"),
and *HH* 23 ("mighty"). Not cited by Holtsmark: B. Kummer,
ed., *Die Lieder des Codex Regius (Edda) und verwandten
Denkmäler*. B. II. *Heldendichtung*. Erster Teil: Die
Dichtung von Helgi und der Walküre (Zeven, 1959), p. 60,
agrees with B. Sijmons and H. Gering (*Kommentar zu den
Liedern der Edda*, II [Halle, 1931]) that irony is intended; but he seems to have in mind a sexual context
for his translation "keck, wie 'nen jungen Kater" in
view of his comment "hier ist an den jungen, werbenden
und noch nichts vermögenden Kater gedacht" and the parallel he cites from *Hávamál* 96ff. (the scorn of *Billings
mey*). But a sexual sense is quite impossible for the
other instances of *neiss* and *óneiss*. Holtsmark has shown
that Gering was wrong about the meaning of *óneiss* in his
Wörterbuch and *Kommentar*, but it is interesting that
earlier in his translation (1892) Gering had rendered the
phrase ironically while omitting *óneiss*: ". . . dass er
wie kater zum König tauge."
   [14] "Kattar sonr. Ein merknad til Helgakviða
Hundingsbana I, str. 18," *MM*, 1971, pp. 50-51.
   [15] *Bjarnar saga Hítdœlakappa*, in *Borgfirðinga sogur*,
ed. by Sigurður Nordal and Guðni Jónsson, Íslenzk fornrit
3 (Reykjavík, 1938), pp. 168-69; and cf. R. C. Boer, ed.,
Bjarnar saga Hítdœlakappa (Halle, 1893), pp. 45-46, 99-
100). A comparable ironic comparison seems to be present in Hallfreðr's *lausavísa* 1 (*Hallfreðar saga*, ed. by
Einar Ól. Sveinsson, Íslenzk fornrit 8 [Reykjavík, 1939],
pp. 146-47, prose order): "Reiði sannargs allheiðins
søkkvis margra troga verðr mér svá nokkvi œgilig fyr
augum, sem ólítill, gamall búrhundr stúri úti fyr búri
alls mest við for gesta; stœrik brag." Hallfreðr's
verse means: "the wrath of Gríss (his rival) seems to my
eyes approximately as fearsome as if a big old housedog
should be barking hard at strangers."
   [16] *HHII* 37: "Svá hafði *Helgi* hrœdda gorva / fiándr
sína alla   oc frœndr þeira / sem fyr úlfi   óðar rynni /
geitr af fialli,   geisca fullar" ("Such the fear   that
Helgi's foes / Ever felt,   and all their kin, / As
makes the goats   with terror mad / Run from the wolf

among the rocks," Bellows, st. 36.)   Cf. *Ǫrvar-Oddr in
Biálkaland* (= *Eddica minora* . . ., ed. by A. Heusler and
W. Ranisch [Dortmund, 1903], p. 75):"sem fyr úlfi
geitr   argar rynni."   Other associations with she-
goats in poetry are contemptuous in a general way: *HHII*
22, *HH* 43, *Skírnismal* 35, *Hávamál* 36, *Rígsþula* 12 (perhaps also in Finnur Jónsson, ed., *Den norsk-islandske
skjaldedigtning* [Copenhagen, 1912], I(B), 167 Anon.
(X), IBl and II(B), 252-53 [Vers af Ragnarssaga, II,
5]); or else insultingly associated with lasciviousness:
Hyndluljóð 46, 5/8.

[17] Holtsmark, p. 150: "No, twist it and turn it as
much as we like, a cat never becomes *óneiss*. . . .   It is
not possible to understand Sigrun's words as anything but
scorn: Hǫðbrodd is as fearless as a cat!"   Cf. Gering-
Sijmons, *Kommentar*, II, 82.

[18] An example parallel in several respects comes from
the saga of Magnús the Good in *Morkinskinna*, ed. by C. R.
Unger (Christiania, 1867), p. 28 (my translation): "King
Haraldr thought it a disnonor to drink with þórir and
'spoke' (*qveþr*) the following to him: 'Be silent, þórir,
/ you are an unreasonable thane; / I heard that your
father / was called Hvinngestr.' þórir was a proud man
and was displeased by the 'squib' (*qviþlingr*)."

[19] *The Saga of the Volsungs*, ed. by R. Finch (London
and Edinburgh, 1965), pp. 14-15; translations from
Vǫlsunga saga (= *VS*) are Finch's.

[20] Ursula Dronke, ed., *The Poetic Edda*, vol. 1 (Oxford, 1969), p. 7; Dronke's translation of the adjective
is consistent with her assumption that Gunnarr and Hǫgni
set out unaccompanied.   However, I prefer Detter-
Heinzel's notion of this as "Held statt Held und
Begleitung" (their commentary to *Atlakviða* 13, 1 [= 12,1],
Voluspá 47, 1 [= 50, 1]; they further point to
Vafðrúðnismál 17-18 and *Fáfnismál* 14); and Dronke's
translation seems to capitulate to the logic of this
view when "at varða þeim Gunnari" (14, 13) appears as "to
watch for Gunnarr and his men," not "Gunnarr and Hǫgni"
as a consistent application of her reading would require.

[21] Adopting Dronke's *húna* for Kuhn's *Húna*; Dronke's
translation follows.

[22] This translation and the next from *Guðrúnarkviða
III* are mine; Bellows has the sense wrong; cf. Kuhn,
Wörterbuch, s.v. *nema*.

[23] Perhaps influenced by the only parallel to *sem
kattar son* she cites: *sem kǫttr í hreysi*.

[24] Johan Fritzner, *Ordbog over det gamle norske sprog*, 3rd ed. rev. by D. A. Seip and Trygve Knudsen (Oslo, 1954-72), s.v. *kråkuungi*; my translation.

[25] Fidjestøl calls this wordplay a *høveskenning* (occasional kenning); but although it is based on a (perceived) kenning, I cannot see that any established poetic term fully accounts for it. It resembles *ofljóst* and name-kennings in requiring a shift based on homophony but reverses the internal order of stages; cf. generally B. Fidjestøl, "Kenningsystemet. Forsøk på ein lingvistik analyse," *MM*, 1974, pp. 32-34; Roberta Frank, "Onomastic Play in Kormakr's Verse: the Name Steingerðr," *MScan*, 3 (1970), 7-34; and "Anatomy of a Skaldic Double-Entendre: Rognvaldr Kali's *lausavísa* 7," pp. 227-35 in *Studies for Einar Haugen Presented by Friends and Colleagues*, ed. by E. S. Firchow et al. (Mouton, 1972).

[26] The parallel offered, *nosgás* = duck (*Heiðreks gátur* [st. 27, 2] in *Eddica minora*), seems inadequate. I have not found a fully convincing parallel, but cf. A. Kjærs' idea that *gofugt dýr* is a similar wordplay on *Sig-(f)røðr* ("Zu Fáfnismál str. 2," pp. 54-60 in *Fest-schrift, Eugen Mogk zum 70. Geburtstag . . .* [Halle, 1924]), which Gering-Sijmons reject abruptly. Bugge (*The Home of the Eddic Poems, with Especial Reference to the Helgi-Lays*, rev. ed., tr. by W. H. Schofield [London, 1899], pp. 38-40) also thought *kattar sonr* a kind of sur-name, but the context (Irish influence) of this agreement with Fidjestøl is generally rejected. Ordinary name-puns (e.g., Skúta = *skúti*, in *Víga-Glúms saga*, Íslenzk fornrit 9: 54) seem distant, and the mysterious insult in *arfr Fiǫrsunga* (*HHII* 20), though perhaps related to the pres-ent passage, explains nothing. The most secure parallel I have found is offered by Gerd Weber's clever interpre-tation of the Altuna-stone ("Das Odinsbild des Altuna-steins," *BGDSL*, 97[1972], 332-33) where a name is inter-preted as a kenning to a referent in ordinary life, which is then produced as a symbol for the name: Arn-fastr = an eagle on his *fastr* or prey, so that a picture of an eagle on his prey in turn = Arnfastr; as Gran-marr = (metaphor for) a cat, so that the word *kǫttr* can refer back to Granmarr.

[27] Quoting the independent and superior version, Íslenzk fornrit 5: 280-90; the short version in *Morkinskinna* gives "Ek em kattar sun"; basic discussion in Holtsmark, pp. 151-55.

[28] This interpretation of dramatic tension between

the king and the Icelander is based on the longer, independent version where it is more pronounced than in the
condensed king's saga version; for Haraldr's concern with
fathers in a context of satire, cf. *Hreiðars þáttr
heimska* and Haraldr's encounter with Magnús the Good and
his brother þórir in *Morkinskinna* and *Flateyjarbok* (ref.
and discussion in Erik Noreen, "Studier i fornväst-
nordisk diktning," *Uppsala Universitets Årsskrift*, 1922,
Filosophi, språkvetenskap och historiska vetenskaper 4
[Uppsala, 1922], pp. 50-51).

[29] *einhaga ylgr* is a scornful kenning that suggests
the animalistic hunger of Arnóra. Cleasby-Vigfusson
treats *grámagi, grámaga* as the female of the lump-sucker,
just as *rauðmagi* is the male; but the male gender in the
poem argues against this as does the phrasing *hrognkelsi
glíkr*. Boer seems to have the right explanation:
"hrognkelse:. . . das männchen dieses fisches heisst,
wie mir Finnur Jónsson mitteilt, rauðmagi, was Bjǫrn
durch grámage ersetzt, um eine gewisse ähnlichkeit, doch
nicht vollständige identität mit dem rauðmagi anzudeu-
ten" (p. 99). I would add that the replacement of *rauð-*
"red" by *grá-* "gray" may be conditioned by the secondary
meaning of *grár* as "evil, malicious," a meaning that is
conspicuous in the opening lines of *Bjarnar saga* itself:
"Ekki var þórðr mjǫk vinsæll af alþýðu, því at hann
þótti vera spottsamr ok grár við alla þa, er honum þótti
dælt við" (p. 112); but since the female of the lump-
sucker is regularly called *grásleppa*, Bjǫrn may simply
have combined the first morpheme of the female with the
second of the male—cf. the androgenous Loki myth cited
below. The quaint resemblance of this stanza to the
verse on the front panel of the Franks Casket is presumably due to the limited language of Old Germanic
verse.

[30] The lump-sucker is a bloating fish that feeds on
the "garbage" of the ocean floor. Is this not a fitting
model for Arnóra, who is pictured as feeding off carrion
on the beach and then swelling in pregnancy? I understand from Icelandic friends that lump-suckers are actually caught on the beach after a storm (Cleasby-Vigfusson
gives *hrognkelsa-fjara* as the name of such a "fishing"
expedition) and that the female is actually eaten in a
ripe condition (like the delicacy *hákarl*, rotten shark).

[31] *auðar gildir* may be no more than a colorless
kenning for "man" (so *Lexicon poeticum*); but both editors
agree in giving it a primary sense "increaser-of-wealth"

(Nordal and Guðni Jónsson: "[sem eykur gildi e-s]: mann-
kenning"; Boer: "vermehrer des reichtums, ein mann"), and
since we expect the equivalent man-kenning to be constructed on the pattern "destroyer-of-wealth," i.e. "generous man," I think there is reason to believe that Bjǫrn
meant to construct a satirical inversion: "increaser-of-
(his own)-wealth," i.e. "miser." For the formula *líta í
augu* ("look into the eyes") cf. *Vǫluspá* 28.

[32] Cf. Stith Thompson motifs Z216, Magic conception
of hero; A511.1, Birth of culture hero; A112, Birth of
gods; A511.1.3.3, Immaculate conception of hero; T500-
599, Conception and birth generally.

[33] *Hyndluljóð* 41; Bellows, st. 43.

[34] Boer translates *at hon ala vildi* as "dass sie
gebähren wollte (d.h. dass ihre stunde gekommen war),"
but Icelandic *ala* means both "give birth" and "rear,
bring up (literally: nourish)." Here the collocation
with *vilja* tells against "give birth," nor would Arnóra
need to announce the wish to give birth to her husband
after the boy has already been born (*sveinn kom í ljós*).
See the second meaning (II, 1) in Cleasby-Vigfusson.

[35] I think the interpretation of Nordal and Guðni
Jónsson is preferable, but the parallels cited below from
HH and *Rígsþula* do not settle the question.

[36] *Commentar*, I, 360.

[37] Cf. Thompson motifs B635.1.1, Eaten meat of bear-
lover causes unborn son to have bear characteristics;
and J1532.1, The Snow Child.

[38] It is not even certain that the attenuated form of
the motif of supernatural conception found in T682 ("Hero
a posthumous son") applies in Helgi's case; for the
legendary-historical development, cf. de Vries, "Die
Helgilieder."

[39] Cf. *ANF*, 41(1925), 277-80, and *MM*, 1966, pp. 1-10.

[40] Cf. *Vǫlundarkviða* 17, 5/6.

[41] So Kuhn, *Wörterbuch*, s.v. *verpa* (with query); Bellows gives "and hounds unleashed."

ORAL COMPOSITION IN MIDDLE HIGH
GERMAN EPIC POETRY

Edward R. Haymes

This paper was originally conceived under the sarcastic title "OK, so it's oral, so what?"—the exasper-
ated outcry of the student of literature after being
flooded with formula statistics and oral-formulaic theory. It is a question which deserves our attention.
What *does* oral composition, or oral form, mean to the
historian or critic of literature? In this paper I shall
use the area best known to me to illustrate some of the
implications of the oral theory for our picture of an
epic poetry and the community which produced it.

The Middle High German period is perhaps unique in
Medieval Europe because it produced simultaneously two
very different traditions of narrative poetry, both of
which are historically associated with the feudal civilization under the Hohenstaufen Emperors. One group traditionally bears the name Heroic Epic and is best represented by its earliest and greatest surviving representative, the *Nibelungenlied*. The other group takes its
materials from contemporary French courtly romances and
includes as its most important representatives the
Arthurian Romances of Hartmann von Aue and of Wolfram
von Eschenbach.

This distinction between heroic and courtly epic is
one of the most universally observed conventions among
historians of medieval German literature. In spite of
this, there is no agreement about the criteria involved.
In his standard multi-volume *Geschichte der deutschen
Literatur*, Helmut de Boor sees the principal difference
in the "closeness to life and density of reality of the
action [in the heroic epics]. The Arthurian epic moves
in a never-never land which leaves all ways open to the
imagination. The *Nibelungenlied* moves with geographic
conscientiousness in the real space of the Rhine and
Danube landscapes."[1] Maurice O'Connell Walsche restricts
himself in his *Medieval German Literature* to a distinction based on sources. The heroic epic is derived from
Germanic sources and the courtly from French and Classical sources.[2] In his handbook on Middle High German
heroic epic, Werner Hoffman lists five areas of distinction: a) the anonymity of the heroic epic, b) the

strophic form (opposed to the couplet form in the courtly
works), c) the vocabulary, d) the style, and e) the
sources of the materials.[3] Hoffmann does not include the
distinction between oral and written composition, since
he does not accept the applicability of the oral theory
to the surviving Middle High German heroic poetry.[4] It
is, however, just this opposition between oral traditional epic and consciously innovative literary epic which
may best explain the intuitively grasped distinction between heroic and courtly narrative poetry.

The heroic poetry of the Middle High German period
is traditional and formulaic in the sense of Parry's and
Lord's oral theory.[5] Although this can no longer be
considered incontrovertible proof of oral (i.e., dictated) origin, it does prove that the poetry in question
is the product of an active oral tradition. The
Nibelungenlied, for example, tells stories which have
their origins in historical events which took place
eight centuries before the Middle High German epic was
written down.[6] The traditional style revealed in its
formulaic language and construction by themes and type-
scenes is, however, one which is a product of its own
time, i.e., of the period around 1200. The written poem
can thus tell us much about the tradition of oral poetry
alive at the time it was composed, even if the surviving
poem itself was the product of a writing poet who only
imitated the oral style (see *Das mündliche Epos*, pp.
14ff.).

Since the technique of "oral verse-making" is the
product of many generations of singers, it is necessarily
very conservative in nature[7]; "for it is of the *necessary*
nature of tradition that it seek and maintain stability,
that it preserve itself. And this tenacity springs
neither from perverseness, nor from an abstract principle
of absolute art, but from a desperately compelling conviction that what the tradition is preserving is the very
means of attaining life and happiness."(*Singer*, p. 220).
This wholly traditional character of oral epic implies a
congruence with the society in which it exists in a kind
of symbiosis.[8] In a pre-literate society, the singer
will be an honored member of the community, since his
art is the repository of the values and history upon
which the society rests (cf. *Singer*, pp. 13-29 and
passim). Some members of the audience may also be singers and the audience as a whole plays an important role
in the preservation of the traditional materials, since

it will not tolerate a significant variance from the traditional way of telling a story (*ibid*., pp. 25ff.).   In
drawing conclusions about the society that produced the
Middle High German strophic epics, we can bear this congruity between oral epic tradition and the structure of
society in mind and see what inferences we can draw from
it.

There has been little research into the level of
literacy prevailing at the courts of Germany before 1200.
The evidence available suggests that it was minimal, so
we can—with relative safety—conclude that we are dealing with a largely pre-literate society.[9]   The clergy
was certainly literate, but they represented a special
caste within society and the ability to read and write
was only one of many special powers they possessed.   If
literate knights had been common, Hartmann von Aue would
have had no need to point out his own literacy at the
beginning of both *Der arme Heinrich* and *Iwein*.   The richness of the oral poetic tradition revealed by the
Nibelungenlied is another indicator that the feudal
society was predominantly illiterate.   This work is
scarcely the product of an impoverished and subjugated
class, but an example of true court (if not "courtly" in
the technical sense of the "courtly" romance) poetry.
The richness of the tradition and its obvious orientation
toward questions of feudal lordship and power help to locate the *Nibelungenlied* socially within the upper reaches
of feudal society.   The innate conservatism of the oral
tradition points to an identification with the defenders
of the status quo.

Contemporary with the *Nibelungenlied*, the poets of
the courtly epic were writing a nontraditional, indeed
almost anti-traditional, style.   These works propagate
social values as revolutionary as their style.   The values of courtly love (*minne*), moderation (*mâze*), generosity (*milte*), and the way of life of the knight-errant,
whose personal honor is independent of feudal responsibility and his place in society, replace the politically
based code of the heroic epics, which emphasized personal
heroism, fidelity to one's feudal lord, and blood revenge.   The courtly epics deal with problems for which
there are no traditional solutions.   The introduction of
a new poetic style thus reflected a whole new set of
values, a set of values which may well be identifiable
with the rising social status of knights within the feudal society in Germany during this period.   The new

ideals proposed seem to coincide most clearly with the
interests of the group of legally unfree knights known
as *ministeriales*, whose legal status made them ideal
tools for the policies of the Hohenstaufen Emperors in
their struggle with the powerful nobility of the Empire
during the twelfth and thirteenth centuries. The Emperor
himself seems to have supported the ideas of courtly society among his knights.[10]   Recent research into the
Arthurian epics by Hartmann von Aue supports this interpretation of the social message of courtly romance.[11]

    If the courtly epic is a product of a "special in-
terest group" within German feudal society and represents
their interests, then it is another instance of the congruence between the poetic medium chosen and the social
message intended by the poet. The innovative style of
the courtly epics might be viewed in this light as a code
which has as its purpose the almost subliminal message
of social innovation. The style thus reflects an attempt
to make the new ideas attractive, or at least palatable,
to a society which was still largely static and unfriend-
ly to social change. The *Nibelungenlied*, which appeared
after the first wave of courtly poetry, may well be the
reaction of the most conservative elements of that society. In any case, it makes sense to seek the origins
of the *Nibelungenlied* in circles inimical to the ideals
being propagated by courtly epic. If it is in the very
nature of oral (or oral-derived) poetry to preserve tradition "as the very means of attaining life and happiness," then the use of traditional poetic composition in
a form apparently intended to compete with nontraditional
epic would represent very effective propaganda for the
retention of traditional social values. The largely pre-
literate audience would respond automatically to this aspect of the heroic poetry. This quality of the poem also
has important implications for our understanding of the
"content" of the poem. It may even be possible to view
the *Nibelungenlied* as an "anti-courtly epic," as I have
suggested elsewhere.[12]

    The logical place to look for the origin of the
Nibelungenlied would be in the circle of hereditary
aristocrats who had the most power to lose to the Imper-
ial *ministeriales* and to the social ascendancy of Imper-
ial over regional power. There is considerable evidence
linking the *Nibelungenlied* to the Bishop of Passau. If
further research shows that he was aligned with anti-
ministerialis or anti-Hohenstaufen interests, then the

case for locating the epic at his court will be strengthened. There is much interesting work to do in this
direction.

The application of oral theory to problems of literary history, sociology, and criticism of the Middle Ages
promises to yield results far beyond the areas I have attempted to outline here. For this to happen, however, it
is still necessary for scholars to realize that pre-literate poetry is not "sub-literate," but potentially as
rich and powerful as anything produced in writing. The
vast majority of the German nobility was illiterate before 1200 and there was certainly no opprobrium attached
to illiteracy. There may even have been a resistance to
the ability to read and write as being unfit for a
knight. The frequent references to the necessity to have
someone come and read a letter to a king or a knight suggest that this was the normal procedure. The mere presence of literacy (restricted in this case almost exclusively to the clergy) does not make a society literate.[13]
The historian of literature must attempt to recreate the
set of expectations that greeted a poem as it was presented the first time to its intended audience.[14] The
judicious application of oral theory in combination with
history and sociology may well bring us a few steps closer to that goal.

University of Houston

NOTES

[1]Helmut de Boor and Richard Newald, *Geschichte der
deutschen Literatur*, II: *Die höfische Literatur*
(Munich, 1969), 159.

[2](Cambridge, Mass., 1962), p. 220.

[3]*Mittelhochdeutsche Heldendichtung* (Berlin, 1974),
pp. 11-25.

[4]*Ibid.*, p. 54. Although Hoffmann devotes a whole
chapter to the oral theory, he totally ignores its implications throughout the rest of the book.

[5]The most complete coverage of the theory is Albert
B. Lord, *Singer*; see also *MHV*. For further literature
see *Haymes* and my *Das mündliche Epos: eine Einfuhrung in
die oral poetry Forschung* (Stuttgart, 1977).

[6]Cf. Gottfried Weber, ed., *Nibelungenlied* (Stuttgart, 1964), pp. 29ff.

[7]See Alois Schmaus, "Formel und metrisch-syntak-

tisches Modell," *WS*, 5(1960), 395–408.

[8] For a somewhat analogous notion applied to musical form, see Alan Lomax, "Song Structure and Social Structure," in *The Sociology of Art and Literature: a Reader*, ed. by Milton C. Albrecht, James H. Barnett, and Mason Griff (London, 1970), pp. 55–71.

[9] The largest collection of material is in James W. Thompson, *The Literacy of the Laity in the Middle Ages* (Berkeley, 1939), which unfortunately excludes vernacular literacy. See also the discussion and literature in Blanka Horacek, "Ichne kan deheinen buochstap," in *Festschrift für Dietrich Kralik* (Horn, 1954), pp. 129–45; and in Herbert Grundmann, "Dichtete Wolfram von Eschenbach am Schreibtisch?" *AKG*, 49(1967), 391–405.

[10] See Josef Fleckenstein, "Friedrich Barbarossa und das Rittertum," in *Festschrift für Hermann Heimpel* (Göttingen, 1971), II, 1023–41.

[11] Gert Kaiser, *Textauslegung und gesellschaftliche Selbstdeutung: Aspekte einer sozialgeschichtlichen Interpretation von Hartmanns Artusepen* (Frankfurt, 1973).

[12] In a paper given at the Twelfth Conference on Medieval Studies, Kalamazoo, Michigan, May 1977.

[13] The situation described in Franz H. Bäuml and Edda Spielmann, "From Illiteracy to Literacy: Prolegomena to a Study of the *Nibelungenlied*," in *OLSE*, pp. 62–73, probably did not exist in Germany until quite late in the thirteenth century.

[14] This is the thrust of the essay "Literaturgeschichte als Provokation der Literaturwissenschaft," in Hans Robert Jauss, *Literaturgeschichte als Provokation* (Frankfurt, 1970), pp. 144–207.

NARRATIVE AS PRECEDENT IN YORÙBÁ ORAL TRADITION

Deirdre La Pin

Perhaps the most recurrent assumption underlying studies of folk literature before the empirical work of Milman Parry and Albert Lord was the view that oral tradition was little more than a body of set texts. The word "folklore" conjured up images of happy illiterate masses reciting tales memorized from time immemorial: an enterprise requiring small effort and less creativity. It seemed that oral societies were incapable of sustaining any activity that was genuinely "literary," conceived and produced by individuals who could be regarded as artists in poetry or prose. Collections demonstrated the existence of variants, but these could be attributed to flaws in transmission or local differences of interpretation rather than a conscious choice made by the artist himself. At the root of this misunderstanding, of course, was a dearth of reliable annotated sources, and it was not until the voices of oral performers could be recorded and compared that the contribution of the individual to tradition could be adequately judged.

Parry and Lord addressed themselves to this task with a remarkable wisdom and precision. Not only did they study variants in the Yugoslav epic art, but they took into account the influence of audience, the conditions of performance, and the singer's expertise on the song that emerged.[1] What was more to their credit was an intent to support these findings (or compare them, at least) with the views of performers about the nature of their relationship to the artistic tradition. That these two lines of inquiry at times yielded conflicting conclusions seems only to have enhanced their force of insight; it brought their work nearer to the imaginative soil from which it grew. If a singer's claim to reproduce a song "word for word and line by line" crumbled against the weight of empirical evidence, it nevertheless expressed a significant cultural notion that offered a clear vision of the criteria guiding individual performance within the framework of tradition (*Singer*, pp. 28-29). Indeed, this tension between difference and sameness became the chief focus of Parry's and Lord's work; it began in the study, was sharpened in the field, and the theories of the formula, system and theme were its result.

Inheritors of the Parry-Lord method, in their preoccupation with text, have tended to overlook the part
that indigenous literary thought once played in their
masters' work. It is in this spirit of cultural inquiry
that the following discussion has evolved. Drawn from a
longer study on Yorùbá storytelling, its aim is to show
that it is wholly possible, and perhaps only proper, to
examine oral literature from within the thought system
that has lent it substance and shape.[2] I shall first
describe the Yorùbá narrative in its natural setting,
where it serves as a precedent for ritual actions, religious beliefs, social customs, and general truths
about man and his world. I shall also describe how this
role emerges naturally from the intrinsic structural
properties of these narratives, how, for example, the
sequence binds the events of the story to particular
phenomena that occur in the present, and how the linguistic organization of narrative furthers a mode of
discourse that argues in favor of a precept or message.
I shall also try to show how these two structures work
in concert to insure the acceptance of the story as a
model for human behavior which may be put to service in
the present.

1. The Narrative in Context

Narrative expression for the traditional Yorùbá includes a diversity of forms which range from the informal
anecdote to stories more appropriately described as folklore. In this capacity they set themselves apart from
other types of prose because they carry the weight of
common consent. The incidents they portray may be taken
as being fictional or real, depending on the mode in
which they are cast. An *àló*, for example, is a "lie"
(*iró*) or a flagrant distortion of reality, while an *ìtàn*
generally offers an account of things that actually took
place. A less common mode is the *àró*, which paints fan-
tastic images of personal success; an *òwe* is a parable
that proves or exemplifies a general truth about life.
Once these stories gain acceptance into the general culture, they enjoy thereafter the custodianship of society
at large, which is responsible for their retention and
transmission. An individually-conceived anecdote or account—told and readily forgotten—is not in this sense
literary. And yet across the great divide which separates the fleeting, personal creation from general social

practice may be found important bridges that link prose
which is lore with prose which is not.

All anecdotes and accounts share two important
functions not fully met by ordinary discourse: first,
they "prove" and second, they "persuade." In an oral
setting where the transmission of information is necessarily intimate and personal, knowledge is related by
its knower. It is not uncommon for a speaker bearing
important news to be asked for further verification.
Often he will resort to a story that recapitulates his
experience of coming to know: how he acquired his knowledge, when, from whom, whether any further evidence is
available. If the audience judges his account to be
plausible and coherent—believable because it is imag-
inatively reliveable—it will be accepted as a reasonable
explanation.

The use of narrative to verify news or facts is a
device that relies in some degree on persuasion. Sum-
moning his skill as a *raconteur*, the teller must create
an account which invites the listeners to share in his
assessment of the events he relates. Let us assume that
he is a man whose crops have been trampled by another
man's goats. To launch an immediate attack against his
wayward neighbor would strike his audience as hasty and
unfair. But by beginning with a full story, the accuser
will be able to guide his listeners through the twists
and turns of his experience in such a way that they reach
a conclusion similar to his own. His story may act as an
appeal for the understanding and support of others, a
drama which persuades the listeners to accept his point
of view.[3]

Yorùbá say that the value of a tale is judged by its
"wisdom" (*ogbón*) or the "weight" (*iwòn*) of its message.
Against these criteria a narrative grounded in personal
experience and told for immediate and private ends is not
considered worthy of general transmission. Yet when a
tale that is collectively known ends this way—"And that
is why we do not marry our daughters to foreigners without knowing their customs," a proof for this social habit
must be offered. It was Aristotle in his *Rhetoric* who
perhaps first pointed out that a story is often more than
a group of characters bound together by plot; it also
carries a message driven home by means of a subtle but
well-hewn argument. In Yorùbá stories such reasoning
generally follows the pattern in which acceptable or poor
responses by the characters are shown to bring about pos-

itive or negative results. The whole story together with
its outcome stands as evidence which the listener may
adopt as a model for later action in his own life.

An important and quite obvious contribution to the
listener's appreciation of narrative, then, is the way
it resembles life experience. Any story is told against
a background of people and events, attitudes and beliefs,
institutions and social structures with which the listener is already familiar. A performance calls for a constant
interplay between the expectations the spectator carries
over from real life and the image of society which the
story presents. Drawing on his personal experience or
that of people around him, he is able to appreciate the
characters' emotions, motives, and attitudes. He receives them as if they were real people—or at least
representations of a category of people—and he therefore accepts the events that befall them as being in
some way credible.

This power to draw on human experience in order to
evaluate and direct future activity is the assumption
that underlies the role of story as precedent. This
function is illustrated most clearly by the place narrative is assigned in Yorùbá divination literature, the
odù Ifá. The voice behind the odù is Òrúnmìlà (sometimes known as Ifá), the god understood to possess full
knowledge of those events that decide human destinies.
His medium on earth is the babaláwo, the "father of se-
crets" or Ifá priest who communicates the oracle's response to the questioner. Each odù is said to contain
sixteen ęsę or set literary pieces portraying a mythical
event that duplicates the petitioner's own point of inquiry.[4] When an odù sign appears on the divining tray
(opón), the babaláwo recites all the ęsę straight through
until the client indicates the one that corresponds to
the problem in question.[5] Agun Jagude, a babaláwo from
(Benin Republic) opens an ęsę belonging to odù Ejì Òsę
with an account of Òrúnmìlà's consultation with a former
babaláwo. (His name appears in the beginning of the
verse as a hyphenated praise poem.) The conditions that
brought him to Ifá are explained, together with the outcome of his reaction to the oracle's advice:

> Let—us—unroll[6]—it—bit—by—bit—until—it—is—worth—
>   twenty—cowries;
> Then—let—us—spread—it—very—wide—so—that—it—is worth—
>   forty.

was the one who cast Ifá for Ọ̀rúnmìlà when he went
to collect a mat from the Kingdom of Benin.[7] It
would bring him riches that would last forevermore.
Ọ̀rúnmìlà was told to make a sacrifice and that the
mat he fetched from Benin would go a long way, that
its bounties would be reaped forever without end.

Often a narrative will follow this synopsis and present a
dramatic image which enhances the petitioner's appreciation of his own plight. It is crucial to the Ifá system
that the listener build an emotional identification with
the experience of the mythical predecessor so that he
gains trust in the solution the narrative suggests. In
a very real sense the story is a mirror in which the petitioner examines his own condition against the reflected
image of another man:

> Ọ̀rúnmìlà went to make a sacrifice and when he had
> finished a large one he went to fetch a mat in the
> Kingdom of Benin. They asked, "Whose mat are you
> coming for?" He replied that it was Olúwo's mat.[8]
> They asked, "Whose mat are you coming for?" He
> replied it was Ojùbọ̀nà's mat. They asked "Whose
> mat are you coming for now?" He replied that it
> was for all future generations of babaláwo's.
>
> They said that was good. The mat they would un-
> roll today would become a never-ending tale that
> would last forevermore, and until the end of the
> world its bounties would not cease to flow.
>
> Ọ̀rúnmìlà took the mat, he went home and cast Ifá.
> When he had cast Ifá, the mat was shared out among
> all the babaláwo's. The mat chosen for Olúwo, for
> Ọ̀jùbọ̀nà, for Ọ̀rọ́ Awo, Ọ̀dọ̀fín Awo, and the sacrifi-
> cers: that mat was the one divided among them all,
> and all of Ifá's bounties reside in the mat of that
> past time.
>
> Whenever anyone casts Ifá in Ẹ̀gbá[9] country he col-
> lects gifts: chicken, firewood, twigs, everything.
> On that day Ọ̀rúnmìlà bought everything and it all
> remains until today. No one requires another mat
> or needs to buy anything in addition for himself,
> because we now have them thanks to what was done.
> What was earned then is still being earned. And
> so it will be until the end of the world. There

will no longer by any worry or hardship because of
what was spent before us. And perhaps all the
bounties we reap until the end of time will be ours
because Ọ̀rúnmìlà procured his own bounties, and as
long as people continue to consult Ifá, nothing else
needs to be done.

Here the idea of precedence is put to double service. It rules the intended effect of the narrative on
the petitioner; but also it operates within the story
itself as a major theme. Past and present are figura-
tively linked through the image of the unrolled mat, "a
never-ending tale that would last forevermore and until
the end of the world its bounties will not cease to
flow." Modern *babaláwo*'s share a common inheritance
borne of Ọ̀rúnmìlà's original gesture, and they pass on
its riches to their clients of present time.

Priest and client may also hear a second message in
the *ẹsẹ*, a truth in the abstract: adequate preparation
yields profit. And lest this more general interpretation be missed by the listener, the performer adds the
following remarks:

It is the same as when a person attends school,
works hard, and finishes his studies; then he sits
peacefully and earns all the money he needs at the
end of every month; if any work comes his way, he
will profit from it.

As Ọ̀rúnmìlà's original sacrifice caused Ifá's bounties to
be spread throughout time, so too will a person's early
training yield happiness and wealth in his later life.
The expanded narrative image of the mythical precedent
persuades the client of the reason behind Ifá's counsel,
and in this way his acceptance of the oracle's response
is fully assured.

2. "Following" a Story[10]

To say that a story serves as a precedent, then, is
to say that it supports actions or attitudes that guide
people's behavior and thought in the present. Prece-
dents fulfill their function only because they command
the general belief of those who hear them. The notion
that the present is the result of, the reflection of, or
the repetition of events that once took place is the

assumption that underlies the role of every Yorùbá precedent. While the connection between past and present is
quite apparent in the case of *ìtàn* (history or myth),
fictional modes also seem to bridge the gap with extraordinary effectiveness, either through implication or by
the attachment of a concluding explanatory statement.
Events in fiction are said to account for such phenomena
as why humans have hair on their heads, why women have
long hair, or why Tortoise has a roughly-textured shell.
Such conclusions, then, are not always meant to be believed, but they may lend support to a more discursive
element in the story by suggesting (if only half-seri-
ously) that certain kinds of behavior can bring about
permanent, and thus significant, results. A statement of
precedence may at times be wholly different from the message or idea the story puts forward (the narrative that
explains why women have hair on their heads, for instance, argues against the maltreatment of orphans).
Both varieties of conclusion, however, must be justified
in terms of the story from which they evolve, and this
assumes from the outset that their development has been
reasonable and clear and that the listener has accepted
their logic throughout. Understanding a story's full impact requires the simultaneous agency of two cognitive
operations. One is "following" the characters and the
action, observing how the early parts of the sequence
tend to establish conditions for events occurring later
on. The other is discursive reasoning or accepting the
story argument as grounds for a particular idea. (This
last will be discussed in the next section.)

Following a story is quite different from grasping
the point of a story, the statements it makes about human experience, or the way it applies to life on the
whole. The interest a story commands, at least in the
beginning, is not in the general, but in the particular
characters and events which the story describes, the way
in which they respond to certain situations, and whether
or not their behavior is intelligible within the bounds
of the story world itself. Tradition in many Yorùbá
speech areas conceives the experience of hearing a story
as a vicarious journey which the storyteller has em-
barked upon and now shares with his listeners. The tale
usually relates the actions and experiences of people he
once joined in a series of encounters which brought
about substantial changes in their lives. Often these
changes plunge the people into a predicament from which

they must be rescued, either through their own efforts or
by the intervention of an outside helper. The response of
other people to this deliverance decides the outcome of
their problems and ends the storyteller's expedition into
their world.

This journey motif recurs regularly in the formulae
and phrases of story-telling vocabulary. If the performer wishes to prepare his audience for a long tale, he
might warn them: *Itàn 'yí, ó jìnnà,* "now this *ìtàn* is going a long way," using the term *jìnnà* in the sense of
"far" or "distant." Similarly, the close of his venture
is marked by a "return," as in the concluding statement:
Ibí mo bá ọn dé kí mo sèyìn 'o ("And that's how far I
went along with them before I turned back"). Joining in
the metaphor, the audience greets his return with the
cry *E káàbọ̀ 'o* ("Welcome!").

Throughout this journey the underlying assumption
is that the characters are wholly unaware of their ultimate destination: they do not know where events will
lead them or how they will get there. But listeners are
often endowed with a greater measure of foresight.
Within a single community stories are generally transmitted as complete plot units, so that the identity of
the protagonists and their possibilities for success are
very nearly settled before the storyteller begins. An
experienced listener, then, sets out on the journey
reasonably sure that he will follow characters 1, 2, and
3 from a point A, through points B, D, or Q, to another
point in or around Z. But if he knows *where* he is going,
he does not know with certainty *how* he will arrive
there. As a living drama, the oral tale may vary to meet
the interests and needs of the audience and performer
every time it is told. In this sense a storyteller is
rather like a dispatcher in a taxi company who regularly
conducts a client to work. The client knows each day
where he is headed and which direction he will probably
take, but he does not always know who will drive him or
the route his chauffeur will choose. Hence the listener's willingness to "follow" is the result of a certain
kind of seduction carried out by the storyteller, for he
may re-draw the story and promise new details or motives
for the events that take place. A listener who knows in
a general way where the characters are bound will on each
journey gain a better appreciation of why.

Nearly every Yorùbá tale begins in a setting that is
commonplace and routine. Elizabeth Ẹkúndayọ̀ of

Ilá'wé-Èkìtì opens her *àlò* (842)[11]:

> Líjéèhún ìyálé nì... ó féràn ìyàwó rè ñ dáadáa;
> ìyàwó náà féràn ìyálé dáadáa. Ọṣìn, òun *líí* soko
> rọn. Ànaṣìn li ìyálé ni í jẹ́; ìyàwó ni .. í jÀmùjí.

At a time long ago, a senior wife was quite fond
of her husband's new bride, and the bride was also
fond of the senior wife. The *ọba* was their husband. Ànaṣìn was the name of the senior wife; the
bride was called Àmùji.

But abruptly the tone changes and the listener is confronted with a clash of wills:

> Àmùjí è léyín sérun kòòkàn. Léèkè kíí Ànaṣìn
> ri... í "Áà! í kú'un ti gbé súnúlé látayé báyé
> leèyi? Ii béè ni, oni kòò bá tọ mó léyín sérun,
> í ẹ̀ẹ̀ fọọ́ sọkọ, í ẹ̀ẹ̀ bọ́kọ í ṣiré. Í ṣe nu yá wí
> ọn Ọṣìn.

Àmùjí didn't have a single tooth in her mouth. When
Ànaṣìn found out... she exclaimed, "Ah! Is this
what I have been lodging in my house all this time?
It is well known that a woman who has no teeth must
never talk to our husband or amuse herself with him.
I'm going to tell the *ọba* about this!"

The journey has begun. The listener leaves his personal world behind to pursue the complex twists and turns
that make up the experience of Ànaṣìn and Àmùjí. The
senior wife reports the deformity to her husband and sets
a date for its revelation. Provided with this information alone, one could readily predict the outcome. And
yet the listener knows that stories are not so simple
that the contingencies and surprises which befall the
characters make for unpredictability in the story. What
will happen next? The hearer's interest is maintained
by two considerations: one is the *ọba*'s query—"And what
if she does have teeth?"; the other is the storyteller's
strong sympathy for Àmùjí shown by her satirical description of Ànaṣìn's repugnant behavior.

The listener sits at a crossroad between two alternative outcomes. His emotions dictate that Àmùjí should
be victorious, but the end is not entirely certain. If
he is able to draw on his experience of similar story
situations, his presentiments will be strongly in favor

of Àmùjí's success. But since the spirit of a story is
that anything can happen, he waits to find out what surprises are yet in store. Thus when a *deus ex machina*
appears—a bird with a new set of teeth for Àmùjí—the
surprise is entirely acceptable to him within the context of the story, but it is not an event which he could
necessarily anticipate. Its occurrence has reduced the
two alternatives to one, and with his predicting power
improved, the listener knows that if the rules in the
story are maintained, it is Ànaṣìn and not Àmùjí who
will lose her head.

Thus, while the itinerary of the story-journey is
not predictable, each incident is nonetheless intelligible in terms of the events that precede. The listener
cannot always foresee where he is going, but he recognizes each major turning point as the result of earlier
conditions already laid down by the storyteller. This
relation in which later events are predicated upon
earlier ones is the bond of logical continuity in a
well-performed tale, and in this respect the listener
follows, not by virtue of prediction, but with the gift
of hindsight.

A cognitive process in which previous events are
viewed as a cause for a later effect holds special implications for the conclusion of the story. For it invites the listener to accept the entire narrative as a
precedent for experiences and events observable in present reality, and he must do so in the same spirit that
has guided his progress through the story thus far. It
remains for the storyteller to point out the exact relationship between the present and the past, and this is
achieved by extending the logical relation of cause and
effect one step further. Here, the listener must embrace
the experience gained from hearing the story as a "necessary"[12] condition for a category of behavior required by
the current social code:

> Àtijéẹ́rẹ̀, àtijẹ̀ẹ̀rẹ̀, òun ní mọ̀ dẹ̀ jẹ́ ọn jowú àjàkú
> lúlé ọkọ 'o. Bẹ́ẹ̀ ni ẹ̀ẹ̀ súun kí ìyàwó re nì, ẹ̀ẹ̀
> súun wí kẹ́ẹ mẹ́ẹ̀ jẹ; ìyàwó rèe nì, òun lí seruú kò
> ó. Sùgbón ó dẹ̀ í wá ònà ìpalóra fun. Òun tìka
> mo mórí diiiii 'o. Bá'yí nì ní mo ṣee 'o!

Ever since then women have no longer felt bitter
jealousy toward one another in their husband's
house. For it wasn't as if the junior wife had

tried to keep her senior from eating. In fact,
she behaved more like a slave to her. And yet
the senior wife sought a way to do her harm. It
was she herself who paid the consequences in the
end. And that is how it was.

The formula *àtijẹ́ẹ̀rẹ̀ àtijẹ́ẹ̀rẹ̀* ("and ever since
then") would on the face of it suggest that the concluding statement shares the same logical texture as the
events in the story so far. Not predictable, it is
posited on all that went before. But on closer scrutiny
it is clear that another logical process has come into
play. What the conclusion does, in fact, is to make a
general statement about jealousy between co-wives on the
evidence of a particular example. The element of con-
tingency peculiar to the rationale of the sequence has
been eliminated, and in this sense the conclusion takes
on the appearance of a rational deduction rather than
the unpredictable result of prior conditions. It is at
this point that the precedent abandons its role as story
and adopts the posture of argument.
      In Yorùbá tradition this connection between the *end*
of a story and its underlying *idea* is expressed by the
word *ìdí*. The term in some contexts denotes "bottom" or
"end" as in *ìdí igi* ("base of the tree"); in other contexts it stands for the "sense" or "meaning" behind something as in *ìdí ọ̀rọ̀ mi ni wí pé...* ("the idea behind my
statement is..."). Story-tellers often mark the end of
a performance by using the formula *ìdí ẹ̀ nuù 'o* ("that's
how it ends"), and in these instances the word always
bears a double signification implying that both the
"end" and the "message" have been reached. Hence a narrative must do more than report past events. Its whole
machinery of character and plot is carefully directed in
support of a specific belief, custom, or idea that justifies the tale's continued retention and transmission.
Today most Yorùbá observe that where the narrative makes
its "point" its real social importance begins.

3. Pattern and Reasoning

As a mirror of experience, a story demands assessment from its audience, not as a cause but as an idea or
collection of ideas. This calls for a question that
goes beyond "What will happen next?" At issue is "Why
did it happen and what does it mean?" To this end a

story manifests a second structure in addition to sequence; this structure is a verbal organization or
"pattern" that divides the narrative material into segments. Generally speaking, the segments foreground[13]
significant actions by the characters and thereby clarify the evolution of the narrative argument.

To assist the listener's perception of pattern
along the journey, a variety of *signposts* are erected
along the route. Signposts are linguistic markers, words
or groups of words that contrast with the narrative's
characteristic structure.[14] Ayọ̀ Bámgbóṣé shows that the
Yòrúba sentence is composed of three parts: (1) the free
clause; (2) the dependent clause; (3) a linking element
between clauses.[15] The common style in narrative consists in a series of free clauses uttered paratactically,
that is, one straight after another without linking elements or connecting words to indicate a relationship of
co-ordination or sub-ordination between them. For example (344):

Ìọn obìnrin náà,	The women,
an gbégba rìan,	they took their calabashes,
an lọ sóko,	they went to the farm,
an laa mí ṣa èkùro	they collected palm nuts at
lú'dí ọ̀pẹ,	the foot of the palm trees,
an ṣàá jọ,	they gathered them together,
ó pò,	it was many,
ó pọ̀ yéye,	it was a vast quantity,
an ì yá mọ́àà ni	they took the midribs,
an télẹ̀,	they spread them out,
an hún,	they wove them together,
an télẹ̀ bẹ́ẹ̀ẹ́....	they laid them flat just
	so....

Connecting verbs may occur within the structure of
the free clause, but they do not constitute markers in
and of themselves. Examples are:

wá(á): ó jẹ ọmọ Ọwá Obòkun, ó *wáá* dìgbà tó òyè
        kàn án.

        he was the son of the Ọwá Obòkun, *and
        eventually* the time came for him to be
        crowned.

sì: ojú ń pọ́n ọkùnrin 'yí, ará *sì* ní.

> poverty and misery afflicted this hunter, *and* he was terribly disturbed.

bá: Ni Àgbìgbò, ló *bá* bèrè; ni Alábahun, ló *bá* bó sí èhìn rè.

> *So* Hornbill steadied himself *and then* Alábahun jumped straight onto his back.

tún: (Having already met Antelope, the hunger...) ó fÀgbònrín sílè... ó *tún* wá kan Èfòn....

> He let Antelope go and he next happened upon Bushcow....

Unlike the connecting verbs above, signposts alter the paratactic style of narrative in several ways, usually by placing a dependent clause before a free clause, by inserting an exclamation of pause between clauses, or by reduplicating the free clause (in whole or in part). Time, the cement that binds the story sequence into a continuous flow, is the chief agent for making patterns. By far the most significant breaks in narrative continuity take place following a *lapse in time* marked by an introductory clause that advances the action by hours, days, months, or years:

> kò rí ñkan tí óò fun obìnrin àtomo rè. Ó wá ronú títí *ñjó kan*....

> he couldn't find anything to give his wife and children. *One day* he began to think.... (222)

> Ó wá jé kó tó *bíi odún'kan*, wón tún jo dóde....

> *About a year passed* and they again went out together.... (67)

Sometimes a transition takes place when the action of the previous segment is shown to repeat itself:

> éè sí lúwèe Ó ì wa *dìgbà kejì*....

> such a person could not be found there. *The next time* for battle came.... (169)

Boundaries between segments may be marked by the *passage of time*, for instance in an opening clause using the verb pé ("to be long"): *ìgbó ì pé ìgbè ni on omo ni,*

ọn kẹ́ sí... ("A while later the children called out...")
or by repeating a free clause, as in travelling: Ó tí
wáá ń lọ ó tí ń lọ títítítí ("And then he went, he went
on and on and on").

Most common among signposts is the introductory dependent clause constructed on the model Nígbà tí ó X, ó
Y ("When he had done X, he did Y").[16] For example:

> Ló bá múu lọ síbi oko 'yí, ló bá gbin ẹ̀pà so.
> Nígbà tó gbin ẹ̀pà sóko....
>
> So he carried them to his farm and planted the
> groundnuts there. *When the groundnuts were
> planted....* (106)

or

> Àwọn ọmọ ogun wá dé, wọ́n mu; wọ́n wá mu fún Ọwá
> Àtàkúmọ́sà. *Nígbà tí an mu dé....*
>
> His soldiers arrived and seized her; they gave
> her to Ọwá Àtàkúmọ́sà. *When she had been brought
> ....*(1000)

The advantage of this construction is that it overlaps
two groups of events in order to highlight transitions
in meaning between them. In the first example,
Tortoise finds his effort to grow groundnuts countered
immediately by Squirrel, who eats up the seed. Such
changes advance the discursive intention of the narrative while at the same time making it more explicit.

A weaker patterning device than the more obviously
time-bound signposts is the emphatic particle *ni* (in
some environments *li* or *l'*). Standing at the head of
a clause it means "so, it was that" or "so, it happened
that" with the implication that the action it precedes
is the result of an earlier condition. It is not uncommon to find *ni* heading several clauses in succession,
each describing an action which is the outcome of a
previous event. For example:

> *So* Hornbill steadied himself; *and then* Alábahun
> jumped onto his back. *Ni* Àgbìgbò, ló bá bẹ̀rẹ̀; *ni*
> Alábahun, ló bá bọ́ sí ẹ̀hìn rẹ̀.

or

> ìgbeẹ̀ *ni* on omo ni, ó kẹ́ sí ọn elegbé rẹ̀, ọn jọ mí
> ṣiré léhìnkùlé ilé rion. *Igbeẹ̀ ni* ọba ìlú 'i, i e

mà soné moríkì 'un nínú gbogbo ìlú 'o, í gbogbo
fon olí'lú gaan i ón 'mó. *Gbeè ni* omo ni, i ǹń
mà moríkì rè béèé 'o....

then the boy called out to his friends and they
started to play in the backyard together. *Then*
the *oba* of the town announced that there was no
one in the town who knew his....

Time is not the only means by which narrative relates events to one another. Segments or incidents may
be distinguished semantically by using relative adjec-
tives such as *náà* ("that") or *'yí* ("this") or with adverbial nouns such as *béè* ("the fact of being thus").
Contrasts or similarities may be indicated discursively
by opening a sentence with the injunction *sùgbón* ("but"),
àmó ("but"), or *nítorí* ("because") and *nítorí náà*
("therefore," "for that reason"). A performer may also
mark turning points in the story by borrowing from a
fixed set of formulaic expressions; he may make personal
comments on the action, ask rhetorical questions, quote
prayers or proverbs, or utter exclamations. He may also
employ nonverbal devices such as volume, tempo, rhythm
or gesture. Not signposts in themselves, these auxiliary
markers nevertheless assist the narrative in developing
a pattern.
     If evaluating and comparing are narrative tools for
argument, signposts make the steps in the logic easy to
discern. For every story manifests a pattern whether it
be subtle or salient, and patterns use signposts to highlight significant actions that relate to the narrative
discourse. But it would be an error to assume that a
listener who is able to compare the meaning of significant actions is necessarily "pattern-conscious." As an
oral performance, a story is told and understood as a
living creation emergent in time. It is composed of actions, but actions fused together in succession; like
words spoken one after another, their boundaries are
often blurred by the rush of meaning their totality conveys. Signposts inform the listener of the meaning and
direction his narrative journey will take. Only secondarily, and with the assistance of memory, can they
describe the length or shape of the segments that make
the story up. Yorùbá narrative structure would suggest
a correlation between the relative weights of the signposts and the *levels* of the segments introduced by

them.[17]   Perhaps the clearest way to examine this relationship would be to compare a narrative which is performed using the signpost alone as boundary-marker with
another version of the narrative that manifests a more
uniform patterning device.   A parable about competition
for power between the rich man's son, the *oba*'s son, and
the herbalist's son will put the hypothesis to the test.
The first version was collected in Lagos from Alágbà
Sóbándé by Professor S. A. Babalọlá of Lagos University.[18]   The second was told to me by Mr. James Ọlá in
the farming village of Aiyégúnlẹ in Ìbàdàn East.[19]   The
Babalọlá version, cast in the *àrọ̀* mode, divides the story
into segments introduced by the call *Mo járọ̀! Mo járọ̀!
Àrọ̀ Màjàgbà* ("I burst into *àrọ̀*! I burst into *àrọ̀*! My
hefty *àrọ̀* tumbles down!") This yields a story in nine
parts:

(1) Three close friends; one becomes *ọba*, another a
    wealthy merchant, the third a poor herbalist;
    all have boys as their first offspring.

(2) The three sons desire to marry the same woman;
    each tells his father who declares that the
    girl will have to make a choice among them.

(3) The woman prescribes a condition for marriage
    requiring that the future husband must commit
    an unprecedented crime and go unpunished.

(4) The *ọba*'s son beheads a butcher in the market-
    place and is released.

(5) The merchant's son beheads a woman selling
    beancakes and a large bribe is paid to the
    judge.

(6) The herbalist's son beheads an old man selling
    cloth. He is tried and found guilty.

(7) The herbalist uses his knowledge of herbs to
    cause an epidemic.

(8) He agrees to end the plague if amnesty is
    granted his son.

(9) The woman finally agrees to marry the herbal-
    ist's son; he has fulfilled her condition and
    of the three sons he is the only one to have
    survived the epidemic.

In comparing this performance with the version told
by Jame Ọlá, the following correspondences in segmentation occur:

Segments (1) and (2) are not included in the Ọlá
        version.

Segment (3) is introduced by the signpost: *ó wáá*
        di ojọ́ náà
        ("The particular day came")

Segment (4) *ó wá jẹ́ kó tó bí osù mẹ́fà*
        ("before six months had passed")

Segment (5) *ó wá jẹ́ tó tó bíi ọdún 'kan*
        ("When about a year had passed")

Segment (6) *Nígbà tó pẹ́, tó tó bí osù mẹ́fà*
        ("After a long time, about six months
        had gone by")

Segment (7) *Olóògùn bọ́ sílé ... bàbá bọ́ sílé*
        ("The herbalist rushed home ... the
        father rushed home")

Segment (8) *Ọba pé ìjòyè*
        ("The ọba called his chiefs together")

Segment (9) *Hẹ́ẹ̀n, ńgbà tó wá dijọ́ tí wọn pàde ẹjọ́*
        ("Well, when the day for the meeting
        arrived")

In the Ọlá version it is clear that each transition
(with the exception of segments 7 and 8) is effected by
a signpost that shifts the action to a new point in
time. The change is plainly stated in terms of days,
months, or years. Transitions using the *nígbà tí* construction, however, generally occur *within* these time-
fixed segments: for example, *Nígbà tí wọn dé ọjà* ("When
they reached the market") or *Nígbà táwọn olọ́'pá dé*
("When the police arrived") or *Nígbà ọ̀n sá mu* ("After
his arrest"). Apparently, overlapping marks segments
which are smaller in proportion than those bounded by
time-lapses, for they fail to show a regular correspondence with the segments in the *àrọ̀* version of the
tale. The *àrọ̀* emphasizes a broad level of division in
preference to subordinate levels. Large segments or
"sequences" of events assist the process of argument by
presenting each time new data for evaluation: the *ọba*'s

son boasts that he can commit a crime and go unpunished;
the merchant's son unexpectedly beheads a butcher, the
herbalist's son does the same, and so on. Each new
point in time inaugurates new conditions in the action,
and by comparing these incidents, the "point" of the
story is more fully understood.

The second test will use an example from a group of
narratives from Kétu known as *orin ìtàn*, "narratives in
the form of song." Characteristic of this genre is a
style that groups together a series of verses, with each
group repeated before main turning points in the plot.
Moreover, each group is initiated by a marker of some
kind. A performance by Láwáni Adékanbí of Ìrókò Oyin
(Kétu region) tells the story of the man Tilélikú who
was falsely accused by the *oba* of having lost a royal
chain (677)[20] :

> Tiléliku padà, ọ́ padà ọ́ lọ ńnúlé,
> Tiléliku wo ṣééni li ṣééni di kiki.
>
> Tiléliku padà, ọ́ padà ọ́ lọ ńnúlé,
> Tiléliku wo ṣééni li ṣééni di kiki.
>
> Tiléliku nawọ́ lẹ̀ lòó họkọ́,
> Á kọ í sódò kọ́ọ lọọ̀ pẹja wálé.
> Ẹín ò ríṣẹ́ Oolódù Ọba
> Li kò réja pa tíítí
> Ẹja í ó mi ṣééni ẹ̀n ló rí pa!
> Lóó mú álé.
>
> Tiléliku nawọ́ lẹ̀ lòó họkọ́
> Á kọ í sódò kọ́ọ lọọ̀ pẹja wálé.
> Ẹín ò ríṣẹ́ Oolódù Ọba
> Li kò réja pa tíítí
> Ẹja í ó mi ṣééni ẹ̀n ló rí pa!
> Lóó mú álé.
>
> Ìgbòó délé nọ́ọn mọbẹ kọ́ kẹja
> Ojú ibẹ mú lọ ṣééni ló kù lau ń wò láyà ẹja, ń wa
>   fufu yeye.
>
> Ìgbòó délé nọ́ọn mọbẹ kọ́ kẹja
> Ojú ibẹ mú lọ ṣééni ló kù lau ń wò láyà ẹja, ń wa
>   fufu yeye.
>
> Tiléliku ǹde ọ́ kọ í sáàfin Ọba
> Tiléliku yọ ṣééni sọọ ńnẹ̀ fufu yeye.
> Àmọ́ ikú Ìtìjú lọba á kú ẹ ò rí.
> Tiléliku joyè Arẹ̀mu.

Tilélikú ǹde ọ́ kọ í sáàfin Ọba.
Tiléliku yọ séèni sọọ ńnẹ fufu yeye.
Àmọ́, ikú ìtíjú lọba á kú ẹ ò rí.
Tiléliku joyè Arẹ̀mu.

Tiléliku went back, went back to his house,
Tiléliku looked for the chain, looked for it in
    vain.

Tiléliku went back, went back to his house,
Tiléliku looked for the chain, looked for it in
    vain.

Tiléliku then took up a hoe
And headed for the river to fish for the house.
You see the good work of Ọba Olódùmarè,
After finding no fish for a long, long time,
He finally caught the fish which had swallowed the
    chain!
Then he took it home.

Tiléliku then took up a hoe
And headed for the river to fish for the house.
You see the good work of Ọba Olódùmarè,
After finding no fish for a long, long time,
He finally caught the fish which had swallowed the
    chain!
Then he brought it home.

When he reached home they cut open the fish
And there in its belly he spied the gleaming white
    chain.

When he reached home they cut the fish open
And there in its belly he spied the gleaming white
    chain.

Tiléliku got up and set out for the *àòfin*.
And with his hand he presented the shining white
    chain.
But the *ọba* died a shameful death, you understand,
And Tiléliku became chief because of his success.

Tiléliku got up and set out for the *àòfin*.
And with his hand he presented the shining white
    chain.
But the *ọba* died a shameful death, you understand,
And Tiléliku became chief because of his success.

Unlike the parable, this performance shows only one
signpost that shifts the action to a completely new point
in time. Segments are identified in several ways:
through overlapping as in *Igbòó délé noón mobe kó keja*
("When he reached home they cut open the fish"); through
repetition, as in *Tiléliků padà, ó padà lọ ḣnúlé*
("Tiléliků went back, he went back to his house"); or
through discursive devices, as in *Àmọ́ iků ìtíjú lọba á
ků ẹ ò rí* ("But the *ọba* died a shameful death, you understand"). Not identical in form, they appear to be similar in weight and indicate segments definitely less
broad than those in the preceding example. These second-
level segments may be described as temporally continuous
groups of actions often separated by a transition, but
never a complete break, in time. Frequently they bring
about a change of place or characters when compared to
the previous segment, but they do not usually introduce
a wholly new situation. Instead they tend to show new
responses to previous conditions. In this respect each
is comparable to a theatrical "scene" marked by its en-
trances of important actors or by a change in location.

"Tiléliků" suggests a yet smaller division in the
narrative material emerging from the breath groups that
comprise Yorùbá verse. Each breath group here describes
one or two basic propositions which shall be called
"actions":

1. (a) The *ọba* sought a way to kill him (b) but he
       found none
2. (a) So he called his wife and (b) set out his
       plan
3. (a) Tiléliků then took up a hoe

In this performance actions are generally marked by the
particle *ni* (*li*, *l'*) as in the Yorùbá original in example 2: (a) *Ló á pàyá ẹ̀* (b) *ló báá dọgbọ́n inú.*

A least three levels of segmentation are possible
in Yorùbá narrative, and each is generally introduced by
signposts of differing weights in keeping with the
"major," "middle," or "minor" positions on the continuum
in Table 1. "Actions," the smallest and most basic units,
combine to form "scenes," which group in temporal series
to give "sequences." These building blocks formulate a
complex grid of human responses, and the resulting grid-
pattern serves to advance an argument in favor of a
fact, an ethical principle, or a code of behavior

Narrative Signposts

Major Transitions in Meaning				Minor Transitions	Connecting Verbs
ojọ́ náá ni "on that day"	nígbà tí "when"	ó lo ó lo títítí "he went on and on and on"	ibi "when"	ní "emphatic"	wáá (i) "and then"
ní ojọ́ 'kan "one day"	nígbà tó yá "in time"	igbó ì pé "after a time"	ibè ni / igbe ni "then"	ń se ni "it happened that"	sí "and"
ó ti dìgbó alẹ̀ "night fell"	nígbà tó se "eventually"	nígbà tó pé "after some time"		bàbá yìí náá "this particular man"	bá "so"
léé kejì ni "the next time"	bàbá 'yì wà "there was a man"				tún "again"
					gbé "manage"

Nonlexical features

- increased tempo at the end of segments
- pauses before segments
- bow at the close of a performance

Auxiliary Markers

Discursive links	Exclamations	Formulae
sugbọ́n "but"	Awé! "Friends!"	dá mà farò ì gún "let's not prolong things"
nítorí náá "therefore"	Bàbá 'o! "Father!"	agúdú fó "things took a new turn"
bá'yì ni "that was how"	Àà! "Oh!"	mo járò, mo járò àrò gìdìgbà "I burst into àrò, I burst into àrò, the hefty àrò tumbles down"
ìdí ẹ̀ ni wí pé "the conclusion is"	Hẹ́ẹ́n "Really!"	

Auxiliary Markers (Contd.)

Discursive links	*Exclamations*	*Formulae*	*Nonlexical features*
àtijéérẹ́ àtijèèrẹ̀ "and ever since then"		prayers proverbs rhetorical questions	

accepted by the story-telling community.

A story is a process; it sets off, moves along, and fades away in time. Its progress resembles the slow advance of the worm, inching its way patiently, action by action, through scenes and sequences until its destination is finally reached. Not far behind it is the listener, on constant alert for the signs and clues that tell him where he is going and what it all means.

I have shown that two kinds of thinking are involved in the experience of listening to a story: one is "following" or recognizing cause-and-effect relationships between the story events; the other is reasoning out an idea presented through pattern, being convinced by the process of argument that its message is correct. The Yorùbá notion that every story is a precedent is made possible by the way sequence and pattern work together. Pattern alone may clarify the relationship between certain actions and good or bad results, yet listening to a story is not a deductive process in which certain premises lead to inevitable results. People, not premises, are the subject of a tale; they are not fixed entities but unpredictable beings; when given a predicament and several characters, one might conceive numerous ways in which their actions might come to an end. But when the means of argument—that is, characters and events—are firmly bound to a sequence, alternatives are no longer possible. For sequence insures that the listener accept the end of the story as the intelligible result of prior conditions, a result which though not necessary is nevertheless so right within the bounds of the story itself that the listener is convinced that it is valid. And this is how a narrative precedent not only provides a link between present and past action, but also creates an image that directs action for the future.

University of Arkansas at Little Rock

NOTES

[1] See Lord, *The Singer of Tales*; "Composition by Themes in Homer and Southslavic Epos," *TAPA*, 82(1951), 71-80; "Homer and Huso I: The Singer's Rests in Greek and Southslavic Heroic Song," *TAPA*, 67(1936), 106-13; "Homer and Huso II: Narrative Inconsistencies in Homer and Oral Poetry," *TAPA*, 69(1938), 439-45; "Homer and Huso III: Enjambement in Greek and Southslavic Heroic

Song," *TAPA*, 79(1948), 113-24; "Homer as Oral Poet,"
HSCP, 72(1967), 1-46; "Homer's Originality: Oral Dictated Texts," *TAPA*, 84(1953), 124-34; Parry, "Studies
in the Epic Technique of Oral Verse-Making. I. Homer
and Homeric Style," in *MHV*, pp. 266-324; "Studies in the
Epic Technique of Oral Verse-Making. II. The Homeric
Language as the Language of an Oral Poetry," in *MHV*, pp.
325-64; "Whole Formulaic Verses in Greek and Southslavic
Heroic Song," in *MHV*, pp. 376-90. A complete bibliog-
raphy of Parry's writings and those of Lord through
1973 is available in *Haymes*; see further J. M. Foley's
Introduction to this volume. Add, especially, Lord,
"Perspectives on Recent Work on Oral Literature," in
OLSE, pp. 1-24.

[2]Large portions of the material in this paper have
been drawn from my "Story, Medium, and Masque: The
Idea and Art of Yorùbá Storytelling," unpub. Ph.D. diss.
(University of Wisconsin/Madison, 1977). The dissertation is based on field data collected with the support
of the Foreign Area Fellowship Program between the years
1971-74; the collecting continued intermittently in
Nigeria until 1977. Recordings of 1,063 narratives are
now housed in the Archives of Traditional Music and
Folklore at Indiana University, Bloomington.

[3]It is still surprisingly common in the West to
equate the art of the *raconteur* with low mental acuity
and class. A notable example of such thinking appears
in F. C. Bartlett's valuable study, *Remembering* (Cambridge, 1932, rpt. 1967), pp. 264-65. To illustrate what
he describes as "low-level type of recall," he draws on
the court testimony of a Swazi woman who had been the
victim of attempted murder. Despite the magistrate's
repeated efforts to bring her account to the precise
moment of the crime, she persisted in recounting a complete story of her activities during the day on which the
incident occurred. But Bartlett is mistaken, I expect,
when he interprets this habit of "rote recapitulation" as
a sign of analytical impoverishment. He says: "Practically all white administrators in underdeveloped regions
agree that this sort of procedure is typical of the native witness in regard to many questions of daily behavior. Forcibly to interrupt a chain of apparently irrelevant detail is fatal.... Indeed, not the African
native alone, but a member of any slightly educated community is likely to tell in this way a story which he has
to try to recall." (*idem*). A trial, it would seem, is an

obvious context for putting to use the power of "persuasion" and "proof" so excellently afforded by narrative.

[4]For further studies in English on Ifá, See Wándé
Abímbọ́lá, *Ifá: An Exposition of the Ifá Literary Corpus*
(Ibadan and Oxford, 1976); *Sixteen Great Poems of Ifá*
(Zaria, 1975); the less useful *Ifá Divination Poetry*
(New York, 1977); William Bascom, *Ifá Divination: Com-
munication between Gods and Men in West Africa* (Bloom-
ington, 1965); "The Relationship of Yorùbá Folklore to
Divining," *JAF*, 46(1943), 127-31; E. M. McClelland, "The
Significance of Number in the Odù of Ifá," *AfricaL*, 36
(1966), 421-30.

[5]Communication between the *babaláwo* and the oracle
commences with a throw of sixteen palm nuts (kola nuts
are also used) or by the toss of an *ọpẹ̀lẹ̀* chain of
eight half-seeds or cowrie shells. The nuts are held in
the palm of the left hand and repeatedly grasped by the
right until one or two nuts remain behind. If one nut
appears in the left hand, two marks are made on the tray
which is dusted with white chalk; two nuts yield one
mark. The action is repeated four times, and the marks
are impressed on the tray vertically, whereupon the complete figure will correspond to one of the sixteen principal *odù*. The *babaláwo* then repeats the operation and
a second figure is placed to the left of the first, a
process yielding a combined *odù* which is one of a possible 256 (16 x 16).

[6]Performance number 740, recorded at mid-day on
July 25, 1973. In the course of this *ẹsẹ*, the word "unroll" carries literal and figurative meanings. When not
in use, a mat is normally rolled up and leaned against a
wall in a corner of the house, and when brought out it
is unrolled. In a figurative sense, "unroll" connotes
the spread of Ifá from its beginnings in the time of
Ọ̀rúnmìlà to its later practitioners, together with the
promise of riches that come in its wake.

[7]In the fourteenth and fifteenth centuries, the
great kingdom of Benin in South Central Nigeria spread
its influence across the eastern city-states of the
Yorùbá-speaking area. Benin's impact left its mark in a
double cultural heritage in which local traditions were
overlain with linguistic, literary, and religious practices brought in by the foreign power. Ifá is not usually associated with Benin (it is said to have originated
in Ifẹ̀, the seat of creation), but the prestige associated with this city may account for its presence in the

ẹsẹ. It is not unlikely that Benin was a significant
mat-making center in the past, since the art is still
common in the Eastern Yorùbá and Ẹ̀dó areas.

[8] Olúwo is the head *babaláwo* of the cult and
Òjùbọ̀nà its female leader; Ọ̀rọ́ Awo and Ọdọ̀dfín Awo are
title-holders in the Ifá organization.

[9] The Ẹ̀gbá are a Yorùbá sub-group occupying the
southwestern part of Yorùbáland. They are bordered on
the north by Ọ̀yọ́, on the west by Ẹ̀gbádò, and to the
east by the Ìjẹ̀bú and Ìbàdàn. Generally, the Kétu are
classed as a separate ethnic grouping not unrelated to
the western Ọ̀yọ́. Here, however, Agun Jagude seems to
assimilate the Ifá practice in this area with that of
the Ẹ̀gbá.

[10] This discussion of "following" is drawn from W. B.
Gallie, *Philosophy and the Historical Understanding*
(London, 1964), pp. 22-50.

[11] Numbers in parentheses refer to items in the
author's personal collection. This was Elizabeth's
first performance of the narrative and it took place
on August 21, 1973 at about 8:00 P.M. A second performance can be seen in the film "Àlọ́ ... àlọ̀: Storytelling
in Yorùbá," made in association with Frank Speed, University of Ifẹ̀, Nigeria.

[12] I am using quotation marks here as a warning to
the reader not to be tempted to view the narrative argument as being identical to the deductive argument in
standard logic. However, Gallie himself makes allowance
for such deduction in parables and other narratives in
which the characters are made to stand for premises or
ideologies.

[13] "Foreground" in this context is equivalent to
"highlight" or "make to stand out" against a background
or norm. This usage is more general than the meaning intended by Jan Mukarovsky, for whom "foregrounding" is a
feature of "poetic" language as opposed to the "standard" language; see his "Standard Language and Poetic
Language," trans. by Paul L. Gavin, in *A Prague School
Reader on Esthetics: Literary Structure and Style*
(Washington, D.C., 1964), pp. 17-30.

[14] A remarkable and meticulous study of pattern in
Native American narrative was recently brought to my attention by its author, Dell Hymes. He distinguishes
four levels of narrative organization: verse, stanza,
scene, and act—each identified by internal features
(such as the "scene-agent ratio") and/or linguistic

markers. See his "Louis Simpson's 'The Deserted Boy,'"
Poetics, 5(1976), 119-55.

[15] Ayọ̀ Bámgbóṣé, *A Grammar of Yorùbá* (Cambridge,
1966), p. 28.

[16] In their study of Tonga historical narratives,
A. M. Jones and H. Carter identify this stylistic fea-
ture as "overlapping" and consider it to be "the main-
stay of the Tonga narrative." See their "The Style of a
Tonga Historical Narrative," *AfrLS*, 8(1967), 113-20;
cited in Dan Ben-Amos, "Folklore in African Society," in
Forms of Folklore in Africa, ed. by Bernth Lindfors
(Austin, 1977), pp. 1-34.

[17] Part of our heritage from Russian Formalism has
been a nonending quest (one that strikes me at times as
being somewhat quixotic) for the mysterious "chunk" of
which narrative (oral or otherwise) is composed. So far
the search has yielded an impressive range of possibilities: the "motif" (Aarne and Thompson), "motifeme"
(Dundes), "image" (Scheub), "eidon" (Colby), "function"
(Propp), "proposition" (Todorov), "formula, system,
theme" (Parry and Lord), "verse, stanza, scene, act"
(Hymes). Lord and Hymes, it seems to me, have come nearer to solving the mystery than many structuralists because they choose to restrict their categories to the
evidence provided by a single tradition (Serbo-Croatian
in the case of Lord, Upper Chinook in that of Hymes) before extrapolating. It is especially noteworthy that
they, unlike others, have settled upon a *hierarchy* of
compositional units as revealed by the inner logic of
the data itself. See, in addition to Lord and Hymes
(notes 1 and 14), B. N. Colby, "A Partial Grammar of
Eskimo Folktales," *AA*, N.S. 75(1973), 645-62; Alan
Dundes, *The Morphology of North American Indian Folktales*, FFC no. 195 (1964); Pierre and Elli Köngäs
Maranda, *Structural Analysis of Oral Tradition* (Philadelphia, 1971); Denise Paulme, "Morphologie du conte afri-
cain," *CEAfr*, 45(1972), 131-63; Vladimir Propp, *Morphology of the Folktale*, trans. by Laurence N. Scott
(Austin, 1968); Harold Scheub, "The Technique of the
Expansible Image in Xhosa *Ntsomi*-Performance," *RAL*, 1
(1970), 119-46; Tzvetan Todorov, *La Poétique de la prose*
(Paris, 1971), trans. by Richard Howard as *The Poetics
of Prose* (Ithaca, 1977).

[18] In S. A. Babalọlá, "Àrọ̀: A Minor Genre of Yorùbá
Spoken Art," paper given at the Ninth West African Language Conference, Freetown, Sierra Leone, March 1970.

[19] Performance number 67, recorded on June 18, 1972 before an audience of twenty-two people. Mr. Ọlá is the head of his village and is especially respected for his acute intelligence and a gift for solving personal disputes.

[20] Performance number 677, recorded in Ìrókò Oyin (Republic of Benin) on July 20, 1973 at 6:30 P.M.

HISPANIC AND SOUTH SLAVIC TRADITIONAL NARRATIVE POETRY AND RELATED FORMS: A SURVEY OF COMPARATIVE STUDIES (1824-1977)

John S. Miletich

Comparative studies of Hispanic and South Slavic traditional[1] poetry have been relatively rare. This is somewhat surprising, since both these traditions offer an enormously rich stock of materials from the past as well as from the modern period, a stock which is to some extent still vital.[2]

As early as 1824 Jacob Grimm commented on the richness of imagery to be found in South Slavic traditional poetry, which was for him, like Spanish poetry, reminiscent of the Orient.[3] He stated further that he esteemed more highly the individual phrases appearing in the South Slavic poems when similar imagery was used in both traditions (*ibid.*, p. 221 and note).

Such Romanticist views, with their tendency toward impressionist criticism and fondness for the exotic, were followed at the end of the nineteenth century by the observations of the Croatian writer and diplomat to Spain, Ante Tresić-Pavičić. He emphasized the sociological parallels existing in the two traditions, which formed the background for the cultivation of similar thematic material, such as, for example, battles between Christians and Moslems.[4]

Almost a half century later Dragutin Subotić dealt with the possibility of direct literary contacts between the two cultures.[5] He indicated, as had Grimm before him, such general features as analogous expressions and whole verse lines as well as similar compact narrative styles and outlook, particularly in the poems dealing to some extent with historical incidents. He did not, however, posit the probability of direct inspiration of individual works but rather implied a general Western European influence—French, Italian, Spanish—on the South Slavic tradition. He based his theory of possible literary contacts with Spain during the fifteenth and sixteenth centuries on the following facts: maritime trade between the latter and the Ragusan Republic (now generally known as Dubrovnik) and the service of Ragusan officers, crews and ships in the navy of the Emperor Charles V (*ibid.*, pp. 153-59). Furthermore, Subotić

supported the strong probability of even earlier contacts in the tenth century between Croatian kings and
Andalusian caliphs.

In accord with the theories of the migratory school
of traditional song, Branislav Krstić suggested that a
Dalmatian ballad of the *Matica hrvatska* collection (vol.
II, no. 34) recorded near Split arose through the influence of the Spanish *Don Bueso romance*, either through
the Sephardim, who may have brought the ballad to Dal-
matia, or by way of the Spaniards, since during the war
of 1538-39 they seized the town of Herceg Novi.[6] Ramón
Menéndez Pidal indicated the existence of a motif found
generally in the South Slavic songs of the Adriatic
coast in German versions from Gottschee, a linguistic
island located in northwestern Yugoslavia. The
motif dealing with the protagonist as a black Moor
appeared in the German versions of the song "Mare" as
the result of the latter's contamination with a South
Slavic song. The Gottschee versions in question contain
more of the basic story content which appears also in
the *Don Bueso romance* of the modern Spanish tradition and
which supposedly has its roots in the earliest versions
of the Kudrun tale.[7]

Of such earlier investigations the most comprehensive by far was William J. Entwistle's work, which gave
a general description of the shorter traditional narrative song of Europe and dealt with the similarity of
motifs occurring in the songs of various national traditions. He grouped together the Spanish *romance*, the
Serbo-Croatian *junački deseterac* (decasyllabic song dealing generally with combat themes), as well as the Russian
bylina, describing them as basically narrative in that
third-person narrative was frequent in all three and that
their exterior form was stichic. These, he indicated,
were to be clearly distinguished from other Romance traditions as well as from those of northern and central
Europe. The latter, according to him, were more "lyrical," by which he designated a number of features such as
the use of first-person narrative and of troubadour
themes and conventions, as well as strophic forms and the
use of the refrain.[8]

In contrast to the initial comparative attempts outlined above, more recent interest in the subject has been
considerably greater. First published in 1952, C. M.
Bowra's work[9] dealing with heroic traditional narrative
song serves as a model at least in principle for future

comparative investigations insofar as the breadth and
variety of its subject matter is concerned. He includes
in his study not only Western and Eastern European traditions, such as the Spanish and South Slavic, but also
those of Asia as well, showing at least some familiarity
with the generally little-known songs of the Achins and
the Ainus in western Sumatra and the northern Japanese
island of Hokkaido, respectively. From such a broad base
he treats such questions as the heroic outlook and its
development, the metrical principles underlying different
traditions, oral composition and transmission of songs,
the relation between heroic poetry and history, the de-
cline of heroic traditional narrative song, and the question of its narrative style.

   The following year Menéndez Pidal, in a discussion
of the influence of the Hispanic *romance* in European literature, assumed a neutral position on Subotić's thesis
of the possible influence of the Spanish tradition on
South Slavic song (*Romancero hispánico*, II, p. 245). It
would appear that an investigation proposing to show direct influence between these two traditions would be
quite hazardous if its point of departure were such general similarities as those aspects of subject matter and
style indicated by Subotić, which may be the result of
general inspiration or of independent development rather
than of mutual contacts. The fluid nature of oral tradition, together with the scarcity of reliably recorded
versions in the earlier periods, are sufficient grounds
for discouraging any search for a significant number of
unique details which, in the matter of direct influence,
would be of prime importance. Finally, as regards especially those songs whose thematic material consists of
international motifs in which general similarities are
abundant and which have migrated in various directions
across Europe, it would be most difficult to establish
direct influence unless a number of unique features in
specific variants of both traditions could be isolated.

   On the question of the development of such types as
epic and the shorter traditional narrative song which he
terms *Ballade*, Erich Seemann proceeds from a fairly broad
base of European and Asian materials similar to but not
as extensive as those of Bowra. He concludes that the
gradual development from an early short song (*Lied*) to
the epos and thence later to a shorter form (*Ballade*)—
which occurs, for example, in the Hispanic tradition (as
was explained by Menéndez Pidal)—is not universally

applicable.[10]   Such exceptions are, for example, to be
found in the South Slavic and Uzbek traditions, in which
the shorter song exists alongside the more extensive type
and both types are cultivated at times by the same singer (*ibid.*, 167-70, 175-76).

Both Ivan Slamnig and Olinko Delorko had drawn attention in separate studies to the fragmentary state of a
number of South Slavic poems and to their similarity in
this respect to the Hispanic *romance*. Slamnig furthermore alluded to similar expressions appearing within the
two traditions.[11]   On a number of occasions Delorko
briefly commented on such broad similarities existing between the two as their motifs, imagery, stylistic techniques, point of view, historical conditions, and the
question of collectors.[12]   Regarding the latter, he indicates his admiration for Menéndez Pidal who, as collec-
tor, editor, and critic, published the older versions of
romances with others which he himself had recorded and
who also compared critically the two groups on the basis
of their diction, style, and aesthetic merits. It must be
added at this point that in the particular collection to
which Delorko is here referring (the *Flor nueva de romances viejos*), Menéndez Pidal clearly reveals with what
freedom and creativity he himself retouched and re-
worked some of the *romances*.[13]

A problem which lies at the root of much of the confusion met with in comparative studies was dealt with in
1965 by Svetozar Petrović. He remarked on the difficul-
ties arising from the use of terms which cross national
frontiers and which are then used as synonyms to designate analogous but not identical literary types in other
national traditions. He stated, for example, that the
Hispanic *romance* may resemble but also at the same time
may differ from the English "ballad" or the South Slavic
"*epska p(j)esma.*"[14]

The work which certainly occasioned the greatest
discussion in recent scholarship dealing with traditional
poetry and related forms was Albert B. Lord's *The Singer
of Tales* (1960) with its thesis of oral composition by
"formula" and "theme" based on the field study of the
South Slavic oral tradition conducted by Milman Parry and
Albert Lord. The implications regarding the oral character of the Homeric poems and of early medieval narrative
poetry led to numerous further investigations broadly
based on the Parry-Lord methodology not only in the study
of literature but also in anthropology and linguistics.[15]

It is beyond the scope of a broad, comparative survey of
this nature to detail even briefly the increasing number
of studies of Hispanic narrative poetry bearing to some
extent on the Parry-Lord oralist thesis. Furthermore,
such reviews are already available in recent studies by
Michael Magnotta, Charles B. Faulhaber, and Alan D.
Deyermond, who deal with the oralist question within the
broader framework of the major theoretical positions on
Spanish epic.[16] Other recent overviews with a more detailed critical emphasis on such specific aspects as
quantitative formulary analysis have been provided by
Margaret Chaplin and John S. Miletich, the former concentrating principally on work in the Spanish epic and
the latter dealing with the problem from a comparative
standpoint.[17] I will, therefore, in this discussion of
oralist theory, make certain necessary refinements of
previous statements by Hispanic scholars regarding the
theory, summarize briefly what appears to be the principal problem in the consideration of Hispanic narrative
poetry in the light of the theory, and discuss what, in
my opinion, is the most fruitful type of work in this
area, namely, investigations that are based on data derived from a study of the original South Slavic texts
themselves or, when this is not possible, at least from
translations suitable for purposes of thematic and motif
study. In order to situate the discussion within its
proper theoretical context, it may be useful first to
outline summarily the three major positions regarding the
composition and transmission of the Spanish epic.

The dominant Spanish school, neo-traditionalism,
maintains that Western European epic originated in the
form of short oral songs in the vernacular which served
to disseminate news of famous events. Eventually the
extensive epic form came into existence and continued to
be sung in variants and to be renewed at times with
greater changes through a process of oral re-working.
The epic tradition was thus maintained through what is
basically the memorization of a more or less fixed story
line.[18] The American oralist theory holds that, through
a system which makes use of "formulas," "formulaic expressions," and "themes," the song is to some extent different each time it is performed, although the basic
story line remains the same. A process such as this,
however, is not to be understood as approximate or
word-for-word memorization (*Singer*, p. 5). The neo-
individualist position, primarily British, affirms

basically that the Spanish epic in its extant versified
forms was composed by a learned poet who to some extent
also made use of oral tradition.[19]   Menéndez Pidal expressed his disagreement with the oralist theory in its
application to the *Cantar de Mio Cid* and the *romances*,
reiterating his neo-traditionalist position and the basic
stability of Hispanic traditional poetry as opposed to
what he understood as greater innovation in the South
Slavic tradition.[20]   Maja Bošković-Stulli suggested that
the basis for the disagreement might be due to Menéndez
Pidal's interpretation of the term "improvisation" as a
kind of marked innovation apart from tradition rather
than the process of oral composition by traditional
"formula" and "theme" as Lord had explained.[21]   She affirmed later that, although Menéndez Pidal's position regarding the role of memory in the composition of traditional song was untenable, the importance he attributed
to tradition needed to be stressed.[22]   Lord, furthermore,
had explicitly affirmed that innovation in South Slavic
song occurred within a traditional framework, stating
that the material and the manner in which it was used
were traditional, although individual styles could be
differentiated within that framework (*Singer*, pp. 63-65).
He had thus, in fact, underscored the fundamental stability of South Slavic song.

    In comparing the critical approaches of Lord and of
Menéndez Pidal with regard to traditional narrative poetry, Edmund de Chasca made the following observations. He
believed that the Hispanic scholar's methodology was more
thorough inasmuch as it considered not only what was common to the tradition but also what distinguished a particular poem within that tradition.[23]   It must be borne
in mind, however, that Lord's purpose was primarily to
explain the process of oral composition, which in itself
requires an emphasis not on differences but on similarities of formulary and thematic material. As indicated
above, however, he did in fact allude to differences in
the styles of various singers and thus did not intend
that traditional song be viewed as a closed structure.

    Future applications of oralist theory will have to
be based on extensive data arrived at from an examination
of the authentic narrative folksong, its deliberate imitations, and literary epic which to some degree draws on
the folk narrative tradition. Otherwise there can be no
empirical basis against which we can assess the data derived from a study of the problematic texts under scru-

tiny. In this regard, it is the recent studies of narrative organization, motifs, and repetition emerging principally from Great Britain and Ireland that deserve attention.

In support of the neo-individualist position regarding the composition of the late fourteenth-century *Mocedades de Rodrigo* epic text, Deyermond compares the references to documents and seals in the latter and in three songs of Salih Ugljanin, relying on the Parry and Lord prose translations.[24] He suggests that a learned notarial or administrative background for the poet of the *Mocedades* is revealed because of the emphasis placed on praising monarchs for the confirmation of documents, the insistence on producing the latter, and the references to visual impressions of them, features which also appear in other learned medieval Spanish works but which are absent in the orally composed Serbo-Croatian poems studied by him.

Additional support for the neo-individualist thesis based on the Parry and Lord texts in translation is offered by Chaplin in her exploratory, comparative study of motifs or Lord's "themes" in Spanish epic (pp. 15-17). She indicates that the Spanish material is generally different from the Serbo-Croatian in three ways. First, in the latter the same motifs are frequently repeated to describe the same situation while in Spanish epic the same situation is treated with greater motif variation. Second, the overall "motif-pattern" or narrative organization is more complex in the Spanish tradition. Third, as a rule (qualification mine) the same "formulas" are not used for the same motif in Spanish as is the tendency in the Serbo-Croatian tradition examined.

On the basis of patterns founded on contrast and irony, Deyermond illustrates further the complex character of the *Cantar de Mio Cid*, suggesting that such intricate patterning is an additional argument for written composition, since such complexity is not evident in the South Slavic translations of orally composed song.[25] It may be useful, however, to compare the structural and stylistic patterning of those songs that are considered generally by Yugoslav scholars to be representative of the flowering of the South Slavic oral epic tradition, namely, the best songs[26] in the somewhat edited, but nevertheless primarily oral-traditional,[27] nineteenth-century collection of Vuk Karadžić, although the latter are not comparable in their generic structure to the extensive

Moslem epic proper of the Krajina.[28]

Relying also on the texts of the Parry and Lord Novi
Pazar collection, Kenneth Adams' interesting proposal regarding the composition of the *Poema de Mio Cid* constitutes a modified oralist position.[29] He suggests that an
unknown portion of an orally composed poem may have survived through dictation when scribal changes were made to
it during the process of dictation. Of special interest
to me is his discussion of repetition in the *Cid* and the
South Slavic poems in view of my investigations of repetition, the barest outlines of which I will attempt to
summarize here.[30]

By organizing repetitions occurring within set metrical boundaries into two specific categories, namely one
in which the same idea recurs and another in which it
does not, it is possible to establish a numerical ratio
of styles differentiating an "elaborate" or recurring
style from an "essential" or nonrecurring style at the
semantic level. In an application of this method to some
14,000 verse lines of narrative poetry ranging from the
twelfth (the earliest widely accepted date for the *Cid*)
to the twentieth centuries primarily in Spanish and
Serbo-Croatian, but also in Russian, and covering both
unedited and slightly edited traditional songs, deliberate imitations thereof, literary epic,and problematic
works, i.e., the *Cid* and the *Mocedades*, my conclusions
are as follows. First, traditional texts as a genre
average together approximately one-third "elaborate
style" repetition while the deliberate imitations and
the two Spanish epics analyzed taken together average
about 16% "elaborate style."   Second, this marked difference in quantity is paralleled in distribution. The
"elaborate style" repetitions tend to be fairly evenly
distributed throughout the traditional texts while in the
other texts such distribution tends to be more sporadic.
Thus, to use Albert Lord's apt term, the "weave"[31] of the
traditional structures is fundamentally different.

Considering Kenneth Adams' suggestion in the light
of the above results, I find it difficult to accept that
a scribe would be physically capable of making what would
have to be extensive, substantial changes in the very
different traditional style during the moments of transcription. Furthermore, if such revision were indeed
possible, the pervasive weave of the traditional style
would be significantly impaired and the result could
hardly be an aesthetically pleasing work similar to the

Cid. Albert Lord has repeatedly emphasized the difference between the poetics of a traditional style and that
of a written style (*Singer*, pp. 132-38; "Perspectives,"
pp. 209-10). For the foregoing reasons, my suggestion
regarding medieval Spanish epic is that it is similar to
pučka književnost,[32] a type of learned literature which
draws with considerable freedom on both oral and learned
traditions, constituting a separate model in itself with
its own distinctive poetics, and not a greater or lesser
revision of a traditional text.

Finally, the work of Béla Bartók and Lord on Serbo-
Croatian traditional song serves well the purposes of
Judeo-Spanish folksong scholarship.[33] Samuel G. Armistead and Joseph H. Silverman, in making a case for the
Balkan character of a number of stylistic exclamations
occurring in Judeo-Spanish balladry, find support in
Serbo-Croatian and Bulgarian folksong.[34] In addition,
the monumental work of Armistead and his collaborators
in anthologizing the voluminous mass of Sephardic traditional narrative and other forms includes treatment of
Bulgarian and Serbo-Croatian as well as Pan-Hispanic and
other European analogs.[35]

In concluding this brief survey, I would like to
emphasize that the course for new directions in the comparative study of traditional narrative poetry and related forms has been well charted by two eminent scholars
of the English-speaking world, Milman Parry and Albert B.
Lord. They relied for their thesis on unedited, authen-
tically traditional texts as must also those who wish to
pursue seriously the suggestions introduced by them.[36]

University of Utah

NOTES

[1]The term "traditional" is used throughout the present study to designate the text that is marked by considerable variation according to set patterns as the result
of sung presentation, whether or not it has been subsequently edited to some minor extent.

[2]R. Menéndez Pidal, *Romancero hispánico (hispano-
portugués, americano y sefardí): Teoría e historia* (Madrid,
1953), II, p. 440; *El Romancero en la tradición oral
moderna*, ed. by Diego Catalán and Samuel G. Armistead
con la colaboración de Antonio Sánchez Romeralo (Madrid,
1973), pp. 304-25; Mira Sertić, "Forma i funkcija narodne

balade," in *Rad JAZU*, 338 (Zagreb, 1965), pp. 318, 321;
Benjamin A. Stolz, "On Two Serbo-Croatian Oral Epic Verses: The *Bugarštica* and the *Deseterac*," *PMMLA*, 1(1969),
153.

[3]"*Narodne Srpske Piesme*, skupio i i na svijet izdao
Vuk Stephanovitch Karadgitch. 2 theil 1823. 1 theil
1824," in *Kleinere Schriften* (Berlin, 1869), IV, p. 218.

[4]Ante Tresić-Pavičić, "Prvi pokušaj prispodobe
hrvatske narodne poezije sa španjolskom," *MHr*, 1(1894),
14-22; along similar lines, Viktor Schirmunski [Žirmun-
skij], *Vergleichende Epenforschung*, I. (Berlin, 1961),
pp. 9-11—in Russian, "Èpos slavjanskix narodov v
sravnitel'no-istoričeskom osveščenii," in his *Narodnyj
geroičeskij èpos* (Moscow and Leningrad, 1962), pp. 75-
194 (latter drawn from: Felix J. Oinas, "Russian Byliny,"
in *Heroic Epic and Saga: An Introduction to the World's
Great Folk Epics*, ed. by Felix J. Oinas [Bloomington and
London, 1978], p. 256) and David Buchan, *The Ballad and
the Folk* (London and Boston, 1972), pp. 17, 46-47.

[5]*Yugoslav Popular Ballads* (Cambridge, 1932), pp.
107-9; a passing reference to the similarity of the
romances to other European traditional compositions,
among which are included those of Serbia, is found in
Ramón Menéndez Pidal, *Flor nueva de romances viejos*
(Buenos Aires, 1963), p. 9, originally published in
Madrid, 1928. See further note 36.

[6]"The Kudrun Story in the Balkans," *SEER*, 28 (1950),
457-59.

[7]Ramón Menéndez Pidal, "Supervivencia del *Poema de
Kudrun* (Orígenes de la balada)," in *Los godos y la
epopeya española* (Madrid, 1956), pp. 147-48, originally
published in *RFE*, 20(1933), 1-59—in German, "Das Fortle-
ben des Kudrungedichtes," in *Probleme der Volksballaden-
forschung*, ed. by Elisabeth Pflüger-Bouillon (Darmstadt,
1975), pp. 139-93, which I have not seen; for a motif in
El Conde Sol and other Western European songs, and its
relation to a Bulgarian analog, see V. Schirmunski,
Vergleichende..., p. 110; for more recent work suggesting
the influence of the Sephardic tradition on South Slavic
(Serbo-Croatian language and Slovenian) traditional songs
dealing with the motif of the warrior girl, see Ljiljana
Pavlović-Samurović, "Motiv devojke-ratnika u španskom
romanseru i u našoj narodnoj poeziji," *NSSVD*, 4/1(1974),
255-69 (summary in French).

[8]William J. Entwistle, *European Balladry* (Oxford,
1939, 1951) and for his preliminary study see, "Some

Comparative Notes on Ballads: Danish, Castilian, Yugo-
slavic," *MÆ*, 1(1932), 197-203 and, later, his "New Light
on the Epic-Ballad Problem," *JAF*, 62(1949), 375-81; for a
different classification of the Hispanic and Slavic
songs, see Schirmunski, *Vergleichende...*, p. 102.

[9] *Heroic Poetry* (London, 1952, 1961, 1964).

[10] "Ballade und Epos," *SAV*, 51(1955), 150-52, 182.

[11] Slamnig, "O komparativnom proučavanju narodne
poezije," *UR*, 7(1963), 58; Delorko, *Narodne lirske pjesme*
(Zagreb, 1963), p. 17.

[12] Delorko, *Hrvatske narodne balade i romance* (Zagreb,
1951), pp. 180-81, 183; Delorko, *Zlatna jabuka: Hrvatske
narodne balade i romance* (Zagreb, 1956), II, p. 181 (latter drawn from: Lj. Pavlović-Samurović, "Motiv devojke-
ratnika...," p. 257, n. 3); Delorko, *Ljuba Ivanova*
(Split, 1969), pp. xviii, xxxvi.

[13] Menéndez Pidal, *Flor nueva...*, pp. 36-38.

[14] Svetozar Petrović, "Rječnik knjiʑevnih termina i
pojam knjiʑevne terminologije,"*UR*, 9(1965), 32; for similar observations, see Mira Sertić, "Forma i funkcija...,"
p. 308, no. 1. For more recent treatment of the problem
of genre and the European learned ballad including discussion of García Lorca's *Romancero gitano* and South
Slavic models, see Radoslav Josimović, "proteiformnost
umetničke balade," *NSSVD*, 4/1(1974), 285-95, esp. 292-93,
and n. 15.

[15] Michael Nagler, "Oral Poetry and the Question of
Originality in Literature," in *Proceedings of the Vth
Congress of the International Comparative Literature
Association*, Belgrade, 1967 (Amsterdam, 1969), p. 451;
Haymes, with additions, pertaining especially to the His-
panic tradition, in Armistead's review, *MLN*, 90(1975),
296-99.

[16] Magnotta, "Per Abat y la tradición oral o escrita
en el *Poema del Cid*: Un ensayo histórico-crítico (1750-
1972)," *HR*, 43(1975), 293-309; Magnotta, *Historia y
bibliografía de la crítica sobre el "Poema de mío Cid"
(1750-1971)* (Chapel Hill, 1976); Charles B. Faulhaber,
"Neo-traditionalism, Formulism, Individualism, and Recent
Studies on the Spanish Epic," *RPh*, 30(1976), 83-101;
Deyermond, "Tendencies in *Mio Cid* Scholarship, 1943-
1973," in *"Mio Cid" Studies*, ed. by A. D. Deyermond (London, 1977), pp. 13-47. Studies of enjambement in Spanish
narrative poetry examined in the light of similar work in
the South Slavic tradition appear in Edmund de Chasca, *El
arte juglaresco en el "Cantar de Mío Cid"* (Madrid, 1972;

enlarged 2nd ed. of 1967), pp. 329-31; and in Orest R.
Ochrymowycz, *Aspects of Oral Style in the "Romances
Juglarescos" of the Carolingian Cycle* (Iowa City, 1975),
pp. 132-44, and on "twinning" (repetition of the same or
similar expressions and concepts as well as of opposing
concepts) and metrical irregularity with reference to the
South Slavic case, pp. 97-131 (esp. p. 100) and pp. 145-
49 (esp. p. 145), respectively, with statistical summary
on p. 153. For an important evaluation of such studies,
see Deyermond, "Tendencies in *Mio Cid*...,"pp. 31-32, and
Deyermond's review of Ochrymowycz in *BHS*, 54(1977), 148-
49, which deals also with Ochrymowycz's application of a
form of Parry-Lord formulary analysis.

[17] Chaplin, "Oral-Formulaic Style in the Epic: A
Progress Report," in *Medieval Hispanic Studies Presented
to Rita Hamilton*, ed. by A. D. Deyermond (London, 1976),
pp. 11-20; John S. Miletich, "The Quest for the 'Formula':
A Comparative Reappraisal," *MP*, 74(1976), 111-23. More
recent analyses dealing with Mexican and Chicano traditions are John H. McDowell, "The Mexican *Corrido*: Formula
and Theme in a Ballad Tradition," *JAF*, 85(1972), 205-20
and a dissertation dealing with an important but relatively neglected area of *romance* scholarship, which establishes the continuity of the Hispanic tradition of
religious balladry of New Mexico and the Canary Islands
principally on the basis of the Parry-Lord formulary system and R. H. Webber's study of formulistic diction (*Formulistic Diction in the Spanish Ballad*, *UCPMP*, 34, no. 2
[Berkeley, 1951]): William H. González, "Aspectos tradi-
cionales en el alabado romancístico de Nuevo México a
base de romances sagrados de las Islas Canarias," unpubl.
Ph.D. diss. (University of Utah, 1977), a portion of
which appears in the present volume.

[18] Menéndez Pidal, "Los cantores épicos yugoeslavos y
los occidentales," *BRAB*, 31(1965-66), 208, 214-15. For
Russian version (through middle of 214 including last two
paragraphs on 224-25) with preface and comments by
V. M. Žirmunskij, see "Jugoslavskie èpičeskie pevcy i
ustnyj èpos v Zapadnoj Evrope," *IAN*, 25(1966), 100-17;
for a Serbo-Croatian summary of Menéndez Pidal's article,
see Ljiljana Pavlović-Samurović, "Jedno mišljenje
Menendesa Pidala o jugoslovenskoj usmenoj poeziji,"
NSSVD, 6/2(1977), 129-37 (summary in French).

[19] P. E. Russell, "Some Problems of Diplomatic in the
Cantar de Mio Cid and their Implications," *MLR*, 47(1952),
340-49; Russell, "San Pedro de Cardeña and the Heroic

History of the Cid," *MÆ*, 27(1958), 57-79; *Poema de mio Cid*, ed. by Colin Smith (Oxford, 1972), pp. xxx-xxxvii; Smith, "Further French Analogues and Sources for the *Poema de mio Cid*," *Cor*, 6(1977), 14-21, which includes references to studies along similar lines since 1971; Smith, *Estudios cidianos* (Madrid, 1977); Deyermond, *A Literary History of Spain: The Middle Ages* (London and New York, 1971), p. 49 [Spanish translation with revisions, *Historia de la literatura española: La Edad Media* (Barcelona, 1973)]; Deyermond, *Epic Poetry and the Clergy: Studies on the "Mocedades de Rodrigo"* (London, 1969); H. Salvador Martínez, *El "Poema de Almería" y la épica románica* (Madrid, 1975).

[20] Menéndez Pidal, "Sobre las variantes del códice rolandiano V4 de Venecia," *CN*, 21(1961), 10-19, and in detail, Menéndez Pidal, "Los cantores épicos...," pp. 208, 210, and 19 of colloquy in same volume; for corresponding sections in the Russian version of the article, pp. 112-14.

[21] "Postojanost epskog modela u dvije pjesme iz dubrovačkoga kraja," *NUm*, 4(1966), 27, n. 23.

[22] "Uz dva članka o usmenoj književnosti," *UR*, 16 (1972), 213 and n. 9.

[23] *El arte juglaresco en "El Cantar de Mío Cid"* (Madrid, 1967), pp. 22-41, esp. 38-41.

[24] *Epic Poetry*, pp. 63-80; *S-CHS* I; although the following exceed the chronological limit of my study, their importance in attempting to refine extreme individualist and traditionalist positions warrants their inclusion here: Deyermond, "The *Mocedades de Rodrigo* as a Test Case: Problems of Methodology," *Cor*, 6(1978), 108-12 and Armistead, "The *Mocedades de Rodrigo* and Neo-Individualist Theory," *HR*, 46(1978), 313-27.

[25] Deyermond, "Structural and Stylistic Patterns in the *Cantar de Mio Cid*," in *Medieval Studies in Honor of Robert White Linker*, ed. by Brian Dutton, J. Woodrow Hassell, Jr., and John E. Keller (Madrid, 1973), pp. 69-71.

[26] Svetozar Koljević, "Varijanta i pesnički izraz u srpskohrvatskoj narodnoj epici," *Knji*, 55(1972), 222-48, and for detailed discussion, Koljević, *Naš junački ep* (Belgrade, 1974); Vido Latković and Nada Milošević, review of Lord's *Singer* in *Prilozi*, 28(1962), 105-9, esp. 108.

[27] Lord, *Singer*, p. 136; Lord, "Homer as Oral Poet," *HSCP*, 72(1967), 12.

[28] Alois Schmaus, *Studije o krajinskoj epici*, *Rad JAZU*, 297 (Zagreb, 1953), pp. 125-32; corresponding section available also in "Studije o krajinskoj epici," in *Narodna književnost*, ed. by Vladan Nedić (Belgrade, 1966), pp. 281-91 and in "Iz 'Studija o krajinskoj epici'," in *Usmena književnost*, ed. by Maja Bošković-Stulli (Zagreb, 1971), pp. 237-45.

[29] "The Yugoslav Model and the Text of the *Poema de Mio Cid*," in *Medieval Hispanic Studies ... Rita Hamilton...*, pp. 1-10. Somewhat similar appears to be the position of Thomas Montgomery, "Grammatical Causality and Formulism in the *Poema de Mio Cid*," in *Studies in Honor of Lloyd A. Kasten*, ed. by Theodore S. Beardsley, Jr. *et al.* (Madison, 1975), pp. 185-98, and his "The 'Poema de Mio Cid': Oral Art in Transition," in *"Mio Cid" Studies...*, pp. 91-112.

[30] Miletich, Dissertation Abstract: "Repetitive Sequences and their Effect on Narrative Style in Spanish and South Slavic Traditional Narrative Poetry" (also appearing in bibliographies as "The *Romancero* and the South Slavic *Bugarštica*: A Study of Repetitive Sequences and their Effect on Narrative Style"), *Olifant*, 2(1974), 146-47; *DAI*, 36(1975-76), p. 8104-A; "Narrative Style in Spanish and Slavic Traditional Narrative Poetry: Implications for the Study of the Romance Epic," *Olifant*, 2 (1974), 109-28; "1974 Annual Meeting of the Société Rencesvals, American-Canadian Branch, Proceedings," *Olifant*, 2(1975), 164-66, 172-73; "The South Slavic *bugarštica* and the Spanish *romance*: A New Approach to Typology," *IJSLP*, 21(1975), 51-69; "The Poetics of Variation in Oral-Traditional Narrative," *FIRL*, 1(1976), 57-69; "The Stylistic Differentiation of Oral and Written Literature: Current Methodologies" (in Serbo-Croatian), *NSSVD*, 6/2(1977), 117-28 (summary in English); "Oral-Traditional Style and Learned Literature: A New Perspective," *PTL*, 3(1978), 345-56; "Elaborate Style in South Slavic Oral Narrative and in Kačić Miošić's *Razgovor*," in *American Contributions to the Eighth International Congress of Slavists*, ed. by Henrik Birnbaum (Columbus, Ohio, 1978), I, pp. 522-31; "Medieval Spanish Epic and European Narrative Traditions," *Cor*, 6(1978), 90-96; "South Slavic and Hispanic Versified Narrative: A Progress Report on One Approach," in the Acts of the Davis, California *Romancero* symposium of May, 1977, forthcoming.

[31] "Perspectives on Recent Work on Oral Literature," *FMLS*, 10(1974), 203 (rpt. in *OLSE*, p. 19).

[32] Bošković-Stulli, "O pojmovima usmena i pučka književnost i njihovim nazivima," *UR*, 17(1973), 149-84, 237-60, esp. 184.

[33] *Serbo-Croatian Folk Songs* (New York, 1951).

[34] "Exclamaciones turcas y otros rasgos orientales en el romancero judeo-español," *Sefarad*, 30(1970), 189-93.

[35] Armistead and Silverman, *The Judeo-Spanish Ballad Chapbooks of Yacob Abraham Yoná* (Berkeley, 1971); for earlier work toward a Pan-European description of traditional narrative song which also includes Hispanic and South Slavic material, see Francis James Child, *The English and Scottish Popular Ballads* (Boston and New York, 1882-1898), vols. I-V, Lajos Vargyas, *Researches into the Medieval History of Folk Ballad* (Budapest, 1967), and "Južnoslovenska narodna poezija i teorija o evropskoj baladi," in *NSSVD*, 4/1(1974), 195-201 (summary in French); for more recent efforts toward a classification system for a typological index of Pan-European ballads, see *El Romancero judeo-español en el Archivo Menéndez Pidal: Catálogo-índice de romances y canciones*, ed. by S. G. Armistead, with the collaboration of Selma Margaretten, Paloma Montero, and Ana Valenciano; musical transcriptions ed. by Israel J. Katz (Madrid, 1978), I, pp. 30-32 (in Spanish), pp. 63-65 (in English). Armistead refers here principally to the Freiburg and the Wilgus-Long systems. Of special interest in the present context is a Slovenian catalog, which follows the former system and makes reference to the Hispanic tradition; see Zmaga Kumer, *Vsebinski tipi slovenskih pripovednih pesmi (Typenindex slowenischer Erzähllieder)*, (Ljubljana, 1974), p. 351.

[36] I am indebted to Samuel Armistead and to Alan Deyermond for numerous helpful suggestions, which I have taken into account in preparing the final draft of the present essay.

The following citations were added after the essay went to press (Ed.): to note 5, Krinka Vidaković, "Kalmi Baruh o Sefardima," *Izraz*, 20(1976), 801-11; for more recent work related to Menéndez Pidal's *Romancero hispánico*, see "El tema del Rey Rodrigo en un poema esloveno," *AN* 7(1974), 53-58 (summary in Slovenian, 68-69); to note 12, Delorko, *Narodne epske pjesme* (Zagreb, 1964), I, pp. 10, 13.

AN EVOLUTIONARY MODEL FOR THE TEXT
FIXATION OF HOMERIC EPOS

Gregory Nagy

Risking the greatest sort of oversimplification, I
begin by confronting a fundamental principle of oral
poetry with a fundamental problem of Homeric Epos. From
the field work of Milman Parry and Albert Lord on the
living poetic traditions of the Southslavic people, we
know that oral poetry is a medium where the composition
can be simultaneous with the performance—or at least,
where the composition becomes a reality only in performance. As we turn our attention to the poetic traditions
of Homeric Epos, frozen in the texts of the *Iliad* and
Odyssey, we ask ourselves exactly how two such monumental
poems came to be composed and how on earth they could
ever have been performed. Surely the diction of Homeric
poetry reveals a formulaic system characteristic of oral
poetry, and Parry's own investigation of the subject remains our definitive guide. To me one of the most decisive factors in this regard is the principle of economy
that we find operating in Homeric diction: from the experience of field work done by Parry and Lord in Southslavic poetry, we know that this principle operates not
on the level of oral tradition in general but rather on
the level of oral *performance* in particular (*Singer*, p.
53). Equally definitive is Lord's investigation of
Homeric themes, which likewise reveal a behavior that
parallels the workings of oral poetry as we find it in
the living traditions of Yugoslavia. The cumulative experience of field work, then, leads us to believe that
Homeric poetry is oral poetry in both form and content.
Still, the question remains: how were the *Iliad* and
Odyssey composed and performed?

What we have here is simply a reformulation of the
Homeric Question, which still boils down to the same
problem—a problem of history. How do we place the *Iliad*
and *Odyssey* in their historical context? For the student
of western literature in general and for the Hellenist
in particular, what comes most readily to mind is that
the factor of poetry must be reconciled somehow with the
factor of writing. From the historical point of view,
there are two fundamental realities that argue for the
factor of writing. One, the Homeric poems have come down

to us as a written *text*; and two, the era reflected by Homeric poetry as the ultimate state of its evolution, namely the eighth century B.C., is the same era that witnesses the wholesale adoption of alphabetic writing by the Greek city-states. In short, the factor of writing is made to account for the fixed texts that we know as the *Iliad* and *Odyssey*.

But here the experience of field work confronts us with a major problem: in the case of the living South-slavic traditions, Parry and Lord have found that literacy undermines and even destroys the mechanics of oral poetry. Albert Lord has proposed a solution to the problem: simply put, "Homer" dictated the *Iliad* and *Odyssey*.[1] This way, Homeric poetry is still oral poetry because "Homer" remains an oral poet; meanwhile, the factor of writing can still motivate the *Iliad* and *Odyssey* as fixed texts stemming from, say, the eighth century B.C.

We are left, however, with an additional problem. How can the Homeric poems be traced back to one time and one place when they are so consistently Panhellenic in orientation? In fact, there is not the slightest provable trace of any reference by the Homeric poems to the time and place of their composition/performance. Rather, what we see time and again from the internal evidence of their contents is that the *Iliad* and *Odyssey* synthesize the local traditions of each major city-state into Panhellenic models that suit most city-states but correspond exactly to none. For just one example, I cite the Homeric concept of the Olympian gods, which incorporates yet goes beyond the localized religious traditions of each city-state.

The Homeric poems are Panhellenic not only in orientation but also in proliferation. At the dawn of the historical period, we find that the *Iliad* and *Odyssey* have already attained their ultimate status as the prime heritage recognized by the various Greek city-states as the very foundation of Hellenic civilization. Since Homeric Epos has such a Panhellenic spread dating from the prehistoric period, we cannot actually establish a chronological distinction between a single event of composition and an ongoing process of proliferation.

In light of these considerations, I would propose that the dictation theory be modified: the text-fixation of the Homeric poems may be due not to the specific factor of writing but to the general factor of Panhellenism. A recent archaeological synthesis[2] has made it clear that

the eighth century B.C., the very era in which the Homeric poems reached their ultimate form, was a watershed in
the evolution of Hellenic civilization: alongside the
emergence of the πόλις (*pólis*, "city-state") as a general
institution with a strong trend of localized traditions,
there emerged a commensurately strong trend on intercom-
munication among the *élite* of the city-states—the trend
of Panhellenism. The Panhellenic institutions that
evolved in the eighth century include the following:

- Olympic Games
- Delphic Oracle
- organized colonizations
- alphabetic writing

Such institutions are of course monumental feats of in-
tersocial organization as also of intercultural synthesis. Significantly, *the same can be said about Homeric
poetry itself*. To repeat, the contents of the *Iliad* and
Odyssey—such as the concept of the Olympian gods—reveals a *social* as well as *artistic* cohesion.

If indeed Homeric poetry is a Panhellenic institution, it follows that the proliferation of such poetry
throughout the city-states need not be looked upon as a
process that merely followed the event of composition.
The Panhellenism of the Homeric poems suggests that proliferation is a factor that must be considered alongside
those of composition and performance.

The social context of Panhellenism implies an audience that is in the end considerably different from the
local folk listening to the after-dinner songs performed
by the singer of tales. The latter context is still reflected in *Odyssey* viii, where the singer Demodokos is
entertaining his local audience with tales about the
quarrel of Odysseus and Achilles, the affair of Ares and
Aphrodite, and the capture of Troy through the stratagem
of the Wooden Horse. By contrast, the earliest attested
context for the actual performance of the Homeric Epos
is the *festival*, where the ῥαψῳδός (*rhapsōidós*) recites a
fixed text. The factor of composition is already lost,
but we may well envision earlier times when the proliferation of Homeric Epos still entailed the existence of
rhapsodes who were composing while they performed, performing while they composed. The point is, however, that
the Panhellenic context of proliferation, within the setting of such institutions as the Panathenaic festival of

Athens or the Panionian festival of Delos, has eventually frozen the dynamic element of composition into the static marvels that we know as the *Iliad* and *Odyssey*. The fixed texts may have evolved, then, without the factor of writing. But once frozen, the Homeric poems could then be kept frozen permanently by having them written down.

Harvard University

NOTES

[1] See Lord, "Homer's Originality: Oral Dictated Texts," *TAPA*, 74(1953), 124-34.
[2] A. M. Snodgrass, *The Dark Age of Greece: an Archaeological Survey of the Eleventh to the Eighth Centuries* (Edinburgh, 1971).

FORMULA AND FORMULAIC SYSTEM IN *BEOWULF*

John D. Niles

It is both the blessing and the curse of the oral-formulaic theory of the composition of *Beowulf*[1] that the theory has come to England via Greece. It is the blessing because, from the beginning, Anglo-Saxonists interested in exploring the oral roots of *Beowulf* have been able to compare the poem not only with modern epic poems collected in the field, but with the far greater poems of Homer. It is the curse because too often both advocates and critics of the oral-formulaic theory have treated the language of Old English epic poetry as if it were fully comparable to the language of early Greek epic poetry. The result has been confusion.

The meter of *Beowulf*, like that of Old Germanic heroic poetry in general, is alliterative.[2] It is based on the linkage of two half-lines (or verses) by the similar initial sound of either two or three stressed syllables. The meter of early Greek epic poetry is quantitative. It is based on a steady flow of dactylic feet, six per line, in a system whereby one long syllable may substitute for the two short syllables of any dactyl. Because of this fundamental difference in meter, the formulaic language of *Beowulf* differs significantly from the formulaic language of Homer. In particular, the stylistic feature of *variation* is much more important in Old English narrative poetry than in the narrative poetry of early Greece.[3]

Let us consider the case of Homer's "winged words." The phrase ἔπεα πτερόεντα προσηύδα ("he spoke winged words") occurs eighty-five times within the thirty thousand or so lines of the Homeric corpus with only one variation, the substitution of the imperfect προσηύδων for the aorist προσηύδα. Each time the phrase occurs, it occupies the same metrical position, from the masculine caesura to the end of the line, according to the following scheme:

$$\text{καί} \left\{ \begin{array}{l} \left\{ \begin{array}{l} \text{μιν} \\ \text{σφεας} \end{array} \right\} \left\{ \begin{array}{l} \text{φωνήσας} \\ \text{φωνήσασ'} \\ \text{λισσόμενος} \end{array} \right. \\ \text{ρ' ὀλοφυρόμενος} \\ \text{ἀγχοῦ δ' ἱστάμενος} \\ \text{τοὺς ὅ γ' ἐποτρύνων} \end{array} \right\} \begin{array}{l} \text{ἔπεα πτερόεντα} \\ \text{προσηύδα (-ων)} \end{array}$$

$$\text{and} \left\{ \begin{array}{l} \left\{ \begin{array}{l} \text{him} \\ \text{them} \end{array} \right\} \left\{ \begin{array}{l} \text{addressing (masc.)} \\ \text{addressing (fem.)} \\ \text{entreating} \end{array} \right. \\ \text{then lamenting} \\ \text{near [him] standing} \\ \text{them urging on} \end{array} \right\} \begin{array}{l} \text{winged words he} \\ \text{spoke.} \end{array}$$

Although the distinguished Homerist George Calhoun had attempted to show that Homer uses the phrase ἔπεα πτερόεντα only at chosen moments, when he wishes to give a speech special emphasis,[4] Milman Parry was able to demonstrate that the phrase is used chiefly for its metrical convenience. The various ἔπεα πτερόεντα lines are used to bring in speech when "the character who is to speak has been the subject of the last verses, so that the use of his name would be clumsy."[5] Given the poet's desire to say "he said" in the second half of a line which does *not* begin with the speaker's name, he will use the phrase ἔπεα πτερόεντα προσηύδα (-ων). No alternative expression occurs. The phrase is thus a good example of a *formula*, under Parry's definition: "a group of words which is regularly employed under the same metrical conditions to express a given essential idea."[6]

Now let us consider an example of formulaic language from *Beowulf*.[7] The word *gedryht* ("body of retainers") occurs six times within the 3182 lines of the poem. Each

time, it occurs without inflection as the second measure
of the off-verse, or *b*-verse:

1.	mid minra secga gedriht	633b
2.	mid þinra secga gedryht	1672b
3.	mid his eorla gedriht	357b
4.	ond minra eorla gedryht	431b
5.	mid his hæleþa gedryht	662b
6.	æþelinga gedriht	118b.

While no two of these verses are exactly alike, all
share a certain resemblance. In each case, the word
gedryht is preceded by a noun denoting "man" or "nobleman" in the genitive plural case (*secga, eorla, hæleþa,
æþelinga*). In the first five verses of the group, the
noun denoting "man" is preceded by two unstressed words,
a preposition or a conjunction (*mid, ond*) followed by a
form of the personal pronoun (*minra, þinra, his*). These
first five verses could reasonably be said to constitute
a single *formulaic system*: that is, a group of verses
which follow the same basic patterns of rhythm and syntax and which have at least one main semantic element in
common. The members of this formulaic system differ from
one another in the number (but not the distribution)
of unstressed syllables, which are not significant from
the point of view of the line's alliteration. In addition, and more significantly, they differ in the choice
of a variable word which carries the alliteration. The
poet speaks of *secgas* rather than of *eorlas* or of
hæleþas not because of a desire to fit the precise con-
notation of a word to a particular context, of course,
but in order to satisfy the alliteration of the line.
When one considers these five verses, one can speak of
no "group of words regularly employed," an essential
criterion for the formula under Parry's definition. One
can speak of no "identical metrical conditions" except
in the case of those verses (1-2; 3-4) which share the
same alliteration. Instead, we are dealing with a group
of verses which are similar in rhythm and syntax and
which are alike in the relative placement of the word
gedryht. Very likely the poet knew these verses not
only as isolated phrases but as verses *of a type*, and we
can imagine that he was able to substitute among them
almost without thinking. The system may be summarized
in an equation:

$$(x)\ x\ x\ \overset{\textcircled{X}}{}\ x\ (x)\quad \textit{gedrýht.}$$

The large X of this equation represents the initial
stressed syllable of a noun in the genitive plural case,
while the small x's represent unstressed syllables (optional ones in parentheses). Here as elsewhere in this
paper, primary stress is marked with an acute accent (´)
and secondary stress with a grave accent (`), while the
alliterating element is encircled.

What then of the sixth verse, æþelinga gedriht?
Despite its general resemblance to verses 1-5, it more
profitably may be considered a member of a different
formulaic system, a system which could be represented
by the equation æþelinga(-es) X̣. Seven members of the
system occur in *Beowulf*:

æþelinga bearn	1408b
æðelinga bearn	2597a
æþelinga bearn	3170a
æþelinges bearn	888a
æþelinges fær	33b
æþelinga gestreon	1920b
æþelinga gedriht	118b.

Like the members of the *gedrýht* system, these seven
verses are of the same metrical type and syntactic pattern. They are related semantically by one constant
element, the word æþeling ("nobleman") in the genitive
singular or genitive plural case occupying the first
measure of the verse. This constant element is fairly
negligible in meaning. In the heroic context of *Beowulf*,
to say that a man is a "son of noblemen" is simply to
say that he is a man; to say that treasure is "treasure
of noblemen" is simply to say that it is treasure. In
the case of this system, then, the constant element supplies the alliteration, while the variable element carries the burden of meaning. The primary function of the
formulaic system remains much the same as before, however: to allow the poet to express his meaning unerring-
ly in the given metrical form.

Aware of the importance of the stylistic feature of
variation in Old English poetry, Donald Fry has proposed
definitions of the formula and formulaic system tailored
to the special conditions of the Anglo-Saxon poetic
line. To Fry, a *formulaic system* is "a group of half-

lines usually loosely related metrically and semantically, which are related in form by the identical relative
placement of two elements, one variable and usually supplying the alliteration of the line and the other constant, with approximately the same distribution of non-
stressed elements."[8] The *formula*, according to Fry,
then can be defined simply as a member (or product) of a
formulaic system. Fry's definitions cut right across
fruitless debate as to the degree of resemblance between
phrases which is sufficient to identify them as "the
same." They direct attention away from the recurrent
phrase to the pattern which underlies both recurrent
phrases and similar phrases which do not happen to recur. According to Fry's definitions, for example, *Beowulf* 633b (*mid minra secga gedriht*) deserves to be considered a formula not only because a nearly identical
verse happens to recur elsewhere in the poem (1672b, *mid
þinra secga gedryht*), but because it is a member of a
well-defined formulaic system. The verse still would be
a formula even if nothing quite like it were to recur,
as is the case with verse 662b, *mid his hæleþa gedryht*.[9]

     In view of the theoretical importance of Fry's con-
cept of the Old English formula, it is to be regretted
that Fry's own application of his definitions has not
been more rigorous. As a result, his concept has not
received the attention it deserves. The main problem
lies in the identification of just what constitutes metrical and semantic resemblance between different verses.
To judge from Fry's own examples, the metrical and semantic resemblance between members of the same formulaic
system may be loose indeed, while the syntactic resemblance may be nonexistent. Fry cites the following
verses as among thirty-one members of what he calls the
"X *muþ*" system in Old English poetry, for example[10]:

recedes muþan	*Beowulf* 724a
þurstige muðe	*Paris Psalter* 61.4.3a
lease muðe	*Paris Psalter* 77.35.1b
ofer seolfes muð	*Andreas* 1300b
hunig on muðe	*Homiletic Fragment I* 21b
þurh þæs deman muð	*Elene* 1283b
rum recedes muð	*Maxims II* 37a.

What common rhythmic or syntactic pattern underlies
these verses? How could such verses have formed part of
a functional formulaic system in the mind of an oral

poet? To be functional, a formulaic system must provide
a poet with the means of expressing his meaning with a
minimum of reflection. The system will not do the
poet's thinking for him, but it will narrow the linguistic choices open to him at a particular moment, and thus
it will facilitate his task of rapid composition. It is
difficult to see how Fry's postulated "X *muþ*" system
could have narrowed the choices of a singer in any significant way. Practically inevitably, if one searched
through a poetic corpus of some thirty thousand lines,
one would find instances of the same word occurring at
the end of a verse. To say that a common word such as
muð ("mouth"), in some inflection, occurs at the end of
a verse thirty-one times in the entire Anglo-Saxon poetic corpus is to say nothing about the formulaic language of a given poet.

Interpreted loosely, Fry's concept of the formula
thus is little more helpful to Anglo-Saxonists than
Parry's. Interpreted with rigor, it may yet provide us
with a satisfactory way of identifying what is formulaic
about Old English narrative poetry. To put the matter
in general terms, a formula in Anglo-Saxon poetry may be
considered a *rhythmic/syntactic/semantic complex one
half-line in length*. It is one of a set of verses (or
formulaic system) of a similar metrical type in which
one main verbal element is constant. Strictly speaking,
a formulaic system is not the same as the sum of its
members. It could be looked upon as a pre-verbal *Gestalt*
which is capable of realization in a number of different
surface forms, not all of which may occur in the extant
poetry. [11] In the case of the *gedryht* system, for example, one reasonably may surmise that if the text of
Beowulf were twice or three times its actual length, the
poet might have had occasion to use such verses as *mid
his gumena gedryht*, or *mid his þegna gedryht*, or *mid
his Geata gedryht*. The fact that such verses do not occur in the text that has come down to us does not mean
that they did not figure in the poet's central concept
of the *gedryht* system. As it is difficult to speak of a
psychological *Gestalt* and impossible to measure it
statistically, however, there is some practical justifi-
cation for considering a formulaic system to be equal to
the sum of its recorded members.

To take such a view of the formula in Old English
poetry is to be in accord with what is known about the
way that oral poets learn the fundamentals of their

craft. According to Lord, singers learn to sing tales
not by a process of rote memorization of formulas, but as
one learns to speak a language, by a process of gradual
assimilation.[12]   The difference between the language of
oral poetry and the language of everyday speech is
solely one of degree: "the former is of the same kind as
the latter, but it is more intensive and specialized
because of added limitations of form."[13]   To Lord, who is
well acquainted with the nature of formulaic language,
having recorded in the neighborhood of 700,000 lines of
epic poetry in the field,[14] a formula is not a fixed
phrase, a dead counter to be shuffled about at will. It
is "a living phenomenon of metrical language" (*Singer*,
p. 30). To put the matter another way, the formula is
"the offspring of the marriage of thought and sung verse"
(*ibid.*, p. 31). Robert L. Kellogg echoes Lord in urging
that scholars turn their attention to the pattern behind
the formula rather than to the fixed formula alone:

> Professor Lord maintains that "in studying the pat-
> terns and systems of oral narrative we are in
> reality discovering the 'grammar' of the poetry, a
> grammar superimposed, as it were, on the grammar
> of the language concerned" [*Singer*, pp. 35-36]. To
> continue his analogy with language, we might add
> that the fixed formula is to the abstract pattern
> of which it is a manifestation as the phonotype is
> to the phoneme. Both the fixed traditional formu-
> las and the phrases invented by the singer during
> a performance will conform to a given number of
> abstract patterns. And it is an elaborate set of
> these patterns, rather than merely the stock of
> fixed formulas conforming to the patterns, that con-
> stitutes the verse-making tradition of oral-formu-
> laic poetry.

Kellogg concludes:

> We now know that the really relevant elements, in
> analysis as in composition, are not the verbatim
> repeats within the corpus, but rather they are the
> abstract patterns governing the construction of
> lines and verses.[15]

Patrick W. Conner has carried the observations of Lord
and Kellogg one step further. Using a concept of the
formula as "the product—one half-line in length—of a

grammar of poetic diction superimposed upon the grammar of the spoken language," Conner has developed a structural model of the "grammar of poetic diction" of Old English poetry which is a refinement of the Chomskyan description of the grammar of a natural language.[16]

A re-examination of *Beowulf* 1-25 from the theoretical standpoint outlined in the previous pages provides a fair glimpse into the working "grammar of poetic diction" of one particular Anglo-Saxon poet. When one reviews these lines, one immediately sees the extent to which flexible formulaic systems rather than fixed formulas formed the core of the poet's traditional vocabulary. In the following table, each head-verse is followed first by a list of the members of the formulaic system to which it belongs, then by an equation which represents the system in abstract form.

FORMULAS AND FORMULAIC SYSTEMS, *BEOWULF* 1-25

System		*Equation*
1a. *Hwæt! We Gardena*		

to Gardenum	601a	
ond Gardenum	1856b	
oððe to Gardenum	2494b	$(x)(x)\ x\ \widehat{\textcircled{X}}-D\grave{e}n\begin{cases}-a\\-um\\-e\\-es\end{cases}$
ðær Hringdene	1279b	
hu hit Hringdene	116b	
Swa ic Hringdena	1769a	
to Westdenum	383a	
to Westdenum	1578b	
lete Suðdene	1996a	
Hæfde Eastdenum	828b	

Cf. verses based on the compounds
Eastdena 392a, 616a; *Suðdena* 463b;
Norðdenum 783b

1b. *in geardagum*

þone on geardagum	1354a	
swa hy on geardagum	2233a	$(x)(x)(x)x\ \widehat{\textcircled{X}}(x)-d\grave{a}g\begin{cases}-um\\-es\\-as\\-a\end{cases}$
næfre he on aldordagum	718a	
swylce he on ealder-dagum	757a	
swa hine fyrndagum	1451b	
Samod ærdæge	1311b	
somod ærdæge	2942b	

1b. *in geardagum* (contd.)

æfter deaðdæge	187a
æfter deaðdæge	885a
ær swyltdæge	2798a
ne his lifdagas	793a
Sceolde lændaga	2341b
þæt hio hyre [heofun]g- [da]gas	3153a
on ðyssum windagum	1062a

Cf. verses based on the compounds
endedæg 637b, 3035b; *lifdagas* 1622a;
lændagas 2591a

2a. *þeodcyninga*

þeodcyninges	2694b
woroldcyninga	1684b
wyruldcyninga	3180b
wuldurcyninge	2795a
sæcyninga	2382b
heahcyninges	1039b
eorðcyninges	1155b
Frescyninge	2503b

$$\widehat{(X)}\;(x)\;-c\grave{y}ning \begin{cases} -a \\ -es \\ -e \end{cases}$$

Cf. verses based on the compounds
guðcyning 199b, 1969a, 2335b, 2563a,
2677b, 3036b; *þeodcyning* 2144a, 2579a,
2963a, 2970a, 3008a, 3086a; *folccyning*
2733b, 2873a; *beorncyning* 2148a;
soðcyning 3055a.

2b. *þrym gefrunon*

æfre gefrunon	70b
godne gefrunon	1969b
hilde gefrunen	2952b
swa guman gefrungon	666b

$$(x)\;\widehat{(X)}\;(x)\;gefr\acute{u}non(-en)$$

3a. *hu ða æþelingas*

siþðan æþelingas	982a
syððan æðelingas	2888b
wæron æðelingas	1804a
ofer æþelinge	1244a
æt ðam æðelinge	2374a
þæt hig þæs æðelinges	1596a

$$(x)\;x\;x\;\acute{æ}þeling \begin{cases} -as \\ -e \\ -es \end{cases}$$

3b. *ellen fremedon*

mærðo fremede	2134a	
mærða gefremede	2645b	$\widehat{X}$ (x) (ge-)*frém* { -*edon* -*ede* -*man*
mærðu fremman	2514a	
geoce gefremede	177b	
geoce gefremman	2674b	
fyrene fre[m]man	101a	
fyrene gefremede	811a	
dæd gefremede	585b	
dæd gefremede	940b	
helpe gefremede	551b	
gryra gefremede	591b	
feohtan fremedon	959a	
arna gefremedon	1187b	
wyrpe gefremman	1315b	
læs gefremede	1946b	
sorge gefremede	2004b	
ænige gefremman	2449b	
sæcce fremman	2499a	
folcred fremede	3006a	

Cf. *oft gefremede* 165b, *oft gefremedon*
2478b, *eft gefremede* 135b, *þenden
fremedon* 1019b, *forð gefremede* 1718a

5a. *monegum mægþum*

manigum mægþa	1771a	*manegum*(-*re*) $\acute{X}$
manigre mægþe	75a	x
manegum maðmum	2103a	
monegum fira	2001b	

6b. *Syððan ærest wearð*

syððan ærest wearð	1947b	
þa ðær sona wearð	1280b	x x $\widehat{X}$ x *wéarð*
swa hyt lungre wearð	2310b	
to hwan syððan wearð	2071b	
Forðam secgum wearð	149b	
he his leodum wearð	905b	
He þær eallum wearð	913b	

7a. *feasceaft funden*

godne funde	1486b	$\widehat{X}$ (x) (*on-*) *fúnde* (-*n*)
hleonian funde	1415b	
weard onfunde	2841b	
sona onfunde	2226b	

8a. *weox under wolcnum*

weold under wolcnum	1770a	
Wod under wolcnum	714a	
Wand to wolcnum	1119a	
won to wolcnum	1374a	
wan under wolcnum	651a	
wæter under wolcnum	1631a	

$\widehat{X}$ (x) *under* / *to* } *wólcnum*

9b. *þara ymbsittendra*

ymbesittendra	2734a
healsittendra	2015b
healsittendum	2868a
fletsittendum	1788a
*flet*sittende	2022b

(x)(x) $\widehat{X}$ -*sittend* { -*ra* / -*um* / -*e* }

Cf. *þæt þec ymbsittend* 1827a

10a. *ofer hronrade*

ofer swanrade	200a
on seglrade	1429b

ofer / *on* } $\widehat{X}$ -*ràde*

10b. *hyran scolde*

healdan scolde	230b
healdan scoldon	704b
bugan sceolde	2918b
bugan sceolde	2974b
wæcnan scolde	85b
þolian scoldon	832b
geþeon scolde	910b
gangan scolde	1034b
mænan scolde	1067b
feallan scolde	1070b
seðan scolde	1106b
wunian scolde	1260b
bicgan scoldon	1305b
mengan scolde	1449b
æfnan scolde	1464b
habban scoldon	1798b
rædan sceoldest	2056b
bywan sceoldon	2257b
gewegan sceolde	2400b
gretan sceolde	2421b
fremman sceolde	2627b
ðafian sceolde	2963b
weorðan sceolde	3068b

$\widehat{X}$ x *scóld* { -*e* / -*on* / -*est* }

11a. *gomban gyldan*

golde forgyldan	1054a
gode forgylde	956a
Grendle forgyldan	1577a
lige forgyldan	2305b

$\widehat{(X)}_{\ x}$ *(for-)gýldan(-e)*

11b. *þæt wæs god cyning*

þæt wæs god cyning	2390b
ac þæt wæs god cyning	863b
þa wæs frod cyning	1306b
wæs þa frod cyning	2209b
þæt wæs an cyning	1885b
swylce self cyning	920b
wolde self cyning	1010a
þa gen sylf cyning	2702b

(x) x x $\widehat{X}$ *cýning*

12b. *æfter cenned*

ær acenned	1356b

$\widehat{X}_{(x)}$ *(a-)cénned*

13a. *geong in geardum*

gamol of geardum	265a
gomen in geardum	2459a
gist of geardum	1138a

$\widehat{X}_{(x)}$ $\left.\begin{array}{l}in\\of\end{array}\right\}$ *(g)éardum*

13b. *þone god sende*

ðe him god sealde	1271b
þe him god sealde	2182b
swylc him god sealde	72b
þæs þe him ær god sealde	1751b
nymðe mec god scylde	1658b
hwæðre him god uðe	2874b

(x) (x) x x $\widehat{(g)od}$ $\overset{\prime}{X}_{\ x}$

14a. *folce to frofre*

non-formulaic, but cf. *hæleðum to helpe* 1709a, 1961a

15a. *þe hie ær drugon*

þe hie ær drugon	831b
þe hie ær drugon	1858b
þa hie gewin drugon	798b
Hi sið drugon	1966b

$\left.\begin{array}{l}þa\\þe\end{array}\right\}$ *hie* $\widehat{X}$ *drúgon*

15b. *aldor*[*le*]*ase*

aldorleasne	1587a
ealdorleasne	3003a
sawolleasne	1406b
sawulleasne	3033b
ðeodenlease	1103a
winigea leasum	1664a
feormendlease	2761b
hlafordlease	2935b

$$(\hat{\bar{X}})_{x} \ -le\acute{a}s \begin{cases} -e \\ -ne \\ -um \end{cases}$$

16a. *lange hwile*

lange hwile	2159b
longe hwile	2780a
lytle hwile	2030b
lytle hwile	2097a
orleghwile	2911a
orleghwila	2427a
læssan hwile	2571b
ænige hwile	2548b
ane hwile	1762a

$$\hat{\bar{X}}_{x} \ (x) \quad hw\acute{\imath}le$$

Cf. *lange þrage* 114a, 1257b,
longe þrage 54b

16b. *Him þæs liffrea*

nefne sinfrea	1934b

$$x \ x \ \hat{\bar{X}} \ -fr\grave{e}a$$

Cf. *agendfrean* 1883a

17a. *wuldres wealdend*

wuldres waldend	183a
wuldres waldend	1752a
sigora waldend	2875a
ylda waldend	1661b

$$\hat{\bar{X}}_{x} \ (x) \quad \widehat{waldend}$$

Cf. *waldend fira* 2741b

18b. *blæd wide sprang*

Hra wide sprong	1588b

$$\hat{X} \ w\acute{\imath}de \ spr\acute{a}ng$$

19a. *Scyldes eafera*

Hreðles eafora	2358a
Hreðles eafora	2992a
Hreþles eaferan	1847b
Wælses eafera	897a
be Finnes eaferum	1068a
uncran eaferan	1185a
angan eaferan	1547a

$$(\text{x}) \; \widehat{\text{X}} \; _\text{x} \quad \acute{e}afera(\text{-}n)$$

19b. *Scedelandum in*

Freslondum on	2357b

$$\widehat{\text{X}} \; \text{-}l\grave{a}ndum \; \acute{i}n$$

20b. *gode gewyrcean*

men gewyrcean	69b
hlæw gewyrcean	2802b
wunde gewyrcean	2906a

$$\widehat{\text{X}} \; _{(\text{x})} \quad gew\acute{y}rcean$$

21b. *on fæder* [*bea*]*rme*

ond to fæder faþmum	188a
on fæder stæle	1479b
be fæder lare	1950b
fore fæder dædum	2059b

$$(\text{x}) \; \text{x} \quad \widehat{f\grave{æ}der} \; \acute{\text{X}} \; _\text{x}$$

22a. *þæt hine on ylde*

þæt hire on hafelan	1521a
þæt ic on þone hafelan	1780a
þæt hire wið halse	1566a
þæt him on breostum	2714a
þæt heo on ænigne	627a
þæt ðær on worðig	1972a
þæt he mid ðy wife	2028a
þæt he bi wealle	2716a
þæt him for swenge	2966a
þæt he to Gifðum	2494a

$$þ\grave{æ}t \left\{ \begin{matrix} h\grave{i}ne \\ hire \\ ic \\ \text{etc.} \end{matrix} \right\} \left\{ \begin{matrix} on \\ wið \\ mid \\ \text{etc} \end{matrix} \right\} \widehat{\text{X}} \; \text{x} \; (\text{x})$$

22b. *eft gewunigen*

eft gefremede	135b
eft gelimpeð	1753b
eft gesealde	2142b
eft gemetton	2592b
eft ne wendon	1596b

$$\widehat{Eft} \; _\text{x} \; \acute{\text{X}} \; _\text{x} \; (\text{x})$$

23a. *wilgesiþas*

swæse gesiþas	29a	
swæse gesiðas	2040a	$\hat{X}$ (x) *gesiðas*
swæse gesiðas	2518a	
swæsra gesiða	1934a	
ealdgesiðas	853b	

24a. *leode gelæsten*

soðe gelæste	524b	
oft gelæste	2500b	$\hat{X}$ (x) *gelæst* $\begin{cases} -en \\ -e \\ -ed \end{cases}$
gilp gelæsted	829b	

25a. *in magþa gehwære*

æt niða gehwam	882a	
Swa he niða gehwane	2397a	
þæt he dogora gehwam	88a	(x) x $\hat{X}$ x (*ge-*) $\begin{cases} hwære \\ hwam \\ hwane \\ etc. \end{cases}$
wið manna hwone	155a	
wið feonda gehwone	294a	
ond on healfa gehwone	800a	
þær mæg nihta gehwam	1365a	
ond þegna gehwylc	1673a	
se ðe meca gehwane	2685a	
þeah ðe he dæda		
gehwæs	2838a	

Study of the foregoing table shows that of the first
50 verses of the poem, 33 are expressions of one or another identifiable formulaic system. Only 9 verses
(2a, 5a, 6b, 9b, 11b, 15a, 16a, and 17a) are repeated
elsewhere in the same form, allowing for differences of
spelling and inflection. In other words, using as a
referent the 3182 lines of the poem itself, the first
50 verses are 66% formulaic and 34% nonformulaic or
doubtful, with 18% reiterated phrases. One could widen
the referent of the analysis to include the entire
Anglo-Saxon poetic corpus, of course.[17]   In this case 9
additional verses (1b, 3a, 3b, 4b, 8a, 10b, 13a, 14a,
and 23a) would qualify as reiterated phrases. Methodologically this step would be unsound, however, for it
means confounding the diction of *Beowulf* with the diction of poems composed in different genres, in different regions, and in different centuries.
    When compared with the more than 6000 verses of the
poem as a whole, of course, 50 verses make up only a

small sample. In order to see whether or not the formulaic density of *Beowulf* 1–25 is representative of that
of the entire poem, I have undertaken an exactly similar
formulaic analysis through *Beowulf* 500. In the case of
each of these thousand verses, just as in the smaller
sample, I have checked each main word against the Smith-
Bessinger computer-generated *Concordance*[18] so as to
identify all formulas and formulaic systems that occur
within these lines. Space does not permit reproducing
here the vast network of formulas and formulaic systems
which was yielded by this analysis. Instead, I shall
summarize my results in the form of a table.

FORMULAS AND FORMULAIC SYSTEMS, *BEOWULF* 1–500

Members of formulaic systems.	632	63.2%
Reiterated verses: 133		
Nonreiterated verses: 499		
Reiterated verses not part of a formulaic system	36	3.6%
Nonformulaic or doubtful verses	327	32.7%
Verses metrically defective	5	0.5%
	1000	100.0%

If one adds the number of reiterated verses which are *not*
members of a formulaic system (36) to the number of reiterated verses which *are* members of a formulaic system
(133), one arrives at a total of 169 reiterated verses,
or 16.9% of the whole. Study of the larger sample thus
verifies our earlier conclusions. Close to *two out of
three* verses in the poem are members of one or another
identifiable formulaic system. In creating these
phrases, the poet not only was working within the linguistic patterns afforded him by the natural language,
he was using more highly specialized patterns which enabled him to compose fluently in the alliterative form.
On the other hand, only about *one verse in six* recurs
elsewhere in substantially the same form. To call these
verses "fixed formulas" would be misleading, for most of
them (almost 80%) are members of one or another flexible
formulaic system. In other words, the diction of *Beowulf* is indeed highly formulaic, but far more important
than the repetition of fixed phrases is the substitution
of one verbal element for another within flexible formulaic systems one half-line in length.

We may conclude that any further development of the
oral-formulaic theory of the composition of *Beowulf* must
be based on an understanding of the poet's tendency to
express his thought in flexible formulaic systems. Any
critique of this theory that is based on the study of
fixed phrases alone, in like manner, is bound to be of
limited value. In particular, the main contention of
Ann Chalmers Watts in her study *The Lyre and the Harp* [19] —
that when closely scrutinized, Anglo-Saxon narrative
poetry is not highly formulaic and therefore has no claim
to be called oral—is unjustified because it is based on
a concept of the formula as a fixed phrase. Watts
rightly discards Parry's definition of the formula as
inapplicable to Old English poetry. Her own definition
of the formula is no more helpful, however. To Watts,
a formula in Old English is "a repeated sequence that
fills one of Sievers' five basic rhythmical types" (p.
90), or in other words, a repeated verse. Watts correctly concludes that the formula *thus defined* is not of
outstanding importance in *Beowulf*, but since her definition is ill chosen, her conclusion has no bearing on the
question of the validity of the oral-formulaic theory.

Objection also must be made to certain of Larry D.
Benson's conclusions in his outstanding essay "The Literary Character of Anglo-Saxon Formulaic Poetry."[20]   By
comparing a number of passages of Anglo-Saxon poetry,
Benson shows that formulas occur in the work of authors
known to have been composing pen in hand. He concludes
that since all Old English poetry is formulaic, there
can be no way of determining the oral vs. written nature
of a given text. Benson has well shown that blind formulaic analysis of a particular passage of Old Fnglish
poetry is no sure proof of its mode of creation. Many a
learned author has been known to use formulas, whether
for rhetorical effect, for atmosphere, or because the
poetic language itself is steeped in them. In the absence of definite information indicating the mode of
creation of a text, one must use great caution in at-
tributing it to a singer. All the same, like Watts,
Benson fails to make a distinction between living formulaic language and the parroting of formulaic tags. In
seeking evidence for the mode of composition of a text,
one must not only count the number of fixed formulas in
the work, for these are easily imitated by a lettered
author. One must look for evidence that the poet in
question made formulaic language his *habitual mode of*

thought. When one compares Book II, Meter 3 of the Anglo-Saxon *Meters of Boethius* with the Anglo-Saxon prose which served as its source,[21] for example, one can see that many of the poem's formulas are mere padding. When the prose author speaks of "all stars," the poet speaks of "all stars *ofer eorðan*" (1.5). When the prose author speaks of "the wind," the poet speaks of "the wind *under wolcnum*" (1.9). When the prose author laments that "no worldly thing long endures," the poet laments that "no worldly thing *on eorðan* long endures" (1.16). Benson has succeeded in showing what has long been known: that the person who translated the meters of Boethius' *De Consolatione Philosophiae* into passable Anglo-Saxon verse used a number of formulaic tags.[22] Benson has not shown that this person used flexible formulaic language as his habitual mode of thought—in other words, that he thought like an oral poet.

In sum, we may conclude that the *Beowulf* poet did not have to search his mind for new and ingenious ways of saying what he wished to say. His tradition not only provided him with a large body of known stories; it also provided him with a method whereby he could sing these stories fluently in verse. To an overwhelming extent, this method did not consist of the poet's parroting fixed phrases or formulaic tags. It consisted of his varying verse-length phrases within a vast interlocking network of formulaic systems. In this way the poet could easily generate new verses on the model of old ones as the need arose. It is the set of abstract verse-making patterns used by the *Beowulf* poet, rather than a body of fixed phrases, which constitutes his true formulaic repertory.

The Dark Ages remain dark, whether in pre-classical Greece or in post-classical Europe, and one cannot be too skeptical of facile theories that attempt to account for the mode of creation of the few archaic epic poems that have come down to us. The passage of time has seen theories of origin rise and fall. All the same, the oral-formulaic theory of Milman Parry and Albert Lord offers hope for future research precisely because it is neither facile nor dogmatic, but is grounded on close study of oral poetic traditions which are still living today. For Anglo-Saxonists, the oral-formulaic theory seems to send beams of light penetrating into the obscurity of early Germanic England. One main task presently facing Old English scholars is to refine

the tools of oral-formulaic analysis so as to approach
Old English poetry in its own terms. Oral poetry differs in style from written poetry, true. In addition,
the evidence is clear that the oral poetry of one tradition may differ in style from the oral poetry of a different tradition. If the oral-formulaic theory of the
composition of *Beowulf* is to bear full fruit, Anglo-
Saxonists must distinguish carefully between the language of the *Beowulf* poet and the language of Homer. In
this way misleading comparisons may be avoided, and the
language of *Beowulf* may be seen for what it is: a rich,
dignified, and supple language uniquely suited to the
Old Germanic alliterative form.

University of California at Berkeley

NOTES

[1]See Francis P. Magoun, Jr., "The Oral-Formulaic
Character of Anglo-Saxon Narrative Poetry," *Speculum*,
28(1953), 446-67; and Lord, *Singer*. The thesis first
was advanced by Lord in his unpublished doctoral dissertation, "The Singer of Tales" (Harvard, 1949), pp.
198-211, and first attracted the attention of Anglo-
Saxon scholars as formulated by Magoun. Long before,
scholars had been in agreement that *Beowulf* was composed to be sung aloud. Once Milman Parry and Lord had
documented the processes of creation of oral story poetry by intensive field work in Yugoslavia, thereby
making a strong case for the oral character of the
Homeric epics, Magoun was able to assert with some confidence that *Beowulf* (and other Anglo-Saxon narrative
poetry) was composed in the process of being sung aloud.
The chief evidence for this assertion was the poem's
highly formulaic diction. Magoun was able to account
for the many formulas in *Beowulf* by suggesting that they
were not merely decorative, they were functional.
If the oral poet is to keep from faltering, he must have
forms and formulas ready to hand. According to Magoun's
statement of the oral-formulaic theory—a rather sim-
plistic statement, as is now clear—the difference between a poem composed in writing and a poem composed
orally is that "the recurrence in a given poem of an
appreciable number of formulas or formulaic phrases
brands the latter as oral, just as the lack of such

repetitions marks a poem as being composed in a lettered tradition" ("Oral-Formulaic Character," 446).

[2]An alliterative verse form is inconceivable except in a language (like Old Germanic or Somali) which has developed a system of stress on the initial or root syllable of a word. A language which favors rising intonation or terminal stress—Old French, for example—is better suited for a verse form based on assonance. In the case of Old French epic poetry, formulas which fill the first hemistich of the line tend to remain "fixed," while formulas which fill the second hemistich frequently are varied in the final syllables for the sake of assonance. Aware of the way in which Old French epic diction is tailored to the assonantal verse form, Joseph J. Duggan wisely has admitted to the status of *formulas* phrases which differ only in the choice of word which supplies the assonance, that is, hemistich-pairs such as *li proz e li curteis* and *li proz e li gentilz*; see his *The Song of Roland: Formulaic Style and Poetic Craft* (Berkeley, 1973), pp. 10-11. In respect to the importance of *variation* of phrases within flexible formulaic systems as opposed to *repetition* of fixed phrases, Old French epic poetry appears to stand somewhere midway between early Greek and Old English epic poetry.

[3]See Donald K. Fry, "Variation and Economy in *Beowulf*," *MP*, 65(1968), 353-56. Klaeber refers to variation as "all-important," as "the very soul of the Old English poetical style" (*Beowulf and the Fight at Finnsburg*, 3rd ed. with 1st and 2nd suppls. [Boston, rpt. 1950], pp. lxix and lxv, respectively).

[4]"The Art of the Formula in Homer—ἔπεα πτερόεντα," *CP*, 30(1935), 215-27.

[5]Parry, "About Winged Words," in *MHV*, p. 414; quoted from his "The Traditional Metaphor in Homer," in *MHV*, p. 372.

[6]"Studies in the Epic Technique of Oral Verse-Making. I. Homer and Homeric Style," in *MHV*, p. 272.

[7]In the present paper, all references to the text of *Beowulf* are to Elliott Van Kirk Dobbie, ed., *Beowulf and Judith*, The Anglo-Saxon Poetic Records, vol. 4 (New York, 1953).

[8]"Old English Formulas and Systems," *ES*, 48(1967), 203. Note also his subsequent "Some Aesthetic Implications of a New Definition of the Formula," *NM*, 69(1968), 516-22, in which he slightly rephrases his definition, omitting the word "loosely."

[9]In "How Free Was the Anglo-Saxon Scop?" in *Franciplegius*, pp. 75-85, Frederic G. Cassidy maintains that of greater importance to a scop than either fixed formulas or formulaic systems would have been abstract "archetypal syntactic patterns," of which he finds twenty-five in *Beowulf*. To judge from Cassidy's examples, however, these syntactic frames include widely disparate verses. *He æt wige gecrang* (1337b) and *ofer sæ sohton* (2380a) are both examples of the "PV frame," for example, while *breostgewædu* (1211a) and *we synt gumcynnes* (260a) are both examples of the "N frame" (pp. 79-80). It is hard to see how Cassidy's syntactic frames would have helped the scop a great deal in the process of rapid composition before an audience. In his discussion of the oral-formulaic theory in his and Richard Ringler's edition of *Bright's Old English Grammar and Reader*, 3rd ed. (New York, 1971), pp. 270-72, Cassidy appears to abandon the concept of syntactic frames in favor of a concept much like that advocated in the present paper.

[10] From "Some Aesthetic Implications of a New Definition of the Formula," 520.

[11] See Michael N. Nagler, "Towards a Generative View of the Oral Formula," *TAPA*, 98(1967), 269-311; for further discussion, see his *S&T*, Chapter 1, "The Traditional Phrase (1): Theory of Production," pp. 1-26.

[12] *Singer*, Chapter 2, "Singers: Performance and Training," pp. 13-29.

[13] Lord, "The Role of Sound-Patterns in Serbo-Croatian Epic," in *For Roman Jakobson* (The Hague, 1956), p. 302.

[14] This wealth of recorded song is now the core of the Milman Parry Collection of Oral Literature at Harvard University. I have arrived at the rough estimate of 700,000 lines by multiplying the *number of discs* of epic poetry which Lord personally recorded by the *playing time per disc*, then multiplying the resulting sum by the estimated average number of lines of poetry sung by an epic singer per minute.

[15] "The South Germanic Oral Tradition," in *Franciplegius*, pp. 67-68. In an article published after the present paper was written, John Miles Foley adds his voice to those of Lord and Kellogg in urging that scholars turn their attention away from the surface phenomenon of the repeated phrase toward the more abstract form which underlies both repeated and non-

repeated phrases. According to Foley, "what we read—
the formula—is only the footprint, the verbal trace" of
the underlying form, which he sees as chiefly metrical
("Formula and Theme in Old English Poetry," in *OL&F*, p.
212).

[16] "Schematization of Oral-Formulaic Processes in
Old English Poetry," *L&S*, 5(1972), 204-20, espec. 206.

[17] As does Magoun in "The Oral-Formulaic Character
of Anglo-Saxon Narrative Poetry," 444-67.

[18] *A Concordance to Beowulf*, ed. Jess B. Bessing-
er, programmed by Philip H. Smith, Jr. (Ithaca, 1969).
As a precautionary measure, I have checked the results
thus yielded against the impressive data amassed by
Robert P. Creed in his "Studies in the Techniques of
Composition of the Beowulf Poetry in British Museum Ms.
Cotton Vitellius A. xv," unpub. Ph.D. diss. (Harvard,
1955).

[19] *The Lyre and the Harp: a Comparative Reconsideration of Oral Tradition in Homer and Old English Epic
Poetry* (New Haven, 1969).

[20] *PMLA*, 81(1966), 334-41.

[21] The two texts are printed *en face* in Benson, 338,
as well as in Roger Fowler, ed., *Old English Prose and
Verse* (London, 1966), pp. 122-23.

[22] As Walter J. Sedgefield notes, the author of the
metra fashioned them "by rearranging the words of the
prose version and inserting poetical commonplaces or
'tags,' to bring the lines into an alliterating form"
(*King Alfred's Old English Version of Boethius' De
Consolatione Philosophiae* [Oxford, 1899], p. xxxviii;
quoted by Benson, 337). The poetic technique of the
Meters of Boethius has been discussed recently by John
W. Conlee, "A Note on Verse Composition in the *Meters
of Boethius*," *NM*, 71(1970), 576-85; Allan A. Metcalf,
Poetic Diction in the Old English Meters of Boethius
(The Hague, 1973); and Pierre Eric Monnin, "The Making
of the Old English *Meters of Boethius*: Studies in Traditional Art and Aesthetics," unpub. Ph.D. diss. (University of Massachusetts/Amherst, 1975). On the facility with which Latin or Old English prose could be turned
into Old English poetry with the aid of empty "fillers,"
see also F. H. Whitman, "The Meaning of 'Formulaic' in
Old English Verse Composition," *NM*, 76(1975), 529-37.
Mistakenly, in my opinion, Whitman would restrict the
term "formulaic" in the Old English context to refer
only to such empty fillers.

ORAL-FORMULAIC CONTEXT: IMPLICATIONS FOR THE COMPARATIVE CRITICISM OF MEDIAEVAL TEXTS

Alain Renoir

If one may paraphrase Jane Austen, it is a truth universally acknowledged that the professional scholar who wishes to carry on with his trade in relative comfort had better be thought willfully wrongheaded than innocently blind. In this light, the most elementary caution urges me to proclaim here and now my full awareness of the fact that anyone who includes the terms *oral-formulaic, context, criticism,* and *text* in the same title is off to a bad start.

Every American teacher of literature today knows that it has been almost ten years since Stanley E. Fish demonstrated to the apparent satisfaction of the world that "the objectivity of the text is an illusion."[1] In the intervening years, the erstwhile function of criticism as a tool to help a given audience understand and evaluate a given text has become as uncertain as the objectivity of the text. At any rate, we may surely be permitted this assumption when we hear one of the very most respected formulators of our current critical canons praise an equally respected practitioner for being both incoherent and subjective. I am referring to Geoffrey H. Hartman's introductory eulogy of Harold Bloom's work as "this dense, eloquent, and experiential brooding,"[2] and I am not the only one to suspect that the respective activities of Hartman and Bloom—as well as those of their colleagues in New Haven and of the French structuralists whose names constantly crop up on their pages—are doing yeoman's service to disconnect criticism from individual works of literature and establish it as a totally independent literary genre.[3] Nor does Hartman prove much more encouraging about the integrity of the context within which a work of literature may be understood, since he assures us that interpretation "implies . . . that a work has become detached from its original context or that criticism helps detach (decontextualize) it. . . ."[4] In other words, the models from whom rapidly multiplying numbers of young teachers of literature are taking their cue have decided that the text is in the reader's mind, criticism is an ineffable experience, and the context changes with the critic's intended audience, location,

and time. Indeed, as Robert DeMaria, Jr., has recently
pointed out, current criticism is increasingly practiced
"to the exclusion, and even the avowed extinction, of
authors and literary objects."[5] Carried to its logical
and no longer very remote extreme, this trend must perforce reduce any critical discussion of literature to the
informatory level of a conversation with Humpty Dumpty.

Perhaps because my own trade as a student of the
early Germanic Middle Ages requires constant attention to
both text and context, and perhaps also because my training has conditioned me to read literature for its own
sake and turn to criticism only when some aspect of literature or its history seems in need of clarification, I
find myself somewhat less than thrilled with the prospects of the situation outlined here. I should be both
dishonest and unfair, however, if I failed to acknowledge
my chagrined realization that the trend to which I object
constitutes a logical response to a historical development and that the unquestionably brilliant manifestations
which grate most harshly against my sensitivities are
perfectly legitimate solutions to a very real problem.
At a time when the explosive growth of communication
and dissemination has caused such a proliferation of important texts available in any one location that no single human being may hope to read more than an infinites-
imal portion of them, the critic attempting to discuss
either a general phenomenon or a broad area of literature has only two choices: one is rigorous selectivity
based on clearly stated principles (but democracy in its
twentieth-century manifestation does not exactly encourage selectivity), and the other is pure theory independent from the chronological and geographic shackles of individual texts (and this method offers the obvious advantage of appealing to a society which agrees with Henry
Ford that history is bunk and has convinced itself that
theory will always come to the rescue in the nick of time
to solve our problems). The rejection of an objective
context may be explained on similar grounds, and professional mediaevalists should be especially attuned to the
process, since they must often work with texts whose
time, place, and original language of composition have
thus far defied identification. As for the integrity
of the text, anyone who has ever glanced at Fredson
Bower's *Textual and Literary Criticism* knows only too
well that even the most elementary physical features of
a modern printed page are open to question[6]; and the

scholar who examines two different editions of the same
mediaeval text will not seldom find discrepancies serious
enough to warrant mutually exclusive interpretations.

In different respects and from a different point of
view, the term *oral-formulaic* is almost as slippery as
the other terms in my title. A few decades ago—say,
after the pioneering views which Milman Parry had published in 1928, 1930, and 1932 had been substantiated by
Albert B. Lord in 1938 and applied to a new context by
Francis Peabody Magoun, Jr., in 1953[7]—it referred to the
recurrence of certain verbal, syntactic, and metrical
patterns whose high density in a poetic text was supposedly indicative of oral composition and whose formal
study was almost exclusively the property of scholars
concerned with Archaic Greek, South Slavic, and Old
English traditional poetry. Today, however, things are
no longer so clear-cut. Primarily as a result of the
formidable impact of Lord's *The Singer of Tales*—whose
first hard-cover edition appeared in 1960 and whose seventh paperback reprint was published in 1976—constant
and energetic research has both deepened and broadened
our understanding of the nature and mechanics of metrical
formulas as well as of such larger oral-formulaic units
as the song and the theme or type-scene; and Haymes' *Bibliography of the Oral Theory* shows that the study has
been extended to materials composed in some twenty different languages whose geography circles the entire globe.

Since 1973, for example, Joseph J. Duggan has drawn
upon the theory and facts of oral-formulaic composition
in order to solve previously insoluble problems in the
Song of Roland and has modified our concept of oral-
formulaic composition in the process[8]; Ching-Hsien Wang
has found in Chinese poetry "clear characteristics and
abundant traces of composition by themes, to an extent
comparable in technique to classical Greek and Old English poetry"[9]; Michael N. Nagler has examined oral-formulaic patterns in Homer as "an expression of the poet's
conscious or unconscious purpose, . . . part of his
'semiotic system'"[10]; John Miles Foley has used computer
analysis to show that "we may have to revise our thinking about 'mistakes' and 'inconsistencies'"[11] in texts
of oral-formulaic origin; Gregory Nagy has shown the relative importance of both synchronic and diachronic approaches "for solving the problem of formula and meter
in the study of oral poetry"[12] ; Jeff Opland has drawn
upon his field work among Xhosa tribal singers to de-

fine the relationship between "general improvising, memorizing, the refined improvising of the *imbongi*, and
writing"[13]; and the list of brilliant contributions could
be extended almost at will. The price of this intense
activity and quasi-geometric increase in scope and knowledge is that the meaning of the term *oral-formulaic* and
its relationship to oral composition are no longer certain. A few years before the publication of the investigations listed here, Walter J. Ong had already argued the
presence of legitimately oral-formulaic elements in Ren-
aissance prose composed in writing for the printing
press,[14] and at the opposite end of the spectrum of
scholarly convictions Larry D. Benson had argued with
equal authority that certain poems with a particularly
high density of oral-formulaic elements could not possibly have been the product of oral-formulaic composition.[15] The situation as it now stands has been neatly
summed up by Donald K. Fry in respect to Old English:
". . . a consensus seems to be emerging that written Old
English poetry used oral forms, but no reliable test can
differentiate written from oral poems."[16] In other
words, the term *oral-formulaic* may now be used by different scholars to refer to different degrees of orality.[17]

Since I have almost conclusively demonstrated that
my proposed subject does not exist, I suppose that I
should bring my discussion to an end right here. But
then, as I shall try to show in the remainder of my discussion, I see no reason to disagree with Lord's recent
statement that "the increase in the last few years in the
number of studies of oral literature is very encouraging."[18] Not only, once again in Lord's words, are we
"learning about many aspects of this phenomenon in many
hitherto either unexplored or inadequately described traditions" ("Perpsectives," p. 24), but the very multi-
plicity of directions taken by this new learning enables
us to draw upon the theories of oral-formulaists in order
to examine aspects of literature whose formal study would
have been assigned to totally different bailiwicks in the
days when the concerns of oral-formulaic investigation
were limited to inquiries into the mode of composition of
certain poems and the description of certain techniques.
For mediaevalists reluctant to reject the ideal of possible textual and contextual integrity—especially for
those engaged in the critical study of literature from a
comparative point of view—I believe that certain aspects

of oral-formulaic composition may occasionally prove
workable substitutes for, or additions to, the often
hypothetical and increasingly discredited geographic
and chronological contexts upon which we have been used
to rely for the interpretation of literary texts. I shall
now try to illustrate my contention and to suggest that,
in contradistinction to its geographic and chronological
counterparts, the oral-formulaic context can often be
stretched in many pragmatically convenient directions
without losing anything of its specificity or validity.

My assumption is that, even though the notion of
context may well be as arbitrary and controllable as
Hartman's argument seems to imply, the recognition of
some kind of objective context is nevertheless necessary
to intelligible interpretation. The context may, of
course, be either extrinsic or intrinsic, but the principle remains the same. In *The Wasps* of Aristophanes,
for example, a modern reader opening the book at the
point where the choryphaeus has urged Philocleon to seek
a way of escaping from his confinement and the latter has
answered "You seek it, for I'd do anything; I so long to
go about small boards with a little mussel" ("Ζητεῖϑ᾽
ὑμεῖς, ὡς πᾶν ἄν ἐγωγεποιοίην· / οὕτω κιττῶ διὰ τῶν
σανίδων μετὰ χοιρίνης περιελϑεῖν."[19]), might well draw upon information gathered from a handbook of tourism to
conclude that the intended context of Philocleon's wish-
ful statement is simply one of the famous seafood bars
of Madrid. Another reader, however, might construct the
extrinsic context from editorial commentary to the effect that in Aristophanes' time a χοιρίνη (*choirínē*) was
a small sea-mussel used by the Athenian dicasts in vot-
ing.[20] We need not surmise here which of the two contexts may prove more appropriate to our interpretation of
the passage, but we must recognize that the tone and in
part the action itself will be decidedly affected by our
choice of one or the other. The same principle applies
to the effect of intrinsic context, as may be illustrated
with Chaucer's use of the auditory image of a thunderclap in both *The Miller's Tale* and *Troilus and Criseyde*.
In the former, the image describes a massive flatulence
delivered point-blank into the face of a ridiculous
small-town parish clerk who has been characterized a little earlier as "somdeel squaymous / Of farting"[21] and has
spent nearly an entire day preparing himself for a bout
of romantic love with a concupiscible young woman. I do
not think that I am offering more than a reminder in

pointing out that, within this context, the image of a
thunderclap clinches the lustily farcical tone of the
whole episode, and I hope to be forgiven for suggesting
that one needs only read Chaucer's words to appreciate
the full olfactory quality of the action:

> This Nicolas anon leet fle a fart,
> As greet as it had been a *thonder-dent*,
> That with the strook he was almost yblent. (3806-8)

In the latter, the very same image describes a blast co-
incident with the glorious death of a proud knight on the
battlefield before Thebes, and it concludes a descriptive
list of the heroes who died there. Within this context,
it inescapably brings to mind the detonation of artillery
as well as the opaque smoke and acrid smell of the black
powder used in the cannons of Chaucer's time; and, in so
doing, it emphasizes the noble futility of heroic reck-
lessness:

> She tolde ek how Hemonydes asterte,
> Whan Tideus slough fifty knightes stoute.
> She tolde ek . . . .
> . . . .
> How Tideus was sleyn, lord of Argeyes,
> And how Ypomedoun in litel stounde
> Was dreynt, and ded Parthonope of wownde;
> And also how Capaneus the proude
> With *thonder-dynt* was slayn, that cride loude.
> (V, 1492-1505)

The image remains the same in both cases, but the action
which it evokes and the tone which it governs in *The
Miller's Tale* are vastly different from their counterparts in the *Troilus*, so that an interpretation totally
unrelated to the factual context of either would probably
be unintelligible to anyone but its author.

We must note that in the foregoing instances the alternative contexts have affected the significance of a
seashell and a loud noise, respectively, by enabling us
to relate these to actually or vicariously familiar situations which are wont to evoke certain predictable responses in us. This function of context happens to correspond precisely to one of the functions which scholars
have attributed to oral-formulaic elements in poetry. As
early as 1955, for example, Stanley Greenfield wrote that
"the association with other contexts using a similar

formula will inevitably color a particular instance of a
formula so that a whole host of overtones springs into
action. . . ."[22]   Since that time, Adrien Bonjour has argued that the effective use of an oral-formulaic theme
makes the audience see things "in advance, and thereby
implies deeper connotations,"[23] and Fry has pointed out
that these themes "provide the audience with a supply of
associations. . . ."[24]   More recently, Foley has shown
that the presence of a particular formula is likely to
affect our reaction to "speech and character by locating
them with relation to archetypal paradigms"("Formula and
Theme," p. 218).   The fact is that—regardless of the
ways in which one may wish to define the term *oral-formulaic*—a given narrative element gets to be labeled "formulaic" as a result of some kind of repetition. We know,
of course, that the repetition need not be immediately
apparent. To draw an obvious example from what is probably the best-known oral-formulaic statement of Old English poetry: "X (nominative) *maðelode, bearn* Y (genitive)," the letters *X* and *Y* may stand for any two of an
almost infinite number of alliterating names, and even
the structure of the statement may be changed along with
the alliterative pattern, as in the case of "X (nominative) *maðelode*, Y (genitive) *sunu.*" Nevertheless, one
need not have been a student of Old English very long to
recognize the basic pattern and to come to expect it under certain circumstances; conversely one soon learns to
expect the circumstances whenever the formulaic pattern
turns up. Unless we wish to assume oral-formulaic poetry
to be usually composed for audiences completely unfamiliar with the system of composition, we have to grant the
likelihood that the audience of that poetry would be better attuned to both the patterns and the circumstances
than most academic students are likely to be,[25] and we
may even suppose that a gifted oral-formulaic poet thoroughly familiar with his materials and techniques might
wish to shape these materials so as to take advantage of
the familiarity and expectations of his audience. To put
the same thing differently, what I am suggesting is that
the particular oral-formulaic elements within a given
poem are likely to be apprehended—at least by the intended audience—within the context of familiar occurrences of the same elements and, under these circumstances, may be said to function very much like the extrinsic and intrinsic contexts which I have discussed in
respect to Aristophanes and Chaucer.

Since I have already mentioned that scholars are by
no means agreed that the presence of oral-formulaic elements should be taken as incontrovertible proof of oral
composition, I should point out now that the validity of
the views which I have advanced does not depend on the
actual mode of composition of whatever texts may happen
to fall under the critic's scrutiny. I should admittedly
be a happier man if I knew for a fact that the texts with
which I must deal were first-hand records of oral performances, but the principles outlined here would apply
almost as well to texts composed on a typewriter, as
long as these texts were demonstrably composed in accord-
ance with oral-formulaic techniques and addressed to an
audience consciously or unconsciously familiar with these
techniques either through the ear or through the eye. In
a different context, Lord has suggested that the transition from heroic to religious poetry in Anglo-Saxon England may well have resulted in the composition of what he
calls "'transitional' or 'mixed'" poems, and he has drawn
on Fry's work to surmise that "the audience for the poems
must have been still enough of a traditional audience to
feel that the working out of these models was right"
("Perspectives," p. 24). I submit that, to a certain
extent, the same principle may be considered to apply to
the transition from oral performance to written composition, unless we posit a situation in which both poets and
audiences forget every aspect of their common tradition
the moment someone brings the first pen and ink within
the community.

Of course, one need not accept the foregoing argument or any part thereof. To the extent that we accept
it, however, we must also accept the concomitant claim
that, for the critical study of both oral and written
texts composed under the conditions outlined here, the
oral-formulaic context can be altogether as specific and
relevant as its chronological and geographic counterparts. Furthermore, because oral-formulaic patterns retain their integrity over long periods of time, attesta-
tions necessarily accumulate in the records and may provide a rich context for works whose immediate chronological context happens to be poverty-stricken. This fact
is precisely what has enabled Fry to produce a particularly masterful study of *Cædmon's Hymn* by, in his own
words, "using post-Cædmonian verses to explain Cædmon"
("Cædmon," p. 60). Since the integrity of certain oral-
formulaic patterns seems to endure in various branches

of the same family, the oral-formulaic context may at
times prove, not merely relevant, but indeed indispensable when the literary critic happens to be a comparatist
working with texts drawn from several literatures; and
whatever truth there may be in my statement becomes even
truer when our hypothetical critic-comparatist further
happens to be one of the many mediaevalists working with
documents whose dates of composition are very much in
doubt.

The point which I have been trying to make may be
illustrated with a brief examination of the function of
the same oral-formulaic theme in the Archaic Greek *Odyssey*, the Old English *Beowulf*, and the Old German *Song of
Hildebrand*. The oral-formulaic quality of both the Greek
and the English poems has received so much attention in
the past few decades that it needs no further discussion
here, and Haymes has convincingly argued that the German
poem "does belong to the improvisory oral-formulaic tradition that produced Old-English epics and the *Heliand*."[32]
Although I readily confess that I have not the slightest
notion regarding the respective dates and places of composition of the poems under consideration, we can safely
say that the received texts were probably copied down
more than a millenium apart.[27] Since there is no compelling reason to think that the composers or scribes of
the English and German texts were directly imitating each
other or the *Odyssey*,[28] and I seriously doubt that Homer
kept annotated copies of *Beowulf* and the *Song of Hildebrand* by his bedside, I submit that we have here a case
where the comparatist may do at least as well by working
within the factual oral-formulaic context as he would
within the hypothetical chronological context.

The theme which I have in mind was first pointed out
by Robert P. Creed in an extremely important essay which
he published in 1962[29] and in which he called attention
to basic but yet unrecognized similarities between, on
the one hand, the performance of the poet Demodocus, in
the *Odyssey*, when he composes orally in front of Odysseus
himself an account of the exploits of Odysseus and, on
the other hand, the performance of an unnamed Danish poet
who, in *Beowulf*, composes in front of Beowulf himself an
account of the exploits of Beowulf. Creed's essay shows
that the resultant type-scene occurs explicitly once in
Beowulf (871b-74a: after the visit to Grendel's Pond, the
morning after Beowulf has wounded Grendel to death) and
twice in the *Odyssey* (VIII, 72-82: immediately before the

Phaeacean Games; and VIII, 499-520: beyond Demodocus' account of the love affair between Ares and Aphrodite, immediately after the reconciliation between Odysseus and
Euryalus).[30]   In addition to the obvious parallelism of
the initial situation, the principal thematic similarities between the Greek and Old English episodes may be
summed up as follows.

1) *In both texts, the narrator within the poem composes a
story orally:* we have in effect a smaller oral narrative
within a longer narrative, or a mini-epic within an epic.

2) *In both texts, the hero whose exploits are recounted
in the mini-epic has travelled far and wide and has only
recently reached the location where the recounting is
taking place:* most recently, Odysseus has sailed from
Calypso's homeland, and Beowulf from his own native
country.

3) *In both texts, the recounting takes place in the pres-
ence of a substantial crowd:* at the court of King
Alcinous in the *Odyssey*, and among riders returning from
Grendel's Pond in *Beowulf*.

4) *In both texts, the hero must face a challenge of
physical strength soon after the completion of the story
to which he is listening:* after the first recounting,
Odysseus is insultingly prodded by Laodamas and Euryalus
into competing in the Phaeacian Games, and after the second recounting and a brief sea-crossing to Ithaka he has
to face the suitors in his own home; the day after the
recounting, Beowulf dives into Grendel's Pond, where he
must meet Grendel's Mother in mortal combat.

5) *In both texts, the occasion has the makings of a joyful scene and is celebrated as such:* in the *Odyssey*, the
first recounting takes place during the feast which King
Alcinous arranges to welcome the stranger Odysseus (e.g.,
VIII, 40-43), and the second takes place during the feast
that follows the Phaeacian Games; in *Beowulf*, the recounting is part of the festivities with which the Danes greet
the undoing of Grendel.

6) *In both texts, the story-teller and the hero are
totally unrelated strangers, but the former nevertheless
succeeds in retelling the latter's adventures as they
really happened:* in the *Odyssey*, both recountings are so
true to facts that Odysseus weeps upon hearing them

(VIII, 92 and 531); and, in *Beowulf*, the hero's adventure is specifically said to be recounted *"on sped"* (873a).

Creed's perceptive analysis reveals additional similarities, but those listed above will do for my immediate purpose. Because his primary concern was the actual act of *singing* rather than the thematic situation regardless of the mode of performance, his essay necessarily kept clear from possible occurrences of the theme in which the story-telling might not explicitly take the form of a song. Because I am primarily concerned with the theme rather than with the explicit mode of performance of the story within the story, I should like to point out that the very same pattern occurs in the flyting between Unferth and Beowulf (499a-529b). In addition to the same initial situation, we find that (1) Unferth explicitly tells (499a) his story orally (2) in front of Beowulf, who has come from far away and has only now entered (402a-403a) Heorot; (3) the recounting takes place in the presence of a large group of Danes and Weders (498a-b); (4) Beowulf answers Unferth's insulting account by reasserting his intention to fight Grendel (601b-6b), whose challenge he will actually meet a few lines later (745b-823a); (5) the occasion is a joyful feast (497b) filled with the laughter of warriors (611b); and (6) Unferth and Beowulf are totally unrelated strangers, but the former nevertheless succeeds in telling a belittling story that has just enough of an air of truth to send the latter flying into a rage and prompt him to offer his own interpretation of nearly the same facts (530a-83a).

Since the *Song of Hildebrand* is not such a familiar part of the common repertory as the *Odyssey* and *Beowulf*, I am outlining its contents here for the same of communication: *Two warriors named Hildebrand and Hadubrand meet alone between two armies. When asked to identify himself, Hadubrand answers that his father, who was named Hildebrand and thirty years ago left a woman and a young child behind to follow Dietrich von Bern in exile, was the best of warriors and is probably long dead. Realizing that he is facing his own son, Hildebrand tries to conciliate him, but the other answers with insults and reasserts his conviction that the real Hildebrand died in battle. Hildebrand then notes the bitter irony in the fact that he, whom no warrior could ever kill in battle,*

must now be killed by his own son unless he kills him
first; and the poem comes to an end with the two oppon-
ents hewing at each other with their weapons. From the
testimony of Saxo Grammaticus and the *Saga of Ásmund the*
Champion-Killer, we know that the Hildebrand of the legend does in fact kill Hadubrand,[31] and it is difficult
not to assume at least a modicum of audience familiarity
with a subject whose lasting popularity with the Indo-
European world is attested by analogues in the Old Irish
The Death of Aife's One Son, the Persian *Book of Kings*,
and some forty Russian variants.[32] The assumption becomes especially tempting when we recall that the episode outlined here is part of the Cycle of Dietrich von
Bern, which remained for centuries a favorite of Germanic
audiences.[33]

Even if one wishes to set aside Matthew Arnold's
version of the story[34] as unrelated to the present argument, the literary critic is thus provided with a familiar context within which to examine the subject matter of
the *Song of Hildebrand*, and there is a statistical likelihood that Germanic audiences would at some point have
shared that familiarity, though obviously not through the
study of texts yet to be composed in languages other than
their own. A similar argument may be advanced in respect
to the theme of the story-teller performing in front of
the live hero of his own story. Although the fact that a
certain pattern occurs twice in an Archaic Greek poem,
twice again in an Old English poem,[35] and once in an Old
German poem might conceivably be dismissed as purely
coincidental, the additional fact that similar recur-
rences of patterns are by no means uncommon between these
two linguistic and chronological areas[36] would seem to
put the burden of proof upon the proponents of coincidence. Even though the scarcity of extant recorded
documents necessarily makes reliable statistics out of
the question, one may reasonably assume the probability
of some kind of audience familiarity with an oral-formulaic theme which—once again barring the likelihood of
conscious borrowing—seems to have exhibited enough vitality to remain in use within the same linguistic family
for over a millenium and probably much longer. The factual presence of a theme within a poem, however, does not
necessarily mean that it will be critically recorded by
the scholar, the reader, or the listener, for recent investigation has demonstrated that consumers of literature
tend to notice mostly those aspects of a given text which

they are cued in to expect or to seek out.[37]   In the case
of the *Song of Hildebrand*, the scholar is cued in to expect formulaic elements with the opening statement—"Ik
gihorta ðat seggen" ("I heard that told")[38] —whose Old
English equivalent has been shown by Magoun to be the
most common oral-formulaic opening statement in the surviving corpus ("Oral-Formulaic Character," 453).

     With these observations out of the way, we may now
turn to the form under which the theme under consideration appears in the *Song of Hildebrand* and to its function therein.   As my outline may have suggested, the
narrator of the story within the story is Hadubrand, who
answers a request for self-identification with a mini-
epic (15a-29) about Hildebrand's wanderings and the cause
thereof (18a-b), his loneliness (24b) away from the woman
and little child necessarily left behind (20a-22a), his
brave deeds in the service of Dietrich (22b-24a; 25a-27b),
his fame among bold warriors (28a-b), and his having presumably met with death by now (29):

> 15) dat sagetun mi   usere liuti,
>   alte anti frote,   dea erhina warun,
>   dat Hiltibrant hætti min fater: ih heittu
>   Hadubrant.
>
> 18) forn her ostar giweit,   floh her Otachres nid,
>   hina miti Theotrihhe   enti sinero degano filu.
>
> 20) her furlaet in lante   luttila sitten
>   prut in bure   barn unwahsan,
>
> 22) arbeo laosa: her raet ostar hina.
>   sid Detrihhe   darba gistuontun
>
> 24) fateres mines: dat uuas so friuntlaos man.
>   her was Otachre   ummet tirri,
>   degano dechisto   miti Deotrichhe.
>
> 27) her was eo folches at ente: imo was eo fehta
>   ti leop:
>
> 28) chud was her . . .   chonnem mannum.
>
> 29) ni waniu ih iu lib habbe.

[(15) Our people told me that—the old and wise ones
who used to be around here—that my father was named
Hildebrand: I am named Hadubrand. (18) He went
east—he fled from Odoacer's hostility—away from

here with Dietrich and many of his warriors. (20)
He abandoned in this country a wretched young son
at his wife's home, (22) deprived of his inheritance: he rode east from here. Eventually Dietrich
stood in need (24) of my father. That was a man quite
without friends; he was utterly furious with Odoacer.
The best of warriors with Dietrich, (27) he was always at the forefront of the host: fighting was always dear to him. (28) He was famous among bold
men. (29) I do not think that he is still alive.][39]

As in the case of the *Odyssey* and *Beowulf*, the initial situation conforms to Creed's description, since the
story-teller recounts the hero's adventures in front of
the hero himself; and, with two important exceptions, the
remaining circumstances likewise conform to the paradigm
which I have drawn from the Greek and English poems. For
the sake of convenience, I am listing each point of comparison in the same order which I used above for these
two texts.

1) *As in the other texts, the narrator within the German
poem composes his story orally*: we are told that "Hadubrand *spoke*" (14a).

2) *As in the other texts, the hero whose adventures are
recounted in the German poem has travelled far and wide
and has only recently reached the location where the recounting is taking place*: Hildebrand has "wandered sixty
summers and winters" (50a-b) since he rode away eastward
(19a; 22b), and the fact that the two warriors have just
met (2a-b) and do not yet know each other's identity
(8b-10) makes it obvious that he has only now arrived on
the spot.

3) *As in the other texts, the recounting in the German
poem takes place in the presence of a substantial crowd*:
specifically, in this case, "between two armies" (3b).

4) *As in the other texts, the hero in the German poem
must face a challenge of physical strength soon after
the completion of the story to which he is listening*:
his attempt at conciliation by offering some precious
rings to his antagonist meets with the intractable answer that gifts from treacherous old men can only be
received "spear-point against spear-point" (38), and the
result of this challenge is the mortal combat in which

the two must face each other at the end of the poem
(63a-68).

5) *As in the other texts, the occasion in the German poem
has the makings of a joyful scene*: in a society that attaches importance to the relationship between father and
son, few things are likely to give greater cause for joy
than the unexpected reunion of the two after a long and
cruel separation. *In contrast to the other texts, however, the meeting results in mortal combat rather than in
joyful celebration.*

6)*Again in contrast to the other texts, the story-teller
and the hero in the German poem are bound by the closest
possible blood relationship, but the former nevertheless
succeeds in including in his story a crucial piece of
gross misinformation*: he states of the man to whom he is
talking, "I do not think that he is still alive" (29).

    I believe that the two differences mentioned here
are central to our critical understanding of the function of the passage under discussion. Since (a) the
several points occur in the order in which I have listed
them, (b) Hadubrand does not actually challenge Hildebrand until eight lines after the conclusion of the story
within a story, and (c) the mistaken statement that he
assumes his father to be dead comes only with the very
last line of the story within a story, an audience consciously or unconsciously used to the implications of the
theme embodied here would initially expect a recognition
followed by the joyful scene appropriate to the occasion.
But an audience likewise familiar with the legend of
Hildebrand would also know that the father must kill the
son, and it would presumably be sensible to the dissonance between the facts of the story and the expectations
created by the oral-formulaic theme. Unfortunately, I
have no means of ascertaining exactly how the dissonance
in question would have affected the Carolingian readers
for whom the only extant text of the *Song of Hildebrand*
was copied down, and I know even less about the audiences
for whom the ancestors of that text were composed.[40] As
a teacher of literature, however, I know very well how
this dissonance affects me in a way which I can communi-
cate objectively to my students. By calling to my attention the unnatural character of the action, it stresses
the deeply moving fact that what ought rightfully to be a
joyful reunion between an old warrior of heroic stature

and his brave son must turn into the ultimate separation
of death, and the tension thus created remains unsur-
passed in Western literature. Even before Hadubrand's
challenge to Hildebrand, the depth of the separation between father and son is emphasized comparatively by the
fact that, in pronouncing the former long dead, the latter makes us see that he knows less about him than his
counterparts in the other manifestations of the same
theme know about perfect strangers. These observations
in turn alert us to a host of details which imply Hildebrand's separation from practically everything dear to
early Germanic warriors and thus enables us to appreciate
his situation against the emotion-charged background of
the many Germanic poems in which a man or a woman must
endure the bitter pangs of separation.[41] This is no
place to defend the implied interpretation of the poem,
but we must note that this interpretation is possible
only if we supplement the completely hypothetical and
practically nonexistent geographic and chronological contexts by the tangibly attested context of an oral-formulaic theme.

A word about my choice of an illustrative theme is
appropriate at this point, for I have argued elsewhere
that—contrary to what might mistakenly be inferred from
the foregoing analysis—the central oral-formulaic theme
of the *Song of Hildebrand* is, not that in which the
story-teller must face the subject of his story, but
rather one known as "the hero on the beach," which is
probably the second most common oral-formulaic theme in
Germanic poetry, is attested in both mediaeval English
and mediaeval German, and has been so often investigated
since 1960 that it no longer needs an introduction.[42] The
reason for my choice of the less appropriate theme was my
wish to suggest an additional respect in which the oral-
formulaic context may prove of special importance to the
literary tradition at the end of the twentieth century.
As already pointed out, the respective dates of the extant recorded texts of the works which I have used to
illustrate the critical implications of the theme span
more than a millennium. If we wish to be somewhat less
cautious and argue on the assumption that the Homeric
poems may have been composed around the seventh century,
B.C., and that the only manuscript of *Beowulf* may have
been copied down as recently as the tenth century A.D.,
we may then venture to say that our theme occurs over a
period of about 1600 years in works which were vital

enough to be the property of the general public rather
than that of a few specialized scholars isolated from
the mainstream of their respective cultures. If we also
keep in mind that the texts examined here have come to us
in three different languages used respectively in three
different geographic locations, we are tempted to conclude that the oral-formulaic approach to relevant works
of literature may provide us with an objective context
while affording us a great deal of freedom from both
geography and chronology. In respect to the Western
World, my statement applies especially to scholars concerned with the Middle Ages and Antiquity, but I am not
at all certain that these limitations are with us to
stay. As David Bynum has reminded us in a recent book,
the amount of oral composition that goes on daily around
the world is much greater than we tend to assume,[43] and
the random samples of research in oral-formulaic composition which I have listed toward the beginning of this essay allow us to entertain some reasonable hope that the
joint efforts of field workers and philologists will
eventually find objectively significant points of comparison between genetically unrelated dead and live traditions. Insofar as the oral-formulaic approach enables us
to handle vast areas of literature, it offers us an alternative to the critical theories mentioned at the outset of this essay, but it differs from them in two essential respects. The first is that it provides a
flexible but *specific* context whose integrity is readily
ascertainable and against which we may in turn measure
the integrity of a given text,[44] about which we are thus
enabled to make reasonably objective statements. The
second is that it provides us with the means for understanding certain aspects of ancient texts through legitimate comparison with more modern texts. In contradistinction, the critical theories which are gaining popularity today make it very difficult to examine ancient
literature, which usually demands close attention to both
text and context, and the fact is that nearly all the
practitioners of these theories are dedicated modernists.
Some years ago, Harry Levin remarked before an audience
of comparatists that, "having taken all literature for
our province, we need special bibliographies rather than
an *omnium gatherum*."[45] For the same reason, we need
special techniques, and the techniques developed by the
students of oral-formulaic composition and related matters are among those that may help us retain something

of our rapidly vanishing literary tradition. For those who would agree with Cicero that a human being without a past is doomed to remain a child,[46] the work of Milman Parry, Albert B. Lord, and their followers may conceivably prove one of the few remaining means whereby literary education can contribute to the formation of culturally responsible grown-ups.

University of California at Berkeley

NOTES

[1]"Literature in the Reader: Affective Stylistics," *NLH*, 2(1970), 140.

[2]"War in Heaven: a Review of Harold Bloom's 'The Anxiety of Influence: a Theory of Poetry'," in Hartman, *The Fate of Reading and Other Essays* (Chicago, 1975), p. 41; this review, incidentally, is not totally uncritical of Bloom's methods. One might wish to note that Hartman's book has itself been praised for its "gleeful unintelligibility" in a review by Richard Poirier, *NYTBR*, April 20, 1975, p. 21.

[3]For discussions of the trends treated here, see, e.g., William H. Pritchard, "The Hermeneutical Mafia or, After Strange Gods at Yale," *HudR*, 28(1975-76), 601-10, who refers to the critical enterprise of Hartman and his colleagues as a "hermeneutical shindig" (610) which "attempts to frisk students of their principles as naive or enthusiastic readers" (601). In a particularly witty and brilliant essay, Gerald Graff, "Fear and Trembling at Yale," *ASch*, 46(1977), 467-78, recognizes the importance of these trends but sees in them a "literary quarrel with the objective way of knowing" (477). Michael André Bernstein aptly points out in the work of one practitioner a "desire to preserve uncertainty from any contamination by 'sense' or'meaning'," in "Jonathan Culler and the Limits of Uncertainty," *Poetics*, 3(1977), 593.

[4]"The Interpreter: a Self-Analysis," in *The Fate of Reading*, p. 14.

[5]"The Ideal Reader: a Critical Fiction," *PMLA*, 93 (1978), 463; an excellent bibliography of the subject is given on 473, n. 1.

[6](Cambridge, 1959). He calls attention to such things as, e.g., "about a hundred inconsistencies and errors in the first printing of Sinclair Lewis's novel *Babbitt*" (p. 19).

[7] Parry, *L'Épithète traditionnelle dans Homère (The Traditional Epithet in Homer)*, in *MHV*, pp. 1-190; *Les formules et la métrique d'Homère (Homeric Formulae and Homeric Meter)*, in *MHV*, pp. 191-239; "Studies in the Epic Technique of Oral Verse-Making. I. Homer and Homeric Style," in *MHV*, pp. 266-324; "Studies in the Epic Technique of Oral Verse-Making. II. The Homeric Language as the Language of an Oral Poetry," in *MHV*, pp. 325-64; Lord, "Homer and Huso II: Narrative Inconsistencies in Homer and Oral Poetry," *TAPA*, 69(1938), 439-45; Magoun, "The Oral-Formulaic Character of Anglo-Saxon Narrative Poetry,"*Speculum*, 28(1953), 446-67.

[8] *The Song of Roland: Formulaic Style and Poetic Craft* (Berkeley, 1973).

[9] *The Bell and the Drum: Shih Ching as Formulaic Poetry in an Oral Tradition* (Berkeley, 1974), p. 128.

[10] *Spontaneity and Tradition: a Study in the Oral Art of Homer* (Berkeley, 1974), p. xxiv.

[11] "Formula and Theme in Old English Poetry," in *OL&F*, p. 231.

[12] "Formula and Meter," in *OL&F*, p. 256. See further his *Comparative Studies in Greek and Indic Meter* (Cambridge, Mass., 1976).

[13] "*Imbongi Nezibongo*: the Xhosa Tribal Poet and the Contemporary Poetic Tradition," *PMLA*, 90(1975), 187.

[14] "Oral Residue in Tudor Prose Style," *PMLA*, 80(1965), argues, e.g., that "the oral elements ... in Tudor prose are akin to those in the *Iliad* and the *Odyssey*" (153).

[15] "The Literary Character of Anglo-Saxon Formulaic Poetry," *PMLA*, 81(1966), argues that we may no longer have "any lingering suspicion that the relative percentage of formulas might be used to distinguish between oral and lettered productions" (336).

[16] "Cædmon as a Formulaic Poet," in *OLSE*, p. 41.

[17] See, e.g., F. H. Whitman, "The Meaning of 'Formulaic' in Old English Verse Composition," *NM*, 76(1975), 529-37.

[18] "Perspectives on Recent Work on Oral Literature," in *OLSE*, p. 24.

[19] Aristophanes, *The Wasps*, ed. by C. E. Graves (Cambridge, 1899), ll. 348-39.

[20] Henry G. Liddell and Robert Scott, *A Greek-English Lexicon*, rev. by Henry S. Jones (Oxford, 1961).

[21] Geoffrey Chaucer, *The Miller's Tale*, ll. 3337-38; this and all subsequent quotations from Chaucer are from *The Works of Geoffrey Chaucer*, ed. by Fred N. Robinson

(Cambridge, 1957).

[22] "The Formulaic Expression of the Theme of 'Exile' in Anglo-Saxon Poetry," *Speculum*, 30(1955), 205.

[23] "*Beowulf* and the Beasts of Battle," *PMLA*, 72 (1957), 566.

[24] "The Heroine on the Beach in *Judith*," *NM*, 68 (1967), 181.

[25] John Miles Foley, "*Beowulf* and the Psychohistory of Anglo-Saxon Culture," *AI*, 34(1977), convincingly argues that "the traditional oral society educates its members—that is, it provides them with necessary information—through the repeated and collective experience of performed epic poetry, by presenting them time and again with a verbal montage of the group's poetic models and thereby with the data which these models encode" (134), and again that "the psychohistorical matrix which underlines and generates the epic narrative remains available to all members of the society through repeated oral performance" (153).

[26] "Oral Poetry and the Germanic *Heldenlied*," *RUS*, 62(1976), 52. From a totally different point of view, the relationship of the German poem to Old English poetic practices was first analyzed in Moritz Trautmann's influential study, *Finn und Hildebrand* (Bonn, 1903), pp. 67-131. I have reconsidered this relationship from the point of view of a central oral-formulaic theme in my "The English Connection Revisited: a Reading Context for the *Hildebrandslied*," *Neophil*, 63(1979), 84-87.

[27] According to Roger A. Pack, *Greek and Latin Literary Texts from Greco-Roman Egypt* (Ann Arbor, 1952), pp. 39-42, the earliest extant papyri of the *Odyssey* are dated in the second century B.C. The only extant manuscript of the *Song of Hildebrand* is usually dated in the early ninth century, e.g., by Elias von Steinmeyer, ed., *Die kleineren althochdeutschen Sprachdenkmäler* (Berlin, 1916), who places it "wahrscheinlich im zweiten Dezenium des 9. Jh." (p. 8). The only manuscript of *Beowulf* is usually dated in the tenth century, e.g., by Elliott Van Kirk Dobbie, ed., *Beowulf and Judith*, Anglo-Saxon Poetic Records, vol. 4 (New York, 1953), who places it "at the end of the tenth century" (p. ix), although scholars generally assume it to be a copy of an earlier text which, as Stanley B, Greenfield writes in his *A Critical History of Old English Literature* (New York, 1965), "probably existed in the middle of the eighth century" (p. 82).

[28] Even if all three poets had known each other, we should keep in mind that modern views on imitation and originality are not readily applicable to poetry composed within an oral-formulaic tradition. As Lord writes in *Singer*, "the truth of the matter is that our concept of 'the original,' of 'the song,' simply makes no sense in oral tradition" (p. 101); even in cases where a story is the object "of direct transmission without any intervening period of time" (p. 102), the resultant text follows the original only "fairly closely in terms of basic story" (p. 102), so that "in a variety of ways a song in tradition is separate, yet inseparable from other songs" (p. 123). In reference to Old English traditional poetry, I have tried to argue in my "Originality, Influence, Imitation: Two Mediaeval Phases," in François Jost, ed., *Proceedings of the IVth Congress of the International Comparative Literature Association* (The Hague, 1966), that "the concepts of imitation, influence, and originality have practically no value for the criticism of the oral-formulaic phase of mediaeval literature" (II, 741). One might, of course, argue the influence of Homer upon *Beowulf* through Virgil, since the case for the influence of the *Æneid* upon the English poem has been given a new lease on life in Theodore M. Andersson's fine *Early Epic Scenery: Homer, Virgil, and the Medieval Legacy* (Ithaca, 1976), with a chapter entitled "The Virgilian Heritage in *Beowulf*" (pp. 145-59). Although Andersson's argument in favor of Virgilian influence is the most compelling which I have read in recent years, I retain on the subject of classical influences on *Beowulf* reservations which I have expressed in my "The Terror of the Dark Waters: a Note on Virgilian and Beowulfian Techniques," *HES*, 5(1974), espec. 147-50.

[29] "The Singer Looks at His Sources," *CL*, 14(1962), 44-52; rpt. in Stanley B. Greenfield, ed., *Studies in Old English Literature in Honor of Arthur G. Brodeur* (Eugene, rpt. 1963), pp. 44-52.

[30] All references to *Beowulf* and the *Odyssey* are, respectively, to *Beowulf and Judith*, ed. by Dobbie, and to *Homeri Odyssea*, ed. by Guilielmus Dindorf (Leipzig, 1899).

[31] Saxo Grammaticus, *Gesta Danorum*, ed. by Jørgen Olrik and Hans R. Rœder (Copenhagen, 1931), I, 204; *Ásmundarsaga Kappabana*, ch. 8, in Ferdinand Dieter, ed., *Zwei Fornaldarsögur* (Halle, 1891).

[32] For discussions of the relationship between

versions in different languages, see, e.g., Georg
Baesecke, "Die indogermanischen Verwandtschaften des
Hildebrandliedes," *NAWG*, Phil.-Hist., n.F., 3(1940),
139-53; Jan De Fries, "Das Motiv des Vater-Sohn-Kampfes
im Hildebrandslied," *GRM*, 24(1953), 257-74; and A. T.
Hatto, "On the Excellence of the *Hildebrandslied*: A Comparative Study in Dynamics," *MLR*, 68(1973), 820-38. A
version with a different ending is recorded in the Middle
High German *Jüngeres Hildebrandslied*, in Elias von
Steinmeyer, ed., *Denkmäler deutscher Poesie und Prosa
aus VIII-XII Jahrhundert*(Berlin, 1892), II, 26-30, and
in the *þidriks Saga af Bern*, ed. by Henrik Bertelsen
(Copenhagen, 1905), V, 348-52 (chs. 407-10).

[33] See, e.g., Georges Zink, *Les légendes héroiques de
Dietrich et d'Ermrich dans les littératures germaniques*
(Paris, 1950), espec. pp. 225-68.

[34] Matthew Arnold, *Sohrab and Rustum*, in *The Poems of
Matthew Arnold*, ed. by Kenneth Allott (London, 1965), pp.
302-31, is based on the *Book of Kings* and treats the
materials of the *Song of Hildebrand* in ll. 1-508.

[35] Since Hrothgar subsequently praises Beowulf's
deeds after the latter's victory over Grendel's mother
(1700a-84b) and we can later learn that he actually composed a song (2105a-15a) on that occasion, one might conceivably wish to argue that the theme in question occurs
implicitly a third time in the poem.

[36] In addition to those works of Lord's already cited
above (e.g., the section on *Beowulf* in his *Singer*, pp.
198-202), see his "Beowulf and Odysseus," in *Franciplegius*, pp. 86-91. In a paper presented before the 1963 annual meeting of the Philological Association of the Pa-
cific Coast, Michael N. Nagler pointed out thematic similarities between Odysseus' encounter with Polyphemus and
Beowulf's encounter with Grendel's mother; a modified
version of this paper is included in his "*Beowulf* in the
Context of Myth," in *Old English Literature in Context:
Ten Essays*, ed. by John D. Niles (London and Totowa, New
Jersey: Boydell-Brewer and Rowman and Littlefield,
1980), forthcoming. In my "Oral Theme and Written
Texts," *NM*, 77(1976), 337-46, I have tried to argue the
presence of the same oral-formulaic theme in the *Odyssey*
and two different Old English poems.

[37] E.g., Norman N. Holland, *Poems in Persons* (New
York, 1973), discusses the ways in which "a reader re-
creates a literary work" (pp. 99-100).

[38] *Das Hildebrandslied*, in Wilhelm Braune, ed.,

Althochdeutsches Lesebuch, rev. by Karl Helm (Halle, 1949), pp. 72-73; the translation is from Haymes' "Oral Poetry and the Germanic *Heldenlied*," 50; subsequent translations are my own.

[39] My translation must perforce be arbitrary whenever the text is ambiguous (e.g., l. 21a, where *prut* has been construed as either a genitive or an accusative), but my argument does not depend on the choice of one alternative rather than another in this passage.

[40] Scholars have argued in favor of ancestors in Old English (Trautmann, *Finn und Hildebrand*, with reconstruction on pp. 121-23), Longobardic (Willy Krogman, *Das Hildebrandslied in der langobardischen Urfassung hergestellt* [Berlin, 1959], with reconstruction on pp. 47-49), and Gothic (Richard H. Lawson, "The *Hildebrandslied* Originally Gothic?" *NM*, 74 [1973], espec. 339). The prevalent opinion is summed up by Hatto, "Excellence," 820, with the statement that the extant text is a "'Saxonized' version of a (scribal) Bavarian version of an original (oral) Longobardic lay."

[41] A documented discussion of this aspect of the poem will be found in my "Germanic Quintessence: the Theme of Isolation in the *Hildebrandslied*," in Margot King and Wesley M. Stevens, eds., *Saints, Scholars, and Heroes* (St. John, 1979), pp. 143-78.

[42] See my "The Armor of the *Hildebrandslied*: an Oral-Formulaic Point of View," *NM*, 78(1977), 389-95. The theme of the hero on the beach was isolated and discussed by David K. Crowne, "The Hero on the Beach: an Example of Composition by Theme in Anglo-Saxon Poetry," *NM*, 61 (1960), 362-72. Crowne's study has been followed by, e.g., my "Oral-Formulaic Theme Survival: a Possible Instance in the *Nibelungenlied*," *NM*, 65(1964), 70-74; Fry, "The Hero on the Beach in *Finnsburh*," *NM*, 67(1966), 27-31; "The Heroine on the Beach in *Judith*," *NM*, 68(1967), 168-84; and "Themes and Type-Scenes in *Elene* 1-113," *Speculum*, 44(1969), 35-45; Janet Thormann, "Variations on the Theme of 'The Hero on the Beach' in *The Phoenix*," *NM*, 71(1970), 187-90; Carol J. Wolf, "Christ as Hero in *The Dream of the Rood*," *NM*, 71(1970), 202-10; and James D. Johnson, "The Hero on the Beach in the Alliterative *Morte Arthur*," *NM*, 76(1975), 271-81. The only theme more commonly attested is that of the Beasts of Battle, first isolated and analyzed by Magoun in his "The Theme of the Beasts of Battle in Anglo-Saxon Poetry," *NM*, 56(1955), 81-90.

[43] *The Daemon in the Wood: a Study of Oral Narrative Patterns* (Cambridge, Mass., 1978), p. 35.

[44] In my "The Kassel Manuscript and the Conclusion of the *Hildebrandslied*," *Manuscripta*, 23(1979), 104-8, I have tried to illustrate the extent to which the oral-formulaic context may occasionally enable us to ascertain the integrity of a given text.

[45] "Comparing the Literature," in Harry Levin, *Grounds for Comparison* (Cambridge, Mass, 1972), p. 89; this essay was originally an address delivered before the 1968 triennial meeting of the American Comparative Literature Association.

[46] Marcus Tullius Cicero, *Orator*, ed. by Otto Seel (Heidelberg, 1952): "nescire autem quid ante quam natus sis acciderit, id est semper esse puerum" (p. 76, XXXIV, 120).

ORAL LITERATURE IN THE MIDDLE AGES
Bruce A. Rosenberg

By the inclinations of their training, medievalists revere the written word: in manuscripts, especially in manuscripts we can date, in archival documents, the letters of royalty and the inventories of castles. Only recently have several scholars of medieval literature bothered to experience the recited word—spoken and sung—in live, authentic oral traditions where narratives are still performed and appreciated. We used to be content with paleography and Latin philology; now an increasing number of medievalists are learning about techniques of interviewing and recording. Harvard University has a long and illustrious history of folklorists and an interest in folklore; and now, stimulated by the research of Albert Lord, David Bynum, and others, oral literature has gained a widespread respectability in American universities.[1] Yet among those academic writers on orality—with medievalists the interest has been largely on composition techniques putatively employing the oral formula—there is an embarrassing ignorance that folklorists and anthropologists have been studying oral literature for well over a century.

The now famous 1933-35 field trip of Milman Parry and Albert Lord to study the Yugoslav singers of tales, the *guslari*, introduced the idea and the importance of oral literature to modern scholars. Parry was, primarily, field-testing his Sorbonne dissertation which had postulated the composition of Homer's *Odyssey* and *Iliad* by the use of formulaic verbal units and epithets. The idea was not entirely new to Professor Parry; oral-formulaic composition had been suggested by Johannes Kail in an 1889 article in *Anglia*.[2] So Parry was field-testing a theory which had never emerged from any library into the clarity of real life, where the tales were actually sung. The oral-formulaic theory was put to the proof among the coffeehouses and taverns of Serbia, Bosnia, and Hercegovina.

The first application of the Parry-Lord theory to medieval literature was made by (another) Harvard scholar, Francis P. Magoun, in a 1953 article in *Speculum*[3] that is in an important sense the patron of many of the essays in this volume—though the ultimate tribute must go, of course, to Professors Parry and Lord. Since

that milestone publication, a galaxy of essays, books, and
theses have applied the theory to the moribund poetry of
ancient Greece, to the Hebrew of the Old Testament, and
to selected works in the corpus of Old Norse, Old French,
Old English, Old High German, even early medieval Arabic.
Folklorists have studied their living counterparts in
eastern Europe, Africa, and Turkey. The *Haymes Bibliography of the Oral Theory*, published in 1973, lists several hundred entries, nearly all of which were published
in the past decade.

But the oral formula is only one manifestation of
orality in medieval narrative. Since early in the nineteenth century, the close relationship between the folktale and epic and romance has been understood (though
not always correctly), and in some cases the relationship
between ballad and romance. Friedrich Panzer's comparative study of the *Beowulf* with more than 200 folktale
versions of some sub-type of A-T 301—"The Bear's Son"—
is the first important, systematic study of this type.
Recently, Utley has made an identification of various
folktales with Arthurian romances, though he did not live
long enough to sustain his initial observations. And
Kenneth H. Jackson's demonstrations of the relations of
the international popular tale with early Welsh literature, and Gwyn Jones' linking of *Culhwch and Olwen* with
hero-and-helpful-animal tales, are the most recent model
studies.[4]

Some variant or other of the oral-formulaic theory
has been accepted by most medievalists, probably because
of the dignity and stature lent this technique by the
claim that none other than Homer composed in this mode.
The idea that medieval narrative may be based on the
plots of traditional folktales has traveled a rougher
road toward acceptance, probably because most medievalists still associate folklore and particularly the folktale with unlettered, unwashed folk of crude sensibili-
ties and even cruder expressive powers. Roger Sherman
Loomis' now widely quoted denial that Arthurian romances
had folk origins is famous in its own circle, partly because of the vigor with which he denounced "the fancies
of plowmen, goose-girls, blacksmiths, midwives, or yokels
of any kind."[5] Parry and Lord may have been more convincing because of the material they recorded, and their
singers actually composed, they argued, as did Homer and
other poets who contributed to the Homeric corpus.

The folktale's existence in the Middle Ages is

somewhat hypothetical, since the only evidence we have of
it is in written narratives—in a form, in short, which
is not folklore—and in analogous folktales collected recently. The relationship between the modern folktale and
that which we believe to have been recited centuries ago
depends upon the folklorist's assumption that these narratives remain stable through multiple transmissions in
time and space. If they did not, the indices would have
no validity. Establishing the folktale's occurrence in
a particular region still will not settle the matter of
priority; and that is not an issue to be argued here.
Enough that the folklorist's assumptions and methodology
be illuminated.[6] So the existence of the folktale in the
Middle Ages is not a simple demonstration, yet it is not
necessarily less real for that, no less tangible than the
myriad so-called "lost French originals" which are the
stock-in-trade of many medievalists.

Beginning as recently as the 1930s, folktale analysis
could be conducted in a systematic, rigorous manner. At
that time the first motif and tale-type indices were com-
piled, and the revised *Types of the Folktale* became
available. During the last century comparisons between
folktales and literary narratives were often random studies, that is, analogues were sought in one nation only,
or isolated portions of narratives were compared with
fragments of others, and editions of medieval literature
often included extensive lists of folklore parallels. An
inane thoroughness resulted; and care was never taken to
determine the precise relationship among these analogues,
either historically or geographically, or in any meaning-
fully structural sense.

Based on more than a century of field work and the
scrutiny of archival holdings, folklorists are now certain that, as the folktale travels from teller to teller,
it retains its essential outline and most of its salient
features. Structuralist analysis of the folktale by
Vladimir Propp in the later 1920s[7] (but not translated
into English until thirty years later) has reinforced the
understanding that, regardless of the minor variations
that do actually occur in oral circulation,[8] the folktale
retains its direction and thrust—the purpose toward
which beginning and middle conspire. Experience with
oral narratives as they are actually learned, told, and
transmitted—not as these processes are imagined or
hypothesized in the academic library study—has demonstrated not only their stability but the extreme improb-

ability of two such tales with the same or analogous narrative structure (the Tale Type) ever being composed independently in two or more locations.[9] Consequently, the
medievalist who understands the basic principles of oral
transmission is justified in identifying folktales with
romances and with epics quite closely if their narrative
structures are of the same type.

Convincing proof requires much more than a super-
ficial similarity of plot, of course; we must be careful
about the form in which the narrative elements, whether
folktales or simpler motifs, appear, and how this configuration compares to narratives in an authentic oral
tradition.[10] For instance, comparisons have been made
in the past between folktales and literary tales on the
basis of analogous motifs only, disregarding the order
of their appearance in the hypothesized "source" folktale. Kittredge's claim that *Sir Orfeo* derived from *The
Wooing of Etain* was based on one analogous motif only:
in both stories the wife of the king is abducted from
amidst a company of armed guards.[11] But Kittredge could
not identify any other portions of the narratives which
were seriously alike, the fatal flaw in his identification. Secondly, we will want to determine, if that is
possible, whether the author had access to the proposed
source folktale. Ideally, we should desire a demonstration of the author's direct familiarity with folklore,
though that is a complex matter in medieval literary
contexts. And we should want to know whether the alleged
folklore item possessed an independent traditional
life.[12]

There is a lesson to be remembered here for the
"discoverers" of yet more oral formulas in medieval narrative. How much evidence do we have for the practice of
the oral formula in the composition of medieval literature? In fact, are we quite sure that we know what this
verbal component, the "oral formula," really is?

In nearly all of the applications of the Parry-Lord
theory to national literatures, the starting point has
been a modification of the original conception, adjusted
to suit the demands of the particular language being
studied and the tradition in which it was being performed. Old English scholars, for instance, found it
necessary to modify the Parry specification of "a group
of words," since some single words (*ymbsittendra,
wuldorfæder*) appeared to be used formulaically.[13] Creed
thought it could be "a single monosyllabic adverb."

The stipulation that the formula be "regularly employed"
also had problems, particularly if one adhered to
Magoun's interpretation of that to mean "repeated."[14]
The body of Anglo-Saxon verse is slight, the sampling
base quite small for such assertions, and few medievalists have been so inflexible. The result has been a
series of very flexible interpretations of "regularly
employed," allowing for inverted word order (in the
definition of Wayne O'Neil) and for the addition of a
word at the middle or end of the formula (Lewis Nicholson).[15]   And, as H. L. Rogers has pointed out, "under
the same metrical conditions" has come to be rendered as
"under no metrical conditions."[16]   The most imprecise
phrase in Parry's now classic definition is the final
one, "... to express a given essential idea."

Is the oral formula a poetic device exclusively?
Professor Ilhan Basgöz has found formulas among the
prose narrative *hikaye* of Turkey which are not metrical
at all—at least not metrically organized throughout
the performance—and actually many of these narratives
are blends of poetry and prose.[17]   Among Black preachers
of the American South and Southwest, I found that metrical
considerations were matters relating to specific performances—how the preacher chose to recite at a particular
time—and not a predictable matter which, when transcribed, could be scanned as one would a narrative prepared for print.[18]   And then, oral performance from the
pulpit was not found to differ qualitatively from the
generation of speech in most other circumstances, leaving
aside musical considerations.

The result of the inevitable modification of the
Parry definition of the formula has been a proliferation
of conceptions, occasionally so diverse as to be mutually
exclusive. And one wonders (or, should begin to wonder)
whether, finally, we are all talking about the same thing.
I personally recall one reaction to the first paper I
gave on the formulaic composition of American folk
preachers at the American Folklore Society meetings in
1967: it was that my idea was interesting, but that I was
not talking about *the* "oral formula." And I certainly
was not talking about the oral formula as it is manifested in Yugoslavia, but a kind of formula all the same.
Now, given the copious proliferation of the formula's
definition throughout the world—in manuscript as well as
among native societies today—one should well wonder at
the ontological status of the formula. Are we talking

about the same thing when we use this noun to describe
the language of the *Chanson de Roland*, the *Beowulf*, the
Nibelungenlied, and the *Mwindo* epic? My answer to that
rhetorical question, as you may have guessed, is "no."
David Bynum is right, I think: the oral formula—as Professors Parry and Lord found and defined it—is native to
the central Balkans, and so is best studied by those who
know the region and the language best.[19] What the rest
of us have been working with are verbal constructs at
best closely related to but not identical with the Balkan discoveries.

Parry, as I have already noted, went to Yugoslavia
to field-test an extant hypothesis. Given the impetus
of his landmark research, recent field workers want, implicitly, to move beyond the initial milestones of the
pioneers. We now know a lot more about oral culture and
oral literature than did Parry in 1934, though our knowledge was often inspired by him and Albert Lord. To begin
with, oral narrative is not necessarily traditional. Oral
poets who compose new and original songs do not necessarily contribute to a tradition. We cannot tell immediately whether their audiences will accept their creations and re-create them, thus making them "traditional." Such singer/composers of original songs thrive in
African cultures, particularly the makers of praise songs
and topical poems. The well-known Hausa Fulani bard,
Mannan Shata, regularly performs throughout Nigeria, accompanying himself with the *kalangu* and a sextet, performing the celebration of weddings, the installation of
kings, the departure of truck drivers. His songs are
seldom performed by others; each new composition relates
to a new situation and to different individuals, though
he does have the competence to create "spontaneously."[20]

The manner of creation and performance differs widely from culture to culture. Professor Daniel Biebuyck
reports that the Nyanga bards are accompanied in performance by "young men who are agnatic relatives, affines,
and/or blood friends of the accomplished. . . ." Their
number varies, but most often is three. By listening to
the master's performances they will be learning, at their
own speed, his repertoire. As they get to learn significant portions of the narrative they may, "whenever necessary, help the bard to remember and to find the thread of
his story."[21] Eventually, when the most talented of
these assistants gains sufficient mastery of the text, he
may replace his mentor. But the audience does not cor-

rect the performer, as we might expect from the European
tale-telling experience: they "merely" clap hands and encourage the bard with short exclamations (p. 13).

When oral narratives (*oralatures*?) have been recorded and analyzed as they were recited in authentic folk
communities, the Yugoslav experience has not been precisely duplicated. Ruth Finnegan has pointed out, for
instance, that the West African Hausa "Wakar Bagauda"
occurs simultaneously in both written and oral form, the
priority of which cannot be determined. Like much
Swahali verse, there is constant interchange between
written and oral versions. Somali "oral" poets frankly
use material they have heard on radio or which has come
to them in writing. A number of Finnegan's Limba poets
both write and recite aloud, indicating that one is hard
put to generalize about the orality of "oral literature."[22]

An equally persuasive array of evidence can be
amassed to demonstrate that performance is not always
precisely the moment of composition. Somali and
Mandinka poets do not perform their poems publicly until
they have finished their products in seclusion. The
famous description of Cædmon's poem about creation, often
cited by exponents of the oral-formulaic theory in medieval literature, suggests that he also may have composed
his hymn in this manner. Donald Fry has very recently
(in this volume, in fact) argued that this hymn was not
composed formulaically but is, rather, like much of
Anglo-Saxon narrative, memorial.[23] Among the poets of
Gambia, Ruanda, South Africa, among the Zulus and in some
instances the Finns (Paul Kiparsky thinks specifically of
those poems richly laden with mythic and ritualistic
freight[24]), in several instances in the American South—
memorization, rather than improvization, plays a major
compositional role. Rasmussen's Eskimo informants la-
bored at great length to perfect, in privacy, verse which
would be performed aloud to their audience. The Gilbert
Islanders pre-compose in the same way as, we believe, did
the Gaelic bards of the early Middle Ages who created in
darkened rooms until they felt in their own minds that
they had gotten their lines "right" (Finnegan, pp. 156-
57).

If a metrical/semantic/syntactic/quantitative definition of the formula has not traveled comfortably beyond
the Balkans, other attempts employing generative-grammat-
ical assumptions do postulate the formula's ontological

status. Paul Kiparsky, in a symposium at the University
of Michigan in 1974 and in the published proceedings of
that meeting, suggests yet another approach, that of a
tripartite taxonomy (pp. 73-106). Kiparsky would classify formulas, as do linguists with "ordinary" utterances,
as "bound," "flexible," and "free." The sermon phrase,
"dry bones in the valley," or Rev. Ruben Lacy's stall,
"God from Zion," is not likely ever to occur in altered
form: it is "bound." But "Moses said to me the other
day" could and does occur in several variations ("Jesus
said to me the other day," "God said to me the other
night," etc.), hence its flexibility. Like flexible
phrases, those that are "free" are generated out of deep
structure while the fixed formulas are ready-made surface structure utterances. But once we have made this
distinction, we may want to know the way in which the
types are really different from memorized formulas
(stalls such as "God from Zion"), and those which we have
in the past termed "improvized." Has our understanding,
rather than our terminology, significantly improved?

Unfortunately, Kiparsky's examples do not come from
oral poetry, but from everyday discourse; they do illustrate the arbitrariness of distribution, but again, not
in poetry. I am not qualified to comment on the importance of knowing that certain phrases derive from the surface with no synchronic deviation, and that others are
generated out of a deep structure. More particularly, I
do not at present appreciate how our understanding is enhanced beyond our present knowledge when we are told,
though in linguist's jargon, that certain phrases are
traditional and/or memorized and others are created anew,
roughly at the moment of performance—though not necessarily so. We knew that. And there the matter rests.
Whatever promises the approaches of the linguists may
have, little (so far as I know) has been published analyzing the texts of actual oral performances. And when
that is done—if it is ever done—hopefully the analysis
will be done in the context of the poetry's sociolinguistic milieu, so that we may compare poetry with discourse.
As I stated at a session on the "oral formula" at the
annual meeting of the American Folklore Society two years
ago, the linguist will yet tell us much because of the
expertise he brings to the study of the articulated utterance.

And I do not despair of help from other disciplines
as well. Some day, it is to be wished, a psycholinguist

will clarify the very casual way in which many of us have spoken of the use of language and formulas "unconscious- ly." The folklorist or anthropologist will tell us more about the responses and expectations of the traditional audience, and not leave these matters on the quicksand of our own speculations. The cognitive psychologist can help us really understand the dynamics of the input, storage, and retrieval processes in memory, surely the most important phenomenal aspect of traditional narra- tive performance, and consequently not an issue to be left to the literary critic's speculations. One day we may turn back upon our own critical traditions and review what T. S. Eliot and others have written about "tradition and the individual talent." And then, perhaps some day some generous Chomskyan will help our understanding of what is really meant by that often carelessly used phrase, to "generate a formula."

And as those professionals who better understand the phenomena of speech, in each of several respects, have not been adequately heard, neither have we as medieval- ists paid enough attention to those of our colleagues who have had "hands-on" contact with authentic, live oral cultures and oral traditions.[25] When Parry wished to demonstrate the hypothesis he had written about in his dissertation, he went to an area where live singers still sang heroic songs. Now, more than forty-five years after that momentous work was begun, we pause to honor those pioneers who made literary scholars aware of orality. I wish to suggest—to *urge*—that as we begin to move for- ward into a second phase of oral/literary scholarship (or a third phase, depending upon how one counts), that we return to an examination of oral traditions in the "living laboratory" where they in life exist; that we cease torturing yet new bodies of poetry (lyrical as well as narrative) into the Parry-Lord mold, itself a product of the observations of South Slavic traditions. After forty-five years it is time to move forward again, armed with that data that the anthropologist, linguist, and psychologist can provide, into a richer understanding of that fascinating phenomenon, oral poetry. When we do that, we will be in a much better position to understand how poetry may have been composed and performed in the Middle Ages.

Brown University

NOTES

[1] David E. Bynum, "Child's Legacy Enlarged: Oral Literary Studies at Harvard Since 1856," *HLB*, 22(1974), 27-48.

[2] "Über die Parallelstellen in der angelsächsischen Poesie," *Anglia*, 12(1889), 21-40. See further the "Introduction" to this volume.

[3] "The Oral-Formulaic Character of Anglo-Saxon Narrative Poetry," *Speculum*, 28(1953), 446-67.

[4] Panzer, *Studien zur germanischen Sagengeschichte* (Munich, 1910); among many articles, Francis Lee Utley, "Arthurian Romance and International Folktale Method," *RPh*, 17(1964), 596-607; Jackson, *The International Popular Tale and Early Welsh Tradition* (Cardiff, 1961); Jones, *Kings, Beasts, and Heroes* (London, 1972), pp. 65-119.

[5] "Arthurian Tradition and Folklore," *Folklore*, 69 (1958), 1-25.

[6] See my "Folktale Methodology and Medieval Literature," *JFI*, 13(1976), 311-25.

[7] *Morphology of the Folktale*, trans. by Laurence Scott (Austin, 1973).

[8] Stith Thompson, *The Folktale* (Berkeley, 1977), p. 436, lists 15 of the most common folktale changes: Forgetting a detail, stringing two or more tales together, multiplication of details, repetition of incidents, specialization of a trait, substitution of material from another tale, character's exchange of roles, adaptation to new environment, etc.

[9] The basic assumption is that the folktale is monogenetic rather than polygenetic.

[10] Propp himself cautioned that his morphology would also describe "certain novels of chivalry" (p. 100).

[11] George Lyman Kittredge, "*Sir Orfeo*," *JAP*, 7(1886), 176-202.

[12] Richard M. Dorson, "The Identification of Folklore in American Literature," *JAF*, 70(1957), 1-8, established these criteria.

[13] For instance, Magoun, "Bede's Story of Cædmon: the Case History of an Anglo-Saxon Oral Singer," *Speculum*, 30(1955), 49-65.

[14] Robert P. Creed, "The Making of an Anglo-Saxon Poem," *ELH*, 26(1959), 445-54.

[15] O'Neil, "Oral-Formulaic Structure in Old English Elegiac Poetry," unpub. Ph.D. diss. (University of Wis-

consin, 1960), p. 32; Nicholson, "Oral Techniques in the Composition of Expanded Anglo-Saxon Verses," *PMLA*, 78 (1960), 91.

[16] "The Crypto-Psychological Character of the Oral Formula," *ES*, 47(1966), 89-102.

[17] "The Tale-Singer and His Audience," in Dan Ben-Amos and Kenneth S. Goldstein, eds., *Folklore: Performance and Communication* (The Hague, 1975), pp. 143-206.

[18] *The Art of the American Folk Preacher* (New York, 1970), espec. Chapter 5, "The Formula," pp. 46-58.

[19] "The Generic Nature of Oral Epic Poetry," *Genre*, 2(1969), 236-58.

[20] Abdulkadir Dandatti, "The Role of the Oral Singer in Hausa-Fulani Society," unpub. Ph.D. diss. (Indiana University, 1975).

[21] *The Mwindo Epic* (Berkeley, 1971), p. 13.

[22] "What is Oral Literature Anyway?" in *OL&F*, pp. 127-66.

[23] "Oral Poetry: Some Linguistic and Typological Considerations," in *OL&F*, p. 99.

[24] See his "The Memory of Cædmon," included in this volume.

[25] In recent years several medievalists have seen the wisdom of studying live oral traditions in the field: John Miles Foley, Robert Creed, Rudy Spraycar, *et al.*

MEMORY, FIXITY, AND GENRE IN ORAL
TRADITIONAL POETRIES

Albert B. Lord

Although the South Slavic epic singers do not memorize a fixed text but "improvize" their verses, does
memory play any role at all in that process?

The answer is that such singers compose their verses
by means of formulas. They remember phrases they have
heard from other singers and that they themselves have
used many times before. This "remembering," however, is
as unconscious as our use of certain phrases in ordinary
speech, and should be distinguished from "memorization."
We have not consciously memorized "please" and "thank
you," for example. We use them by an unconscious "remembering." At a given stimulus such phrases come to our
minds as a learned reflex. So it is with formulas. The
weaving of formulaic diction exclusive of the formulas
themselves, the exact repetitions, is also but a special
extension of the processes of everyday speech, a special
extension that embraces sung verse as a means of communication of a special set of ideas appropriate to the epic
genre of story-telling. This, of course, sounds particularly easy, but it is in reality a complex art which requires considerable time to master. I repeat, then, that
the formulas and the diction of the poetry, the elements
that enter into the making of verses, are no more consciously memorized or even "remembered" than the phrases
and structural elements of any other kind of speech. In
everyday speech an idea seems to produce the word or
words to express it. The same process occurs in composing verses in oral traditional epic style, except that
the idea must be expressed under given metrical conditions. As in everyday speech but with the added necessity of meter, the same idea is expressed in much the
same words, often in exactly the same words each time it
is needed for the story. It is because of the regular
response to a given stimulus that formulas and the formulaic style are so readily discernible and so suscepti-
ble of analysis, even statistical analysis. The phrases
look as if they had been consciously memorized and repeated, but I submit that that is not so.

There is nothing new in what I have just said, but
it bears repetition because it is sometimes not complete-

ly understood or its consequences fully realized. Does the same principle of "unconscious remembering" hold for units larger than a verse, or at most two or three verses? Anyone who has compared several texts of the same song by the same singer of an oral traditional epic is aware that there are passages of varying length that are either identical or nearly so in all the texts. They seem to be a regular response to a given stimulus. Let me give some examples.

We have three texts of the *Song of Bagdad* from Salih Ugljanin of Novi Pazar.[1] The first five lines of the story are either identical or nearly so in all three texts.

1 & 2		3

Jednom vaktu a
  starom zemanu,
		Jednog vakta od
		  starog zemana

1	2	3

Sultan Selim rata
  jotvorio
	Car Sulejman
	  rata jotvorijo
		Sultan Selim otvorijo
		  rata

1,2,3
Sa kraljicom od grada
Bagdata.

1 & 2		3

Spremi sultan sto
  hiljada vojske,
		Opremijo sto hiljada
		  vojske,

1	2	3

Jenjičara sina
  njegovoga,
	Jenjičara, sužnja
	  nevoljnoga,
		Janjičara sve sina
		  njegova,

*	*	*
Once in olden times,		Once in olden times

Sultan Selim opened
  war
	Sultan Sulejman
	  opened war
		Sultan Selim
		  opened war

With the queen of the city of Bagdad.

The sultan sent an
  army of 100,000
		He sent an army
		  of 100,000

Janissaries,
  his sons,
	Janissaries,
	  unwilling
	  captives,
		Janissaries,
		  all his sons,

After these five lines some greater variety begins to appear, especially in the order of lines:

1
A sa vojskom kuhvet i
 topove.
                        2
          A za njima paše i veziri.   3
Spremi š njima paše   I pred njima paše i vezire,
 i vezire,
                              2
          Pa him tajin ide, pa   I sa šnjima od rata
                  kuhveta,   topove,
          A za njima kuhvet i   I za njima tajin i
                  topovi,   djephana,

        *   *   *

And with the army power
 and cannon.
          And after them pashas and
                  viziers.
              And before them pashas and
                      viziers,

He sent with them pashas
 and viziers,
          Then came provisions and
                  power,
              And with them cannon of war,

          And behind them power and
                  cannon,
              And behind them provisions and
                      ammunition,

     It seems clear that Salih had not memorized this
passage. He remembered, unconsciously, the elements that
make it up and, to some extent, the order of the elements: the army of a hundred thousand, then Janissaries,
the pashas and viziers, the cannon and ammunition. The
order varies after the Janissaries have been mentioned,
but the three elements in the seven or eight lines are
present in each version. Not memorized, not improvized
either, not even exactly repeated, but presented in "more
or less the same words," while expressing the same essential ideas. The text is not really fixed, yet because
the essential ideas have remained constant, it is "more
or less fixed."

     This holds true for the first eight lines of the
story as seen above. Notice, however, that one line,
with the essential idea of "provisions" (the key word is
"*tajin*") is missing in text 1 from the couplet that depicts "cannon" (*topovi*) and "provisions" (*tajin*). Or in

other words, of the three elements following "Janissaries," i.e., "pashas and viziers," "cannon," and "provisions," in text 1 provisions are not mentioned.   In texts
2 and 3 all three elements are present, although the
wording is not the same.   *"Topovi"* (cannon), an essential
idea, is expressed in 1 and 2 as *"kuhvet i topovi"* (power
and cannon), but in 3 as *"od rata topovi"* (cannon of
war), both demonstrable formulas.   The essential idea of
"provisions" (*tajin*) is coupled with "power" or "force"
(*kuhvet*) in 2 and with "ammunition" (*djephana*) in 3. But
the essence of the lines remains the same.   Moreover,
note that the order of "provisions" and "cannon" in 2 is
the reverse of what it is in 3, and that the order of
"cannon" and "pashas and viziers" of text 1 is the reverse of what it is in texts 2 and 3.   This shortening,
together with metathesis (found also in line 2 ["otvorio
rata" and "rata *j*otvorijo"] on the level of the phrase),
form two of the most common elements of the "more or
less" similar relationship between texts; i.e., a line
omitted, and lines or phrases metathesized.
     Let us follow the three performances for a few more
lines:

              1   3
Pa sidoše do grada   Pa pod Bagdat kraljici
   Bagdata.   na grada,
                         2
              E! pod Bagdatom bijeljijem gradom,
              E, da biju kraljici Bagdata,
                                                   3
                                       Pa s' kraljicom kavgu
                                          otvorijo
                         2
              Kad šljegoše do grada Bagdata,
              E, tresahu carevi topovi.
              E, biju Bagdat bijeloga grada,
              E, biju ga topom i kuhvetom;
              1   3
Bijo Bagdat dvadeset godina   Bagdat bijo dvadeset
Bez promena danjem i po noci,   godina.
Nit' mu vara nadje *j*o' duvara.   3
                                       Ni odbijo vara o'
                                          duvara,
                         2
              Nit' odbiju vara *j*od duvara,

                    1   3
A deljatim da učini kvara.   Ni Bagdatu učinijo kvara,
                             2
             A deljatim ućinjeti kvara;
                                                      3
                                 Ni Bagdatu nalazijo vrata,
                          2
          Niko ne zna koljiko vremena,
          Nikomu nać' od Bagdata vrata,
          E! Biše Bagdat dvadeset godina,
          Dvades puno a više četiri.
             1   2
Uhalji se careva
   ordija.
             Pobolje se careva ordija.   3
U ordiju boljes pogodila.   I na vojsku boles'
                                        udarila.

            *   *   *

Then they went to the   Then to Bagdad, the
   city of Bagdad   queen's city,
             To Bagdad the white city
             To attack the queen's Bagdad.
                                 Then he opened battle
                                    with the queen.
             When they came to the city of Bagdad,
             The imperial canon rumbled.
             They attacked Bagdad the white city,
             They attacked it with cannon and
                    forces;
He attacked Bagdad for   Bagdad he attacked for
   twenty years   twenty years;
Without ceasing day and
   night.
He did not find the mortar   He did not strike the
   of the walls,   mortar from the walls,
             They did not strike the mortar from
                    the walls,
To say nothing of doing   Nor did he do Bagdad any
   harm.   harm,
             To say nothing of doing harm;
                                 Nor did he find the
                                    gates of Bagdad;
             No one knows for how long,
             Nobody could find the gates of
                Bagdad.

> They attacked Bagdad for twenty
>   years,
> Twenty full years and four more.
> The imperial army fell ill.
> Illness struck the army.   Illness hit the army.
>   The imperial army fell ill.

The relationships in this third group are more complicated. In the second text Salih expands a bit. He seems actually to be feeling his way. The basic elements are:

1) they went to Bagdad
2) they attacked Bagdad for twenty years
3) they could not disturb the mortar from the walls, so how then do any real harm?
4) sickness came upon the army.

Those elements are in each text. Salih remembers them (unconsciously probably) from one singing to the next, but the lines are not exactly the same; the texts are different. Would one still call them "more or less the same"? Perhaps, but one is reaching the breaking point in credibility.

Singers will vary in the closeness of the wording of a text from one singing to another. The degree of closeness depends in part on the frequency of the singing of that song, or the themes used in it, or even— though, I think, to a less extent—on the length of the interval between singings. In that regard it is interesting to note that Salih's texts above were spaced as follows:

> No. 1 Nov. 22, 1934 - sung
> No. 2 July 24, 1934 - sung
> No. 3 July 23, 1934 - dictated

If each section of the poem exhibits this kind of relationship—although we must recognize that sometimes the text will be closer than at other times—we could safely say for the whole song that Salih has not either memorized or even "remembered" a *text*, but he has remembered the essential elements in each section, and he has remembered the story. It is in *these* areas, i.e., essential elements in the themes or segments and the overall story, that memory plays its role.

For brief runs, therefore, there may be (apparent)
fixity of text. How long that fixity would exist in a
singer's practice is hard to say. It would depend in
part, of course, on how often the song or the theme is
sung. In short, even fixity of text may be an unstable
element in the Serbo-Croatian oral epic tradition.
Nevertheless, it is not by any means absent, though,
paradoxically, it may not be long-lasting.

If we saw three manuscripts from the Middle Ages
with correspondences such as I have indicated above,
what would we, as medievalists knowledgeable in manuscript traditions, say about the relationship among
them? We might construct a stemma with at least one x
in it. If we were to some degree conversant with oral
traditional literature, we might think they were three
oral versions of the same song by three different singers. What we most surely would not say is that they
were three tellings of the same song by the *same* singer.
But that is what they are!

*

Were we to look at parallel passages from the same
song from two singers, one of whom "learned" the song
and heard it many times from the other, what would be
the result in terms of text? Would there be *more* or
less "fixity" than in the preceding case?

Suljo Fortić learned his *Song of Bagdad* from Salih
Ugljanin. We have two singings of it from him, one
November 24, 1934, two days after Salih's singing of
one of the above, the other May 17, 1950.

Suljo begins the song with the gathering of pashas
and viziers by the sultan, an action which occurs in the
Bagdad story shortly after the passages used above.

1	2
	Jedno jutro rano *j*osvanulo,
	*J*osvanulo, sunce *j*ogrijalo,
Podranijo sultan Sulejmane,	Podranijo sultan Sulejmane
Podranijo na bijelu dvoru,	
	*J*u Stambolu gradu bijelome,
Pa saziva paše *j*i vezire,	Pa poziva paše i vezire,
Paše svoje *j*i vezire svoje.	
	Pokupio paše *j*i vezire,
Dok dodjoše paše *j*i veziri,	
Pa *h*im care dugo besedijo:	Pokupio, pa *h*im govorijo:

```
     *                    *              *
```

                    One morning it dawned early,
                    Dawned early and the sun
                      grew warm.

Sultan Sulejman arose early, Sultan Sulejman arose early
In his white courts.

                    In Stambul the white city.

Then he summoned the pashas   Then he summoned the pashas
  and viziers,   and viziers,
His pashas and his viziers.

                    He gathered the pashas and
                      viziers,

When the pashas and viziers
  had come,
The sultan spoke to them at   He gathered them and said
  length: to them:

    Let us turn now to the same passage in the three
texts of Salih Ugljanin's song. In them the sultan receives a letter from the army commander seeking advice
as to whether they should return to Stambul or not. When
he receives this the sultan gathers his counsellors together.

```
          1                  2                  3
```
Pa pokupi paše i vezire,   Car pokupi cijelu voćelju,
         Ta put sultan pokupi vučelju,
                Sve $h$islama svojega imama,
         Kupi paše a kupi vezire,
Redom lalje a redom
   ridžalje,
         Pa pokupi trides delibaša,
         E pokupi paše i ridjale.
Pa pašama sultan   Pa im sultan vako
  besedaše: besedaše:
         Sve hi pred se zovnu na divana.
         Sultan pita paše i vezire:

```
          *                  *                  *
```

Then he gathered the pashas   The sultan gathered his
  and viziers,   whole council,
         Then the sultan gathered his
            council,
                    The pontiff of all Islam,

> He gathered the pashas and
>   gathered the viziers,
The nobles and officials
  in order.
>   Then he gathered thirty heroes,
>   He gathered the pashas and
>   the officials.
Then the sultan spoke to   Then the sultan spoke thus
  the pashas: to them:
>   He called them all before him in
>   audience.
>   The sultan asked the pashas and
>   viziers:

There is about the same degree and kind of fixity
in Suljo's two singings that we have seen in the examples from Salih, but we can note that the two singers
vary greatly from one another. It would be necessary to
carry this analysis much further to make the experiment
meaningful in detail, but the tendency is abundantly
clear: on the whole, passages vary much more from one
singer to another than they do in the singing of a given
bard.

In other words, a *kind* of "fixity" may be attained
in the work of a single singer, but that fixity is not
transmitted to another singer. At an early stage each
has learned the art and comes up with his own responses
in the traditional diction. Each develops his own passages within measurable and describable parameters. The
art is transmitted but not passages of text.

I must emphasize that I have been speaking of the
Serbo-Croatian tradition, of sung epic narrative, but
the principle is applicable in those other traditions
which are composed and performed in the same manner as
the Serbo-Croatian.

But since memory may play a somewhat different role
in different genres, it seems necessary to take genre
into account in discussing fixity. Obviously, shorter
lyric songs tend to greater fixity of stanza than long
epics. If one were to generalize about fixity from the
observation of it in lyric poetry and apply the result
to epic, the conclusions drawn would not be accurate.
The reverse, of course, is true. In general the smaller
the unit the greater the degree of fixity, whether one
speaks of lyric, or praise song, or whatever. Often *non*-
narrative poetry consists of a series of short units
which may be more or less fixed, but their order is

customary, rather than fixed, and metathesis is frequent.

Finally, there are, I understand, cases where a poem is composed in the poet's head without benefit of writing—and memorized and recited. This applies to short poems. It should not be cited as a model for oral traditional epic composition. Such an application would be false on two grounds. First, only in the most literal sense of the word is such poetry oral. If the description of the process is correct, in its method of composition it is the same as written poetry and should be considered as such. Secondly, the shorter genres to which such poems belong tend to fixity anyway and should not be compared to long narrative compositions.

In sum, in oral traditional epic in the Slavic Balkans memorization in the strictest sense plays little or no role. Nevertheless, some degree of fixity is attained in some passages in the epics in the singing of individuals, although it may not be permanent. The shorter genres and strophic units may exhibit greater fixity than the longer ones.

Memorization does occur at a later stage in the Serbo-Croatian tradition. That is to say, at a time when published, therefore fixed, texts were available and their prestige established, some traditional singers began to memorize the printed texts, and some who were not singers did the same. The latter were mere memorizers and performers, and except for lapses of memory such as we all have, stayed with the text. The former group is not uninteresting. When their memory failed them, they were still able to compose in the traditional way, and therefore, to continue to sing. Such a combination of processes results in "mixed" texts, i.e., partly memorized and partly not.

Memorization is not a great boon to traditional singers. It is too restrictive for them. Memorization requires a fixed text, and is impossible in the oral traditional narrative poetries with which I am acquainted, because in the tradition's natural state, there are no fixed texts to memorize. The singers of the South Slavs are creators and not rhapsodes as is sometimes erroneously averred by those who do not comprehend their art.

Harvard University

NOTES

[1]Quotations from Salih Ugljanin's three versions of the *Song of Bagdad* (*Pjesma od Bagdata*) are taken from *S-CHS*, II, nos. 1, 2, and 3; those passages cited below from Sulejman Fortić's two versions of the same song are taken from *S-CHS*, II, nos. 22 and 23.

OTHER BOOKS FROM SLAVICA PUBLISHERS

American Contributions to the Eighth International Congress of Slavists. Zagreb and Ljubljana, Sept. 3-9, 1978. Vol. I: Linguistics and Poetics, ed. by Henrik Birnbaum, 818 p., 1978; *Vol. 2: Literature,* ed. by Victor Terras, 799 p., 1978.

Balkanistica: Occasional Papers in Southeast European Studies, ed. by Kenneth E. Naylor, *I(1974),* 189p., 1975; *II(1975),* 153p., 1976; *III(1976),* 154p., 1978.

Henrik Birnbaum: *Common Slavic Progress and Problems in Its Reconstruction,* xii + 436 p., 1975.

Henrik Birnbaum and Thomas Eekman, eds.: *Fiction and Drama in Eastern and Southeastern Europe Evolution and Experiment in the Postwar Period,* ix + 463 p., 1980.

Malcolm H. Brown, ed.: *Papers of the Yugoslav-American Seminar on Music,* 208 p., 1970.

Ellen B. Chances: *Conformity's Children: An Approach to the Superfluous Man in Russian Literature,* iv + 210 p., 1978.

Catherine V. Chvany: *On the Syntax of Be-Sentences in Russian,* viii + 311 p., 1975.

Frederick Columbus: *Introductory Workbook in Historical Phonology,* 39 p., 1974.

Dina B. Crockett: *Agreement in Contemporary Standard Russian,* iv + 456 p., 1976.

R.G.A. de Bray: *Guide to the Slavonic Languages. Third Edition, Revised and Expanded,* in three parts: *Guide to the South Slavonic Languages,* 399 p., 1980; *Guide to the West Slavonic Languages,* 483 p., 1980; *Guide to the East Slavonic Languages,* 254 p., 1980.

Paul Debreczeny and Thomas Eekman, eds.: *Chekhov's Art of Writing A Collection of Critical Essays,* 199 p., 1977.

Bruce L. Derwing and Tom M.S. Priestly: *Reading Rules for Russian A Systematic Approach to Russian Spelling and Pronunciation With Notes on Dialectical and Stylistic Variation,* vi + 247 p., 1980.